David Bjork's four decades of disciple-making and theological education experience in Europe and Africa earn him the right to write on the subject. I agree with David that, "...most currently available discipleship resources either minimize or completely ignore the element [of theological reflection]." Therefore, we desperately need a resource that profoundly addresses the issue of a biblical theology of discipleship. Putting on the Lord Jesus: A Gospel-Driven Theology Discipleship, *accomplishes that mission. Scholars, students and practitioners will find this resource very helpful.*

Felix Niba, National Director for Cameroon/Regional Represent for Central and West Africa of The Bonhoeffer Project and Resident Coordinator of the West Africa Advance School of Theology (WAAST), Cameroon Campus

A great deal of available evangelical literature on Christian discipleship tends, on the one hand, to focus on the usefulness of the motif in enhancing church growth, mentoring and Christian maturity (pragmatic approach); and, on the other hand, to highlight methodological processes (how to) for making disciples (methodological approach). However, often, little attention is paid to anchoring views and practices of discipleship in solid biblical theology. In this book, Dr. David Bjork contends that a Christ-centered and gospel-driven theology is the substratum that should undergird, shape and inform evangelical conceptualizations and practices of discipleship to Christ. As such, a recovery of an accurate understanding of the person of Jesus, the Christ, and His gospel as portrayed in Scriptures is vital for delineating a biblical outlook of discipleship. I strongly recommend this book to theologians, mission activists and pastors. In it, they will find a fresh as well as a thought-provoking perspective on discipleship to Christ.

Emmanuel Oumarou, doctoral student at Cameroon Faculty of Evangelical Theology (FACTEC), Yaoundé, and member of Lausanne 4 Global Listening Team. Founder and president of the Theological Institute for Mission and Intercultural Studies (TIMIS), Bamenda, Cameroon.

In today's multicultural pluralistic world, Christians stand at the crossroads of deciding between many notions of the gospel and must carefully examine the content of the gospel they believe and have been commissioned to communicate to the world. David Bjork has adequately probed these issues through many decades of missionary and scholarship experience. In this book, he has presented some fascinating findings that demand a paradigm shift especially in the aspect of the gospel's relationship to discipleship.

Fuhbang Emmanuel Tanifum, Lecturer, Intercultural Studies, Cameroon Faculty of Evangelical Theology

REGNUM STUDIES IN MISSION

Putting on the Lord Jesus

A Gospel-Driven Theology of Discipleship

Series Preface

Regnum Studies in Mission are born from the lived experience of Christians and Christian communities in mission, especially but not solely in the fast growing churches among the poor of the world. These churches have more to tell than stories of growth. They are making significant impacts on their cultures in the cause of Christ. They are producing 'cultural products' which express the reality of Christian faith, hope and love in their societies.

Regnum Studies in Mission are the fruit often of rigorous research to the highest international standards and always of authentic Christian engagement in the transformation of people and societies. And these are for the world. The formation of Christian theology, missiology and practice in the twenty-first century will depend to a great extent on the active participation of growing churches contributing biblical and culturally appropriate expressions of Christian practice to inform World Christianity.

Series Editors

Paul Bendor-Samuel   Oxford Centre for Mission Studies, Oxford, UK
Tony Gray   Words by Design, UK

REGNUM STUDIES IN MISSION

Putting On the Lord Jesus
A Gospel-Driven Theology of Discipleship

David E. Bjork

First edition published 2021 by Regnum Books International

Regnum is an imprint of the Oxford Centre for Mission Studies
St. Philip and St. James Church, Woodstock Road
Oxford, OX2 6HR, UK
www.regnumbooks.net

09 08 07 06 05 04 03 8 7 6 5 4 3 2 1

British Library Cataloguing in Publication Data
A catalogue record for this book is available from the British Library

ISBN: 978-1-5064-8912-4
eBook ISBN: 978-1-5064-8913-1

Typeset by Words by Design

Distributed by 1517 Media in the US, Canada, India, and Brazil

Acknowledgments

This book is the fruit of more than four decades of cross-cultural witness to the Lord Jesus, first in Europe and then in Africa. I cannot name here the many men and women of diverse ethnic, cultural, educational, and Christian backgrounds without whose support and encouragement that experience, and the theological reflection that accompanied it, would have been impossible.

I want to thank the leadership of World Partners, Dave Mann, Tami Swymeler and Rick Dugan for backing my wife and me through this project. Dr. Danny McCain, in association with Global Scholars, allowed me to teach much of the material in this book for almost a decade in Africa, for which I am grateful. I am also appreciative of Dr. Samuel Kwak and the graduate students of the Cameroon Faculty of Evangelical Theology who helped me to develop the contents of this book both in the classroom and in countless conversations.

Joshua Roberts played a vital role in directing me to important sources as I researched the material in this book. A special thanks goes to Bruce Barron whose editorial expertise, and gracious assistance were invaluable.

I am grateful to Dr. Paul Bendor-Samuel and Regnum Books for publishing this work.

I am especially grateful for my wife Diane, whose love, patient commitment and confidence in our Lord Jesus over the past 48 years, has enabled me to grow in my understanding of our Lord's call to follow him.

Contents

Preface

Many programs of discipleship are available, but not many theologies of discipleship have been suggested. This book addresses such a significant need. While discipleship programs can be contextualized in different cultural contexts, a theology of discipleship should be deeply rooted in the biblical understanding of faith. A more essential and cross-cultural foundation is needed in this task.

Dr. David E. Bjork focuses on the gospel in his theology of discipleship, which corrects many church-oriented programs of discipleship. We must focus on the gospel of Jesus Christ rather than any other institutional centers of activity. I think this point is an evangelical focus. Discipleship can have eternal values when it is based on the transcendental norms of the gospel.

Bjork interprets that "loving God (with all one's heart, with all one's soul, with all one's mind and with all one's strength) means following Jesus." This perspective clearly integrates the essential biblical teachings with the task of discipleship. Bjork goes on to stress that "God is glorified when we give Jesus Christ his appropriate place in our lives," adding that "this seems to be what the Apostle Paul and the early Jesus-followers taught." It is noteworthy that according to Bjork, "recognizing Jesus' lordship fulfills the Father's purpose and so brings glory to God." He further posits that "giving glory to God is the same thing as discipleship or growth in Christ-likeness."

Bjork's theology of discipleship is deepened by the exegesis on the nature of faith in relation to discipleship. We can easily comprehend the point that genuine faith entails discipleship. True discipleship comes from a genuine biblical faith in Jesus Christ. Pragmatism in discipleship programs seems to neglect this foundation of discipleship, which should be corrected with this new yet central understanding of discipleship. This book provides the theological foundation for many programs of discipleship, connecting the possible missing link between faith and discipleship in many programs.

Bjork understands *pistis* as a fundamentally relational concept and practice to suggest translating it by allegiance with quotes from other sources. He prefers "understandings that specifically link discipleship to the person of Jesus of Nazareth, the Christ". In Bjork's perspective, the often missing link between salvation and life under Christ's rule can be connected by the practice of Christian identity in discipleship as a mandatory requirement for being a

Christian. He goes on to point out that "this passion to see Christ in his followers motivated Paul's mission".

This book makes a contribution to our theological understanding of discipleship by explaining the essence of the Christian faith with up-to-date yet authentic exegesis of the biblical teaching relating to the Christian faith and followership in Christ. Rich and succinct exegesis and interpretation of the essence of the faith characterize this book. The author's long-time reflections in different ministerial contexts in North America, Europe, and Africa seem to have brewed such a deep flavor.

A sense of order is desirable in understanding the task of discipleship practically. The theology of discipleship should come before any programs or practices of it. This book is a must-read for all who want to understand what it means to live out the Christian faith as a follower of Christ Jesus. A solid understanding of the biblical faith and followership could facilitate more active participation in discipleship as life or even in a program. The impressive theological congruence found in this book could consolidate and integrate our essential understanding of discipleship within the Christian worldview. Bjork's main challenge seems to be *to critically examine our preconceived notions that base our practices and foster intentional apprenticeship to Christ firmly grounded in the gospel.*

This theological position is significant in many ways. The following four points could summarize them:

First, the concept of gospel-driven theology of discipleship is balancing between the lordship and saviorhood of Jesus Christ. Jesus is not only our savior, but also our Lord. His lordship must be recognized fully and wholly in our lives if we believe in the saving grace in his name. The balance between the two interrelated poles is an important strength of this theological standpoint.

Second, the uniqueness of Jesus Christ is reaffirmed through this theology of discipleship. No other center than Jesus is recognized in our faith. In the relational understanding of the world and life, the concept of center is important. Jesus is *the* center. He is the center of our movement forward relationally. He is the center of our worship and adoration. He is the center of our lives and practices.

Third, Bjork's theology of discipleship clarifies the fuzziness in popular misunderstandings about the relationship between faith and life. The problems of fuzzy worldviews are addressed in this book with the integrated nature of faith and life clarified well in Bjork's theology. This integration prevents us from becoming a vampire who only emphasizes the saving power of the blood of Jesus, neglecting the importance of the genuine practice of faith.

Fourth, Bjork's theology of discipleship is clear about the concept of boundary in a legalistic understanding of the world and life. The sense of boundary defines what is lawful and acceptable, which however is limited in expressing the essence of a worldview. The concept of the boundary explains our understanding of the Christian worldview in part, but does not cover its essence fundamentally. The boundary contingently exists in its relation to the center that is Christ Jesus. Our relationship with the center that is our Lord Jesus Christ explains the essence of the worldview we actually embody. In this sense, Bjork's theology does not lead to legalism, but to the grace and faith in the Lord Jesus.

I hope this book will be read widely by people who are interested in learning the essence of the Christian faith in terms of discipleship. It helps our understanding of why we do what we do as followers of Christ.

Steve Sang-Cheol Moon, PhD
Founder and CEO, Charis Institute for Intercultural Studies
Professor and Director of PhD Program in Intercultural Studies,
Grace Mission University

1. Why a Gospel-Driven Theology of Discipleship?

In November 2019, at their assembly in Indonesia, delegates at the General Assembly of the World Evangelical Alliance (WEA) decided to approach the decade from 2020 to 2030 as a "decade of disciple-making." They urged the churches, networks, commissions, and national and regional members of the WEA to re-examine, re-align, and re-commit their mindset, processes, and structures in accordance with Jesus' Great Commission in Matthew 28:18–20. The WEA recognizes that disciple-making should not be limited to this ten-year period but should be a permanent part of our mission. However, the delegates at this General Assembly seem to have felt that this emphasis needs to be highlighted.

The C. S. Lewis Institute, which describes its own mission as the development of "disciples who will articulate, defend and live their faith in Christ," maintains that several things must done to "start this Decade of Discipleship" (C. S. Lewis Institute, 2020). This evangelical think-tank mentions, among other things, a sustained effort, a focus on the heart and mind, mentoring, and awareness. However, it does not explicitly mention a need for theological reflection. The institute can hardly be faulted for this, since most currently available discipleship resources either minimize or completely ignore this element.

My missionary experience in Europe and in Africa over the past decades has convinced me that our appreciation of discipleship and disciple-making tend to be more pragmatic than theological. In other words, we often embrace those notions because of their usefulness. For example, the leaders of the mission that sent my wife and me to France to begin a church in the early 1970s initially overcame their uneasiness with the fact that we were actively making disciples instead of planting a church because they could see that people were being converted and becoming passionate about following Jesus. For many years I also actively embraced discipleship and disciple-making primarily for that reason.

Do not get me wrong. I am not against fruitfulness in our witness for the Lord Jesus. However, when I look back on what I was doing, I see that all too often I was attempting to prescribe in American evangelical Protestant terms what discipleship to our Lord Jesus should look like to people living in a different cultural and Christian context. I taught others to apply the same spiritual disciplines that I had been taught and applied successfully in my mother culture. I innocently assumed that the practical forms of obedience to the Lord Jesus I had adopted were biblical and universal. At best, this may have been a subtle form of colonization or religious naivety. At worst, it might have been an expression of spiritual and religious arrogance. In either case, I have discovered that although the theology of discipleship to the Christ is biblical and universally true, the forms that discipleship and disciple-making take are not. Surprisingly neither Jesus of Nazareth who sends us out to make disciples, nor the Apostle Paul who instructed many of the primitive Christ-followers, did not give a detailed description of what that looks like in pragmatic terms.

My point is that the reasons for intentional discipleship to the Lord Jesus are often misunderstood. In the series of studies contained in this book, I seek to answer a simple question: what biblical and theological reasoning justifies recognizing intentional discipleship specifically to Jesus of Nazareth, as he is represented in the gospels rather than vaguely to God the Father, as the goal of our mission and not just evangelism and building the church?[1] Our response to this question demonstrates our understanding of the gospel and of spiritual growth. It is also crucial to our evaluation of the impact and vitality of our church programmes and activities, to our interpretation of both the Old and New Testaments, and to how we do systematic or practical theology.

New Testament scholar Michael Bird (2013, p. 21) contends that we need, as a matter of pastoral and missional importance, "an authentically evangelical theology—that is, a theology that makes the evangel the beginning, center, boundary, and interpretive theme of its theological project". With Bird, I unabashedly believe that the Good News of the Lord Jesus of Nazareth, the Christ cannot be limited to his death on the cross and resurrection, and the offer of salvation. It must also encompass all the doctrines of the faith – the incarnation, the resurrection, Lordship, the need for whole-life commitment to Jesus, and so on.

The Natural Link between the Gospel, Theology and Discipleship

The title of this book suggests a link between several notions that are often joined in some important ways, yet considered separately: gospel, theology, and discipleship. For instance, sometimes the gospel is understood as the proclamation of the death of Jesus of Nazareth on the cross for our sins. This understanding is often tied to the idea of personal faith and acceptance of the gift of salvation. The concept of discipleship is then perceived as something that sometimes follows this initial conversion experience as the new believer grows in his or her faith. Theology is seen as something that is done primarily

---

1 For an initial examination of the relationship between theology, discipleship see Appendix A.

by church leaders to help the faithful to hold firmly to sound doctrine and refute those who oppose it.

These fundamental understandings contain many invaluable elements. Yet I believe that they will be greatly enriched by re-examining them separately and then seeing how the first followers of Jesus, the Messiah, put them together in their time and cultural setting.

Developing a Biblical Theology

The Christ-centred biblical theology that I seek to develop here is different from systematic theology in that it does not gather all the biblical texts on God, humanity, sin, Christ, salvation, and the last things in an attempt to bring them into conversation with the tradition of the church and formulate doctrine (Treat, 2014, pp. 34–35). The emphasis of systematic theology is the construction of a coherent whole beginning with solid exegesis of the texts used. It sees this systematization taking place within the Scriptures and works according to its own logic to construct a coherent whole. In contrast, biblical theology also draws on actual exegesis of the text used, but it seeks to make sense of the unfolding of the Creator's plan in human history. Granted, the difference I am describing here between systematic theology and biblical theology is one of emphasis, not an absolute contrast. Both disciplines pursue coherence and presuppose the central truths attested to by the first Jesus-followers. However, they do not pursue the same goal and are distinct in their emphases.

I like the way in which Graeme Goldsworthy (2012) defines biblical theology. After recognizing that evangelicals are not in agreement on a definition, he writes:

> Biblical theology ... is the study of how every text in the Bible relates to every other text in the Bible. It is the study of the matrix of divine revelation in the in the Bible as a whole. ... Biblical theology, then, is the study of how every text in the Bible relates to Jesus and his gospel. Thus we start with Christ so that we may end with Christ; he is the Alpha and Omega (Rev. 22:13). Biblical theology is Christological, for its subject matter is the whole Bible as God's testimony to Christ. It is therefore, from start to finish, a study of Christ. But, since Christ is the mediator who makes the Father known, biblical theology is also *theological* and not solely Christological. (p. 40)

Goldsworthy identifies two evangelical approaches to doing biblical theology. First, he describes what he calls "synchronic biblical-theological study" (Goldsworthy, 2012, p. 39), which focuses on the biblical text or texts from a particular limited time-frame. Such studies inevitably involve questions concerning the cultural, historical, and theological context of the particular text. In this phase or approach, the biblical theologian builds on textual exegesis. He or she reflects on the information gleaned from exegesis in the light of canonical narrative, and on the epoch or epochs preceding and following the redaction of the text (Butner, 2018, p. 6). For example, G. K. Beale (2011, p. 9) describes his project in these terms:

> A biblical-theological approach to a particular text seeks to give its interpretation first with regard to its own literary context and primarily in relation to its own redemptive-historical epoch, and then to the epoch or epoch preceding and following it.

In the same way, when comparing New Testament theology to systematic theology, I. Howard Marshall (2004, p. 44) remarks that in biblical theology "The New Testament must be understood first of all and so far as possible on its own terms, as an expression of thought within the ways that were possible in the first century."

Robert Yarbrough (1996, p. 61) defines biblical theology as "the study of the Bible that seeks to discover what the biblical writers, under divine guidance, believed, described and taught in the context of their own times." Kaiser and Silva (2007, p. 11) affirm that "the term 'biblical theology' has clarity only when it is understood to mean theology as it existed or was thought or believed within the time, languages and cultures of the Bible itself." In other words, it must rest on beliefs and meanings that were conveyed by the texts at the time of their original writing. What Irenaeus, Calvin, or Barth thought about the Bible is something quite other than biblical theology as understood here.

The second aspect of approach to developing a biblical theology seeks to represent the underlying storyline of the literary genres and theological themes of the Scriptures. It presupposes that the biblical literature and its historical storyline together provide the vehicle for God's revelation of himself and his purposes for creation (Goldsworthy, 2012, p. 28). Goldsworthy identifies four elements in our biblical and theological training that hinder us from taking hold of the unity of biblical theology. First, he mentions our tendency to concentrate on individual books, focusing on literary matters and exegesis and a close reading of the text (p. 33). Second, he notes the "usually accepted division" between Old and New Testament teaching:

> Theological curricula have, at least since the nineteenth century, divided the courses in a way that allows for scholarly specialization in one or the other Testament. This is reflected in the fact that most of the biblical theologies written since then have been either of the Old Testament or the New Testament. ... Many, perhaps most, [evangelical seminaries] are heirs to the conventional theological curricula that impose a hermeneutical barrier between the Testaments that is more like the Berlin Wall than a freely negotiable border crossing. (Goldsworthy, 2012, p. 34)

Goldsworthy also claims a lack of consensus in evangelical seminaries about the nature, principles, and method of biblical theology. He suggests that for this reason, seminaries do not know how to design even a one-year introductory curriculum that covers these matters and provides practical guidance for preachers and teachers (2012, p. 35). Finally, Goldsworthy argues that biblical studies have been dominated by the Enlightenment distinctions between dogmatics and biblical theology, which have further diminished the importance of the unity of scriptural interpretation (2012, p. 35).

In the following studies, I will rely on both the synchronic biblical-theological and the underlying storyline approaches to doing biblical theology. In so doing, I will attempt to keep in view both the diversity of the texts and their unified theological content. In other words, I will try to systematically understand what the Bible teaches, but in the context of the Bible's own focus on the crucifixion, resurrection, and enthronement of Jesus the Christ in the kingdom he proclaimed. As I stated earlier, Jesus of Nazareth, the Christ is the center and point of the biblical message. The primary leitmotiv, the metanarrative, of the Bible involves placing our faith in Jesus and learning how to live in the saving relationship of subjects to our king.

I am not attempting to create a theology independent of the biblical texts! Instead, I seek to examine the theology of what the biblical authors actually thought or intended. This process is in some sense descriptive, and it obviously involves biblical exegesis. And although I will focus primarily on the New Testament, we need to remember that Jesus of Nazareth and the Apostles indicated clearly that the Old Testament Scriptures are about the Christ (Clowney, 2003; Goldsworthy, 2000, 2012; Hunter & Wellum, 2018; Murray, 2013). Like R. S. Rosner (2000, p. 10), I hold that a biblical theology must seek to remain fixed on the Bible's overarching narrative and Christo-centric focus. The person of Jesus of Nazareth, the Christ is the basis of the unity of Scripture and the essence of biblical theology.

My Goal

Several years ago, philosopher, pastor, and university professor, Dallas Willard (2010, p. 236), claimed that our disciple-making endeavours lack clear teaching on how our spiritual growth should continue, without interruption, from conversion into a deepening life in the kingdom of God.

My goal is to look more closely at that process. I believe that a theology of discipleship to Jesus of Nazareth exists and can be found in the Scriptures. But to see it, we must rid ourselves of some preconceived ideas and understandings that dominate our religious world. We will need to go back to the origins and begin interpreting the biblical texts as they were understood by those who first read them some two thousand years ago. So instead of introducing new ideas, I propose that we recover some ancient ones.

I wish to stimulate a discussion based on an understanding of the biblical texts as they were initially understood by their authors and first readers. I believe that if we carefully discern the original meanings of those texts, we will begin to see reference points that will center our theology, our spirituality, and our practice more fully in intentional discipleship to Christ.

My Perspective

My parents were active in an evangelical community church during my early years. When I was a teenager, after moving to a different part of the United States, we faithfully attended a Holiness Church that had been shaped by the North American Methodist revival, the Mennonite tradition, and fundamentalism. This small denomination, called the Missionary Church, had a very strong commitment to world missions that marked my life in a significant way. I came to personally trust Jesus for my own salvation in my childhood, and at age 17 I felt a call to missionary service.

I have served Christ overseas for most of my life since receiving that call, first in France and then in Cameroon. After 16 years of disciple-making ministry in France, I began theological studies, which I pursued both at Catholic seminaries and universities in France and at evangelical seminaries in North America. During my 15 years of study, I continued to accompany men and women in their apprenticeship to Jesus. My ministry and study in the French Catholic context brought me to better understand the sacramental vision[2] and fostered in me a deep appreciation of the rich and varied tapestry of our common heritage as followers of the Lord Jesus. I taught for a year at an interdenominational seminary in North America, then for four years at a state university in Africa and for eight years in evangelical seminaries in Cameroon. Today I am a professor of Intercultural Studies and direct the doctoral programme of the Cameroon Faculty of Evangelical Theology.

As for my theological leanings, first and foremost I am a follower of Jesus of Nazareth, the Christ. Second, I call myself an evangelical. I consider myself fortunate to have received graduate training in trans-denominational Protestant environments in North America (Fuller Theological Seminary in Pasadena, California; Trinity Evangelical Divinity School in Deerfield, Illinois) and in French universities at the Ph.D. level (École Pratique des Grandes École, Sorbonne IV, Paris; Université de Strasbourg). I was also privileged to do graduate studies at French Catholic institutions (Grand Séminaire de Caen; Institut Catholique de Paris). This ecumenism and multi-disciplinary formation are mirrored in my practices. I am a Protestant, yet I participate with reasonable

---

2 For a good understanding of how evangelicals can profit from a recovery of a sacramental worldview, see the excellent work of Hans Boersma (2011, 2016) who holds the J. I. Packer Chair in Theology at Regent College in Vancouver, British Columbia, Canada.

comfort in a Catholic context. Almost 50 years of cross-cultural ministry among avowed atheists and nominal Christians have also equipped me to understand the worldview of people who have yet to embrace the Lord Jesus. In various seasons of life, I have regularly and gladly worshipped at charismatic, Baptist, Presbyterian, Catholic, Mennonite, and non-denominational churches. I believe that these experiences have helped me to engage the Scriptures more appropriately and from more diverse angles than might have been possible had I been steeped in only one Christian tradition.

I am not a systematic theologian by specialty. I cut my scholarly teeth in the realm of the theology of missions. Along with theology, my graduate research was in the spheres of ecclesiology, cultural anthropology, sociology of religion, church history, and Christian unity. That research was born out of almost 20 years of personally accompanying men and women as they became and grew as followers of Jesus of Nazareth, the Christ. At that time personal evangelism, church-planting and church growth were the focus of missions, and intentional one-on-one and small-group forms of discipleship to Christ were not yet fashionable in the evangelical world I lived in. They were seen more as means to the end of church growth, and the church programmes and activities were thought to produce fruitful disciples of Christ. Even while researching the biblical, theological, historical, and cultural aspects of my experience, I continued to make it the centre of my ministry despite the misunderstanding and opposition it often provoked from many church leaders.

Today the evangelical world more readily embraces the idea of Christian discipleship as the focus of missions and ministry. One example of that new-found openness is the position of the World Evangelical Alliance, which, as noted at the beginning of this chapter, declared 2020 to 2030 to be a "Decade of Disciple-Making." The idea of discipleship and disciple making is not new by any means, but it has now been put at centre stage. And that concerns some people, such as C. Anderson (2020). He is not upset at all that evangelicals have decided to give discipleship a more central place in their theology and missionary practice. Rather, he is concerned by the lack of agreement among evangelicals about what that means. He recognizes that people are easily excited by the idea of making disciples without grasping really what that involves. I contend that such a shift is necessary, and that among other things it will entail a return to a gospel-driven biblical theology and an adjustment of many of our underlying assumptions.

A Gospel-Driven Theology of Discipleship Is Not a Western Idea
The General Assembly at which the WEA declared its "Decade of Disciple-Making" was attended by delegates from 92 countries. The multi-cultural, multi-linguistic, and multi-ethnic nature of those delegates introduces the last point I wish to make about the character of a Christ-centred biblical theology of discipleship. Although I write from my own experience as a North American

evangelical Christ-follower, the gospel-driven biblical theology we will explore applies to followers of Jesus regardless of their ethnic, cultural, or linguistic origin.

Jesus of Nazareth, who calls us to learn from him, himself had a multi-cultural lineage. Efrem Smith (2017, p. 87) has written these powerful words:

> The Son of God, Alpha and Omega, was multiethnic, multicultural. In the family tree of Jesus were the indigenous inhabitants of Israel, Palestine, Ethiopia, Egypt, the Sudan, Libya. If that is true, we need to present it, remember it. Then we need to ask what it means for us, through the Holy Spirit, for that Christ to live in us. We must wrestle with what it means to follow that Jesus, to surrender to that Jesus, to represent that Jesus. He walked our earth as a multiethnic, multicultural, Jewish human being. But we have reduced him from that. In our culture, we have made Jesus look like whoever we are instead of who he is.

This is certainly true of the Jesus we Western missionaries have carried with us around the globe. We have made him white, Western, European, urban, handsome. Despite this error of which we must repent, I maintain that the call for a gospel-driven biblical theology is not a white, Occidental argument for following a Jesus we have wrongly made to look like us.

The Pentecost story further demonstrates that a gospel-driven theology of discipleship applies to people of any culture, ethnicity, language, or social class. The book of Acts explicitly mentions some of the diverse groups who received the gift of the same Holy Spirit on that day: "Parthians, Medes and Elamites; residents of Mesopotamia, Judea and Cappadocia, Pontus and Asia, Phrygia and Pamphylia, Egypt and the parts of Libya near Cyrene … Jews, Cretans and Arabs" (Ac. 2:9–11). Why are the Scriptures so explicit on this point? Perhaps one reason is so that we will realize that as we grow in our understanding and obedience to our Lord Jesus of Nazareth, the Christ, we do so together with people from every tongue, nation, ethnic group, skin colour, and social class. We have the same Saviour and Lord; we have received the same Spirit; we have been given the same mission; we study the same Scriptures; and we share the same destiny. For this reason, the Apostle Paul could write to the Christ-followers in Galatia that in Christ "there is neither Jew nor Greek, slave not free, male nor female, for you are all one in Christ Jesus" (Gal. 3:28).

Finally, a gospel-driven biblical theology of discipleship keeps in view the glimpse we have into the celestial Kingdom in the book of Revelation. There we see that before the throne and in front of Jesus of Nazareth, the Lamb of God, there is a great multitude "from every nation, tribe, people and language." They are wearing white robes, and they cry out in a loud voice, "Salvation belongs to our God, who sits on the throne, and to the Lamb" (Rev. 7:9–10). This is the aim toward which all creation is moving. It was first promised to

Abraham when *Yahweh* pledged that in him all ethnic groups on earth would be blessed.

Overview of the Book

Many excellent, recent books by biblical scholars have explored various subjects that I examine in the following studies. Two books by Matthew Bates are notable: *Salvation by Allegiance Alone* (2017) and *Gospel Allegiance* (2019). I also have appreciated Scot McKnight's important study *The King Jesus Gospel: The Original Good News Revisited* (2011) and Jackson Wu's *One Gospel for All Nations* (2015). There have also been several significant studies focused on the person of the Lord Jesus and what it means to follow him, including *Christ is King* by Joshua Jipp (2015) and *Slave of Christ* by Murray Harris (1999). Graeme Goldsworthy's *Christ-Centered Biblical Theology* (2012) and *Christian Dogmatics* by Cornelis van der Kooi and Gijsbert van den Brink (2017) are also frequently cited sources. The present studies are my attempt to construct a cumulative argument based on the work of these and many other widely recognized scholars.

In chapter 2, I look at the rabbi Jesus of Nazareth in his historical Jewish context to see some of the ways in which he fit the pattern of what his disciples could expect of any rabbi, as well as ways in which he blatantly violated his own religious customs. I contend that our understanding of discipleship (or, if you prefer, growth in godliness, sanctification, or spiritual maturity) is largely determined by our mental image of Jesus of Nazareth. I explain the importance of the specific meanings of the titles we use to identify him. And I examine his dialogue with the specialist of the Law (Mk. 12:28–31), highlighting the importance of Jesus' amendment of the *Shema* both in affirming his authority and in calling others to allegiance to himself. This opening study is designed to alert us to some of our preconceived notions that hinder us from developing a gospel-driven theology of spiritual growth.

In chapter 3, I briefly examine the gospel of Matthew, the gospel that is perhaps most closely tied to the specific cultural setting within which it was written. The key affirmation here is that a gospel-driven theology, along with the discipleship that grows naturally from it, does not begin with God—at least not as that word is commonly used to indicate the Deity. Instead, we will examine the unique authority given to the resurrected Jesus of Nazareth, and his relationship as the incarnate eternal Son of God with the other persons of the Trinity. I believe that from the outset we must put to rest an ancient heresy that erodes our commitment to Jesus of Nazareth, the Christ, our Lord.

Chapter 4 looks at the difference between understanding that God is *in* Jesus and that God is accessible to us *through* Jesus. Our beliefs in this regard are foundational to the role we assign to the person of Jesus of Nazareth, the Christ in our personal and corporate worship and service. The difference between these two ideas (God *in* or God *through* Jesus) and the preference we give to one or to the other color our way of viewing Jesus of Nazareth and the role we allow him to play in our sanctification. We must come to grips with the subtle yet fundamental difference between these two affirmations to comprehend the importance of the mission that the resurrected Jesus of Nazareth, the Christ, our Lord, has assigned to all whom he has called.

What exactly did the first followers of Jesus of Nazareth understand when on the mountain-top in Galilee, shortly after his crucifixion and resurrection, he told them to make disciples among all the peoples of the world, teaching them how to follow him? What did being someone's disciple mean in Palestine so many years ago? What was the typical relationship between a disciple and his or her "teacher"? And how was the relationship between Jesus and his followers similar or different? These are some of the questions we will consider in chapter 5. My purpose is to demonstrate why discipleship to our Lord Jesus of Nazareth, the Christ is not optional. It is not something reserved for missions or outreach. It is not reserved for leaders, but is for everyone everywhere, all the time.

The commission to accompany others in obedience to Jesus of Nazareth seems to be absent from the gospel of John. Instead, in the sending of his first followers the resurrected Christ says, "As the Father has sent me, I am sending you" (Jn. 20:21). In chapter 6, I argue that in John's thinking and writing the relationship and responsibilities of the one who has been sent are precise and profound. I will demonstrate that the eternal Son of God, having been sent by his Father and becoming flesh in Jesus of Nazareth, perfectly incarnated that relationship and assumed those responsibilities. I will argue that he is the model as the *Father*'s "sent one" for us as *Jesus'* sent ones.

The commission that the resurrected Jesus gave to his first followers, as described in the gospel of Mark, seems to centre on his identity as the Redeemer. That commission tells us to go into the world and proclaim the gospel. In chapter 7, I examine the meaning the Apostle Paul attached to the word "gospel" and its core elements as they are detailed in Romans 1:1–5. I also describe some of the undesirable results of inadvertently separating personal evangelization, from intentional discipleship to the Lord Jesus. I argue that we can find many of these negative results in our own faith communities. And I demonstrate that when we correctly understand the nature of the gospel, its relationship to discipleship becomes evident.

How is the identity of Jesus of Nazareth tied to the kingdom of God? And how is the kingdom of God linked to the gospel? In chapter 8, I look at these questions and the messianic identity of Jesus of Nazareth. I argue that in Jesus, the rabbi from Nazareth, the dynamic regal activity of *Yahweh* is operative, bringing salvation and the transformation of the universe. I also propose that framing our understanding of the gospel with the biblical theme of the kingdom may help us to better promote intentional discipleship to Jesus.

Jesus of Nazareth often referred to himself as the "Son of Man." Some have suggested that he used that title to say that he was truly human, the divine element being similarly denoted by the title "Son of God." Others see in that enigmatic title Jesus' way of claiming to represent the people of God. Still others, combining these notions, maintain that by this phrase Christ represented himself as the head, the type, the ideal of the race. In chapter 9, I look at this phrase from yet another perspective, which I believe to have been the dominant understanding of that term in the minds of the people who first heard it on his lips. I will demonstrate why Jesus' use of the title "Son of Man" was Good News to those first followers and can continue to keep us focused on the Good News of the gospel today.

In chapter 10, I examine the Good News that the first Jesus-followers communicated to their world. They did not have the Four Spiritual Laws or the Roman Road or any of the tools so familiar to us. What did their presentation of Jesus of Nazareth, their recently crucified and resurrected Lord, focus on? And why is it important that we remember these things today? I argue that the first believers' understanding of the Good News of Jesus the Christ was the basis of their allegiance and commitment, as the Apostle Paul put it, to "gain Christ and become like him" (cf. Phil. 3:7–10).

After looking at how the gospel message was communicated by the first followers of their Lord Jesus of Nazareth, the Christ, I turn my attention to their understanding of one of the most important yet one of the most misunderstood, distorted, and misused words in our vocabulary. It was also one of the key words of the Protestant Reformation and one that we would do well to examine afresh. I am referring to the concept of faith. Leaning on the best of recent New Testament scholarship, I argue in chapter 11 that our understanding of what it means to believe in Jesus could be significantly enriched by considering what faith or belief meant to Jesus and his first followers, and to Paul and those to whom he addressed his letters. From a theological perspective, such an enlargement of our understanding will also strengthen the link in our thinking, teaching, and practice between justification and sanctification (that is, between conversion and growth in Christ-likeness or discipleship).

In chapter 12, I examine how the Apostle Paul describes participation in the rule of the Lord Jesus to his "faithful" followers living in the region of Colossae. I show how his words in the epistle to those believers help us to understand his all-consuming goal of presenting "everyone perfect in Christ" (Col. 1:28). This helps us to define discipleship, or as he puts it, "Christ in you" (1:27). And I maintain that Paul uses the Christ-hymn of Colossians 1:15-20 to center our theology, devotion, worship, and daily living explicitly on the humanity of the Lord Jesus of Nazareth, the Messiah, and our participation in him. I also examine Paul's use of "glory" and how it helps us to understand what he means when he writes in Romans 8:29 that God's purpose is that we be "conformed to the image of his Son."

In chapter 13, my argument is that the Spirit's activity mirrors his own disposition and the work in the Creator's project of restoration. As such, I maintain that the Spirit is never the goal of discipleship. The Spirit empowers us as we seek to learn more about Jesus of Nazareth, the Christ, and conform our lives to him. I demonstrate how Paul contrasts this with those Corinthian believers who mistakenly believed they could best follow Jesus by living according to the Old Testament Law. In the process I look at the role of the Spirit and of Scripture in the renewal of the heart. I also examine the relationship between the pre–existent *Logos* (Jn. 1:1) and the biblical text. In this study I also look at what it means to be led by the Spirit into "all truth."

In chapter 14, I look at the context in which those who live under the reign of the Christ, enabled by his Spirit, learn together and from each other how to practise his words, and conform their daily relationships to his "law." My underlying argument in this chapter is that *Christology* must determine *ecclesiology*, and not the other way around. In this study I examine the meaning of the word *ekklēsia* in the world of the New Testament authors. A detailed study of Ephesians 4:11–12, in the context of its surrounding passages is the heart of this chapter. I look at who it is that Paul designates as those who do the work of "perfecting" the saints or "building-up the body of Christ." I argue that the Lord Jesus of Nazareth is the measure by which spiritual growth is measured, and that growth in likeness to him is the measure of the *ekklēsia*. And I maintain that together, the "ministers" (Eph. 4:11) and the "saints" (4:12) serve the goal of learning a new lifestyle from and with each other.

Drawing primarily from the example of Paul's disciple-making relationship to Timothy, in chapter 15, I maintain that, like the Apostle, everything in our understanding of mission is, or should be, gospel-driven. After looking at Paul's gospel-driven lifestyle, I demonstrate why a gospel-driven theology of discipleship is by its very nature a theology of mission. Then I explain why a gospel-driven theology of discipleship spontaneously fosters "church growth." In the process, I look quickly at the erosive effects of Christendom on such an understanding. I also maintain that a gospel-driven theology of discipleship builds on the paradigm of the One living and true God who acts in a fundamental and absolute unity (as described by the Greek word *perichoresis*). As such, I argue, a gospel-driven theology of discipleship is particular, participative, and purposive.

In short, this book is about the relations between Jesus of Nazareth, the Christ and the whole of reality: both the Creator God and the world. This is the theological task of the follower of the Christ. Each of us is called to reflect upon our existence in the light of the eternal *Logos* who became flesh in that man from Galilee. This thinking takes shape in the context of revealed certainties, yet it deals with truths which remain hidden and provoke a sense of "wonder." It is a complex task because it rejects formulas that seem clear and plausible at the cost of leaving things out, or of ignoring or selecting from what has been given to us in the Christ.

As we enter into this conversation, we must consciously resist the natural craving of our human spirit for a clear, transparent and definite system. Gospel-driven theological reflection deals with reality and not primarily with doctrine or methods to be adopted. It concerns the meaning of the world and will be undertaken only by one who has not just learned his Christianity but has let the Lord Jesus, the Christ, become real in him or her.

A gospel-driven theology of discipleship deals with mystery, yet it seeks precision and clarity in thought and word. This is much needed today! I can illustrate this with the analogy of cooking and baking. Both cooking and baking are terms that we probably hear often. However, when asked what the difference between the two is, not all of us can give a straight answer. Both involve heat and are methods to prepare food. Yet there is a difference. In general, cooking is considered an "art" because you are free to change the measurements or ingredients based on your preference. Baking, on the other hand, is considered a "science" because it generally calls for accurate and precise measurements of the ingredients. In this sense a gospel-driven theology of discipleship is more like baking than it is like cooking.

Clarity and accuracy form an important standard of a gospel-driven theology of discipleship. We must be clear in how we communicate our thoughts, beliefs, commitments and reasons for those commitments. Careful attention to language is essential here. This involves working hard at getting the issues that foster, or detract from, devotion to the Christ before our minds. Our beliefs, communication, and actions must be consistent. This means that we must engage in deep and thorough thinking and evaluation, avoiding shallow and superficial reflection about Jesus of Nazareth, and what it means to follow him. It is my hope that this book will assist in that process.

Questions to Think About

1. I introduce this book with the plea made by the delegates at the General Assembly of the World Evangelical Alliance in 2019 to re-examine, re-align, and re-commit our processes and structures in accordance with Jesus' Great Commission in Matthew 28:18–20. Why do you think these representatives from 92 countries felt that this is especially needed today?
2. In the introduction I talk about the importance of developing a gospel-driven theology of discipleship. How would you express the main elements of your own theology of discipleship?
3. This chapter presents biblical theology in relative contrast to systematic theology, suggesting that biblical theology is Christo-centric whereas systematic theology is theocentric. Do you agree? If so, what might be the implications for developing maturity in Christian discipleship?
4. I mention a number of life experiences that have shaped the development of my understanding of discipleship. As you reflect on your life, what are some of the key experiences and relationships that have shaped your views of discipleship?
5. Just before I present an overview of the chapters which follow, I highlight the fact that a gospel-driven biblical theology is not a white,

Occidental argument for following a Jesus we have wrongly made to look like that. Why do you think it is important that people from all ethnic groups on earth think seriously about the theology behind discipleship and disciple-making?

2. The Creed of Jesus of Nazareth

You undoubtedly noticed in the introduction to this series of studies that I referred repeatedly to "Jesus of Nazareth, the Christ" instead of just to "Jesus" or "Jesus Christ."[1] This was intentional! As we will see in the following studies, it is important that we recognize that "Christ" is not Jesus' name. It is, rather, an honorific title with a very distinct and important meaning.

This observation about our misuse of the title "Christ" is also true of our appropriation of many key words of the faith, such as gospel, faith, church, etc. These and other important terms have become a bit untidy in our thinking, teaching, and worship over the past few decades. And this impacts our theology and our practice.

The problem becomes even more troublesome when we consider how we think and talk about the person Jesus. For instance, what do we mean when we affirm that "Jesus is God" or that "Jesus is the name which is above all other names"? Especially when we consider that the Hebrew spelling *Yeshua* (which translated from Hebrew into Greek becomes *Iēsous*) was a common alternative form of the name (*Yehoshua* – Joshua) in the later books of the Hebrew Bible and among Jews of the Second Temple Period. As a result, some other rabbis of that period were also called "Jesus." That being the case, how does this alter our understanding of Paul's affirmation that he has been exalted by God to the "highest place" and given "the name that is above every name?" Does it matter? I will demonstrate in the coming studies why it does.

Here is another example. When we teach that Jesus (the name refers to the man from Nazareth) always existed with the Father, even before he was born of the virgin Mary in Bethlehem, is this sufficiently clear? Who was it exactly who was incarnated as the man Jesus of Nazareth? If we prefer to say that it was "God" who took on flesh to dwell among us (cf. Jn. 1:14), are we as precise as the Evangelist John was when he used the term "Word" (*logos*)? I maintain that precision in the words we use to identify Jesus of Nazareth does matter in our thinking and in our communication.

As we will see throughout this series of studies, the *identity* of Jesus of Nazareth and the *titles* given to him by his first followers are of utmost

---

1 In his lifetime Jesus was called Jesus son of Joseph (Lk. 4:22; Jn. 1:45, 6:42), Jesus of Nazareth (Ac. 10:38), or Jesus the Nazarene (Mk. 1:24; Lk. 24:19).

importance. In many significant ways, those titles, which explain his identity, enable us to give clear meaning to the other words we so commonly use. This is important because thinking and talking about the identity of the one we confess to be truly God and truly human is not easy! Over the centuries, even theologically trained, spiritually sensitive individuals have struggled with how Jesus and the Father can be distinct but at the same time one. In these studies, I will not survey the major Christological challenges that have arisen over the centuries when people have attempted to hold these two aspects of the identity of Jesus in focus. There are many good resources you can consult for that information.

Reflecting on the identity of Jesus of Nazareth is the key to the entire project of theology. It was also of utmost importance to Jesus himself (cf. Mt. 16:15; Mk. 8:29; Lk. 9:18–20). We may think that we have settled this question, and that it is not really something we have to struggle with because we confess that he is God. However, we must avoid the trap of answering the question of the identity of Jesus too hastily and superficially. When we do, we can end up communicating things like "God was born in Bethlehem" or that "God and Jesus are the same."

I do not pretend to fully understand the relationship between the man Jesus of Nazareth and the God he called Father. In the gospels, he is portrayed as distinct from his Father in heaven, to whom he addressed his prayers (he did not pray to himself). In fact, he consistently focused everyone's attention away from himself and directed it to his Father. His relationship with the divine person of the Holy Spirit is also beyond my grasp. My purpose is simply to help us to clarify, as much as possible, the meaning of the words we use to describe the identity of the God-man from Nazareth and what it means to follow him.

Jesus of Nazareth, the Rabbi

Throughout the gospels, Jesus is called "teacher" or "rabbi" by those who surrounded him. The members of the early church were universally called "disciples." They were *mathētai* (Greek for students or apprentices), those who followed the "way" of life that was traced out by Jesus. In describing his relationship with a rabbi, Arhey Leib Sarahs says:

> I did not go to the rabbi to learn interpretations of the Torah from him but to note his way of tying his shoelaces and taking off his shoes. … In his actions, in his speech, in his bearing, and his faithfulness to the Lord, man must make the Torah manifest. (quoted in Tverberg, 2012, p. 28)

Jesus trained his disciples by inviting them to follow him. He invited them to literally walk behind him—to accompany him, to live with him, and to learn from him in the process. His disciples joined him in the activities of life, observing his reactions and imitating his way of living out the Word of God, the Torah. In this, they were like the disciples of all the other rabbis of their day.

Although their apprenticeship was like that of other disciples, they were also surprised by some aspects of their experience, perhaps more than we realize. Jesus of Nazareth did not call them only to a life of faithfulness to the Almighty and to a manifestation of the Law in their daily life. No, in following Jesus they were invited to learn something even more important. That something is precisely what we will examine in this study.

What should someone who has been trained in Jesus' school look like? I am not referring to the spiritual disciplines such as prayer, fasting, and silence. Rather, I am aiming more at the *goal* of these spiritual disciplines, which we see in the life of Jesus and which we often associate with growth in spiritual maturity or discipleship.

We can see what constitutes the heart of Jesus' own spiritual life in the answer he gives when interrogated by a specialist in the Torah:

> One of the teachers of the law came and heard them debating. Noticing that Jesus had given them a good answer, he asked him, "Of all the commandments, which is the most important?" "The most important one," answered Jesus, "is this: 'Hear, O Israel, the Lord our God, the Lord is one. Love the Lord your God with all your heart and with all your soul and with all your mind and with all your strength.' The second is this: 'Love your neighbor as yourself.' There is no commandment greater than these." (Mk. 12:28–31)

This core of the Torah—namely, to love God with all our heart, soul, mind, and strength—was clearly the heart of the spirituality and practice of Jesus of Nazareth.

The specialist in the Law was not trying to trap Jesus by asking a tricky question. On the contrary, he asked a question that was widely discussed by the rabbinic teachers of his time. He was probably intending to ask something like this: "What is the essence of the divine law? What principle summarizes all divine teaching?" (Tverberg, 2012, p. 33). For example, the Babylonian Talmud contains a conversation between rabbis[2] who were attempting to summarize the 613 commandments of the Law in the fewest precepts:

> Micah came and reduced them to three [principles], as it is written, It hath been told thee, O man, what is good, and what the Lord doth require of thee: [1] only to do justly, and [2] to love mercy and [3] to walk humbly before thy God. ... Again

---

2 Actually, the title "rabbi" was not used formally before the year 70 CE. For this reason, biblical scholars hesitate to use it, preferring the title of "wise." However, during the time of Jesus, "rabbi" was a respectful way to address a religious teacher because it meant "my master." Places where Jesus is called "rabbi" in the gospels include Mk. 9:5; 11:21; Jn. 1:37; 3:2; 4:31; 6:25; 11:8.

came Isaiah and reduced them to two [principles], as it is said, Thus saith the
Lord, [1] Keep ye justice and [2] do righteousness [etc.]. Amos came and reduced
them to one [principle], as it is said, For thus saith the Lord unto the house of
Israel, Seek ye Me and live. ...— But it is Habakkuk who came and based them
all on one [principle], as it is said, But the righteous shall live by his faith.
(Talmud, Makkoth 24a)

This conversation between rabbis allows us to understand that when the
specialist in the Law questioned Jesus, he was raising a subject that was
important at that time. By means of this question, the rabbis sought to identify
the heart of the will of God (Vermes, 1993, pp. 37–45).

We Must Remember Jesus' Jewish Culture

The first commandment given by Jesus in his response to the specialist in the
Law is a profession of faith, a prayer, and a pledge of allegiance to the one
God. Known as the *Shema*,[3] this profession of faith is pronounced by Jews
every day at sunrise and sunset, both to praise God and to implore him to act. It
is the first prayer a Jewish child learns. Traditionally, it is the last words a Jew
says before death.

Even today, Jews recite the *Shema* before reading the Torah on the Sabbath
and festival days. They also recite the *Shema* at the end of what they consider
the holiest day of the year, Yom Kippur.[4] The words of the *Shema* are written
in the *mezuzah*[5] that they attach to the lintels of their doorways and in the
tefillin that they fix on their arms and on their foreheads.

The complete *Shema* is composed of three paragraphs of the Torah. The
first, Deuteronomy 6:4–9, quoted by Jesus, deals with the concepts of God's
love, the study of the Torah, and its transmission to children.

We can therefore summarize the creed of Judaism as "Loving God by
putting the Torah into practice." This is the opinion of rabbi Yoel Kahn, who

---

3 *Shema* (Hebrew for "hear") is a shortened form of the full prayer that appears in
Deuteronomy 6:4–9 and 11:13–21, as well as Numbers 15:37–41. This same Hebrew
word is often translated by our word "obey" (see for instance Dt. 11:13 and Ex. 24:7).
This fact helps us to appreciate the expression with which Jesus of Nazareth often ended
his teaching: "He who has ears to hear, let him hear" (Mk. 4:9).
4 According to tradition, the first Yom Kippur took place after the Israelites' exodus
from Egypt and their arrival at Mount Sinai, where God gave Moses the Ten
Commandments. Upon descending from the mountain, Moses caught his people
worshipping a golden calf and shattered the sacred tablets in anger. Because the
Israelites atoned for their idolatry, God forgave their sins and offered Moses a second
set of tablets. Yom Kippur—the Day of Atonement—is considered the most important
holiday in the Jewish faith (History.com Editors, 2009).
5 The *mezuzah* is a parchment inscribed with religious texts and attached in a case to the
door-post of a Jewish house as a sign of faith.

asserts that the most profound component of a Jew's existence is his "attachment to God, and to his Torah" (Loubavitch, 1993–2020).

Jesus Amends the *Shema*

Like every good Jew, Jesus recited the *Shema* daily. There is nothing shocking about that. In his day, Jesus of Nazareth and all who followed him were Jews (or, to use the correct ancient terminology, Israelites). They practiced Jewish rituals, and other Jewish practices. They were shaped by the beliefs and values, the historical and political loyalties that constituted the allegiance of the people of Israel.

Since almost everyone recognizes today that Jesus of Nazareth was a Jew who respected the practices of ancient Judaism, we are not surprised by his response to the Torah expert. But we should be! For Jesus of Nazareth, good believing and practicing Jew that he was, did the unthinkable. Instead of simply quoting the *Shema* when the expert of the Law asks him to identify the first and greatest of all the commandments, Jesus amends it! In doing so, he touches what was considered most precious in the eyes of his contemporaries.

When questioned by the Torah expert, Jesus answers by quoting the *Shema*, but he then adds a verse: Leviticus 19:18. Here then is the "creed of Jesus" (McKnight, 2009). For Jesus, love of God and neighbour is at the heart of his teaching. This is the purpose of what he teaches his disciples. We are so accustomed to this that it does not surprise us. But we must take note of what Jesus is doing. When he changes the *Shema*, he alters not a secondary element of Judaism, but its heart, its very essence. It is true that the idea of loving others is in Judaism, but it is not at the heart of Judaism. What Jesus gives is not a "cling to God" *Shema* but a "cling to God and to your neighbour" *Shema*. This shows that for Jesus, love of others is at the core of the spiritual formation of his disciples.

Nicholas T. Wright (2011, p. 302) helps us to understand the importance of this seemingly innocent transformation of the *Shema*: "Instead of being under the Torah itself, the summons was now to be under Jesus. The young man was being summoned to join an Israel that was no longer defined by Torah." This notion that the followers of Jesus of Nazareth, the Christ are defined by allegiance to him, and by life under his "law" is something we will come back to time and again as we progress through these studies. This is an underlining theme which ran through the entire ministry of Jesus of Nazareth, of the Apostle Paul, and of the gospel itself. The Jesus of Nazareth "revised *Shema*" completely overturned the disciples' worldview.

Most importantly, the act of transforming the *Shema* indicates Jesus' *authority*. To understand the magnitude of this act, we must situate it in the context of Jewish traditions and ways of thinking. Every time Jesus of Nazareth claimed to be equal to and to have the same authority as his Father, this claim provoked the anger of his Jewish fellow citizens (cf. Jn. 10:30–33). In altering the *Shema*, the Law, Jesus was presenting himself as equal to the Law-giver. For who can renew or rework God's Law other than God Himself?

The Incident of the Heads of Grain Torn Off on the Sabbath Day

This answer to the Torah expert helps us understand how Jesus of Nazareth perceived himself. We see his self-understanding also in an incident often referred to as "the incident of the heads of grain being plucked on the Sabbath." In this account, some Pharisees see Jesus' disciples picking heads of wheat and eating the grain as they walk on the Sabbath. These Pharisees then challenge Jesus to justify this Sabbath violation, which seems to be due to inadvertence or arrogance:

One Sabbath day, Jesus was walking through wheat fields. As he walked, his disciples began to pluck ears of grain. The Pharisees said to him, "Look! Why do they do what is not allowed on the Sabbath?" Jesus answered them, "Haven't you ever read what David did when he was in need and hungry, he and his companions? He entered into the house of God in the days of the high priest Abiathar, ate the consecrated bread that is not allowed for priests to eat, and even gave some to his companions!" Then he said to them, "The Sabbath was made for man, and not man for the Sabbath, so that the Son of Man is the Lord of the Sabbath" (Mk. 2:23–28).

In his response to the Pharisees, Jesus claims full authority. We do not find Jesus violating the Torah, but rather we see Jesus of Nazareth exercising his authority over the Torah. This can be seen in the fact that Jesus proclaims himself the "Son of Man"[6] with the authority to decide how to further extend and interpret the Sabbath law. Let us remember the role of the Sabbath for the Jews: "The children of Israel shall keep the Sabbath to celebrate the day of rest in their generations by a perpetual covenant. This is a sign between me [the Lord] and the children of Israel forever" (Ex. 31:16–17a).

Here is another interesting verse because it seems to say that no one may add to God's word:

Now therefore, O Israel, hear these statutes and these ordinances, which I [Moses] teach you to do. You shall not add to the word which I speak unto you, neither shall you diminish from it; that you may keep the commandments of the LORD your God, which I command you. (Dt. 4:1a, 2).

Jesus' response in defence of his disciples who pick heads of wheat and eat the grains as they walk on the Sabbath day looks very much like an attack against the Law or at least like a condemnation of so-called Pharisaic legalism. However, it can also be legitimately seen as a declaration of a new Lord, the

---

6 This is a particularly important and precise title that we will look at closely in chapter 9.

Son of Man, who has received authority over the Law itself. The sovereign, heavenly one who has become a human being is the one who can make exceptions to the Law when he deems it necessary or appropriate. This idea would have been rejected by many Jews, not because they did not believe it, but because they did not believe that Jesus of Nazareth was the incarnation of that heavenly being (Boyarin, 2012, p. 70).

"Let Me Go and Bury My Father First"

Another incident serves as a further illustration of Jesus' authority. In Luke 9:57–62, we read:

> While they were on their way, a man said to him: "Lord, I will follow you wherever you go." Jesus answered him: "Foxes have dens and birds of the air have nests, but the Son of Man has no place to lay his head." He said to another, "Follow me." And he said, "Lord, let me go and bury my father first." But Jesus said to him, "Let the dead bury their dead and you go and proclaim the kingdom of God." And another said, "I will follow you, Lord, but first let me go and bid farewell to those in my house." Jesus answered him, "Whoever puts his hand to the plough and looks back is not fit for the kingdom of God."

The Importance of Grief in Judaism

To fully understand what Jesus of Nazareth demands of this man, who is ready to follow him but only after having buried his father, we must appreciate the importance of mourning in Judaism.

In Jesus' day, burials were done in two stages. First, immediately after the father's death, the family (led by the eldest son) put the body in a coffin and then in a tomb so that the body could decompose. Once they had returned from the burial, the first-degree relatives were given the status of *Avelim* (mourners). This status lasted for seven days, during which family members gathered in a house and received visitors. They spent those days sitting on the floor or on uncomfortably low chairs mourning their deceased: three days to mourn him, four days to remember his merits in this world.

During this week of mourning, the following activities were prohibited for family members of the deceased (Kolatch, 1990; Ouaknin, 2002):

- They could not do any form of work except cooking and cleaning the house (and only if no one else could do it). This of course included professional occupations, commitments, etc.
- They could not wear leather sandals.
- They could not have sexual relations.
- They could not study the Torah except to learn the laws of mourning, recite psalms, or read the book of Job or the book of Lamentations.

- They could not greet anyone ("hello," "goodbye," and especially not "*shalom*"), but after the first three days, they could answer those who asked about their health.
- They did not wash their clothes, and they did not put on clean clothes.
- They could sit only on the floor or on cushions.
- They could not leave the house except to go to the synagogue on *Shabbat*.
- They could not shave or cut their hair or nails for 30 days.
- They could not take part in joyful occasions for 30 days, or 12 months if they had lost one of their parents.

The corpse was left in the tomb for one year to decompose. The bones were then removed from the coffin and tomb, placed in an ossuary, and buried again. This time it was permanent. This is how good Jews showed respect for their fathers, and how they applied the God-given commandment to honor their parents. It was their way of loving God by following the Torah.

Many contemporary biblical scholars believe that Jesus' encounter with this man took place between the first and second burials. It is unlikely that a family member who was observing the week-long mourning period for first-degree relatives (referred to as "sitting *shiva*" in English) would be outside the house. During the period of *shiva*, mourners remain at home. The ancient process allowed for the individual to confront and overcome grief and express sorrow. It is difficult to imagine Jesus refusing such a sacred obligation. If this reasoning is correct, then the man was asking in effect if he could wait up to a year before starting to follow Jesus.

This person finds himself in a dilemma created by Jesus' call: should he follow Jesus or what he understands to be the requirements of the Torah? Jesus calls the man to follow him, and in doing so, he affirms that *loving God (with all his heart, with all his soul, with all his mind and with all his strength) means following Jesus.*

The Importance of Studying the Torah

To further understand the importance of what Jesus demands, it will be helpful to examine the importance of the Torah for Jesus and for the Jews of his day.[7]

Jesus probably began reading and memorizing the Torah, and many other Hebrew scriptures, at the age of five or six. This was typical for Jewish boys. After age ten, he would have begun to learn the oral Torah, the rabbinical traditions passed down from generation to generation that explain the interpretation of the written Torah.

---

7 "Ben (son of) Bag Bag said: Turn the Torah over and over for everything is in it. Look into it, grow old and worn over it, and never move away from it, for you will find no better portion than it." *Ethics of the Fathers* (*Pirkei Avot*) 5:26.

By age thirteen, most boys would have completed their formal Torah studies and then started learning a trade. The most talented among them were encouraged to continue their studies during their teenage years at the *bet midrash* (house of interpretation) of the synagogue until they were married at about eighteen or twenty years of age. Only the most talented would go on to become disciples of a chief rabbi (Safrai & Stern, 1976, p. 968).

In Jesus' time, knowledge of the Scriptures was widespread. Even ordinary people devoutly studied the Torah in the synagogues. For women, as for men, the synagogue was the center of life (Spangler & Tverberg, 2018, p. 29).

Each Sabbath, a member of the congregation read Scripture and offered a commentary on the day's texts. Gifted rabbis, like Jesus, who were in town would also be called upon. In the first century CE, many people were involved in applying and teaching their faith, not just a few. The Jewish historian Shmuel Safrai writes:

> The study of the Torah was one of the outstanding features of Jewish life during the Second Temple period and in the period after. It was neither limited to the formal context of schools and synagogue, nor was it reserved to the wise, but became an integral part of ordinary Jewish life. The Torah was studied on every occasion, even for very short periods. ... The sound of learning Torah often resounded from homes at night. When people gathered together for joyous feasts such as circumcisions or weddings, groups might form in seclusion to engage in the study of the Law. (Safrai & Stern, 1976, p. 968)

When Jesus demands that the man choose between obeying him and obeying the Torah, he is doing something extraordinary for a Jew. He is doing something that the rabbis of his time never did! He is not just redefining allegiances. He is also testing their understanding of who he is! Both men mentioned in Luke 9 acknowledge Jesus as Lord with their mouths, but their attempts to delay obedience to his call reveal that their affirmation is superficial.

The Purpose of Discipleship

The question that has been at the heart of this study is what someone who has been trained in the school of Jesus should look like. In asking this question, we wanted to discern the purpose of discipleship. The answer we found may surprise us, for we sometimes think that the purpose of discipleship is to apply the moral teaching of Jesus.

And there is a grain of truth in that view. After all, Jesus of Nazareth amends the creed given by the Almighty, the *Shema*, by adding the love of neighbour. What Jesus does by changing the *Shema* is more dumbfounding than we are prone to recognize. It demonstrates Jesus' self-understanding as much more than a rabbi explaining the Law of Moses.

In the study of the incident of the ears of wheat pulled up on the Sabbath day, and in looking at the demands of discipleship on the bereaved man, we see that the purpose of discipleship is not only to follow the example of Jesus. That is, the purpose of discipleship to Jesus cannot be only to incorporate spiritual disciplines; it also involves becoming conformed to his wisdom, love, holiness, and his way of relating to those around him. This will not really happen until we come to grips with the truth that he is the perfect expression of what it means to obediently live according to the Creator's intention.

We have become accustomed to seeing Jesus of Nazareth as the key to God's identification with us in our death-doomed existence. And rightly so. My argument, however, is that a biblical, gospel-driven theology sees him as the true model of how we are to respond to God, to our fellow human beings, and to creation. This means that the purpose of discipleship is not primarily to conform to the Christian norms that we have learned.

The evangelical author A. W. Tozer states, "What comes to mind when we think of God is the most important thing about us" (1961, p. 1). I think that this should be modified to read: "What comes to mind when we think about Jesus of Nazareth is the most important thing about us." In our next study, I argue that what we think about Jesus of Nazareth is also the most important thing about our perception of God and our life as Jesus' followers.

Questions to Think About

1. I argue in this chapter that the words we use when we think and talk about the person of Jesus are of utmost importance. What are the words your local congregation or your denomination most commonly use to describe the identity of the God-man from Nazareth and what it means to follow him?

2. Why is it important for our spiritual lives and for our understanding of discipleship to keep in mind Jesus' Jewish culture?

3. I propose that when Jesus amends the *Shema* during his discussion with the Torah expert he is doing something of utmost importance for our understanding of discipleship. What tendencies—in his own day and in ours—does this act counteract?

4. I propose three examples: the incident of the heads of wheat torn off on the Sabbath day, the man who wanted to bury his father before following Jesus, and the study of the Torah to illustrate Jesus' challenge to those he encountered. How might Jesus present the same challenge to people living in your culture today?

5. In what ways do you think that responding to God the Father, to our fellow human beings and to creation like Jesus did might be different than conformity to the Christian norms where you live?

3. The Authority of Jesus

In our previous study, we looked at the enigma of Jesus of Nazareth. He was a Jew like those around him. He prayed the *Shema* several times a day and went to the temple and to the synagogue like other Jews. He ate and clothed himself like everyone else of his day. He was educated and he taught like others. And he died on a Roman cross like thousands of other Jews of his time. Yet he was also different from everyone around him! He claimed the authority to amend the prayer that lies at the heart of Jewish religion. He maintained that he was above the Sabbath, and he called others to follow him immediately, even when that meant not honouring their parents according to how the religious leaders interpreted God's instruction.

Our first study examined the mysterious identity of Jesus of Nazareth, because this is the foundation of all biblical theology and of spiritual growth or discipleship. Another reason I began with Jesus' identity is that this is the first of the four key questions to which the gospel responds: (1) Who is Jesus of Nazareth? (2) What did Jesus of Nazareth do? (3) Why is Jesus of Nazareth important? (4) How should we respond to Jesus of Nazareth? (adapted from Wu, 2015, pp. 55-75). To formulate a biblical theology, we should not start by asking who God is. I believe that the respected evangelical theologian John Piper, for example, is wrong when he maintains that "God is the Gospel" (2011). Rather, I believe that evangelical theology and any theology of discipleship should start by focusing more specifically on the identity of Jesus of Nazareth.

The Pre-eminence of the Gospel of Matthew

In this session, we will examine the gospel that comes first in the New Testament, even though it is not the oldest, that place being occupied by Mark. Voltaire aptly called Matthew "the most circumstantial gospel that we possess" (1943, p. 110). It is also the best known of the canonical four, so comprehensive in scope that it is called, paradoxically, both "the Church's gospel" and "the Jewish gospel," and so influential—if not always popular— that it must be considered one of the most important books in world history. Howard Clarke labels it the "teaching gospel," reminding us that words from Matthew have been "pronounced, prayed, and intoned more often than those of any author we know; and when we hear the words "the Bible says," we will hear more often from Matthew than from any other book of Scripture (Clarke, 2003, p. xxi).

According to biblical scholar Raymond Brown (1997), Matthew has been considered from the first century onward as the foundational document that grounds the followers of Christ in the teaching of Jesus. Matthew has grouped his Master's teaching into five major sermons[1] that take up a little more than a third of his text.[2] One of the best known of all biblical texts is found at the end of this gospel. In it, the resurrected Christ orders his followers to make disciples who will live according to his teaching, from among all the peoples of the world (Mt. 28:16–20). This biblical text continues to play a pivotal role in the life of Christ's followers today. But to really understand the significance of this "Great Commission" we must establish a clear understanding of the author of this gospel and the groups of believers to whom it was originally addressed.

Matthew and His Community

Most contemporary scholars identify the author of this gospel as a member of the Judeo-Christian community that had fled from Judea shortly before the beginning of the Jewish War (66–70 CE) and established themselves among a largely Gentile population, probably either in Antioch or elsewhere within the province of Syria.[3] Although we cannot be sure of the first gospel's place of composition, it seems to have been composed in a Greek-speaking context with a substantial Jewish population (Clarke, 2003, p. xxii). At the beginning of their presence in this new setting, the Jesus-followers seem to have participated fairly actively in the cultural and religious life of their Jewish neighbors, for they did not see their attachment to Jesus of Nazareth as something that separated them from their former practices (Tomson, 2008). They most likely saw themselves as a renewal movement within Judaism.

However, by the end of the 70s and beginning of the 80s, the situation had evolved considerably. Within the Jewish circles that surrounded this

---

1 These sermons or teaching are on (1) what it means to live like his disciple (chapters 5–7); (2) the mission of the Twelve (chapter 10); (3) how the kingdom will arrive (chapter 13); (4) the correction of the disciple who errs (chapter 18); and (5) false teachers and the end of this age (chapters 23–25).

2 Matthew, also called Levi (Mk. 2:4–17; Lk. 5:27–32), is mentioned in all the lists of the Apostles (Mt. 10:3; Mk. 3:18: Lk. 6:15; Ac. 1:13). His name in Hebrew can be translated as "Theodore" or "God-given." In the account of his calling as a disciple of Christ, we learn that he exercised the profession of tax collector for the Roman government (Mt. 10:3) in the Galilean town of Capernaum, which was Jesus' headquarters for much of his public ministry.

3 Many scholars believe that this gospel comes from Syria, and more particularly from Antioch where there were sizable populations of Jews and of Christ-followers. Paul preached in Antioch on two consecutive Sabbaths (Ac. 13).

community of Christ-followers, a violent debate took place between the Pharisees and the followers of Jesus who were of Jewish origin. We have an indication of this in the "Twelfth Benediction," which reads: "May the Nazarenes and the heretics be destroyed all at once. ... May their names be erased from the Book of Life, and may they no longer be counted among the just" (quoted in Bosch, 1995, pp. 79–80).

When Matthew wrote his gospel, the followers of Jesus were facing an identity crisis, unprecedented in its magnitude. How should they see themselves in the coming years? Could they continue to follow Jesus while remaining active members of the Jewish community? Many scholars date the writing of Matthew between 80 and 100 CE, which would be about a decade after the fall of Jerusalem and the destruction of the Temple by the Roman army of the emperor Titus. That event had an enormous impact on the Jewish community, which, deprived of its Temple and its religious institutions, had to redefine itself primarily based upon observance of the Law. The Pharisees, who took refuge in Jamnia, were the artisans of this reorganization, which would have a negative impact on the young community of Christ-followers (Rasmussen, 1989, p. 179). How should they respond to the increasing importance of the Law of Moses within Judaism? Should they stop seeing Jesus as other than a Jewish prophet? Should they abandon their mission to make disciples of Jesus among their Jewish brothers? These followers of Jesus of Nazareth did not agree with each other on what direction they should take. Some argued that they should observe all the Law of Moses, even in the smallest details. Others insisted that they had received miraculous gifts from the Holy Spirit and that they should now be freed from the Law. Most of the believers were likely somewhere between these two views. It is probable that Matthew did not write his gospel simply to put together a "life of Jesus," but to respond to the crisis being faced by these Jesus-followers and to help them understand their identity and their mission.

Matthew's Description of Jesus

Matthew sought to describe the life of Jesus of Nazareth in a way that would help his followers scattered across the Syrian province to best understand their identity and their mission. To accomplish this, from start to finish, his gospel expresses the understanding that Jesus of Nazareth calls men and women from every tribe, nation, and land to become his disciples. Each part of that mission is firmly grounded in the story of Jesus as explained in this gospel. In fact, nowhere does Matthew allow any room for doubt about his fundamental conviction: Jesus of Nazareth is the Lord who must be worshipped and obeyed. Two details reveal that conviction. They are more important than they seem at first glance.

The first is the way in which Matthew uses the verb (*proskuneō*), which means to pay divine homage, to worship, or to bow in adoration (Mounce,

1993, p. 339). Of course, bowing was (and should still be) a common recognition of superiority and a display of extreme humility and submission. We find this word in Matthew 28:16–20, which indicates that when the disciples saw Jesus, they "worshipped him."

Worship is commonly defined as "the act or feeling of adoration or homage; the paying of religious reverence as in prayer, praise, and so forth." It is derived from the Old English *weorthscipe,* the act of ascribing worth to someone or something.[4] When we analyse the Aramaic and Greek words for worship, however, we perceive a somewhat deeper meaning of the act of worship. The Aramaic word for worship, *segad,*[5] means to bow oneself down, to fall flat, to reverence, or to do obeisance, and it has the connotation of total submission to a superior (e.g., the king). The Greek translation of this word, *proskuneō,* means to prostrate oneself in homage or, more graphically, to "kiss as a dog would lick its master's hand."[6] Matthew is particularly fond of this word. He uses it 13 times, whereas it appears only twice each in Mark and Luke. It refers to a position of submission and adoration that is to be reserved for respect to the Creator God Himself. When Jesus was tempted by Satan in the desert, for instance, he explicitly said that one must worship God alone to the Evil One (Mt. 4:10, which is a quotation of Dt. 6:16). In the story of Jesus walking on the water, Matthew is the only evangelist to mention that when he climbed into the boat with the disciples they "fell prostrate before him," saying, "Truly you are the Son of God" (Mt. 14:33). In Matthew's opinion, Jesus of Nazareth was much more than a master surrounded by his admirers. He was the Lord in the full sense of that title.

This brings us to the second significant detail concerning the identity of Jesus in Matthew's gospel: the way in which he is identified as *kyrios* or "Lord." This Greek word has several different meanings. It can mean sir, master, or owner, or it can even refer to an idol.[7] However, on a few occasions it is the Greek equivalent of the Hebrew word *YHWH* (which orthodox Jews render as G-d out of reverence). In Matthew's gospel, Jesus is addressed as Lord uniquely by his disciples and by suffering people who plead with him to come to their aid. Jesus' adversaries, in contrast, call him "Master" or "Rabbi." Matthew systematically makes this distinction. In those places where Mark and Luke have the disciples addressing Jesus as "Master" or "Rabbi," Matthew has them calling Jesus "Lord." The result is that Jesus' adversaries never call him

---

4 According to the *Merriam-Webster Dictionary*, this word evolved to *worshipe* in Middle English. See http://www.merriam-webster.com/dictionary/worship.

5 This word is used of bowing to kings, idols, and God. It is found only 11 times in the Bible, exclusively in the book of Daniel (2:46; 3:5, 6, 7, 10, 11, 12, 14, 15, 18, 28).

6 Joseph H. Thayer (1996, p. 548) observed that by the time of the New Testament, *proskuneō* denoted a "kneeling or prostration to do homage (to one) or make obeisance, whether in order to express respect or to make supplication."

7 Strong (2009, no. 2962), see also Bauer et al. (1969, p. 459).

"Lord" and his disciples never address him otherwise. [8] In other words, for Matthew, Jesus was more than just a leader of men, as Moses was. Instead, he is the Lord of his disciples, and the One to whom all authority in heaven and on earth has been given (Mt. 28:18).

Although Matthew emphasizes that Jesus of Nazareth is the sovereign Lord before whom we must fall prostrate in adoration, he also highlights Jesus' proximity to his disciples. They appear throughout his gospel like students surrounding their Master. This observation perhaps explains why Matthew does not represent the resurrected Jesus of Nazareth only as the One who ascended to his place of authority at the right hand of the Father, and who will return in the same way at some future date (cf. Ac. 1:11). Matthew does not find it necessary to say that Jesus will come back again. How could he "return" when he is with his disciples "always, to the very end of the age" (Mt. 28:20)? Jesus of Nazareth is "Immanuel," God with us! (Mt. 1:23).

Matthew's interest remains focused on the present situation of the followers of Jesus of Nazareth, and not on the end of history. In his view, the Jesus-followers' experience of their risen Lord is so life-transforming that it encompasses the future. The risen Lord is present wherever two or three of his followers come together to learn how to live as his disciples (Mt. 18:20). This is undoubtedly one of the most surprising affirmations of all Scripture. Jesus offers this promise at the end of a teaching he had given about sin, conflict, the need to hold one another accountable for our actions, and repentance. In doing so, he goes far beyond giving the simple promise that he would be present when people gather in a faith community. He speaks specifically of his presence in the midst of two or three persons who have come together to learn how to live as his disciples (Bjork, 2015, p. 173).

In his commentary on this text, Robertson (1910) stresses that Jesus deals in small numbers, not due to modest expectations but because they suit the present condition, and out of jealousy for the moral quality of their lives. Meyer (1832) maintains that Jesus' promise is not so much that he will be present when his followers meet; rather, it is tied to the reason why they meet. According to Meyer, when a few of Jesus' followers meet with the specific motive of learning how to confess and honor him in their way of living, Jesus promises to be present. This is what spiritual growth or discipleship is all about: learning to live like Jesus. Jesus commanded his followers to go into all the world and make disciples, and he promised to be present whenever they became involved in that process.

---

8 The only exception to this pattern is Judas Iscariot, who calls Jesus "Rabbi" twice during the betrayal (Mt. 26:25, 48).

Make Disciples

The word "disciple" plays a more central role in Matthew's gospel than in Mark or Luke. It is found 63 times in Matthew, 46 times in Mark, and only 37 times in Luke. In fact, it is the only word used in the gospel of Matthew to designate those individuals who accompany Jesus. The verb which is the most frequently associated with "disciple" is *akolutheō*, which means "to accompany, go along with, follow, obey." Michael Wilkins (1992) describes the notion of a disciple in this way:

> The word disciple is the term that is used the most often in the Gospels to designate those who follow Jesus, and who are called believers, brothers/sisters, followers of the Way, or saints by the early church. ... This word was used in this specific sense at least 230 times in the Gospels and 28 times in the Acts of the Apostles. (p. 178)

Wilkins argues that Matthew's gospel can be seen as a manual on discipleship, for four reasons: (1) the major teaching sections are directed at least in part to the disciples; (2) most of the sayings directed to the disciples are in fact teachings on discipleship; (3) unlike the gospel of Mark, the disciples are portrayed in a positive yet realistic light; and (4) the disciples are called, trained, and commissioned to carry out their ultimate mandate to make disciples (Wilkins, 1992a, p. 183).

For Matthew, the Twelve Apostles are a sort of prototype of all who would follow Jesus, even the members of the communities to which he was writing. In other words, for Matthew there is continuity between the first followers of Jesus of Nazareth and those who are following him later. And what connects them is Jesus' command to make disciples who "observe all" that Jesus has commanded. The adherents of the earthly Jesus were to accompany others so that they too would conform their way of living to his example and teaching (Przybylski, 1980, p. 112). And it is precisely this process that connects us to the first followers of Jesus and to each other. Each of us serves the Master, but not alone. Every disciple of Jesus is a member of the brotherhood of disciples, or else he or she is not really a disciple of Jesus at all. For Matthew, being a disciple of Jesus of Nazareth means conforming ourselves to the example and teaching of Jesus in the concrete details of our daily life. This is, in fact, the central theme of all the New Testament revelation of God (Ridderbos, 1978). It is summed up in Jesus' teaching about the kingdom of heaven.

The Kingdom of Heaven Was at the Heart of Jesus' Teaching

Everyone knows that Jesus' favorite form of teaching was his parables, many of which set forth the kingdom of heaven. In explaining this form of teaching, Jesus himself described the content of the parables as "the mysteries of the kingdom of heaven" (Mt. 13:11). Usually, the parable is introduced by the words, "The kingdom is like unto ...." In Luke 4:43, Jesus said that communicating about "the kingdom of God" was the very purpose of His ministry.

We will look again at the notion of the kingdom of heaven in chapter 8, but it is important to examine it briefly here because it was at the heart of Jesus' teaching. I contend that the resurrected Jesus' divine authority is the key to understanding the "mystery" of the Father's will (cf. Eph. 1:9–11). This is in line with Matthew's presentation of discipleship as learning to live under the rule of Jesus of Nazareth in the kingdom of heaven.[9]

The Kingdom of Heaven in the Creator's Plan

John the Baptist's message that "the kingdom of heaven is at hand" (3:2) is the first of 29 distinctly Matthean references to God's "kingdom," a concept almost completely absent from the Hebrew Scriptures. It may strike us as strange, but I find it highly significant that although it is God's kingdom, God (the Father) is never referred to as its king. Matthew, unlike Mark and Luke, usually calls it the "kingdom of heaven" rather than of "God" (Clarke, 2003, p. 31).

Moreover, not only is the kingdom of heaven a major theme in Matthew's gospel, but I maintain with Thomas Schreiner that "the 'kingdom of God,' if that term is defined with sufficient flexibility, fits well as a central theme of the entire Bible" (2013, p. xii). Schreiner explains that the phrase "thematically captures, from a biblical theology standpoint, the message of Scripture" (2013, p. xiii). A close relationship exists between God's kingdom and his goal or project in creation. Indeed, the Scriptures tell how, after being usurped by Satan, the Creator's rule is reinstated by the life, death, and resurrection of the eternal Son incarnated in Jesus of Nazareth. That rule is worked out in the lives of the followers of king Jesus with the aid of his indwelling Spirit. The divine project moves toward a new heaven and a new earth where the Creator's kingship is fully worked out.

The Creator Is on a Mission

The Apostle Paul teaches that the Creator is the primary actor in the universe. For Paul, God (the eternal Father, Son, and Spirit) does not intervene haphazardly in our world. He does not decide on his plans on the spur of the moment, devising extra parts of his purpose as human history unfolds. Rather, the triune God had a complete plan formulated from the beginning of creation. His actions are not isolated incidents, unrelated to each other. And the dramatic events that so often take us by surprise are no shock to Him. On the contrary,

---

9 J. Andrew Overman observes that the Matthean community understood itself in certain respects as the reflection and embodiment of the kingdom that is in heaven. In other words, the disciple of Jesus is to live out the order and values of the heavenly society of which he or she is already a member (1990, p. 131).

Paul was convinced that God supervises and guides human history with great attention, and toward a specific goal. In the first of his sermons of which we have a record, for example, he argued that David had "served God's purpose in his own generation" (Ac. 13:36). Later, when he was preparing to leave the elders in Ephesus, he explained that he had not hesitated to explain to them the "whole will of God" (Ac. 20:27). The Greek word used in both verses, *boulē*, means "design, project, resolution, plan, will or intention." It refers to what God has decided, that which he has determined to accomplish. For Paul, the Creator God has a specific design, a particular project that he is in the process of bringing to completion. In 2 Corinthians 5, Paul underscores two aspects of that project: (1) the centrality of Jesus of Nazareth, the Christ, and (2) the goal of the reconciliation of heaven and earth under his rulership. Let us take a close look at these two important elements of the Creator's plan.

The Centrality of Jesus of Nazareth, the Christ

In 2 Corinthians 5:14, Paul explains that *"Christ's* love compels us." (Notice that here he does not say that we are motivated or driven by *God's* love. His argument is that since Jesus of Nazareth, the Christ, died for us, each of us must no longer live for ourselves, but for him (Christ) who died and was raised again (verse 15). Then Paul speaks of our being *"in Christ"* (verse 17), of God's working *"through Christ"* (verse 18), of God reconciling the world to himself *"in Christ"* (verse 19), of our being *"Christ's* ambassadors" (verse 20), and of our imploring others "on *Christ's behalf"* (verse 20). In this way Paul stresses the centrality of Jesus of Nazareth, the Christ, in God's plan.

Jesus of Nazareth is, of course, the central pivot of the gospel (Rom. 1:1–4). But the Scriptures indicate that it was even on Jesus' account that creation was brought into existence in the first place. Hebrews 1:1–2 says of Jesus, "On account of him, the Creator made the universe."[10] The Greek word for *universe* here means "ages." Literally it reads, "On account of him he made the ages," meaning not only that creation happened on account of Jesus of Nazareth, but also that the eternal Son incarnated in the person of Jesus of Nazareth is in control of the triune God's plan and programme throughout all time. This statement points to Jesus as the beginning point of the universe, of history, and of all things. It includes everything that exists within time. Everything in the Creator's programme within the domain of time is in Jesus' control, and the Son incarnate operates the universe through its successive ages and dispensations (Fruchtenbaum, 2005, pp. 19–20). As the Bible discloses, God reveals his plan and programme through time, but the times and ages through which the Creator God's purpose and plan are revealed and unfolded lie under the control of the Lord Jesus of Nazareth, the Christ.

---

10 The Greek words translated "through whom" in the NIV are better translated "on account of" (Peeler, 2014, p. 13).

Not only is Jesus the beginning of all creation and the one who operates it according to the Creator's plan, but in Colossians 1:15–17 Paul makes the startling statement that Jesus of Nazareth is, as it were, the goal or purpose toward which the created world is destined to move (Moule, 1991, p. 59). We will come back to this idea a little later. At this point, let us simply affirm that Jesus of Nazareth existed in the Creator God's mind and purpose from the beginning, although he came into existence physically only by his birth through Mary. 1 Peter 1:20 sums it up: Jesus of Nazareth, the Christ, "was chosen before the creation of the world but was revealed in these last times."[11]

It is important that we understand clearly what is and is not being affirmed. The human Jesus of Nazareth did not pre-exist his virginal conception in the womb of Mary as a human being. As Oliver Crisp (2009) clearly states:

> No human being pre-exists its conception as a human being. (If the human 'part' of Christ has a first moment of existence like other human beings have a first moment of existence, then the human 'part' of Christ cannot pre-exist that first moment of existence as a human being.) It is the Word who assumes human nature at the Incarnation. In so doing, the Word takes to himself the human nature of Christ and becomes a human being. (p. 56)

In this book I will intentionally distinguish between the human Jesus of Nazareth and the eternal Son of God, or Word. The eternal Son is that member of the triune Creator, who voluntarily took it upon himself to become a flesh and blood man in the person of Jesus of Nazareth, and thereby become the mediator of human salvation.

Two Ways of Understanding the Authority of the Eternal Son and the Authority of God the Father

We must pause to examine two ways in which evangelicals interpret the authority of the eternal Son incarnated in Jesus of Nazareth in relation to the authority of God the Father, because this influences their understanding of his current role in the kingdom of heaven. If, as I have just demonstrated, Jesus of Nazareth, the incarnate eternal Son of God, is central to the divine plan, and if the kingdom of heaven is a major theme of Scripture, then this is a vital subject.

Although they all confess the trinitarian affirmations of the creeds, a gulf has formed dividing evangelicals on the question of *authority* within the members of the Trinity (McCormic, 2016, p. 1). I am convinced that how we understand the authority of Jesus influences all our theology, our reading of Scripture, our worship, our ecclesiology, and our understanding of our mission.

---

11 Although a literal rendering might identify Jesus the Christ as "foreknown" (NASB, NET, ESV), other translations speak of him as "chosen" (NIV, TEV) or "destined" (RSV) (Dubis, 2010, p. 33).

Both perceptions of the authority of Jesus are founded on Scripture, but each one reads those scriptures differently.

The Son is Eternally *Submitted* to the Father

The first way in which some evangelicals understand the authority of Jesus of Nazareth, the incarnate Son, and the authority of God the Father recognizes an ontological equality between the members of the Holy Trinity while holding that there is an eternal submission in their way of functioning. Wayne Grudem, one of the most influential evangelical theologians today, expresses that position. He writes, "The Son and Holy Spirit are equal in deity to God the Father, but they are subordinate in their roles" (1994, p. 249). Grudem's idea of the subordination of the trinitarian roles of the Son and the Holy Spirit is not tied to the particular work of the divine persons but refers directly to that of commanding and obeying (2016, p. 20). Grudem writes that "the role of commanding, of directing and of sending is that of the Father ... and the role of obeying, of leaving as the Father sends him, and of revealing the Father is that of the Son" (2016, p. 251). Grudem leans heavily on those biblical texts that identify the Father as the initiator of divine activity and projects in the world (for example, Eph. 1:9–12). He also finds scriptural support in the gospel of John, where Jesus is seen as the one sent by the Father (Jn. 3:16) and the one who does the Father's will (Jn. 6:38).

Grudem is not alone in this view. We find the same preeminence of the Father in the trinitarian thought of other evangelical theologians, such as Charles Hodge, an extremely influential voice in the late nineteenth century. In his systematic theology, Hodge affirms the divinity of the Son, yet unceasingly speaks of his subordination to the Father (1952, p. 445). Hodge argues strongly for the eternal subordination of the Son to the Father, linking it to the self-revelation of the divinity as Father, Son, and Spirit (McCormic, 2016, p. 13). McCormic also points to August Strong who maintains that the formulation of the Nicene Creed, "Jesus Christ, the only Son of God, eternally begotten of the Father, God from God, Light from Light, true God from true God, begotten, not made, of one being with the Father," supports the subordination of the Son to the Father in his personality, rank, and operations (2016, p. 15).

More recently, Bruce Ware has held similarly that the Son is subordinate to the Father, even if he prefers the words "eternal submission" to subordination. Ware maintains a traditional understanding of the Trinity in which each member of the Godhead is fully and eternally divine—not three gods but three persons forming one deity (2005, pp. 15–22). He underscores forcefully, however, the structure of authority and submission which, he writes, "marks even the eternal nature of the deity" (Ware, 2005, p. 37). And he rightfully looks at Matthew 28:19 and maintains that the order (*taxis*) of Father, Son, and Holy Spirit should in no case be reorganized or upset. He sees here an eternal hierarchical order. Since the supremacy of the Father is revealed in this way,

Ware teaches that the Father should also receive the most glory and honor in our worship and prayer (2005, p. 61).

I cannot emphasize strongly enough how this teaching has fashioned our current practice. It is in direct opposition to texts such as Matthew 28:18, where the resurrected Jesus of Nazareth claims to exercise all authority in heaven and on earth. This conviction that the Son is eternally submitted to the Father diminishes the significance of the incarnation, and of the exaltation of the incarnate Son who reassumed equality of authority with the Father.

The Son is Eternally *Equal* to the Father

The resurrected Jesus of Nazareth, the incarnated eternal Son, affirmed that supreme authority has been given to him by the Father. The Apostle Peter made this same claim in his sermon on the day of Pentecost:

> David did not ascend to heaven, and yet he said, "The Lord said to my Lord: 'Sit at my right hand until I make your enemies a footstool for your feet.'" Therefore let all Israel be assured of this: God has made this Jesus, whom you crucified, both Lord and Christ. (Ac. 2:34–36)

In his letter to the Colossians, the Apostle Paul writes that "Christ is seated at the right hand of God" (Col. 3:1). In Psalm 110:1, quoted by Peter and by Jesus himself (Mt. 22:41–45), we find the same language. Hebrews 1:3 states similarly, "After he [the Son] had provided purification for sins, he sat down at the right hand of the Majesty in heaven." Grudem maintains that the position at the right hand of God the Father indicates a place of subordination and thereby reveals that Jesus does not possess the same authority as the Father (McCormic, 2016, p. 29). But the evangelical theologians to whom I will turn now argue that other biblical texts communicate that the throne of God is occupied by the fullness of the trinitarian nature of the deity. These authors quote, for example, the witness of Revelation, which affirms that the heavenly throne is "the throne of God and of the Lamb" (Paul, 2019).[12]

Kevin Giles (2006) points out the serious problems that follow from teaching that the Son incarnate is eternally submitted to the Father. But he is not alone in arguing forcefully for the full equality of the three persons of the divinity (Cunningham, 1998, p. 113; Erickson, 1995, p. 331; Torrance, 1996). Tom McCall (2010, p. 186) summarizes the "mistake" committed by those theologians who deny the equal authority of the Father and the Son: (1) they read back into the immanent or eternal Trinity the subordination seen in the

---

12 As the Overcomer, the incarnate Son speaks of "my throne" (Rev. 3:21a) and, again, as having "sat down with my Father on his throne" (Rev. 3:21b). Twice he is seen "in the centre" of the divine throne (Rev. 5:6; 7:17). The divine presence on the New earth is described as "the throne of God and the Lamb" (Rev. 22:1, 3).

incarnation, (2) which leads them to develop a robust subordination characterized by a hierarchy within the divinity, (3) and which in turn, consequently, identifies the Son as possessing less glory and majesty than the Father.

Adesola Akala (2019) acknowledges that the gospel of John, which unquestionably presents the submission of the Son to the Father in the economy of salvation more than the other gospels do, is at the heart of the debate. Yet, based on an in-depth study of the prologue of that gospel (Jn. 1:1–18), the pericopes that detail the conflicts between Jesus and the religious leaders (Jn. 5:17–24; 6:1–13, 28–57; 7:14–18; 10:1–38, 12:37–49), his last instructions to his disciples (Jn. 13:1–16), and his sacerdotal prayer (Jn. 17), Akala argues that John ingeniously reveals the eternal Son's equality with the Father while accomplishing his saving mission. He concludes that the eternal divinity of the Son and his equality with the Father are in no way compromised by his mission in the world.

In her study of another important text in our discussion, Amy Peeler (2019) demonstrates how the epistle to the Hebrews uses paternal and filial language to illustrate the intimate and unique relationship that exists between the Son and the Father. Peeler maintains that according to the epistle to the Hebrews, there has never been a moment when the authority of the Father was distinct from that of the Son, since they are portrayed as mutually dependent. She insists that the language of the sender and the sent one in no way indicates the submission of the Son to the Father. On the contrary, according to Peeler, that language expresses only their differentiated roles in the accomplishment of one unique will. This is an important element to note! If each divine person has his own will, which is implied by the affirmation that the Son must submit to the Father's will, the unity of the Godhead is destroyed (Giles, 2006, p. 30). Instead, Peeler concludes that a theological reading of the epistle to the Hebrews reveals mutual authority and no submission. This is true because the authority given by the Father to the enthroned and exalted Son is a reiteration of the glory, will, and power that the Son shares equally with the Father throughout eternity. The synopsis offered by Fred Sanders (2010, p. 62) on this topic is helpful: "God's way of being God is to be Father, Son and Holy Spirit simultaneously from all eternity, perfectly complete in a triune fellowship of love." E. A. Johnston (2016, p. 5) adds, "God is eternally and inseparably three divine persons within the one divine essence. If God were lacking this 'eternal threeness' in the ceaseless unity of his one divine essence, he would not be the God that he is." And a careful study of Scripture reveals that it always speaks of the singular will of God, not a divided will or multiplicity of wills, one for each divine person (Sommer, 2016).

Arguing from the doctrine of divine simplicity, Dennis Jowers (2012, pp. 384–385) affirms eternal equality of authority among the persons of the Godhead. The Father, Son, and Holy Spirit have one will. Because there is only one divine will, it follows that the Father cannot issue commands to the Son, and God the Son cannot submit to them.

Glenn Butner (2018) also centres the debate on the question of the unique will of the deity. He shows that 1 Corinthians 15:28 is the only text that uses the Greek word for the submission of the Son outside of the life and ministry of Jesus of Nazareth. This verse reads: "When he has done this, then the Son himself will be made subject to him who put everything under him, so that God may be all in all." Butner maintains that this refers clearly to the eternal Son in his assumed role as the second Adam. Butner (2018) writes:

> Though the biblical authors do not have questions of the eternal intra-trinitarian relations between Father and Son in mind, many texts referring to Christ's submission during his incarnate life are best interpreted in light of such second Adam Christology. (p. 193)

For the evangelicals who hold this position, the subordination seen in the incarnation does not reveal the eternal relationship between the Son and the Father. Instead, they argue, when the eternal *Logos* "became flesh" he freely chose to "submit" to the Father for our salvation, but that plan included his exaltation by the Father to the highest place, where every tongue will confess that he is Lord after his resurrection and enthronement (cf. Phil. 2:9–11). This is an important concept to hold on to as we think about the kingdom of God and the divine plan.

The Second Adam Christology in 2 Corinthians 5

Now we can come back to our discussion of 2 Corinthians 5, where Paul points out that the reconciliation God is accomplishing in the Christ is both personal and universal. He writes in verse 17, "Therefore, if anyone is in Christ, he is a new creation, the old has gone, the new has come." We often interpret this verse in the context of personal conversion to Christ. We say that when someone is united to Christ by faith, he or she is recreated. His or her old state of being is left behind; what he or she was previously has disappeared, and the new has already come. There is certainly some truth in this interpretation. However, the Greek text of 5:17 does not contain the words "he is." Instead, it says literally, "If anyone is in Christ, new creation." For this reason, some biblical scholars suggest that we should interpret this verse as meaning, "If anyone is in Christ, the new creation has come." This interpretation would be in accordance with several Old Testament texts, such as Isaiah 43:18–19, 65:17, and 66:22, which announce that God will do a new thing, a "new creation," and that His new creation was already beginning (see Stamm, 1992, pp. 96–97; Keener, 2005, p. 185). Understanding the verse in this way, and considering Paul's comparison between the resurrection of Christ and the creation of Adam in 1 Corinthians 15:45, these scholars read Paul as affirming that when a person is in Christ, he or she already belongs to the eschatological reality of the new creation.[13] In other words, belonging to Christ by faith, being united to him, and living under his control mean already participating actively in the creative work that God the Father began at the resurrection of Jesus, and which continues to influence all things. When a person is in Christ, the new creation that took place at the resurrection of Jesus takes effect (Barrett, 1968, p. 174). So according to this understanding, in the death and resurrection of Jesus an old, rebellious way of existing as human beings came to an end and a new way of being has become a possibility.

This picture of the new creation is tied to the biblical understanding that if we are followers of Jesus, our Heavenly Father has "rescued us from the dominion of darkness and brought us into the kingdom of the Son he loves" (Col. 1:13). Because of this rescue from the power of darkness, we have the blessing of learning from the eternal Son made flesh in Jesus of Nazareth, and of being empowered by his Spirit, so that we begin to. live differently. This is what living in the kingdom of heaven is all about. Growing in discipleship consists of learning how to live in the kingdom of heaven, which is the kingdom of Christ and of God the Father. In 1 Thessalonians 2:12, Paul tells us that God has called us into "*his* kingdom," that is, the kingdom of God the Father. The kingdom "of the Son he loves" (Col. 1:13) and the kingdom of God the Father (1 Th. 2:12) are one and the same. Ephesians 5:5 calls the kingdom by both names: "the kingdom of Christ and of God."

Matthew argues that the disciples of Jesus must learn how to live within the kingdom of heaven. He wants nothing to do with a gospel that is detached from the earthly Jesus, either through a legalistic attachment to the Torah or through an enthusiastic connection to the Holy Spirit. Making disciples of Jesus, for Matthew, is to add members not to some existing congregation or denomination but to the kingdom of heaven. For Matthew, we are disciples of Jesus of Nazareth, and we make disciples of Jesus because he is the one to whom ultimate allegiance is due. He is the acting king in the kingdom he proclaimed in his teaching.

The assertion that Jesus of Nazareth is currently reigning over the kingdom of God is problematic for many evangelicals, because we focus so intently on Jesus as the Lamb of God who takes away the sin of the world. Our theology appropriately highlights the unique role of Jesus of Nazareth in our salvation, but he is often eclipsed as the centre of our theology and practice. In our next study, we will examine some of the words of Jesus that have fashioned our current evangelical theology.

---

13 Paul writes in Romans 8:19–22 that because of its "subjection to frustration"—its "bondage to decay"—creation "groans". Not only does it groan, but it is also in labour, for something new is being brought to birth.

Questions to Think About

1. I state at the beginning of this chapter that any theology of discipleship should start by focusing specifically on the identity of Jesus of Nazareth, and I quote another scholar who claims that this is why the gospel of Matthew has been considered from the first century onward as the foundational document for the followers of the Christ. How can this perspective function as a corrective to imperfect models of discipleship and Christian growth?

2. What are some of the ways that Matthew expresses his fundamental conviction that Jesus of Nazareth is the Lord who must be worshipped and obeyed? Why is it important for our spiritual lives to keep this perspective in mind?

3. What is Matthew's purpose in highlighting discipleship in his gospel? What tendencies—in his own day and in ours—are counteracted by the notion of discipleship to Jesus?

4. This chapter presents two possible ways of understanding the authority of the eternal Son and the authority of God the Father. Which one do you believe represents the authority of the eternal Son today, and what are the implications of this for discipleship?

5. The last section of this chapter presents the Second Adam Christology in 2 Corinthians 5, and ties it to Colossians 1:13 and 1 Thessalonians 2:12. How should this reality affect our lives, both individually and in our interactions with others?

4. God *through* Jesus, or God *in* Jesus: What's the Difference and Why Does it Matter?

In our previous study, we looked at the understandings of the authority of the resurrected Jesus of Nazareth that are debated in evangelical circles today. What does it mean that after his resurrection he received all sovereign authority in both heaven and on earth? I believe that our answer to that question influences our understanding of spiritual growth and discipleship. Now I want to delve more deeply into that assertion.

Our relationship to God as it is mediated by Jesus the Christ is not some optional topic on the disciple-making agenda. It goes beyond the question of how we come to personal salvation and influences how we read the Bible, how we worship, and our understanding of what discipleship is all about. In fact, this issue lies at the root of most if not all the other issues that are frequently discussed in theology. The relationship between the gospel and discipleship is, at its heart, about our relationship to God as it is mediated by Jesus. So are such matters as the role of the Holy Spirit, listening to God's voice, recognizing God's beauty, or tasting God's goodness. All these questions may seem at first to be only indirectly connected to Jesus and only remotely tied to discipleship and disciple making. But a closer examination reveals otherwise.

Take for instance the question of giving glory to God. Several years ago, I reflected on how Jesus' command to make disciples might fit with Paul's instruction to do everything for the glory of God (1 Cor. 10:31). How do these two seemingly different objectives fit together? To answer that question, I explored the concept of glory in the Bible (Bjork, 2015, pp. 111–128). I concluded that God is glorified when we give Jesus the Christ his appropriate place in our lives. This seems to be what the Apostle Paul and the early Jesus-followers taught. They affirmed that recognizing Jesus' lordship fulfills the Father's purpose and so brings glory to God (cf. Phil. 2:11).

Their thinking seems to have been that since we have been called by God the Father into "the fellowship of his Son, Jesus Christ our Lord" (1 Cor. 1:9), then it must be by our identity in and conformity to the indwelling Messiah in our daily living that our Heavenly Father receives His rightful glory (cf. 1 Pet. 4:11; Col. 3:17; Rom. 13:12–14; Gal. 3:27–28). God is glorified when we become like Jesus the Christ who is "our righteousness, sanctification and redemption" (1 Cor. 1:30), for Jesus is "the radiance of the glory of God and the exact imprint of his nature" (Heb. 1:3). In this sense, then, giving glory to God is the same thing as discipleship, or growth in Jesus' likeness (cf. 2 Cor. 3:18; Gal. 4:19), for God is remaking us into his image, and he is doing so by conforming us to the One who is that image. Therefore, the entire divine project is focused on our complete participation in Jesus' life, which joins us to the life of our triune God and enables us to give glory to God. And when God accomplishes our glorification in Jesus the Messiah, "we will be participants in that one stupendous act of union in which things in heaven and earth will be reconciled to God through Jesus of Nazareth the Christ, through whom and for whom all things were created" (Johnson, 2013, p. 187; see also Bjork, 2015, pp. 111–128).

In this study, I continue to explore how we understand our relationship to both God the Father and Jesus the Christ. This understanding is critical to our personal discipleship[1] and to the future of the disciple-making movements or gatherings we are involved in. My concern will not be to explore why we believe in the deity of Jesus; I will assume that the reader is already convinced that Jesus the Christ (or Messiah), is the Son of God.[2] Nor will I enter into the intense and at times bloody debate over the relationship of Jesus the Christ, the eternal Son, to God the Father, which was finally settled by the Council of Nicea.[3] My focus will be on how we, as followers of Jesus, might best understand and communicate our relationship to God.

The words we choose to describe this relationship are not neutral. Rather, they transmit prepackaged ideas and operative definitions about God that can often distort the nature of discipleship to Jesus the Christ. For example, we cannot accurately summarize the goal of discipleship to the Messiah by saying, "The goal of discipleship to Jesus is that people might be forgiven of their sins that separate them from God and come to have a personal relationship with

---

1 I use the word "discipleship" to refer to the state of being consciously and intentionally apprenticed to Jesus the Christ, choosing to follow and obey him, and being taught by his Spirit and others how to live as he did—loving God the Father and loving people. I distinguish this from the notion of disciple making, or discipling, which I use to refer to the act of accompanying others in this same process.

2 To examine the issue of Christ's deity, see Boettner (1943); Bowman & Komoszewski (2007); Bruce & Martin (2018); and Gurbikian (2011).

3 In the fourth century CE, the newly legalized network of Christ-followers was rocked by a bloody and seemingly intractable theological argument that involved Roman emperors (Constantine, Theodosius) as well as bishops (Arius, Eusebius of Nicomedia, Athanasius, St Jerome) and brought about synods (Councils of Nicea and Constantinople), official confessions of beliefs (Nicene Creed) and accusations of heresy (Arianism). At issue was the exact nature of the divinity of Christ, specifically whether he was a created being or unbegotten and emanating from one same substance. To examine the debates surrounding this question in detail, see Hurtado (2005); Jenkins (2010); and Rubenstein (2013).

Him," (Answers, 2019), or "Christians today must truly 'go all out' to show God that they genuinely seek first His Kingdom. This must be the primary goal of a Christian's entire life!" (Meredith, 2007).

Although these statements do contain important partial truths, they confuse the content of discipleship to Jesus the Christ and the true nature of disciple making (which is probably not even the best term to use).[4]

The Question of "God *through* Jesus" or "God *in* Jesus" and Discipleship

There are two basic evangelical understandings of our relationship to God the Father and to the Lord Jesus, the Christ. The two paradigms can ground their rationale in the words of Jesus to either Thomas or Philip, respectively, as recorded in John 14.

The biblical foundation for the first understanding (Figure 1) is found in Jesus' response to Thomas's request to be shown the way to the Father,[5] Jesus replied, "I am the way, and the truth, and the life. No one comes to the Father except *through* me" (Jn. 14:6, *italics* mine). In these words can be found the basis for understanding our relationship to God the Father and to Jesus the Messiah that I will call the "God *through* Jesus" model.

A Description of Discipleship in the "God *through* Jesus" Model

Several factors make this perspective appealing, not the least of which is its simplicity. The logic it expresses is not complex: God, who is a personal being,[6] created us for relationship with himself (Hordern, 1969, pp. 132, 153). Our fall into sin fractured our relationships with God and with one another (cf. Gen. 2:17; Rom. 3:23; 6:23). God has fixed what we have broken by reconciling our relationship with Himself *through* Jesus (cf. Rom. 5:1, 10; 2 Cor. 5:18; Eph. 2:15–17; Col. 1:20–22).[7] The following figure illustrates this perception.

---

4 I define this process as occurring when two apprentices of Jesus (one perhaps mentoring the other), for a short or longer period of time, voluntarily and freely decide to encourage, exhort, and build up each other with the goal of becoming more like their Master, under the direction of the Holy Spirit (Bjork, 2015, p. 140).

5 The word "Father" occurs approximately 118 times in John's gospel. But "Father" is not simply the Fourth Gospel's preferred name for God; it is the primary metaphor for shaping theological discourse (O'Day & Hylen, 2006).

6 Note that orthodox thought does not conceive of God as personal. It speaks of personality *in* God rather than of the personality *of* God. It conceives of God as consisting of a unity of three personalities, not as one personality (Baillie, 1990, pp. 138–139).

7 That Jesus endured on the cross what sinners should have endured seems simple enough. The Apostle Paul emphasizes this throughout his correspondence with the first Jesus followers (e.g., Rom. 6:23; 2 Cor. 5:14, 21; Gal. 3:13). This was such a central

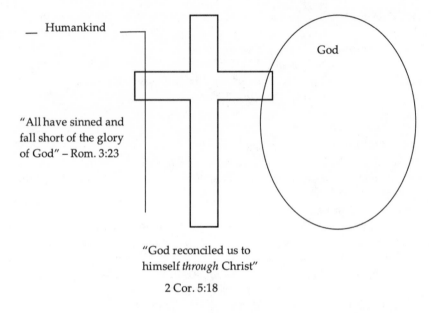

"All have sinned and
fall short of the glory
of God" – Rom. 3:23

"God reconciled us to
himself *through* Christ"

2 Cor. 5:18

Figure 1: God through Jesus Model

Beyond its simplicity, this understanding is also attractive because it clearly distinguishes between God the Father and the eternal Son whom he has sent into the world.[8] In this way, it makes a very difficult subject easier to understand or explain to others. For instance, Jesus claimed to be one with God the Father in John 10:30. Emphasizing that we come to God *through* Jesus highlights that although Jesus is one with the Father, he is not the Father; they relate to each other but are not "the same." Moreover, it fits the image of Jesus the Christ who now serves as our great High Priest in the heavenly sanctuary (Heb. 4:14; 8:1, 2). It also stresses that Jesus is the only way to access the divine presence. There is no other means of salvation (Ac. 4:12; 1 Tim. 2:5).

Finally, this way of interpreting our relationship with God *through* Jesus fits the Old Testament pre-Exile pattern of the ancient Hebrews relating to *Yahweh*: people—temple sacrifice—divine presence. Prior to the destruction of the first temple in 587 BCE, the people (represented by the high priest) came into the

---

element in his understanding of the message he was to communicate that he claimed to know nothing else (1 Cor. 2:2). He says of himself and his colleagues, "We preach Christ crucified (1 Cor. 1:23), and he referred frequently to the centrality of the cross (e.g., 1 Cor. 1:17–18; Gal. 5:11; 6:12, 14; Eph. 2:16; Phil. 2:8; 3:18; Col. 1:20; 2:14).

8 There has been a tendency among Anglican theologians to sharpen the distinction between the persons of the Trinity, regarding them as distinct personal beings between whom there can be a "social" relationship. In the Patristic age, the Cappadocian Fathers, the two Gregories, and Basil went farthest in this direction.

place of God's presence *through* (or by means of) the various sin offerings outlined in Leviticus 4–5. Because the ancient Hebrews could properly meet with the living God only *through* their sin offerings (cf. Ex. 25:22; 29:42; 30:36; Lev. 26:11–12; 1 Sam. 4:4), it is easy to draw a parallel with the person and ministry of Jesus the Messiah as he died for our sin. Even as the substitute animal had to be perfect and without blemish, so Jesus himself was perfect (1 Pet. 3:18). Even as the substitute became sin for the offeror through identification and had to die, so Jesus, when he identified with us, bore our sins in his body on the cross, thereby dying for our sins (1 Pet. 2:24).[9] Just as the substitute animal died, giving its life to the offeror, so likewise, when Jesus died, he gave believers access to his life (Jn. 17:2–3; Rom. 5:10). Since the principles of atonement do not change from pre-Exile Judaism to the New Testament,[10] we often conclude that the intention of our worship is to meet with the living God *through* Christ.

This perspective highlights some important truths, but it also distorts our understanding of our relationship to God and to Jesus the Messiah in a way that undermines discipleship to Jesus.[11] This is because it primarily views Jesus the Messiah as the *means*, and *not the goal*, of our salvation. In other words, it views Jesus as merely the means of our rescue from damnation and the One *through* whom we can enter a relationship with a superior reality we call God. As important as these truths about the salvific work of Jesus of Nazareth are, this understanding tends to separate Jesus the Christ from the goal of our salvation. In this way, the "God *through* Jesus" understanding fosters what might be labeled "a Godward life" or a pursuit of "the supremacy of God in all

---

9 Peter has much to say about Jesus' saving work, but he also speaks of his resurrection (1 Pet. 1:3; 3:21) and his enthronement in the place of power and authority (1 Pet. 3:22; cf. Ps 110:1; Rom. 8:34). "With angels, authorities and powers" now under him, he is the supreme Lord (cf. Rom. 8:38–39; 1 Cor. 15:24ff.).

10 After the destruction of the temple, the study and practice of the Torah increasingly became the focal point of Jewish worship. It was for millions of ordinary Jews a "movable temple" (see Sanders, 1990, chaps. 2–3). According to Wright (1992, p. 228), the Pharisees in particular, in conjunction with the burgeoning synagogue movement, developed the theory that the study and practice of the Torah could take the place of temple worship. "Where two or three gather to study Torah, the *Shekinah* rests upon them" (Aboth 3.2, cited by Danby, 1980).

11 For example, this position often mistakenly assumes, as we have seen in our previous study, that because of the functional subordination of the Son to the Father during the incarnation, the Son continues to be inferior to the Father in some way. Although Jesus says in John 14:28 that the Father is greater than he is, this must not be understood as a superiority of the Father to the Son in his divinity (see the linking of the Father, Son, and Holy Spirit as equals in the baptismal formula of Matthew 28:19 and the Pauline benediction of 2 Corinthians 13:14). In the incarnation, Jesus emptied himself of equality with God, not of the form of God (cf. Phil. 2:6–7). He did not cease to be in nature what the Father is; rather, he became functionally subordinate to the Father for the time period of his incarnation (see Erickson, 1995, p. 735).

of life," which ultimately softens the centrality of Jesus of Nazareth and discipleship to him.

Problems Created by the "God through *Jesus" Theological*
Understanding in Our Discipleship and Disciple Making

Paul Hertig, Professor at Azusa Pacific University and author of articles on Matthew's experience of discipleship and the Great Commission, describes his exegetical study of Matthew 28:16–20 as an exploration of the "post-resurrection declaration of God's universal reign" (Hertig, 2001, p. 343). His approach is a good example of the kind of confusion that happens when discipleship to Christ is embraced in a "God *through* Jesus" paradigm. For instance, following David Bosch, Hertig correctly maintains that the resurrection of Jesus led to the final mission mandate, which "demanded the surrender to Jesus' Lordship" (Hertig, 2001, p. 347). He also properly stresses that the goal of making disciples can only "refer to the process of transforming into the likeness of Jesus" (Hertig, 2001, p. 343). So far, so good. However, immediately after writing this, Hertig changes his vocabulary and emphatically affirms that discipleship is "total submission to God's reign." In contrast, as I have already noted, Jesus of Nazareth now holds the supreme place in the kingdom of heaven.

The understood goal of the "God *through* Jesus" perspective emerges clearly when Hertig writes, "Once the 'disciples are made' they are brought into a new fellowship of 'worshipers of God' through baptism" (see also Bruner, 1990, p. 1102). In his opinion, this makes the disciple of Jesus "a servant of God under the authority of God" (Hertig, 2001, p. 347). Promoting discipleship to Jesus the Christ within the "God *through* Jesus" perspective leaves Hertig attempting to maintain on one hand that Jesus continues to have all authority over all aspects of life, because He is the embodiment of God's reign, while also arguing that "God" has that authority. As we noted at the beginning of this study, the contemporary use of the word "God" is ambiguous, and this haziness shows up here.

This lack of clarity about "God" and Jesus of Nazareth has found its way into much of our thinking and worship. Jesus of Nazareth occupies a certain position in the divine hierarchy or pyramid, but he is certainly not at the top. He is divine, but not in the sense that he shares in the identity of the one God of Israel. This can be seen for instance, in the testimony of Andrew Herbek, who was working in the Instructor Development Department of *Perspectives* a fifteen-weeks' course designed by Frontier Ventures around four different aspects of God's global purpose while pursuing graduate studies at Trinity Evangelical Divinity School. He says, "God has cultivated in me a love and a passion for Himself. It is this passion for Him that causes me to labour to see Him known, loved and obeyed by a people from among all the peoples of the earth." The author of the article in which the quotation appears summarizes

Herbek's perspective when he writes, "Andrew's heart passion is God Himself, and his calling is to mobilize God's people towards His global purpose" (Perspectives in Practice, 2019). Note that these references to God are detached from any explicit mention of the Lord Jesus. In the "God *through* Jesus" theological understanding, the emphasis moves easily from making *Jesus of Nazareth*, the Christ, "known, loved and obeyed" among "all the peoples of the earth" to making *God* known, loved, and obeyed among all the peoples of the earth.

The attempt to insert discipleship to Jesus into a "God-oriented" church setting also produces some creative biblical interpretation. My wife is currently working her way through a manual entitled *The Mind of Christ*. The stated purpose of the authors of this workbook is to help their readers to grow in Christlikeness. One example from their manuscript (among many) will suffice to illustrate my point. The authors affirm with conviction, based on Ephesians 6:5, that "You can do the *will of God* with 'singleness of your heart'" (Hunt & King, 1998, p. 100; emphasis mine). However, Ephesians 6:5 does not speak at all of doing the will of God; instead, it explicitly mentions "being obedient … to the Christ." A bit further on, these authors write:

> Willingness frees God to reward divinely. You are to obey with all your heart, "knowing that from the Lord you will receive the reward of your inheritance" (Col. 3:24, NASB). Identifying your will with *that of God* establishes a spiritual likeness. (Hunt & King, 1998, 100; emphasis mine)

A spiritual likeness to whom? These authors seem to be describing our spiritual likeness as to God (whom they appear to be identifying with "Lord" in this text). But the Apostle Paul consistently affirms that we are to grow in likeness to Jesus the Christ. Even the verse these authors refer to, Colossians 3:24, explicitly names "the Lord Jesus" and has no mention of "God."

Though the "God *through* Jesus" model is easily understood, does not confuse the persons of the Father and the Son he has sent into the world, and reflects the Old Testament pattern of reconciliation of sinful persons to God through sacrifice, it does not seem very conducive to discipleship to Jesus or to disciple-making.

A Description of the "God *in* Jesus" Model

Immediately after stating to Thomas that he is the way, the truth, and the life, Jesus went on to declare that he had adequately presented the Father in his own person (Jn. 14:7). Philip, who apparently had a deep desire to experience God with his own senses—perhaps he had in mind such a manifestation of God as "the angel of the Lord" who appeared to Jacob at Peniel (Gen. 32:24, 30) and to the parents of Samson (Jdg. 13:3–22) or the experience of Moses on Mount Sinai (Ex. 34:4–8)—was not satisfied with this response. Understanding that the one Jesus called the Father is the Ultimate Absolute (Tenney, 1981, p. 145), he requested that he and his associates might see him. "Lord," he said, "show us the Father and that will be enough for us." The "God *in* Jesus" model is grounded in Jesus' response to this request:

> Don't you know me, Philip, even after I have been among you such a long time? Anyone who has seen me has seen the Father. How can you say, 'Show us the Father'? Don't you believe that I am in the Father, and that the Father is in me? (Jn. 14: 9–10)

The "God *in* Jesus" model is based on the conviction that *in* the Lord Jesus, the Messiah, we experience God, the Ultimate Absolute, in all his fullness. Jesus of Nazareth has been, is, and always will be the image of God (cf. Col. 1:15). He cannot be superseded. The nature and being of God are perfectly revealed *in* him (cf. Jn. 1:18; italics mine). This is what Thomas declared emphatically when he addressed the risen Jesus as God, crying out, "My Lord and my God" (Jn. 20:28; Greek *ho kyrios mou kai ho theos mou)*.

This understanding also forms the climax of Johannine teaching found in the confessional formula of 1 John 5:20, which asserts the full identity of essence between Jesus the Christ and God the Father: "And we know that the Son of God has come and has given us understanding, so that we may know him who is true. And we are in him who is true by being in his Son Jesus Christ. He is the true God and eternal life." This translation is a literal reproduction of the Greek words. An alternative translation is "This [Christ] is the true one, God and eternal life" (Schneider, 1976, p. 82; Marshall, 1978, p. 254).

The "God *in* Jesus" model can also be supported by the words of Titus 2:13: "while we wait for the blessed hope—the glorious appearing of our great God and Saviour, Jesus Christ." The words "great God and Saviour Jesus Christ" can be interpreted in various ways, but I believe the proper interpretation views the entire expression as referring to Jesus alone.[12] Ethelbert Stauffer is doubtless correct when he writes, "The Christology of the New Testament is carried to its logical conclusion with the thorough-going designation of Christ as *theos*" (Stauffer, 1977, p. 106).

---

12 Several arguments favor referring the expression "God and Saviour" to Christ alone. (1) Grammatically, this is the most natural view, since both nouns are connected by one article as referring to one person. (2) The combination "God and Saviour" was familiar to Hellenistic religions. (3) The added clause in verse 14 refers to Christ alone, and it is most natural to take the entire preceding expression as its antecedent. (4) In the Pastorals, the coming epiphany is referred to Christ alone. (5) The adjective "great" would be rather pointless if applied to God but highly significant if applied to Christ. (6) This view is in full harmony with other passages, such as Jn. 20:28; Rom. 9:5; Heb. 1:8; and 2 Pet. 1:1. (7) It is the view of the majority of the Church Fathers (Hiebert, 1978, p. 441).

For these reasons, Paul can boldly state that we have "the light of the Good News of the glory of Christ, who is the image of God" (1 Cor. 2:14; 2 Cor. 4:4, 6). Figure 2 illustrates this model.

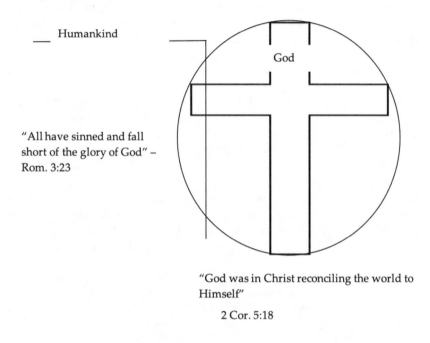

Humankind

"All have sinned and fall short of the glory of God" – Rom. 3:23

God

"God was in Christ reconciling the world to Himself"

2 Cor. 5:18

Figure 2: God in Jesus Model

One factor that commends the "God *in* Jesus" model to those of us who are attempting to deliberately foster discipleship to Jesus of Nazareth, the Christ, is that this was the dominant understanding of the first network of Christ-followerships.[13] N. T. Wright (1992, p. 475) has argued convincingly that this was the heart of their new worldview, and that it even constituted for them a new way of saying "God." It went beyond recognizing that the death and resurrection of Jesus represented the great divine act for which Israel had been waiting, it also meant "that Israel's god, the world's creator, had made himself known uniquely in Jesus." Wright argues that this recognition of God *in* Jesus is what pagans and Jews alike refused to acknowledge. And based on 1 Corinthians 12:1–3 (which is immediately followed by the implicitly trinitarian 12:4–6) and Galatians 4:8–11 (immediately preceded by the implicitly trinitarian 4:1–7), Wright demonstrates that this understanding is important because it was essential for those first Messiah-followers to communicate that

---

13 I have borrowed this term "Christ-followership" to designate the primitive groups of Jesus-followers from Minna Shkul (2009).

they were not referring to a different god when they used the words "Jesus" and "Christ." To do otherwise would have amounted to "idolatry."

Not only was the "God *in* Jesus" understanding the heart of the worldview of the first Jesus-followers, but it also served as the basis for their worship, spirituality, and discipleship. Their discipleship was founded on the conviction that if God in some measure lives and acts in us, it is because first, and without measure, he lived and acted *in* Jesus (Baillie, 1990, p. 128). For this reason, the Apostle Paul could claim that he no longer lived, but that *Christ* lived in him (Gal. 2:20). He could also say of the first Jesus-followers, "You are of Christ, and Christ is of God" (1 Cor. 3:23). And he could argue explicitly that it is God's purpose that people be conformed to the image of his Son (Rom. 8:29).

This conformity to Jesus the Christ was Paul's consuming passion in his own life, and for those he accompanied. He did *not* write, "What is more, I consider everything a loss because of the surpassing worth of knowing *God* my Lord, for whose sake I have lost all things. I consider them garbage, that I may gain *God*" (Phil. 3:8; italicized words are altered). Why not? Because he experienced, loved, worshipped, and obeyed God *in* Jesus the Christ. This explains why Paul would say, "I want to know Christ" (Phil. 3:10). How different this perspective is from the following viewpoint:

> We are made partakers in divine life through the power of the Holy Spirit, as we grow in conformity to the image and likeness of God (1 Pet. 2:4; 1 Cor. 3:18). The heart of Christian life is the encounter with a personal God who makes possible both our union with God and communion with each other. (Fiorenza & Galvin, 1991, p. 155)

The "God *in* Jesus" model understands that growth in likeness to Jesus of Nazareth the Messiah is growth in conformity to the image and likeness of God. Why is this so? Because Jesus of Nazareth is the visible manifestation of that in God which is invisible and incommunicable (Phil. 2:6; Heb. 1:3; Jn. 1:18; 14:9; 2 Cor. 4:4; 1 Tim. 3:16). Jesus of Nazareth is the *Logos* of God (Jn 1:1). He does not merely present God; he embodies God, he *is* God. He is the very substance of God. He is the perfect and total expression of God, possessing all the elements and attributes of God's nature. He is the complete and absolute manifestation of God. Only God Himself can fully reveal God. Jesus reveals more than the will of God or the character of God; he reveals the fullness of God (Col. 2:9). He is the visible image of the invisible God (Col. 2:3). And because he epitomizes in absolute form God's overall intent with respect to us, he gives that intent a concrete shape we can follow (Tanner, 2010, p. viii).

Have We Embraced a Biblical Discipleship Understanding
of Our Relationship to God *in* Jesus?

In 2 Timothy 2:2, we find words of direction for implementing our call to disciple making that are often referred to as a model or guide for our practice: we are to entrust the gospel to faithful men and women who will be able to teach others also. This model emphasizes spiritual multiplication as the desired end product of disciple making and describes the type of people who should be discipled—namely, faithful people.

Although we refer often to this Pauline *model* or *method* of disciple making as it is outlined in 2 Timothy 2:2, I wonder how carefully we have considered his *basis* for or *focus* of discipleship and disciple making as he sketches it in 1 Timothy 3:16:

> Beyond all question, the mystery from which true godliness springs is great: He appeared in the flesh, was vindicated by the Spirit, was seen by angels, was preached among the nations, was believed on in the world, was taken up in glory.

I cannot examine in detail here all the clauses of this ancient hymn of the first Jesus-followers.[14] However, it is evident that the earliest disciples of Jesus the Messiah, who repeatedly sang such words as these, must have firmly believed and taught that Jesus the Christ is what our "godliness" or "religion" is all about (Schwetze, 1998, p. 63). Jesus of Nazareth, in all his aspects, is himself "the mystery of godliness," or what I refer to as the focus of discipleship and disciple-making (cf. Jamieson-Fausset-Brown, 2019; Stamm, 1983, pp. 69–71). This was the opinion of John Calvin, who wrote, "Godliness does not deal with ordinary matters, but with the revelation of God's Son, 'in whom are hidden all the treasures of wisdom and knowledge' (Col. 2:3)" (Calvin, 1998, p. 62). In other words, the object, goal, or focus of our discipleship is growth in knowledge of, obedience to, and worship of "Christ according to the flesh who is over all, God blessed forever" (or "Messiah, who is God over all, forever praised" (Rom. 9:5).[15]

A closer look at just one phrase of this ancient hymn should suffice to illustrate my argument. The English words "was seen" in the phrase "was seen by angels" translate a single Greek verb (*ōphthē*), and this verb appears in the Greek rendition of the Old Testament with God as subject and in a context of worship (Gen. 12:7; 17:1–3; cf. 26:24-25; 31:13; 35:1; Ex. 3:2–5). This suggests that after his resurrection and return to the Father's right hand, Jesus was, in his glorified humanity, visible to angels, who before had never looked

---

14 Fragments of similar hymns centred on Christ are found in 2 Tim. 2 :11, and perhaps also in Eph. 5:14.
15 The *NIV Study Bible* (1985), in a note on Romans 9:5, calls this verse "one of the clearest statements of the deity of Jesus Christ found in the entire NT, assuming the accuracy of the translation."

on God.[16] And it indicates that they worship him (the glorified Lord Jesus, the Messiah): "We do not need to ask when the Lord appeared to angels, whether immediately after the resurrection or after the ascension. Whenever he appeared to angels we may assume that they fall on their faces in worship" (Ward, 1974, p. 65).

My purpose has been to demonstrate that our underlying theological understanding of how our relationship to God is mediated by, or in, Jesus has significant discipleship and disciple making implications. Sloppiness in our thinking or in our vocabulary will not foster an environment where discipleship to Jesus of Nazareth, the Christ can flourish.

For that to happen, we must purposefully follow the example of Paul and the other early Jesus-followers who made the Lord Jesus the subject of their discussions, teaching, and worship (cf. Ac. 28:31). We will need to be convinced that we learn about the one true God *in* Jesus of Nazareth (Stackhouse, 2000, p. 45). And we will need to work diligently to keep the Good News we communicate focused on Jesus Christ the Lord, and thereby avoid the trap of centring it on "God."

Our Lord Jesus, the Christ

The New Testament records two early and widespread confessions made about Jesus of Nazareth: "Christ" and "Lord." "Christ" was a title of honour focusing on his identity as the long-awaited Jewish (but universally significant) king (Bates, 2019, p. 47). Because the kingship of Jesus is the most essential fact of the gospel, Matthew Bates argues that when we see "Jesus Christ" we should resist the temptation to think of a person with the first name Jesus and the last name Christ. He writes (2019, p. 47):

> "Christ" is not a last name nor merely a way to refer to a specific person. It is an honorific title. It is like the term "doctor" in our contemporary society. ... It means something far different to refer to "Jesus of Nazareth" than to refer to Jesus Christ." the "of Nazareth" is closer to our contemporary ideas of a last name, and it is generally spoken by those who do not yet recognize him as the Messiah or when it otherwise needs to be specified precisely which "Jesus" is in view (e.g. Mt. 21:11; 26:71; Lk. 18:37; Jn. 1:45; 18:5–7).

Meanwhile, he is "Jesus Christ" throughout our early Christian literature because authors want to stress his royal office. Jesus of Nazareth, born of the virgin Mary, is the Messiah, the one in whom the Father has chosen to rule over his kingdom.

It has been observed that the Apostle Paul never refers to Jesus as "king" and rarely speaks of Jesus reigning (Wenham, 1995, p. 120). Therefore, one

---

16 See also Eph. 3 :10–11; Heb. 1:6; 1 Pet. 1:12.

might think that Jesus should be *primarily* seen as our Saviour and the one *through whom* we have access to God, as in the "God *through* Jesus" paradigm. Paul's constant use of the title "Christ" almost as a proper name leads some people to assume that the kingly role of Jesus of Nazareth is no longer prominent (Wenham, 1995, p. 120; Schreiner, 2013, p. 544). In opposition to this position, I agree with David Wenham (1995, p. 121) who maintains that for Paul and the first followers of Jesus of Nazareth, his kingship was a "fundamental given," accepted without question. Jesus of Nazareth is the sovereign one in whom God the Father rules even now from heaven (Schreiner, 2013, p. 544). This is his primary identity and role and the basis for the "God *in* Jesus" paradigm.

I also base this affirmation on the meaning and use of the title "Lord" given to Jesus by the first of his followers, and their understanding of Jesus as the one God of Israel (Fitzmyer, 1983, p. 203). The title "Lord" (Greek *Kyrios*) is essentially a functional term that became the most common title for Jesus of Nazareth after his resurrection (van der Kooi and van den Brink, 2017, p. 126). *Yahweh* is the sovereign possessor of all things because he is creator and sustainer; the same thought lies behind the bestowing of the title "Lord" upon Jesus of Nazareth, the Christ (Martin, 1967, p. 237). He is the one in whom, by whom, and for whom "all things were created," and "in him all things hold together" (Col. 1:16–17).

This coincides perfectly with the train of argument developed in the ancient hymn that Paul cites in Philippians 2:6–11. There the argument is that the eternal Son of God, in his pre-existence, declined to grasp what might have been his possession, viz, equality with God. At the close of his mission he returns to his Father's presence and is given the exact counterpart of what proved to be the substance of his choice. He is exalted to the rank of dignity of God as the Father's equal, exercising the very authority which God alone may properly exercise (Martin, 1967, 237).

Johannes Weiss sees, in the granting of the "name which is above every name" to Jesus the Messiah, "endowment with the power which the name denotes," and he concludes that now "Christ definitely takes the place of the almighty God" (Weiss, 2010, p. 52). This is so remarkable because *kyrios* in the Septuagint (the Greek translation of the Old Testament writings) is the Greek translation of *Yahweh*. This understanding can be seen in Paul's way of applying Old Testament statements about *Yahweh* to Jesus (Wenham, 1995, p. 122). For instance, in Romans 10:13 Paul uses the promise of Joel 2:32 that "everyone who calls on the name of *Yahweh* (the LORD) shall be saved" when speaking of faith in Jesus of Nazareth. And in Philippians 2:6–11, when Paul speaks of every knee bowing to the enthroned Christ, he echoes the words of Isaiah 45:23 about knees bowing to *Yahweh*. And as the Reformed dogmatic theologians Cornelis van der Kooi and Gijsbert van den Brink so aptly point out:

Paul writes in an astonishing paradox that "they crucified the Lord of glory" (1 Cor. 2:8), that is, the *YHWH* of the *kabod* (glory). We see here how the person of the crucified and risen Jesus Christ puts an abiding stamp on our concept of God. (2017, p. 127)

"Slaves of God" and "Slaves of Christ"

Another line of evidence also supports the view that our relationship to God the Father, our worship, and our discipleship should be centered on the Lord Jesus, the Christ. This evidence is that the followers of Jesus of Nazareth are called both "slaves of God" and "slaves of Christ" (Harris, 1999, p. 133). I will not look in detail here at the references to the expression "slaves of God" in the Greek Old Testament.[17] However, in the New Testament the expressions "slave(s) of God" and "slave(s) of Christ" appear dozens of times in reference to the individual followers of Jesus of Nazareth.[18]

We might find it difficult to understand this New Testament use of the word "slave" for our relationship to either God the Father or Jesus of Nazareth in whom the Father rules over the kingdom. Even our Bible translations prefer the word "servant" over "slave" and the expression "total commitment" over "total surrender." However, as Murray Harris observes, there is an important difference: "A servant gives service to someone, but a slave belongs to someone. We commit ourselves to do something, but when we surrender ourselves to someone, we give ourselves up" (1999, p. 18). And when the New Testament authors and original readers used slave terminology to describe the human-divine relationship, they shared the common understanding that a slave is someone whose person and service belong wholly to another (Harris, 1999, p. 25). As followers of Jesus of Nazareth, we recognize that we are his purchased possession and are wholly devoted to his person (Rom. 14:8). Harris underscores three things that this complete devotion to Jesus the Messiah

---

17 For an excellent study of the use of *doulos* in the Septuagint, see Harris (1999, pp. 173–175).

18 The expression "Slave of God" is found nine times: twice concerning an angel (Rev. 19:10; 22:9), once for Moses (Rev. 15:3), twice for the Apostles (Tit. 1:1, Paul; Rev. 1:1b, John), once for a Christian leader (Jas. 1:1, James), and *three times for individual believers* (Lk. 1:38, 48, Mary; Lk. 2:29, Simeon). "Slaves of God" occurs 13 times: once for Christian martyrs (Rev. 19:2), three times in reference to the Apostles (Rom. 1:1a; 6:11; 7:3; 19:5; 22:3, 6), and *nine times for any or all Christians* (Ac. 2:18; 4:29; 1 Pet. 2:16; Rev. 1:1a; 6:11; 7:3; 19:5; 22:3, 6). "Slave of Christ" appears ten times: three times in reference to Apostles (Ro. 1:1 and Gal. 1:10, Paul; 2 Pet.), six times for Christian leaders (Col. 1:7 and 4:12, Epaphras; Col. 4:7, Tychicus; 2 Tim. 2:24, for any Christian leader; Jas. 1:1, James; Jude 1, Jude), and *once for any free person* (1 Cor. 7:22). "Slaves of Christ" is found three times, once in reference to Paul and Timothy (Phil. 1:1), *once for any slaves who are Christians* (Eph. 6:6), *and once for Christians in general* (Rev. 2:20) (Harris, 1999, p. 133, emphasis in original).

includes: humble submission to him, unquestioning obedience to his will, and an exclusive preoccupation with pleasing him (1999, p. 143).

My central concern is that the "God *through* Jesus" perspective gives the impression that Jesus of Nazareth's primary identity is that of a Saviour who makes our humble submission, unquestioning obedience, and exclusive preoccupation with pleasing *God* possible. Jesus, in that view, is the Saviour who enables us to be true "slaves of God." The "God *in* Jesus" perspective, on the other hand, highlights the understanding that to be slaves of Jesus of Nazareth, the Christ, is to do the will of the Father. In this way the same person can be said to be simultaneously "a slave of God and of the Lord Jesus Christ" (Jas. 1:1). This is like what Jesus of Nazareth told Philip—namely, that to know him is to know the Father (Jn. 14:7) and that to see him is to see the Father (Jn. 14:9). This perspective understands the primary identity of Jesus of Nazareth as that of a Lord who saves (or, if you prefer, our saving King). This view of the identity of Jesus of Nazareth was clearly that of Peter who declared on the day of Pentecost, "God has made this Jesus, whom you crucified, both Lord and Christ" (Ac. 2:36). And what was the result of this declaration of the identity of the resurrected and enthroned Jesus of Nazareth? People were cut to the heart and asked what they must do to be saved.

Questions to Think About

1. I argue in this chapter that a gospel-driven theology of discipleship is based more on Jesus' answer to Philip's question (Jn. 14:9-11) than on his answer to Thomas' (Jn. 14:6-7). How do you understand Jesus of Nazareth's affirmation that anyone who saw him had seen the Father (Jn. 14:9), and that he is in the Father and the Father is in him (Jn. 14:10)?

2. Why is it important for our spiritual lives to keep in mind that the Lord Jesus, the Christ, is not just the *way* to the Father, but that he is also the *goal* of our salvation?

3. Would you say that the Christians you encounter view Jesus' primary identity more as being their crucified and resurrected *Saviour*, or as their crucified and resurrected *Lord*? What impact do you think this has on discipleship and mission?

4. In the last section of this chapter, I quote another scholar who describes the kingship of Jesus as the most essential fact of the gospel. What is your response to that statement? How do you explain your reaction?

5. Walking in the Dust of Rabbi Jesus of Nazareth

In our last study, I argued that in Jesus of Nazareth we encounter God in all his fullness. That conviction is grounded in the New Testament witness of the first followers of Jesus and their self-understanding as the slaves of God and of Jesus, the Messiah. In the previous studies, we have considered the supreme authority that Jesus claimed to possess.

Now I want to take a step back to be sure that we have fully perceived the significance of what we have already established. My fear is that we have become so accustomed to using the title "Christ" and thinking of Jesus as the "Son of God" that we neglect the importance of his humanity. In the same way, I find that our history keeps us from recognizing the importance of the commission he gave his disciples to go to all the ethnic groups of the earth and accompany others in their apprenticeship to him. In this study, we will examine how the notion of discipleship was understood in the Jewish society of Jesus' day. Even if this aspect of our journey is a bit more historical than theological, it will help us in our understanding and interpretation of the biblical texts.

Jesus of Nazareth, a Rabbi Like the Others

The way in which Jesus trained his first disciples is not unique! In many ways, it fits into a tradition that had begun several centuries before his birth. Jesus did not teach his disciples in a classroom, and he did not follow a pre-established curriculum. Instead he called his first disciples individually to follow him— literally, to "walk behind" him. He invited them to accompany him along the dusty Palestinian roads, living with and learning from him. His disciples engaged with him in life's daily activities, observing his actions and reactions and imitating how he put the Word of God into practice.

In Jesus' day, one of the greatest compliments a person could receive was "You are covered in the dust of the rabbi." That compliment meant that the person followed the rabbi so closely in his travels by foot from village to village that the dust raised by his sandals clung to the clothes of the disciple.[1]

---

1 This compliment based on the *Mishnah*, Ethics of the Fathers (*Pirkei Avot*) 1:4 is attributed to rabbi Yosai ben Yoezer of Tziraidah, who lived in the second century before Christ. The text says, "Make your house a meeting place for the Sages. Cling to

Rabbinical literature preserves several discussions between rabbis and their disciples that took place during such travels. The rabbi always led the way. Here is how one of those scenes took place a century and a half before the birth of Jesus:

> Once rabbi Ishmael, rabbi Eleazar and rabbi Akiva were walking along the road followed by Levi the net-maker and Ishmael the son of rabbi Eleazar. The following question was discussed by them: "Whence do we know that the duty of saving a life supersedes the Sabbath laws?" (Mekhilta, *Shabbeta* 1, on Exodus 31:13)

Apparently, as the scholar Lois Tverberg (who has been researching and teaching about the Jewish background of Christianity for years) observes, three scholars decided to confer on an issue as they journeyed together, while two of their disciples followed closely behind, taking mental notes (Tverberg 2012b). In earlier periods, discussions between sages and their disciples are often set within daily life—while sitting under a tree, in a marketplace, sharing a meal, or walking along a road. Only about a century after Christ did rabbinic study become confined to study halls and synagogues (Rubenstein 2007).

The historians of religions tell us that the disciple making that Jesus initiated was part of an old tradition that had been present for several centuries (Lenoir, 2008, pp. 113–114, 120–122). So we can expect similarities between the rabbi Jesus' relationship with his disciples and that of other rabbis. But we will also see some ways in which the unique authority of Jesus redefined discipleship.

The Life of a Rabbi

In the centuries preceding the birth of Jesus, certain men stood out from the others because of their deep desire to study and teach the Torah. During Jesus' day, a person honored these wise men by calling them "my teacher," or *rabbi* in Hebrew. [2]

---

the dust of their feet, and drink in their words thirstily." The Hebrew of the text literally reads, "dust yourself with their dust" (Tverberg, 2012, n. 24). This phrase could also refer to the fact that the disciple sat at the feet of his master, in the same way as the Apostle Paul did at the feet of Gamaliel (Ac. 22:3). Nevertheless, the Jewish scholar Shmuel Safrai (1976, p. 965) maintains that it probably refers to the trips taken together along dusty paths.

[2] A different account of the origin and the signification of the titles is given in the Tosefta to 'Eduyot (end): "He who has disciples and whose disciples again have disciples is called 'Rabbi'; when his disciples are forgotten [*i.e.*, if he is so old that even his immediate disciples belong to the past age] he is called 'Rabban'; and when the disciples of his disciples are also forgotten he is called simply by his own name" (Singer et al., 2002-2011).

Sometimes Jesus was called "rabbi" in this way; however, since he lived about 70 years before what is called the "rabbinical period," some contemporary scholars prefer to say he was a "sage."

Whatever the case, we find in Jesus of Nazareth many similarities with other sages or rabbis of his time. For example, most of those teachers did not come from the upper classes of Jewish society or from among the priests. Instead, they came from the lower classes. They might have been blacksmiths, stone workers, vineyard labourers, water carriers, tanners, makers of sandals, shepherds, or (of course) carpenters (Safrai & Stern, 1976, p. 953). Many of them were seasonal labourers who traveled during the months when they were free to do so.

The rabbis interpreted the Torah, explained the Scriptures, and told parables. Some of them traveled from village to village, teaching in the synagogues. They relied on the hospitality of others, and they were never paid. Often they were accompanied by their disciples, who studied under them for years. The teaching sessions frequently took place outside—in the vineyards or markets, or alongside a path or a field (Safrai & Stern, 1976, p. 965). Once trained, the disciple left and began teaching his own disciples.

Most Jews married young, often between eighteen and twenty years of age.[3] But the rabbis spent many long years studying the Torah and got married much later. David Bivin (2005, p. 67) maintains:

> An unmarried rabbi was not as strange in the first-century Jewish society as it might seem. The rabbis spent many long years far from home, first as students and then as itinerant teachers. It was not unusual that these men got married between the ages of thirty and forty.

This observation is completely in line with Jesus' reference to those who have "renounced marriage because of the kingdom of heaven" (Mt. 19:12). It is also echoed by the Apostle Paul, who writes that the disciples of Jesus of Nazareth, like himself, chose not to marry "for the sake of the gospel" (1 Cor. 7:7, 38; 9:23). Celibacy was not mandatory but did demonstrate the rabbi's profound commitment.

Jesus among the Rabbis

As far as we know, Jesus of Nazareth did not belong to any of the religious groups of the first century—the Sadducees, Zealots, Essenes, or Pharisees. Among those groups, however, his teaching most closely resembled that of the Pharisees, the group that reestablished Judaism after the destruction of the Temple in 70 CE and from whom today's rabbinical Judaism descends. For example, Jesus not only maintained the habit of praying the benediction after the meal as the Torah requires (Dt. 8:10), but he also blessed the food before

---

3 Danby, 1980, Ethics of the Fathers (*Pirkei Avot*) 5:22.

eating (an innovation of the Pharisees; see Bivin, 2016). Another parallel is that the three commandments the most important in the eyes of the Pharisees were giving to the needy, prayer, and fasting. Among these, the most important was giving to the needy. Bivin observes that Jesus presents the same trio in the Sermon on the Mount (giving to the poor, Mt. 6:1–4; prayer, Mt. 6:5–15, fasting, Mt. 6:6–18). Even if Jesus emphasized that these disciplines should not be done "before men to be seen by them," his reference to them does teach us something about his theology. Jesus underscored the same commandments that were precious in the eyes of the Pharisees (Bivin, 2020).

Sometimes we get the impression that Jesus was hostile to the Pharisees of his day because he called them "hypocrites" on at least one occasion (Mt. 23:13), and because what he did was contrary to their teaching and practice. Spangler and Tverberg (2018, p. 33) remind us, however, that debate was a central element in Jewish studies and that the rabbis thought that a good student should know how to debate. Brad Young (1995, p. xiii) quotes a rabbi who lamented the death of his most skilled adversary because with his disappearance the rabbi lost someone who had forced him to refine his thinking. Even if some sought to trap him with sly questions, others simply debated with him because that was how the study of the Torah took place (Frankovic, 1994).

The gospel of Luke tells us that Jesus of Nazareth taught in the synagogues even before beginning his ministry (Lk. 2:41–52). Spangler and Tverberg (2018, p. 33) note two things that this fact reveals about Jesus. First, Jesus must have been quite learned by the standards of his time. Were that not the case, he would not have been allowed to teach. Even his most ardent critics never questioned his scholarship. Second, Jesus of Nazareth must have been observant of the Torah. Otherwise, he would not even have been able to enter the Temple or the synagogue, let alone speak there (Evans & Brackney, 2007, pp. 41–54).

Jesus lived during what many consider the "Golden Age of Study," which produced the basis for contemporary Jewish thinking (Spangler & Tverberg, 2018, p. 34). Two of the most influential Jewish thinkers, Hillel and Shammai,[4] taught during the years immediately preceding Jesus' birth (between 30 BC and 10 AD). Many of the debates between Hillel and Shammai are recorded in the *Mishnah*,[5] and more than once Jesus was asked to comment on their

---

4 Both Hillel and Shammai were disciples of Shemaya and Avtalyon. Hillel and Shammai were so honoured by the Jewish people that even the odious Herod was afraid to do them harm. In addition, Hillel's devotion to Torah study was legendary.
5 During the seventh generation after Hillel Hazaken lived rabbi Yehouda Hanassi, who was the head of the Sanhedrin. During his time, decrees against the Jews were multiplied, and the Jewish people began to move throughout the Roman Empire. Rabbi Hanassi (also called Rabbi Judah the Prince) observed that people were finding it difficult to remember the words of the oral Torah, so he decided to compile the body of

conclusions. For instance, when Jesus was questioned as to what he thought about divorce (Mt 19:3–11), it was to find out which of those two rabbis he sided with (Instone-Brewer, 2002). Sometimes Jesus agreed with other rabbis, and sometimes he started with their thoughts but went further (see Instone-Brewer, 2004, pp. 28–40; 1999).

The Rabbis Used Parables

In many ways, Jesus taught like other rabbis and made disciples like other rabbis. For example, Jesus traveled, entered into debates, interpreted the Scriptures, and used parables as did the other rabbis of his day.

It might surprise you to learn that Jesus wasn't the only rabbi who used parables to teach. Most rabbis used common themes to illustrate their teaching—for instance, a king, a shepherd, or a farmer with a vineyard might represent God. The rabbis drew these images directly from the Scriptures.[6] Consider the words of one rabbi:

> When a sheep strays from the pasture, who seeks whom? Does the sheep seek the shepherd, or the shepherd seek the sheep? Obviously, the shepherd seeks the sheep. In the same way, the Holy One, blessed be He, looks for the lost. (From rabbi Haggai bar Eleazar; Young, 1998, p. 192)

Do these words remind you of Jesus' parable of the lost lamb (Mt 18:12–13)? Like Jesus, this rabbi says that God looks for us when we are lost. Jesus and the rabbi Haggai bar Eleazar both based their parable on the Scriptures.

Consider another rabbinical parable:

> There are four types among those who sit in the presence of the rabbis: the sponge, the funnel, the strainer, and the sieve. "The sponge," which soaks up everything. "The funnel," which takes in at this end and lets out at the other. "The strainer," which lets out the wine and retains the dregs. "The sieve," which

---

that teaching. This formed the Mishnah, the first written record of what was the Oral Law. As the name implies, the Oral Law was never written down as a formalized text or permanent record. It had been passed on from one scholar to the next, from one generation to the next. In each generation there were experts in different areas of the Oral Law. One scholar was an expert in the laws of the Sabbath, for example, whereas another man was an expert in torts and damages. Altogether, they were the ones who transmitted the full body of the traditions of Moses down through the centuries to the Jewish people. The Mishnah would finally be published in an organized, authoritative form a generation after rabbi Meir by the great Rabbi Judah the Prince. Rabbi Judah did not start from scratch, however. He was the redactor or editor of the Mishnah, not its creator. (See https://www.jewishhistory.org/the-Mishnah/).

6 For example, the image of God as king is found in 1 Sam. 8:7; Ps. 24:47; as a shepherd in Is 40:11; Jer. 23:31; Ez. 34; and as a farmer or vineyard owner in Ps. 80 and Isa. 5.

removes the chaff and retains the fine flour. (Danby, 1980, Ethics of the Fathers [*Pirkei Avot*] 5:15)

This is called a "four types" parable, because it compares four types of people according to their way of living. It reminds us of Jesus' parable in Luke 8:4–11 about the four kinds of soil the seed falls on: the path, the rock, the thorns, and the good soil. The parable illustrates the ways in which people respond to the Word of God.

In the parable found in the Ethics of the Fathers, the rabbi is saying that despite what we might think, the best disciple is not the sponge who retains absolutely everything. On the contrary, the best disciple is the sieve, who filters the teaching and retains only the best. This reminds us that we are not called to be parrots who do nothing more than repeat without reflection what we have been taught. Instead, we are called to exercise discernment and wisdom, continually asking questions and weighing the answers, in our pursuit of a better understanding of the Word of God and the traditions we have received from other followers of Christ.

This brief look at Jesus in his identity as a rabbi could be further deepened by analysing his way of assembling texts from the Torah (Spangler & Tverberg, 2018, pp. 40–49). By this line of explanation, I am suggesting that when the eleven Apostles heard the resurrected Jesus of Nazareth tell them to make disciples, they were not surprised. That is exactly what any rabbi expected from his disciples (Bjork, 2015, p. 66). The making of disciples continues in the Jewish tradition even today. In fact, rabbis are commissioned to make many disciples during their ordination ceremony (Danby, 1980, Ethics of the Fathers [*Pirkei Avot*] 1:1). This practice dates back to the time of Jesus (Spangler & Tverberg, 2018, p. 58).

The Characteristics of Discipleship in the Rabbinical Tradition

What is the source of rabbinic understandings of discipleship? Even if discipleship did not become established as a form of religious instruction until sometime between the seventh and fifth centuries before Christ (Lenoir, 2008, pp. 113–114), Jewish contemporaries of Jesus found their model in the Scriptures, especially in the relationship between the Prophets Elijah and Elisha. According to Spangler and Tverberg (2018, p. 277, n. 5), Elisha is often held up as the prototype of a disciple, especially for his humble service and commitment to Elijah.[7]

---

7 See also the Babylonian Talmud, Berakhot 7a and rabbi Manashe Bleiweiss,"Elisha ben Shaphat: The Wonder Years," http://nebula.wsimg.com/0a1ab8e2288e9b6dacaf2e56081e2b2c?AccessKeyId=DFFED 978B208E263454C&disposition=0&alloworigin=1.

Elisha, a man of God and son of Shiphat, was a farmer. While he was tilling his field, the Prophet Elijah chose him to be his disciple and servant. Elisha followed his master from the moment they met. When he saw his master disappear in a fiery chariot, going up to heaven without dying first, he rent his clothes. He knew then that he was to carry on the great prophetic work of Elijah. As his disciple, Elisha sought not only to be taught by Elijah but to become like him so that he could continue the mission.

Several elements in Elisha's life prefigure discipleship during Jesus' time. First, Elisha was a young man. The first disciples of Jesus were too—probably adolescents when they were called to follow him.[8] Second, Elisha left his home to live with Elijah for several years. As the historian Shmuel Safrai explains, a disciple "did not grasp the full significance of his teacher's learning in all its nuances except through prolonged intimacy with his teacher, through close association with his rich and profound mind" (Safrai & Stern, 1976, p. 964). The disciple learned everything from and about his master. He learned his stories, his habits, his way of honouring the Sabbath, and most of all the way in which he understood and applied the Torah in his daily living.

Total Allegiance

Unlike the disciples of the rabbis in Jesus' time, Elisha began following Elijah after he received a specific call (1 Kings 19:19–21). Elisha hesitated, however, to respond to that call. He wanted first to take the time to kiss his father and mother goodbye. But when Elijah questioned his allegiance, Elisha took a pair of oxen, which he sacrificially slaughtered. He burned the plowing equipment to cook the meat and gave it to the people. He then left everything and set out to follow Elijah. He left behind wealth, home, family, and even his livelihood. Jesus alludes to this incident when a potential disciple wanted to follow him— but not immediately (Lk. 9:61).

Jesus often spoke of the need to abandon everything to follow him. He said that he had "no place to lay his head" (Lk. 9:57–58). By these words, he indicated that he was serving *Yahweh* traveling from place to place. Here is how another rabbi describes that life:

> This is the path of the Torah: a morsel with salt shall you eat, and you shall drink water by measure, and sleep upon the ground, and live a life of painfulness, and in Torah shall you labour. If thou do this, happy shall you be, and it shall be well with you. (Danby, 1980, Ethics of the Fathers [*Pirkei Avot*] 6:4)

---

8 Along with the fact that the education of a young Jew in Jesus' time finished at age 15, scriptural indications also lead us to this conclusion. For example, on three occasions Jesus calls the disciples "children" (Mt. 11:25; Lk. 10:21; Jn. 13:33). Moreover, Peter seems to have been the only one who had a wife, and Jews married after reaching age 18 (Mt. 8:14–15).

The Rabbi-Disciple Bond

Spangler and Tverberg (2018, p. 63) maintain that with the passing of time, the relationship between Elijah and Elisha developed to become like that of a father and his son. We can see this bond in the way Elisha followed his master everywhere during his last day of earthly life, as if he was hoping to keep him on earth a bit longer. The biblical text tells how when the heavenly chariots finally separated them, Elisha cried out in anguish, "My father! My father!" (2 Kings 2:12). He was obviously overwhelmed by grief at the loss of his beloved mentor.

This kind of solid bond between the two Prophets was expected between a rabbi and his disciple. That bond of affection and confidence was considered essential in the training process. And at the time of Jesus, the disciple viewed his rabbi as like his father, and even more. According to Spandler and Tverberg (2018, p. 63), it was said, "Your father brought you into this world, but your rabbi brings you into the life of the world to come!" (from *Baba Metsia*, *Perek* 2, *Mishnah* 11). Spandler and Tverberg also quote such statements as these: "If a man's father and his rabbi are both taken captive, a disciple should ransom his rabbi first," and "If his father and his master are carrying heavy burdens, he removes that of his master, and afterward removes that of his father (*Baba Metsia*, *Perek* 2, *Mishnah* 11). These statements reveal the total devotion expected of the disciple toward his rabbi. The rabbis were also deeply committed to their disciples, as the following words reveal: "If a disciple is sent into exile, his rabbi should go with him" (Babylonian Talmud, *Makot* 10a).

The Disciple Follows the Rabbi with Others

One well-known rabbinical counsel during Jesus' day states, "Assume for yourself a master, acquire for yourself a *haver*" (Danby, 1980, Ethics of the Fathers [*Pirkei Avot*] 1:6). The word *haver* can be translated by either "friend" or "companion." In this saying, it means someone who is ready to join in seeking to understand the Scriptures and the rabbi's teachings.

Just as it was important to learn by following a rabbi, it was also considered paramount that one or two people accompany the learner in that apprenticeship. Rabbi Nehorahi would say, for instance, "Exile yourself to a place of Torah; do not say that it will come after you, that your colleagues will help you retain it. Rely not on your own understanding" (Danby, 1980, Ethics of the Fathers [*Pirkei Avot*] 4:14).

During the first century CE, once a young man was admitted as a disciple, he entered a community of rabbinic apprentices. Since he was a *talmidh* or beginner, he was obliged to stay behind the others and could not participate in the discussions. His next stage of development was to become a distinguished student who could draw near the master and ask him questions. After that phase, he became a sort of associate disciple who could sit behind the rabbi during prayer. Finally, he reached the highest level, disciple of the sages, and was considered the intellectual equal of his rabbi (Wilkins, 1988, p. 123). This entire progression took place along with other disciples whom he could observe and with whom he could seek to gain deeper understanding.

We can see just how important the communal aspect of discipleship was when we consider the words of some of the first rabbis, who taught that "Two who sit and no words of Torah pass between them, this is a session of scorners. ... But two who sit and exchange words of Torah, the Divine Presence rests amongst them" (Danby, 1980, Ethics of the Fathers [*Pirkei Avot*] 3:2). Several centuries later, rabbi Chalafta the son of Dosa, of the village of Chanania, would say, "Ten who sit together and occupy themselves with Torah, the Divine Presence rests amongst them" (Danby, 1980, Ethics of the Fathers [*Pirkei Avot*] 3:6).

These words readily remind us of those pronounced by Jesus: "Where two or three come together in my name, there I am with them" (Mt 18:20). The similarity with the words of the rabbis is apparent. Like the other rabbis of his day, Jesus emphasized the need to learn alongside others how best to follow him. Moreover, he promised that he would be present whenever two or three met together in that kind of relationship (Mt. 28:20).

The Uniqueness of the Discipleship Jesus Initiated

So if Jesus of Nazareth dressed like other rabbis, prayed like other rabbis, taught other Jews about the best way to live according to the laws given by *Yahweh* to Moses, debated like other rabbis, and made disciples like other rabbis, was he different from the other rabbis? In my opinion, he was more different from than similar to the others. The importance of that difference can be seen in the type of discipleship to which Jesus called his followers.

David Bosch (1995, pp. 36–39) suggests four areas where discipleship to Jesus and discipleship to other rabbis were fundamentally different:

The Disciples of the Rabbis	The Disciples of Jesus
The disciples of the rabbis could choose their own teacher and attach themselves to that teacher.	None of Jesus' disciples attached himself to that teacher of his own volition. Those who followed him did so only after receiving his call to "Follow me!" The choice belonged to Jesus, not the disciples.
The law, the Torah, stood at the center of Judaism. The candidates for discipleship attached themselves to a rabbi so as to better know the Torah, and uniquely for that reason. The Torah was the ultimate authority in the relationship, not the rabbi.	Jesus called his disciples to forsake all, not for the sake of the Law, but for him alone: "He who loves father or mother more than me is not worthy of me; ... and he who does not take his cross and follow me is not worthy of me ... and he who loses his life for my sake will find it" (Mt. 10:38–39).

In Judaism, discipleship was merely a means to an end. Being a disciple, a student of the Law, was no more than a transitional stage. The student's goal was to become a rabbi himself.	For the disciple of Jesus, the stage of discipleship was not the first step forward toward a promising career. It was in itself the fulfillment of his destiny. A disciple of Jesus never graduates into a rabbi.
The disciples of the rabbis were only their students, nothing more.	Jesus' disciples were also his servants, something quite alien to the Judaism of his day. They did not just bow to his greater knowledge; they obeyed him. He was not only their teacher, but also their Lord.

I would add to these comparisons the fact that nothing indicates that Jesus carried out a systematic interpretation of the Torah. Unlike the other rabbis of his time, for example, he did not engage in debates about the distinctions between kinds of civil disobedience with his fellow rabbinic sages. Instead, the gospels specify that he "taught with authority" (Mt. 7:29). What does that mean? Clearly, Jesus' teaching was not simply the repetition of Torah verses or of other people's interpretations. His teaching is powerful because it conveys not just truths to be believed, but truths he lived out himself, which stimulates in his followers a different way of life. That is the meaning of the word "authority" with which his contemporaries qualified his teaching. In the root of the word "authority" in both Greek and Latin, there is no idea of submission, commanding, being superior to another, or giving commands. Instead, the foundational meaning is of stimulating growth (*augere* in Latin, to "increase"), developing, making fertile and fruitful. That is the authority of Jesus' teaching, and it represents the goal of our accompaniment of others in his name.

In each of our studies to this point, I have stressed the importance of Jesus' authority. Here I once again take up this important subject, because immediately before he sent his initial followers into the world to accompany others in obedience to him, the resurrected Jesus of Nazareth claimed that all authority in heaven and on earth had been given to him (Mt. 28:19).[9]

Jesus' Claim to Possess Divine Authority

Even though the rabbi Jesus claims to have received absolute authority in heaven and on earth only after his resurrection, that does not mean that he had no authority previously. Wittman explains, "As man, the Son receives an

---

9 Although Jesus states in his great high priestly prayer (Jn 17:2) that he had already received "authority over all people" before his death and resurrection—to give eternal life to those who had accepted him—after those decisive events his authority extends over everyone and everything in heaven and on earth.

authority economically from the Father without abdicating the same authority he shares with the Father as God" (2019, p. 157). John Owen (1968, Vol. 1, p. 326) makes a similar point when commenting on Philippians 2:6–7. He writes that in the form of God, the Son "had dominion over all, owed service and obedience to none, being in the 'form of God,' and equal to him." This is so because "he was in the form of God, he must be equal with God; for there is *order* in the Divine Persons, but no *inequality* in the Divine Being" (italics added).

The Eternal Son Made Himself Nothing[10]

Even as we declare the equality between the Father and the Son within the Divinity, we must recognize the change in rank and authority that the Son temporarily accepted when he assumed humanity. First, however, we must come to grips with the truth that although Jesus of Nazareth came to exist in time and space at his birth in Bethlehem, the Son of God was already present at the time of creation.

Several important passages stress this truth. For instance, in 1 Corinthians 8:6 Paul writes, "Yet for us there is one God, the Father, from whom are all things and for whom we exist, and one Lord, Jesus Christ, through whom are all things and through whom we exist." Although Paul does not speak explicitly here of the "eternal Son" who became man in the person of Jesus, we can legitimately use that language. This conclusion has great significance not only for Christology, but also for the doctrine of God. Cornelis van der Kooi and Gijsbert van den Brink (2017, p. 429) summarize this brilliantly:

> This is the step from the economic to the immanent Trinity ... the step from Jesus as Lord and Son of God to Jesus as God the Son. The Trinitarian scheme becomes the mold that shapes the entire history of salvation. The Father, the Son, and the Spirit existed from the beginning. What appears before our eyes in time is actually a manifestation of what God already is- of the eternal, triune God.

These theologians go on to write that Jesus of Nazareth, the incarnate eternal Son, is not "of secondary importance but belongs to God in an essential manner" (2017, p. 429), which is to say that "Jesus' acts in time manifest who God is." We will come back to this issue in later studies. But it is important to recognize here that ever since the incarnation of the eternal Son in the person of Jesus of Nazareth, Israel's God can no longer be detached from Jesus. As van der Kooi and van den Brink state, "God's identity is definitively and irreversibly defined by Jesus. Anyone who wants to say something about God will also have to say something about Jesus" (2017, p. 383).

The acknowledgment of the high place and status of the rabbi Jesus of Nazareth dates from his very first followers. Whenever the followers of Jesus

---

10 This section is adapted from Bjork (1997, p. 71).

have reflected on the mystery of the Incarnation, they have interpreted it as an act of divine self-emptying or limitation (cf. Phil. 2:6–7). What has mystified and astonished Christ's followers for nearly two thousand years is the incarnate eternal Son's willingness to set aside his divine privilege and status for our salvation. This mystery means that in an act of self-emptying called *kenosis* (from the Greek *ekenosen*), the promise of Emmanuel, God with us (cf. Mt. 1:22), was fulfilled. In the rabbi Jesus of Nazareth, the incarnate eternal Son, God speaks and acts for our salvation. In him he offers "his life-giving presence and his forgiving love in a definitive and irreversible way" (van der Kooi & van den Brink, 2017, p. 382).

We might say, then, that the existence of the Son of God has a three-phase history: his pre-existence as equal with the Father, his existence in the person of the rabbi Jesus of Nazareth on earth, and his "post-existence" exaltation with God. Roy Hoover stresses this point in his detailed study of the Greek word *harpagmon*, which is used in Philippians 2:6 to speak of the Son's not considering equality with the Father "something to be grasped". Hoover maintains that this Greek word should be translated by the idea of "profiting from something."

Jesus' self-emptying consisted, therefore, in adding something. The eternal Son limited himself by taking on our humanity in the person of Jesus of Nazareth. Thomas Schreiner (2001, pp. 172–173) offers his way of understanding this act:

> The text nowhere says that he surrendered his divinity or left it behind in the incarnation. The idea is that he did not exploit the advantages of deity, which were his by nature. As a man he lived in dependence on the Holy Spirit, in the same way other human beings do. He did not use the prerogatives of deity but depended on the Spirit to strengthen him. Contrary to Adam, he lived for the sake of the glory of God and surrendered himself for others.

Throughout the centuries, men and women have marvelled that the eternal, pre-existent *Logos* would willingly choose not to profit for a time from his divine status, but instead would assume our humanity. This astonishment produced reflection on Jesus of Nazareth, the Christ, which is the key project of theology (van der Kooi & van den Brink, 2017, p. 401). Why is this the primary concern of theology? Because our understanding of the identity of Jesus of Nazareth opens the door to our understanding of both the Father and the Spirit. It also provides the biblical answer to the question, "How does God redeem the world?" The affirmation found at the very heart of the Christian faith is that in Jesus Christ, God has freely and totally given Himself (Dawe, 1963, p. 20). The divine *kenosis* of the eternal Son is the key to the whole drama of human salvation. The double (soteriological and theological) role of our reflection on the identity of Jesus the Christ (Christology) is highlighted by van der Kooi and van den Brink in these terms: "Theology must do full justice to the drama of salvation, and at the same time wholly recognize that Jesus the Christ fully determines in every respect our reflection on who God is in his essence" (2017, p. 429).

My purpose here is not to trace the various streams of kenotic teaching in the New Testament or church history (for this information, see Bruce, 1955; Dawe, 1963; Erickson, 1991; Richard, 1982). Rather, I intend simply to underscore the importance of the declaration by the resurrected Christ, when he met his disciples, that he had received all authority in heaven and on earth. This way of beginning his statement means that no other authority could alter the command that he was about to give them. It also implies that what he was about to say is the most important thing his followers can do. It is perhaps for this reason that the command he then gave has been received throughout history as the most complete and definitive definition of the mission he conferred on his followers (Bjork, 2015, p. 43).

The Lord Jesus Sends Us

Go and make disciples of all nations, baptizing them in the name of the Father and of the Son and of the Holy Spirit, and teaching them to obey everything I have commanded you. (Mt. 28:19–20)

The first part of the mission the resurrected Jesus gives to those he sends is to "go." This is an apostolic action. In other words, an apostle is not simply someone who has been sent or who "goes" on mission. The command found in Matthew 28 is sometimes called the Great Commission; the word "commission" means attributing a specific mission to someone. In our next study, we will explore in more detail the responsibilities of one who has been sent relative to the one who sends him. However, let's take a few moments to examine the specificity of what Jesus just said.

The resurrected Jesus sent his disciples to do a specific, distinct work. And what Jesus says here is not an option, but an absolute command: go and do what it takes to make true followers of him among the men and women of all the nations. This command contrasts sharply with the teaching given for centuries to the Israelites, that they should keep themselves separate from the surrounding pagans. The example of Jesus the Christ and the order he gives after his resurrection reverse the situation. Now, instead of keeping themselves apart from non-believers, those who follow him will go everywhere and enter into contact with others, with the goal of helping them to live according to the model and teachings of rabbi Jesus of Nazareth.

And his first disciples understood what he meant! As we have seen, Jesus made disciples and sent them to make other disciples according to a model that was very well understood during his time. They also understood that they wouldn't replace their rabbi and could never consider themselves his superiors (Mt. 10:24-25). They did not make disciples of themselves. Instead, like the

Apostle Paul after them, they consecrated their energy toward the goal of seeing the life of Christ "formed in" other people (cf. Gal. 4:19).

This being the case, how should we understand the other elements that compose the missionary mandate of Matthew 28? We know that the disciples of John the Baptist received baptism at his hands. How then should we understand the baptism "in the name of the Father, and of the Son, and of the Holy Spirit" that the Apostles were to administer to those they accompanied? And in what way does that specific baptism reinforce the centrality of Jesus of Nazareth, the Christ, in our understanding of the Divinity?

Baptism and the Development of a Christocentric Understanding of the Trinity

Often, when we read Jesus' instruction to "baptize them in the name of the Father and of the Son and of the Holy Spirit," our attention is drawn to the ecclesial or soteriological importance of baptism. Several years ago, two evangelical theologians wrote a book titled *The Water That Divides: The Baptism Debate* (Bridge & Phypers, 2008). In this book, they explore four different evangelical interpretations of the importance of the act, its sacramental value (or lack thereof), the validity (or invalidity) of baptizing children, and the place of baptism in the liturgy, among other topics. I will not enter into those debates here. Instead, I seek to show the tie between that trinitarian formulation and intentionally centring one's life, worship, and ministry on the person of Jesus of Nazareth, the Christ.

The Apostle Paul associates the Father, the Son, and the Holy Spirit at least 30 times in his letters, but this text from Matthew affirms with even greater clarity that the Divinity exists in the unity and in the differentiations between three persons (Giles, 2006, p. 108; Schaberg, 1982). I believe that this text also indicates how we should understand the authority of the resurrected and exalted Jesus of Nazareth in relationship to the other members of the Trinity from a discipleship perspective (Hartman, 1997, p. 152). And I maintain that this is of utmost importance for a proper understanding of our daily living and our mission, if we consider ourselves his followers.

We can see the nature of Jesus' authority in the Great Commission in three ways. First, the expression "baptizing them in the name"[11] is used by the first disciples exclusively with reference to Jesus, the Christ. In the Acts of the Apostles (Ac. 2:38; 10:48; 19:5) and in the Epistles, people are baptized "in the name of Jesus Christ." How do we explain this occurring so soon after Jesus gave the explicit order to baptize in the name of the Father, and of the Son, and of the Holy Spirit? This is not a trivial question! Some groups use these texts to

---

11 Three different Greek expressions are all translated by the words "in the name": *eis to onoma, en to onomati,* and *epi to onomati.* Some experts in the Greek language find nuances of meaning between them. I maintain that the three Greek propositions *eis* (Mt. 28:19; Ac. 8:16), *en* (Ac. 10:48, Col. 3:17), and *epi* (Ac. 2:38; 5:40) are interchangeable when used with "name" (see Baggott, 2012).

affirm that anyone who has been baptized "in the name of the Father, and of the Son, and of the Holy Spirit" must be re-baptized. However, I contend that the difference between the two baptismal formulations signals that Jesus the Christ is the center of our discipleship. We are not disciples of the Father, nor of the Holy Spirit (directly).

Second, the text of Matthew 28:19 very much resembles the words of Jesus of Nazareth recorded in Matthew 18:20: "For where two or three come together in my name, there am I with them." In this text, Jesus does not say that either the Father or the Spirit is in the midst of his gathered disciples (even if they are present indirectly). In commenting on the parallel between Matthew 28:19 and 18:20, Porter and Cross (1999, p. 78) point out that to "be gathered" or "baptized" in the name of Jesus means to be identified with him, to be faithful to him, to belong to him, and to be submitted and to have the intention of acting for him. As we have seen in this study, those are the choices made by a disciple. For this reason, Beasley-Murray (1962, p. 175) sees a direct link between the notion of discipleship to Jesus and the use of his name, while excluding the other two persons of the Trinity, in the baptismal expression.

Finally, to be baptized in the name of someone was, for the Jews, a way to indicate publicly that an individual accepted that person as his or her teacher and guide in life—that the follower was willing to be "covered in his dust." In this way, proselytes to Judaism were "baptized into Moses" (cf. 1 Cor. 10:2) and taught how to live according to the Torah. The rabbi Jesus continued this practice in the formulation of his Great Commission, instructing his disciples to teach others to put into practice everything that he had taught them (Mt. 28:20). In this study, we have seen precisely what it means to learn how to live according to the model and the teachings of a rabbi like Jesus.

The Promise of the Presence

The resurrected Jesus finished his commission with a promise as surprising as it is reassuring: "And surely I am with you always, to the very end of the age." That promise corresponds to the one at the beginning of Matthew's gospel: "The virgin will be with child and will give birth to a son and they will call him Immanuel—which means, 'God with us'" (Mt. 1:23).

David Kupp (1996) makes several important observations about this promise. First, he notes that Jesus the Christ, to whom all authority in heaven and on earth has been given, does not give that authority to his disciples! Rather, he incarnates it in their midst. The accomplishment of their mission depends entirely on his own presence among them (Kupp, 1996, p. 105). Second, he highlights the designation of the Eleven and the new Christ-followership that is to be created from *panta ta ethne*, as the place where his people will be finally defined (Kupp, 1996, p. 106). And we must not lose sight of the fact that the declaration of his presence "to the very end of the age" carries an eschatological dimension and solves the problems created by his physical absence within that community. For the reader of the gospel, that final commission marks both the beginning and an end, and the promise of Jesus' presence applies as much to the presumed readers of the gospel as to the first disciples (Kupp, 1996, p. 107). In the same way, the commission given by Jesus to the first disciples becomes the Great Commission for everyone who recognizes the resurrected Emmanuel, the Christ. We can conclude from this that the authority and presence of Jesus are not imposed or forced on anyone; on the contrary, they remain an invitation to obedience (Kupp, 1996, p. 108).

The importance of Christ's presence in the midst of his disciples did not disappear after Pentecost; rather, it was intensified by the experience of the Spirit. The time in which we live is marked by God's having placed his Holy Spirit within the assembled disciples, by whom he empowers them to respond to their calling as followers of their rabbi. The gift of the Spirit was intended, among other things, to equip them for a life of witnessing to him (Ac. 1:8). With this apostolic calling and equipping, his followers would go into the world. This present age, in which we live as followers of the rabbi Jesus of Nazareth, is pervaded because he has come to us in the Spirit, equipping us with the desire and the power to live as he did. Paul calls followers of Christ to be filled with the Spirit of Christ (Eph. 5:18). The gospels and the Epistles alike call us to live in line with that new way. In the Sermon on the Mount, Jesus called his disciples to be a city on a hill, a light on a candlestick (Mt. 5:14–15). In the Epistles, we find repeated calls to "clothe" ourselves with "the Lord Jesus Christ," as if we were putting on a garment (Rom. 13:14). This is what walking in the dust of the rabbi was all about.

Questions to Think About

1. I state that sometimes we become so accustomed to using the title "Christ" and thinking of Jesus as the "Son of God" that we neglect the importance of his humanity. How would you describe the importance of Jesus' humanity to a theology of discipleship and disciple-making?

2. What does the fact that Jesus was a rabbi like the others of his day add to your understanding of discipleship? In what ways are the differences between his relationship with his disciples and that of other rabbis important for our spiritual lives?

3. This chapter presents two important aspects of discipleship: the rabbi-disciple bond, and the importance of following the rabbi with others. What are the implications of these dimensions of Christian discipleship for keeping it focused on Jesus?

4. I argue that since the incarnation of the eternal Son, anyone who wants to say something about God will also have to say something about Jesus, and I quote another scholar who describes Jesus' acts in time as who God is. How can these truths function as a corrective to imperfect models of discipleship and Christian growth?

5. The last section of this chapter presents the Great Commission as an affirmation of Jesus' authority and ongoing presence in the midst of his disciples. Do you agree? If so, how should this reality influence our lives, both individually and in our interaction with non-Christ-followers?

6. The Sending of the Disciples in John's Gospel

In our last study, we saw how the rabbi Jesus of Nazareth sent his disciples into all the world to accompany others in centering their entire existence on him. His method of equipping his first disciples to make other disciples corresponded to the customs of other rabbis of his day. However, one surprising aspect of his instruction is the precise moment when he gave this mission to these men! He did not do it before he could claim that all authority in heaven and on earth had been given to him. In this study, we will explore the responsibilities of a person who had been sent out toward his sender, in the thinking of rabbi Jesus and those who surrounded him. To this end, we will look closely at the sending out of the disciples as recorded in the gospel of John.

The gospel writers clearly did not attempt to give an account of all the details of Jesus' life. Their works are not biographies, history books, or treatises. They are not even the earliest records of what was known and believed about Jesus shortly after his Resurrection.[1] Those biographical memories were present from the outset but were put in order by the authors of the gospels so that their readers might believe that Jesus of Nazareth is the Messiah, and that by believing they might have life in his name (Jn. 20:30–31). Despite the different backgrounds of the authors and the diversity of the early faith communities for whom the gospels were originally intended, there is fundamental agreement on the basic understanding that Jesus of Nazareth is at the very heart of what the Creator God is doing in our universe.

Matthew summed it up at the end of his gospel with the words of the resurrected Jesus: "All authority in heaven and on earth has been given to me" (Mt. 28:18). Because of the place of preeminence that has been given to Jesus Christ, we are to teach all people how to follow him (Mt. 28:19). In this chapter, I examine the way in which John's gospel underscores the authority of

---

1 New Testament scholars have identified a number of passages, especially in the Pauline literature, that contain earlier statements of belief. See for example Robert Jewett & Kotansky's *Hermeneia Commentary on Romans* (Jewett & Kotansky, 2007, pp. 24, 340–341, 361), in which he identifies a number of New Testament passages as including earlier formulae embedded in Acts and the Pauline works, including Ac. 3:15; 4:10; 13:30; Rom. 4:24; 5:6, 8; 8:10; 14:15; 1 Cor. 8:11; 15:3, 2 Cor. 5:14–15; Gal. 1:4; 1 Th. 4:14; 5:9–10.

Jesus, the nature of our mission, and the importance of our relationship to the One who has sent us. These are the elements that stand out in his description of the appearance of the resurrected Jesus to his disciples.

John's Account of Jesus' Sending of His Disciples

The context in which Jesus sends his disciples on mission is interesting. We have two accounts of that evening's meeting, and they remarkably supplement each other. They deal with two different parts of the occasion. John begins where Luke ends. Luke dwells mainly on the disciples' fears that they were seeing a ghostly appearance, and on the removal of these fears by the sight, and perhaps the touch, of Jesus' hands and feet (Lk. 24:33–40). John says that the entire incident begins with "the disciples together, with the doors locked fearing the Jews" (Jn. 20:19). The resurrected Jesus comes and stands among them and says, "Peace be with you!" At this point we can already make several observations.

Fear Imprisons Us

Several hours earlier Peter and John, along with Mary Magdalene, had visited the empty tomb (Jn. 20:1–9), and after Jesus had appeared to Mary she had even gone to the disciples to tell them that she had "seen the Lord [Jesus]" (Jn. 20:10–18). However, instead of believing her, and carrying that news to others, the followers of Jesus were shut up by fear. This situation reminds us of two facts.

First, on the positive side, we are reminded that the early *ecclesia* did not look at all like how we "do church" (Bjork, 2015, pp. 174–177). Instead, it was an illegal, relational, and informal network, a clandestine movement whose members had the threat of the sword hanging over their heads. Pliny the Younger, giving an account of the first Christ-followers in a letter to the Roman emperor Trajan, says that "they were accustomed to meet together on a stated day before it was light, and sing among themselves alternately a hymn to Christ as God" (*Letters* 10.96–97). The reality that the *ecclesia* existed until the fourth century primarily as a movement might encourage us to reexamine our current missional emphasis on church planting (we will look at this more closely in chapter 15).

Second, on the negative side, the fact that Jesus' disciples were huddled together behind closed doors out of fear reveals that they were more focused on Jewish opposition than on their risen Lord. Indeed, fear is at the crux of so many of our locked-up moments. When Martin Luther was led in front of the Emperor Charles V and accused of heresy, the choice he faced was clear. He knew that if he renounced his spiritual beliefs he would be offered a prestigious place in European society. He also knew that if he refused to renounce his beliefs, he would be persecuted and excommunicated. Luther is a dramatic example of the spiritual courage that produces growth and progress. That courage is born from an ardent desire to progress in the knowledge of him who is the truth (Jn. 14:6; Phil. 3:10). Fear keeps us from progressing with the Master. What we need when we are blocked in that progression, just as the disciples needed, is a new encounter with the Lord Jesus! We need to get re-focused on him.

When Jesus appears among his disciples, instead of scolding them for their fear or challenging them to get their act together, he says, "Peace be with you!" He is not saying here, "May you be spared from trouble and conflict." Rather, his words mean "May God grant you fullness, harmony, and fulfillment."[2] And they remind us of Jesus' previous promise to his disciples: "Peace I leave with you, my peace I give unto you. I do not give to you as the world gives. Do not let your hearts be troubled and do not be afraid" (Jn. 14:27). A sense of fullness and the experience of harmony and fulfillment are inseparable from Jesus' presence. They come with him, and they are the atmosphere wherever he reigns (cf. Rom. 14:17). As they focused on Jesus once again, the disciples' fear was expelled, and the text tells us that they rejoiced.

John tells us that the disciples were "overjoyed" when they saw the Lord (Jn. 20:20). However, Jesus did not come among his disciples only to encourage and reassure them. He repeats his salutation, "Peace be with you!" Then he goes on to invest them with a sacred mission: "As the Father has sent me, I am sending you" (20:21).

In fact, the gospel of John highlights the ways in which Jesus compares his relationship to his Father with the relationship between his disciples and himself. For instance, Jesus says in John 6:57, "Just as ... I live because of the Father, he who feeds on me will live because of me." In John 10:14-15, he testifies: "Just as the Father knows me, and I know the Father ... I know my sheep and my sheep know me." He affirms again in John 15:9, "As the Father has loved me, so have I loved you." It is therefore not surprising that the two texts on the commissioning of the disciples in this gospel (Jn. 17:18 and 20:21) tie the way in which that Jesus sends his disciples to the way in which he had himself been sent by his Father.

An Important Detail Given by Luke

Luke's account also helps us in another important way. John says simply that "the disciples were gathered together" (Lk. 20:19), which could refer to the Eleven only. Luke is more specific and tells us something that is of prime importance for understanding the whole incident: "the Eleven ... and they that

---

2 The Greek *eirēnēn* corresponds to the Hebrew *shalom*. According to Strong's Concordance 7965, *shalom* means completeness, wholeness, health, peace, welfare, safety soundness, tranquility, prosperity, perfectness, fullness, rest, harmony, and the absence of agitation or discord. *Shalom* comes from a root verb meaning "to be complete, perfect and full." See also Harris, Archer, and Waltke (1981, p. 931).

were with them" were assembled (Lk. 24:33). The book of Acts leads us to understand that this might have been a group numbering about 120 (cf. Ac. 1:15). This observation is important because it means that Jesus was not sending only the Eleven on mission. When Jesus says, "As the Father has sent me, I am sending you," his words apply to everyone who is counted among his followers, not just the Apostles.

In the remainder of this study, I will look closely at what Jesus really means by the words, "As the Father has sent me, I am sending you." My reflections are based largely on the excellent study of this phrase done by Andreas Köstenberger (2007). Along the way, I will emphasize that in the gospel of John, the way in which God the Father sent Jesus is both the model and the foundation for Jesus Christ's own sending of disciples.

The Gospel of John Insists that Jesus Was Sent by the Father

In answer to the question, "Does the Father do anything in John besides sending the Son?" the New Testament scholar Paul Sanders replies, "Not much!" (1990, p. 34). Sanders explains that most of the Father's actions in John's gospel are tied directly to the Son's mission. In fact, John records Jesus referring to "the Father who has sent me" or "the one who has sent me" 33 times.[3] This "having-sent-me-Father" legitimizes the Son's mission. It can be argued that God is identified primarily in John's gospel not in terms of ontological aspects of being, but by the active aspects of doing, the most important of which is launching the Son's mission (Anderson, 1999, p. 35). In other words, the main thing the Father is portrayed as doing in John's gospel is sending the Son, and the central aspect of the Son's mission is his "sent-ness" from the Father (Anderson, 1999, p. 36).

The Characteristics of Jesus' Sending by the Father

The gospel of John sheds light on four important characteristics of the one who is sent:

1. He must glorify the one who has sent him.
2. He must do the will of the one who has sent him, do his works, and speak his words.
3. He must faithfully witness to and represent the one who has sent him.
4. He must maintain an intimate relationship with the one who has sent him.

Let us look briefly at how Jesus lived out each of these characteristics with relation to the One who had sent him.

---

3 Jn. 3:16–17, 34; 4:34; 5:23–24, 30, 36–38; 6:29, 37–40, 44, 57; 7:16–18, 28–29, 33; 8:16–18, 26, 28–29, 42; 9:4; 10:36; 11:42; 12:44–45, 49–50; 13:20; 14:24; 15:21; 16:5; 17:3, 8, 18, 21–25; 20:21.

Jesus Had to Glorify the Father Who Had Sent Him

First, the one who is sent must glorify the one who has sent him. To glorify or give glory to someone probably means to give praise and honor, but in its biblical sense it also signifies to manifest divine presence and power (Nixon, 1994, p. 424). For that to happen, the one who has been sent must give up all pursuit of his own glorification (Jn. 5:41; 7:18). Jesus often contrasts himself with others on this point (cf. Jn. 5:41–44; 7:18; 8:50, 54; 12:43). For example, he says, "He who speaks on his own does so to gain honor for himself, but he who works for the honor of the one who sent him is a man of truth" (Jn. 17:18, see also 8:50, 54; 12:43). In his way of living, Jesus always sought to bring honor and glory to the Father who had sent him.[4] He even declared that the glory of the One who had sent him was the major objective of his mission (cf. Jn. 11:4, 40; 12:28; 13:31; 14:13; 17:1, 4, 5). At the end of his life, just before his death on the cross, Jesus affirmed in his high priestly prayer, "I have brought you [the Father] glory (*edoxasa*, aorist tense) on earth by completing (*teliosas*, aorist tense) the work you gave me to do" (Jn. 17:4). The glorification of the Father, or in other words revealing his presence and activity, was the distinctive trait of his life throughout the Fourth Gospel.

Jesus Had to Do the Will of the Father Who Had Sent Him, Do His Works, and Speak His Words

Jesus the Messiah is the perfect example in this domain. For Jesus, doing the will of the One who had sent him was his very "food" (Jn. 4:34). And he calls on the works that his Father had given him to accomplish as the proof that he had really been sent (Jn. 5:36).

The works that prove that the eternal Son incarnate in Jesus of Nazareth had been sent by the Father are his normal activities; in other words, his daily way of living is a demonstration to others of the Father's character. His way of living is also a proof of his covenant with the Father who sent him (cf. Jn. 7:3; 9:3; 10:25, 32; 14:10). It is the work (*ergon*) of the Father (Jn. 4:34; 17:4). It was given him to do by the Father. That idea is often expressed: "The Father ... has placed everything in his hands" (Jn. 3:35); "The Father ... has entrusted all judgment to the Son" (Jn. 5:22, 27); "As the Father has life in himself, so he has granted the Son to have life in himself" (Jn. 5:26, cf. Jn 17:2, 6, 9, 12, 24; 18:9). The works of the Father given to the sent One incarnated in the person of Jesus of Nazareth include, but are not limited to, miraculous healings, the multiplication of bread and wine, and the raising of the dead (Jn. 7:3, 21; 9:3–4; 10:25, 32, 37–38; 14:11; 15:24). Everything that Jesus of Nazareth did constituted the work of the Father and witnessed to the Father who had sent him.

---

4 Cornelis Bennema (2002, p. 116) points out that the Father and Son mutually glorify one another (Jn. 13:31–32; cf. 8:54; 14:13; 17:1,4–5).

In another place he states that "as long as it is day" he must do the work of the One who had sent him (Jn. 9:4). And he added, "The Son can do nothing by himself; he can do only what he sees his Father doing, because whatever the Father does the Son also does" (Jn. 5:19).

Jesus claims in effect that the One who had sent him did his own work through him and that this is a sign of his love (Poole, 1985). Jesus does not confuse himself with the Father who had sent him. On the contrary, there is a clear distinction between himself and his Father. At the same time, his words reveal a unity of action with his Father, and they also affirm that his actions are voluntary and thought out (Jamieson, Fausset, & Brown, 1999). Jesus claims therefore that the Father does nothing without the one he has sent. The Father shows the one he has sent everything he does, and through his sent One he reveals himself and shows himself to men (Gill, 1979).

And this is not only a question of what Jesus did, his words were also those of the One who had sent him. John the Baptist noted this when he proclaimed, "The one whom God has sent speaks the words of God" (Jn. 3:34). Jesus asserted, "My teaching is not my own, it comes from him who sent me" (Jn. 7:16). Summing up his entire teaching ministry Jesus claimed, "I did not speak of my own accord, but the Father who sent me commanded me what to say and how to say it. ... So whatever I say is just what the Father has told me to say" (Jn 12:49–50). Later He would say, "These words you hear are not my own; they belong to the Father who sent me" (Jn. 14:24).

Jesus Had to Faithfully Witness to and
Represent the Father Who Had Sent Him

The third characteristic of the one who has been sent, according to the gospel of John, is that the one who has been sent must faithfully witness to and represent the one who has sent him. We see clearly how Jesus did this in John 13:20: "I tell you the truth, whoever accepts anyone I send accepts me; and whoever accepts me accepts the one who sent me." We find it again in John 12:44-45 where Jesus cries out, "When a man believes in me, he does not believe in me only, but in the one who sent me. When he looks at me, he sees the one who sent me." In fact, frequently throughout the gospel of John, the Son is portrayed as the delegated representative of the Father who had sent him. John 10:36-38 states explicitly that the Son, while in the capacity of being sent into the world, is one with the sender. The rabbis understood this concept to mean that the sent one is "like the one who sent him" to the extent that "he ranks as the one who has sent him." In other words, Jesus is, according to rabbinical law, "as [the] one who sent him" (Borgen, 2014, p. 169). This explains why he asks the Jews why they accused him of blasphemy when he said he is the "Son of God" (Jn. 10:31–36).

One illustration of this relationship is the authority Jesus claimed to have as the one sent from the Father. For example, in John 17:2 he prays, "Father ...

you granted your Son authority over all people that he might give eternal life to all those you have given him" (see also 13:3). Jesus, as the sent one, had authority over life: "For just as the Father raises the dead and gives them life," he said, "so the Son gives life to whom he is pleased to give it" (Jn. 5:21). In like fashion, the Father has given the Son whom he has sent the authority to judge (Jn. 5:22, 27). Notice also that the Son shares with the Father the authority to give the Holy Spirit (Jn. 7:37–39; see also 3:3, 5, 8; 4:10, 13–14; 20:22).[5]

Jesus Had to Maintain an Intimate Relationship with the Father Who Had Sent Him

Finally, according to the gospel of John, the one who has been sent must maintain an intimate relationship with the one who has sent him. Jesus said that he knew well the One who had sent him. "I know him," he cried out to the hostile crowd in the temple courts, "because I am from him and he sent me" (Jn. 7:29). John highlights this knowledge of the sender by the one who is sent in his prologue to the gospel: "No one has ever seen God, but God the One and Only, who is (Greek *ho on*, present participle) at the Father's side, has made him known" (Jn. 1:18). By these words, John indicates that the intimacy that the Word enjoyed with the Father did not cease when he became flesh in Jesus of Nazareth.[6] The fact that the eternal Son incarnate in Jesus as the sent one enjoyed an intimate relationship with the Father who had sent him is evident in his declaration, "I am not alone, I stand with the Father who sent me" (Jn. 8:16; see also 8:29). Knowing that soon his disciples would abandon him, Jesus said, "A time is coming when ... you will leave me all alone. Yet I am not alone, for my Father is with me" (Jn. 16:32).

Our Sending by Jesus Is to Be Like His Sending by the Father

Now let us return to the sending of the disciples by the resurrected Christ in John 20:21: "As the Father has sent me, I am sending you."[7]

It is important to grasp that Jesus, not the Father, is sending us on mission here. Moreover, he doesn't say, "As *God* has sent me, *God* is sending you." For

---

5 Rabbinical interpretation today views the sprinkling of the water at the end of the Feast of Tabernacles as symbolizing both the gift of late rain, which often took place during that season, and also the Holy Spirit.

6 Jesus identifies himself with the Father more than 120 times in the gospel of John. See Morris (1989, pp. 126-144); Mlakuzhyil (1987).

7 Although I will not develop this point here, the fact that Jesus links our sending to his own sending means that this is not a double mission—i.e., first Jesus' mission and then afterwards our mission. Rather, it is a single action in two phases: that of the Son in his incarnate life, and then of the risen Son by his Spirit through his disciples. See Milne (1993, pp. 298–299).

the followers of Jesus of Nazareth, the Christ, the word "God" does not refer to a universal divine being, but to someone who has the face of Jesus (van der Kooi and van den Brink, 2017, p. 79). For this reason, all the attributes of the God of Israel are enlightened by that man. Jesus of Nazareth in a particular way is the "exegesis" of the God of Israel. Jesus of Nazareth, the resurrected Christ, reminds his disciples of this by referring to him as his "Father."

Even if the entire ministry of Jesus was undeniably theocentric, in the gospel of John the Christ maintains, as we have seen, that everything he did was for the glory of his Father (Jn. 8:49-50). This way of designating God as his Father underlines his divine sonship. Richard Longenecker (1970, p. 96) observes that if Jesus designated God in this way, that indicated that he considered God is uniquely his Father . He adds that the data indicates that it was this conviction that formed his entire ministry.

In the gospel of John we find the deepest and most complete reflections on the links between Jesus of Nazareth and God the Father. Van der Kooi and van den Brink (2017, p. 84) explain:

> From the resurrection on, the Father has glorified the Son (see Jn. 17:5) by giving him a name that is above every other name (Phil. 2:9). This name can be only the divine name. Furthermore, he has given Jesus a mandate and full power in heaven and on earth (Matt. 28:18) and has taken him into his heavenly glory (Lk. 24:51; Eph. 1:20; 4:10). There he has put all things under his feet (1 Cor. 15:27; Eph. 1:22). From that moment on, the Father puts the Son in the spotlight. Just as the Son had always pointed to the Father, so the Father now constantly points to the Son. Everything in the New Testament is now about Jesus.

We must avoid the trap of overlooking this transfer of power.

Whereas the Apostle Paul speaks often of Jesus of Nazareth as the "Son of God"[8] John speaks more concisely of "the Son" (e.g., 5:19–23).[9] It seems that

---

8 There are places where Paul speaks indisputably of Jesus as God (see for example Rom. 9:5; 1 Th. 1:12; Tit. 2:13), yet he prefers to distinguish between the supreme Father and the obedient Son while maintaining the divinity of Jesus (Wenheim, 1995, p. 118). With the other first Christ-followers, Paul displays a marked preference for the titles "Lord" (around 230 times) and "Christ" for the resurrected Jesus. Most often, Paul reserves the word "God" to designate the Father, while he uses "Lord" (or "Son of God") to designate Jesus. "In its highest most religious sense," affirms O'Collins (2008, p. 143), "'Lord' designates Jesus rather than the Father in Paul's letters."

9 John uses the title "the Son" 22 times in his gospel. In John, Jesus is the eternal preexistent Son who was sent from heaven into the world by the Father (3:17; 4:34; 5:24, 30, 37). He is conscious of his pre-existence with the Father (8:23, 38, 42). He is one with the Father (10:30; 14:7) and loved by the Father (3:35; 5.20; 10:7; 17:23–26). The Son possesses divine power to give life and to judge (5:21–22, 25–26; 6:40; 8:16; 17:2). Through his death, resurrection, and exaltation, the Son is glorified by the Father (Jn. 17:1, 5, 24). His glory did not exist only during the time of his incarnation to reveal the Father (Jn. 1:14) but preexisted also before the creation of the world (Jn. 17:5, 24).

the difference between Jesus of Nazareth and all others is to be found in his obedience and consecration to his Father. Van der Kooi and van den Brink (2017, p. 426) maintain that it is precisely that relationship which pushed the first Christ-followers to affirm that he was without sin (Heb. 4:15).

Jesus *does not* say "As *God* has sent me, *God* is sending you." Nor does he say "As the Father has sent *me*, the *Father* is sending *you*"! We must be absolutely clear on this point. Jesus, not the Father, has sent us on mission. Make no mistake about it, we are *sent*. But it is the Lord Jesus of Nazareth the resurrected Christ who sends us, and not the Father. We see the confirmation of this in the prayer of Jesus recorded in John 17:18, where he prays to his Father, "As *you* sent *me* into the world, so *I* have sent *them* into the world" (emphasis mine). And Jesus sends us in the same way in which He was sent by the Father.

We Are Expected to Bring Glory and Honour to the Lord Jesus, the Christ, Who Has Sent Us

The One who sent us expects us to bring him glory and honor. In other words, just as Jesus did all he could to make his Father's presence and activity known, we are called to do the same thing for Jesus Christ. Jesus said as much in his high priestly prayer: "I have brought you glory on earth ... and glory has come to me through those you gave me out of the world" (Jn. 17:4, 10). Jesus glorified the Father who sent him, by making his goodness visible,[10] and we are sent to glorify Jesus by making his goodness visible, for he is the One who sends us! A bit further in the same prayer, Jesus says, "I have given them the same glory you gave me ... I in them and you in me" (Jn. 17:22–23). Notice once again what Jesus *did not* say. He did not say "*you* in them and you in me"! No, he specifically says "*I* in them and *you* in me."

The inward experience of a new creation, the actual formation of Christ, in each of his disciples is what makes his goodness visible. Paul said as much when he wrote that Christ in us is our "hope of glory" (Col. 1:27). And Paul called everybody to a similar experience. Few words have ever carried a more touching appeal than that intimate personal call to his wavering friends in Galatia: "My little children, for whom I am again in the pains of childbirth until Christ is formed in you" (Gal. 4:19). To the Roman Christians he says, "If anyone does not have the Spirit of Christ, he does not belong to Christ" (Rom. 8:9). To the Corinthian believers he says, "Your body is a temple of the Holy

---

Where Paul and the author of the letter to the Hebrews present Jesus almost as the firstborn of the eschatological family of God (Rom. 8:14–17, 29; Heb. 2:11–12), John insists more on the qualitative difference between the sonship of Jesus and of other people. Given that he is the "only" Son of God (Jn. 1:14, 18; 3:16, 18), he enjoyed a unique and exclusive relationship with the Father (O'Collins, 2008, pp. 137–138).

10 When Moses desired to see the glory of God, saying, "Now show me your glory." God answered, "I will cause all my goodness to pass in front of you" (Ex. 33:18–19). The glory of God can therefore be understood as all His goodness made visible to us.

Spirit who is in you" (1 Cor. 6:19). The Ephesian prayer carries us almost beyond what can be asked or thought—that "Christ may dwell in your hearts" (Eph. 3:17).

The one who sends us, Jesus the Christ, expects us to glorify him. But doesn't Paul instruct us to do everything for the glory of God (1 Cor. 10:31)? The best answer to this question is that God (the Father) is glorified when we become like Jesus of Nazareth the Christ, who is "our righteousness, holiness and redemption" (1 Cor. 1:30). This is so because he (Jesus the Christ) is "the radiance of God's glory and the exact representation of his being" (Heb. 1:3). In other words, he demonstrated in a definitive way who God is. He is the true image (Greek *eikon*) of God (see also 2 Cor. 4:4). Understood in this way, giving glory to God is the same thing as discipleship or growth in Christ-likeness (cf. 2 Cor. 3:18; Gal. 4:19). God the Father is remaking us into his own image, and he does this by conforming us to the one who is that image. Only in this way do we truly glorify God. The entire divine project is focused on our participation in the life of Jesus the Christ, because it is in him that we participate in the life of our Three-in-One God. And when God accomplishes our glorification in the Christ, "we will be participants in that one stupendous act of union in which all things in heaven and on earth will be reconciled to God through Christ, through whom and for whom all things were created" (Johnson, 2013, p. 187; see also Bjork, 2015, pp. 111–128).

We Are Expected to Do the Will and the Work of the Lord Jesus, the Christ, Who Has Sent Us, and to Speak His Words

We are sent to do the will of the One who sends us, Jesus the Christ, and to perform his works and speak his words. In my book *Every Believer a Disciple* (2015, pp. 57–58) I highlight the fact that Jesus of Nazareth distinguished clearly between those who place their faith in him and those who, following that act of faith, attach themselves to his teaching. After hearing Jesus speak of the manner in which he would die on the cross (Jn. 8:28), many people believed in him (verse 30). If it is purely by such faith that one is saved, then we could say that many of those people were "born again"—i.e., that they "became believers," or were "converted." Addressing himself to these people, Jesus called for more than faith. He said in effect, "If you live in my teaching, if you allow my words to define your way of making sense of life, and if you live in conformity to what I say, you will be my disciples. You will understand what is real, and that understanding will free you from illusion" (vv. 31–32).

The Jews who had believed in Jesus were not bad Jews. They followed the Law of God, and they came to Jesus of Nazareth enthusiastically and believed in him, but they continued to understand him according to their preconceived ideas and sought to live out the Torah the same way as they had done before meeting him. They failed to realize that they had before their eyes the appropriate way of interpreting and applying that Law in their daily behavior

(Spangler & Tverberg, 2018, p. 176). For that reason, Jesus told them that to be his disciples, they must dwell in, hold to, remain permanently in, live within, and continue to exist in his teaching.

Have you ever wondered why the gospel of Matthew is the first gospel in the New Testament? For Raymond Brown (1997), Matthew has long been considered the foundational document tying the Christ-followerships to the teaching of Jesus of Nazareth. It seems that Matthew even organized his gospel in a way that highlights the fact that a follower of the rabbi Jesus of Nazareth lives in his teaching. All the major teachings of Jesus in this gospel are addressed to his followers (Mt. 5:1; 10:1, 36; 18:1; 23:1–3). Matthew highlights the fact that the teaching of Jesus brings understanding to his followers (Wilkins, 1992b, p. 183). Jesus communicates things as they really are, and those who follow him learn to conform their way of living to his teaching. According to Matthew, such total obedience to the teaching of Jesus, sometimes called *justice* (5:17–20) and sometimes *love* (22:37–40), is the distinguishing trait of his followers.

The one who is sent must also do the work of the one who sent him (Jn. 13:14–16, 20, 34, 35; 14:12–14, 15, 20–21, 23–24; 15:9–17, 27; 16:1, 4, 23–24, 33; 17:6–26; 18:36; 20:21–23). We are sent by Jesus the Christ who testified that he had finished the work that he had been sent by his Father to do. His prayer indicates that the formation of his own disciples was at the heart of that work (Jn. 17). It is equally clear that his will for us is that we will accompany others as they learn to follow him. Jesus said that all those who dwell in him, drawing strength and vitality from his own life, glorify the Father by reproducing in the life of others that same attachment to their Master (Jn. 15:8). And he warns that any of his followers who do not do this will be disciplined so that he or she conforms to the will of the one who has sent him or her (Jn. 15:2). We are called, and sent, to accompany others in obedience to Jesus. No one is excluded. All who have responded to Christ's call to follow him have also been commissioned by him to extend his reign. We know this because the Lord Jesus the Christ made disciples and ordered his disciples to do the same thing.

We Are Expected to Witness to and Faithfully Represent the Lord Jesus, the Christ, Who Has Sent Us

Jesus Christ witnessed to the One who had sent him—the Father—and represented him faithfully. We are called similarly to witness to the One who has sent us, the Lord Jesus the Christ, and to represent *him* faithfully. This does not only mean that we are to represent him by acting in his name; we must also re-present him, in the sense of allowing him to shine through us by his Spirit. This is highlighted by what Jesus did after he told his disciples that he was sending them just as he had been sent by the Father. The text from John tells us, "With that he breathed on them and said, 'Receive the Holy Spirit'" (Jn.

20:22). Days earlier he had told them that he would not leave them as orphans, but that he would come again to them in the person of the Spirit (Jn. 14:18).

Note that the gift of the Spirit is entirely submitted to the work of Christ and inseparable from the sending of Jesus' disciples (Vellanickal, 1973). He was sent by the Father so that we might experience the actual presence of the Christ (Hull, 2016, pp. 98–100).[11] Van der Kooi and van den Brink (2017, p. 108) succinctly and forcefully state that there is "no Son without the Spirit" and "no Spirit without the Son." They add, "All those who believe that they can bypass Jesus in a spiritual way talk about another *spiritus* than the Spirit of the Father and the Son." This is the case because the Spirit continues the earthly mission of the incarnate Son. He puts people in relationship with Jesus (Jn. 16:14) and urges them to continue the proclamation of the kingdom that the Lord Jesus announced and initiated (van den Kooi & van den Brink, 2017, p. 85). This explains the close association in the Scriptures between the presence of the Spirit and the presence of Christ; indeed, the Spirit is even called "the Spirit of Christ" (Rom. 8:9–11; cf. Gal. 4:6; Phil. 1:19). The Holy Spirit is the Spirit of Christ. He has come neither to transmit his own presence, nor to glorify his name, nor to teach us about himself, nor to form the "body of the Spirit." He has come to make known, glorify, and teach about the Lord Jesus the Christ,[12] and to gather the Lord's followers into the body of Christ (cf. Jn. 15:26; 16:14–15; 1 Cor. 2:14–16; 12:13). As the people whom the Lord Jesus the Christ has sent, our first responsibility is to make visible his presence and his activity by allowing the fruit of his Spirit to shine in our daily behavior (Gal. 5:16-26).

The Spirit is the one who makes us capable of faithfully representing the Lord Jesus the Christ today (Jn. 14:16–18, 25–27; 15:26; 16:7-16). For he communicates to us the intentions, thoughts, and actions of Christ. Jesus the Christ remains our hope and our perfection (Col. 1:27–28), and it is by the person of the Holy Spirit that he lives in our hearts (Eph. 3:17).

---

11 In his entry about the Holy Spirit in the *New Bible Dictionary*, J. D. Dunn (1962, pp. 1140–1141) maintains that the tie between the Spirit and Christ distinguishes the Christian understanding of the Spirit from the "more primitive and less developed concept." He writes, "The Spirit is now definitively the Spirit of Christ (Ac. 16:7, Rom. 8:9; Gal. 4:6; Phil. 1:19; also 1 Pet. 1:11; cf. Jn. 7:38, 39; 20:22; Ac. 2:33; Heb. 9:14; Rev. 3:1; 5:6), the other Comforter who continues the role of Jesus on earth (Jn. 14:16; 16:7; cf. 1 Jn. 2:1). This means that Jesus is now present in the life of the believer uniquely in and through the Spirit (Jn. 14:16-28; 16:7; Rom. 8:9; 1 Cor. 6:17; 15:45; Eph. 3:16f.; cf. Rom. 1:4; 1 Tim. 3:16; 1 Pet. 3:18; Rev. 2–3)."

12 The first followers of Jesus of Nazareth very quickly recognized that it was the Spirit who urged them to attribute the title "Lord" (Greek *Kyrios*) to him (cf. Rom. 10:9–10). Van der Kooi and Van den Brink (2017, p. 85) note correctly that apparently the Spirit does not play the Father against the Son. He acts rather to bring them together. These authors consider that it is for that reason that in the New Testament we find interchangeable references to the Spirit as the Spirit of the Father and of the Son.

We Are Expected to Maintain an Intimate Relationship with the Lord Jesus,
the Christ, Who Has Sent Us

Jesus not only glorified the Father who sent him, did his will, and testified to him by representing him faithfully, but he also maintained an intimate relationship to him. In like manner, we are called to live in a relationship of openness, trust, and intimacy with the One who has sent us, Jesus Christ. In the second half of John's gospel, we see this aspect of Jesus' relationship highlighted in the way he refers to his disciples. They are "his own" (13:1); his "little children" (13:33); his "friends" (15:15); those the Father had given him out of this world (17:6); his "brothers" (20:17). In explaining his future relationship to the disciples in the person of the Spirit, Jesus stresses that the Spirit will unite the disciples to his resurrected self in a new intimacy of communion (14:17–21). "I will come to you ... you are in me, and I am in you," he explains.

Jesus' parable of the vine and the branches also underscores his close relationship with those he sends and the resulting fruitfulness in their lives. Temple (1961, p. 423) eloquently describes the fruit-bearing function of the vine: "The vine lives to give its life-blood. Its flower is small, its fruit abundant, and when that fruit is mature and the vine has become, for a moment, glorious, the treasure of the grapes is torn down and the vine is cut right back to the stem."

This function of the vine and the branches is reflected in Jesus' stress on fruit-bearing (explicitly in Jn. 15:2, 4–5, 8, 16). Reflecting on this, D. A. Carson (1991, p. 518) insists that that the ultimate purpose of our intimacy with the One who sends us "remains bracingly objective and missionary." As Bruce Milne (1993, p. 220) states, "The disciples are sent into the world, as was Jesus, to carry on the task in his absence. That is the principal implication of Jesus' saying, I am the vine; you are the branches."

In other words, we are sent into the world by the Lord Jesus the Christ so that he can continue his mission through us by his indwelling Spirit.

It should be clear by now that the identity of Jesus of Nazareth has the utmost theological significance. To paraphrase the words of Michael Bird (2013, p. 383), absolutely everything—kingdom, church, salvation, and mission—rests on the singular fact that the eternal Son became a human being.

Questions to Think About

1. I argue in this chapter that in the gospel of John, the way in which God the Father sent Jesus is both the model and the foundation for Jesus Christ's own sending of disciples. How can that truth function as a corrective to imperfect models of discipleship and mission?

2. How could a proper understanding that all the attributes of the God of Israel are expressed in the man, Jesus of Nazareth, enable the local church to thrive spiritually and in their outreach?

3. Review the characteristics of our sending by Jesus. Which of the characteristics do you think your patterns of discipleship to the Lord Jesus most faithfully follow? What shape does this take?

4. Which of the characteristics of our sending by Jesus underlined in this chapter do you think need to be strengthened in your patterns of discipleship to the Lord Jesus? What can you begin to do to reinforce that element of your relationship to the one who has sent you?

7. The Relationship between the Gospel and Discipleship

When I introduced this series of studies, I claimed that to be truly evangelical, our theology must be "gospel-driven" from start to finish. Perhaps by now you are wondering why, up to this point, I have given so little attention to the death of Jesus of Nazareth on the cross to pay the penalty for our sins, and to reconcile us to his Father. After all, is not the centre of the gospel the justification of sinners, the church and the love of God? And if that is the gospel, what is its relationship to intentional apprenticeship to Jesus of Nazareth, the Christ?

Before we turn to this important matter, we must consider a methodological question. What is at issue is fundamentally the way in which we understand the relationship between the triune Creator God (the Communicator), the message itself, and the medium through which it is communicated (the Word incarnate and the word inscripturate), along with how the communication is to be understood and applied (hermeneutics and discipleship) (Goldsworthy, 2006). In other words, what are our presuppositions[1] about the primary identity and role of Jesus of Nazareth, the incarnate eternal Son, in the Creator's plan? And how does his fundamental identity influence the way we are called to follow him?

Should we opt for a *functional* comprehension of Jesus of Nazareth that sees him first and foremost as the mediator between God and humanity? Or should we rather understand him more *ontologically*, in his identity as the divinely exalted agent who truly reigns over the cosmos, and who allows those who belong to him to participate in his rule?

I acknowledge, in asking this question, that the function and the ontological identity of Jesus of Nazareth are inseparably linked to each other. Moreover, both ways of understanding the primary identity of Jesus of Nazareth have solid biblical foundations.

---

1 I use the term "presupposition" as defined by John Frame (1987, p. 41): "A presupposition is a belief that takes precedence over another and therefore serves as a criterion for another. An ultimate presupposition is a belief over which no other takes precedence."

The functional understanding of the primary identity of Jesus of Nazareth, for example, can point to 1 Timothy 2:5: "For there is one God and one mediator between God and men, the man Christ Jesus." Classically, one would respond to the question of how Jesus of Nazareth, the Christ acts as the mediator between God and men by saying that he does it in his *functions* as prophet, priest, and king. That response tends to find the primary and ongoing identity of Jesus of Nazareth in his expiation. The functional understanding correctly recognizes that in the person of Jesus of Nazareth, we find the reality that God is with us and for us.

However, as we will see in this study, there is an important problem with this way of describing the primary identity of Jesus of Nazareth. Emphasizing his *functions* does not foster a theological environment favorable to discipleship. This functional understanding of the identity of Jesus of Nazareth also hinders us from fully understanding the gospel.

I believe that a fully biblical theology accords *ontological* priority to Jesus of Nazareth as the center and focus of the Creator's plan and the goal of our experience as his followers today. Some may fear that this path might lead to what is often called Christo-monism—that is, inappropriately separating the person and work of Jesus of Nazareth from God the Father and God the Holy Spirit. But that extreme can be avoided. Instead, I maintain that we must allow the testimony of the gospel to lead us to a Christo-centric Trinitarianism, one that asserts the distinct role of the eternal and incarnate Son in the divine project. This certainly includes the forgiveness of sins and our redemption. However, there is so much more than that.

If this is truly the case, as the Scriptures affirm, then Jesus of Nazareth, in his perfect humanity, is both our representative and the goal of our creation. This would explain why the Apostle Paul's passion was to know Jesus of Nazareth and to become like him (Phil. 3:7–10).

The unique nature of Jesus of Nazareth, "perfect in divinity, and perfect in humanity, true God and true man" according to the formulation of the Council of Chalcedon (451 CE),[2] serves as a healthy expression of the implications of the testimony of Scripture. I have already claimed that when the Son or the *Logos* is described as the *subject* of the incarnation, that does not mean in any way that he was passively submissive in that incarnation. The incarnation was a personal, voluntary choice of the *Logos* who "took the form of a servant" (Phil. 2:7, NKJV). He "became poor" (2 Cor. 8:9).

But what is the relationship between the two natures of Jesus of Nazareth the God-man? In other words, what is the meaning of the expression in John 1:14 that the Word "became flesh" (NIV), "was made flesh" (KJ21), or "became a human being" (Phillips)? We are undoubtedly more comfortable

---

2 For the text of the Council of Chalcedon, see
https://sourcebooks.fordham.edu/basis/chalcedon.asp.

with the expression "took the form of" (from Phil. 2:7) because we are convinced that God does not change. God is immutable, whereas "becoming" or "being made" something implies change, and we suppose that there is no becoming or changing in God. However, that is the word that John uses, and we must take that into account. In the incarnation of the eternal Son in the man Jesus of Nazareth, a real change occurred.

While continuing to be divine and to possess all of God's attributes, the eternal Son entered the sphere of time and space, of experiences and of relationships of his own creation. He experienced life in a human body and in a human soul. He experienced human suffering, temptation, injustice, poverty, solitude, and humiliation. He tasted death. He became the son of Mary and of Joseph, the brother of James, the rabbi of Peter and of John. Before the incarnation, the *Logos* knew these things. But in the incarnate Son, he truly and personally experienced what it means to be human.

For this reason, we can affirm that the eternal Son became what he had never been. This ontological question related to the incarnation is eminently important for our justification, for our worship and for our mission. It is also fundamental to our understanding of the gospel—the "Good News."

Having made these preliminary observations, we are now ready to examine the aspect of the gospel that relates to the most important convictions of evangelicals. We maintain that we should seek to offer salvation to every person, and that for this reason the Good News must be proclaimed (cf. Rom. 10:9-10). For many Evangelicals, that is the gospel. It is therefore logical for Evangelicals to argue that the goal of their calling in Christ is the proclamation of the gospel and the salvation of souls.

What Words Come to Mind when You Hear the Word "Gospel"?

How we answer this question is important for at least four significant reasons.

First, we Evangelicals tend to reduce the gospel to what we believe about personal salvation, and we reshape it to facilitate decisions for salvation. I hear African pastors and seminarians talking all the time about the "gospel of salvation" or the "Good News of salvation." In this they are not alone, and they undoubtedly reflect a tendency of Christians world-wide. This popular equating of salvation with the gospel is so prevalent that, as Scot McKnight argues in his book *The King Jesus Gospel* (2011), we have often become "salvationists" rather than Evangelicals.[3] This has happened because our understanding of

---

3 This judgment is in line with the observations of other researchers who have studied the dominant characteristics of the Evangelical movement. These observers confirm that Evangelicals are not fully Christ-centred, in that they focus on his exclusive mediation as a propitiatory sacrifice (cross-centred) as a fundamental and unquestionable element of contemporary Evangelical faith. On this point, see for instance Balmer (1998, pp. 27–

salvation has often dislocated it from the living person Jesus, the Christ and made it a blessing or set of blessings that exist and are given independently from our being joined to the incarnate, resurrected, ascended, and enthroned Lord himself.[4] In this respect, Augustus Strong's words continue to ring true more than a century after he wrote them: "The majority of Christians much more frequently think of Christ as Saviour outside of them, than as a Saviour who dwells within" (1974, p. 795).

But as we have seen, the resurrected Jesus of Nazareth did not commission his followers simply to evangelize and save souls! Contrary to this contemporary tendency to reduce the gospel to a message of personal salvation, Bill Hull (2016) underscores its connection to discipleship when he affirms that "The gospel we preach determines the disciples we produce." His basic argument is that we have so disconnected evangelism, as a matter of conversion and salvation, from discipleship that we find it difficult to produce healthy disciples. Hull writes:

> A majority of those who make a decision through a tract or evangelistic meeting and pray the sinner's prayer do not decide to follow Jesus. The reason they do not decide that is that discipleship is not connected to the decision they are asked to make. (2016, p. 31)

Dallas Willard (1998) adds that this misunderstanding of the gospel preaches a Christ who exists for our benefit alone:

> His only work is to redeem humankind without requiring any further obligation from them. This understanding tends to foster what some have called "vampire Christians." They only want a little blood from Jesus for their sins but want nothing more to do with him until heaven. (pp. 35–36)

When Jesus sent his disciples to "make disciples of all nations," he spoke of a process much more encompassing and transforming than the saving of souls. When we affirm that the goal of our mission is evangelization and the salvation

---

28); Bebbington (1992, pp. 2–3); Bloesch (1983, p. 17); Kuen (1998, p. 44); Mouw (2000, p. 21); Ruegger (1996, p. 2); Willaime (2000, p. 293).

4 Much of contemporary Evangelical theology attaches the salvific merits of Christ's life and death that are imputed to us by grace through faith (the doctrines of atonement, salvation, and justification) to the person of Jesus, and our ensuing growth in holiness (the doctrine of sanctification) to the work of the Holy Spirit. It is customary to think of Jesus as the Saviour and the Spirit as the sanctifier. I agree wholeheartedly with Marcus Johnson, who argues that this view needs serious revision "lest we begin to imagine that the work of the Spirit in some way eclipses or replaces the work of Christ" in our growth in discipleship. "Jesus does not send the Spirit to the church in order that she might become holy in Jesus's absence. Rather, Jesus sends the Spirit in order that he, through the Spirit, *might be present as her holiness*" (Johnson, 2013, p. 126; emphasis in original).

of souls, and not obedience and conformity to the teaching of Christ and conformity to his character, we have deviated from the true goal.

McKnight (2016) claims that just as we Evangelicals often fall into the trap of thinking that the gospel and "making decisions" are synonymous, we also wrongly attempt to link together the notion of the kingdom of God with the "Plan of Salvation."[5] McKnight refutes this false connection:

> They are two different sets of categories. The kingdom vision of Jesus isn't simply or even directly about the Plan of Salvation, as though the kingdom vision entails or implies or involves the Plan of Salvation, and without the Plan of Salvation the kingdom doesn't work. (p. 41)

Our struggle, McKnight explains, is that we are trying to put the Plan of Salvation into the kingdom vision in a way that Jesus never attempted to do. Rather, the gospel includes the complete story of the crucial events in the life of Jesus of Nazareth as Messiah, as Lord, as Saviour, and as Son (McKnight, 2016, p. 55).

We must understand clearly that although personal salvation is crucial, it is not the complete gospel of the New Testament. The Plan of Salvation leads to one thing only: salvation (McKnight, 2016, p. 40). Justification, often called "new birth,"[6] consists of the divine declaration that we are forgiven. However, contrary to what many of us believe, this does not inexorably or spontaneously lead, like a sort of automatic reflex, to a life of goodness and lovingkindness, or to the formation of a personality that is progressively more conformed to that of Jesus of Nazareth, the Christ. If it did, all Christians would manifest the fruit of the Holy Spirit (cf. Gal. 5:22) in their growth in Christ-likeness.

This observation leads us to the second reason why we must be clear in our understanding of the gospel: how we understand the gospel determines the role we allow Christ to play in our daily living and in our worship. Typically, when we think of the Trinity, we view Jesus as the Saviour by whom we have forgiveness of sin and a restored relationship of union and communion with God. We also tend to associate the person of the Holy Spirit with the Father's

---

5 McKnight defines what he calls the "Plan of Salvation" as "the elements or ideas that we find in the Story of the Bible that many of us, but not just evangelicals, bring together to explain how a person gets saved, gets forgiven, and gets reconciled to God, and what that person must do in order to get saved" (2016, p. 38).

6 The expression "new birth" is not found as often in the New Testament as we might think. It is found in Mt. 19:28 (in relationship to an eschatological cosmic event), in Titus 3:5 (in relationship to baptism), and in 1 Peter 1:3 and 23 (with essentially the meaning commonly attributed to the term today). By far the best-known text containing this expression is John 3:3, where, in a discussion with Nicodemus, Jesus of Nazareth declares that no one can enter the kingdom of God "unless he is born again." This is undoubtedly an important declaration, but it must not be taken out of its context.

power, viewing the Spirit as a sort of replacement for Jesus in his absence.[7] This perspective overlooks or obscures the practical, daily importance of our calling, by God the Father, into "the fellowship of his Son, Jesus Christ our Lord" (1 Cor. 1:9). Marcus Johnson (2013), Associate Professor of Theology at Moody Bible Institute, says of this fellowship:

> To experience fellowship with the Son is to be made alive in Christ, justified in Christ, sanctified in Christ, seated in the heavenly realms in Christ, built up into Christ, and given fullness in Christ. Those joined to Christ are "members of Christ," "crucified with Christ," "included in Christ," "baptized into Christ," and the "body of Christ." They eat and drink Christ; they are one with Christ; Christ dwells in them and they dwell in him; and they can do *nothing* apart from him. Salvation is realized and appropriated in the lives of fallen humans only as they apprehend Jesus Christ, who gives himself and all his blessings to us in our Spirit-empowered faith response to his Gospel. Through this Gospel, God the Father incorporates us into Jesus Christ, who is the sum of all blessings: "And because of [God] you are *in Christ Jesus*, who became to us wisdom from God, righteousness and sanctification and redemption" (1 Cor. 1:30). (pp. 38–39)

Our discipleship to Jesus of Nazareth, the God-man, is grounded in the newness of life we have in him. This consists of more than the forgiveness of sin and the promise of eternal life. It is no wonder, then, that Paul can write that God predestined us "to be conformed to the image of his Son" (Rom. 8:29). Even the Spirit serves this divine project. He was sent by the Father so that we might enjoy the actual presence of Christ (Hull, 2016, p. 44; Bjork, 2015, pp. 94–95).[8] This explains the close association of the presence of the Spirit and that of Christ in the Scriptures, where he is even called the "Spirit of Christ" (Rom. 8:9–11; cf. Gal. 4:6; Phil. 1:19). The Holy Spirit is the Spirit of Christ. He did not come to mediate his own presence, to glorify his own name, to teach us about himself, or to form the body of the Spirit. He came to make Christ known, to glorify Christ, to teach us about Christ, and to form us together as

---

7 See note 5 above.

8 In his article on the Holy Spirit in the *New Bible Dictionary*, J. D. Dunn (1962, pp. 1140–1141) maintains that our tie to Christ distinguishes the Christian understanding of the Spirit from the "earlier, less well-defined conception." He writes, "The Spirit is now definitively the Spirit of Christ (Acts 16:7; Rom. 8:9; Gal. 4:6; Phil. 1:19; also 1 Pet. 1:11; cf. Jn. 7:38; 19:30; 20:22; Acts 2:33; Heb. 9:14; Rev. 3:1; 5:6), the other Counsellor who has taken over Jesus' role on earth (Jn. 14:16; cf. 1 Jn. 2:1). This means that Jesus is now present to the believer only in and through the Spirit (Jn. 14:16–28; 16:7; Rom. 8:9f.; 1 Cor. 6:17; 15:45; Eph. 3:16f.; cf. Rom. 1:4; 1 Tim. 3:16; 1 Pet. 3:18; Rev. 2–3)."

the body of Christ (cf. Jn. 15:26; 16:14–15; 1 Cor. 2:14–16; 12:13).[9] Karl Barth (2010), asks, for instance:

> Why is it that he is the Holy Spirit *per definitionem*? ... The answer is staggering in its simplicity. He is the Holy Spirit in this supreme sense—holy with a holiness for which there are no analogies—because He is no other than the presence of Jesus Christ Himself. (Vol. IV.2 § 128)

The Holy Spirit is the personal manner or mode of Christ's dwelling in us (Johnson, 2013, p. 44).[10]

A third reason why it is important for us to understand the gospel correctly is that this understanding governs how we read and interpret the Scriptures. None of us would deny the importance of the Bible in discipleship and disciple making. Not only have we defended the Bible, its authority, its inspiration, its infallibility and its inerrancy, but we have also placed it at the heart of our spirituality. The problem is that because of our abridged understanding of the gospel, we tend to use the Bible inappropriately. At times we even inadvertently place the authority of the Scriptures over that of Jesus. My seminary students, for instance, more commonly affirm that something should be believed, or put into practice, "because the Bible says it" (the word inscripturated) than "because Jesus says it" (the Word incarnated). And it is more common for them to refer to the authority of Scripture than to the character or model of Christ in issues of ethics or morality. This happens even when they are referring to the very words of Jesus as contained in one of the gospels. Whenever we do this, our discipleship becomes more like that of the rabbis than of the early Christ-followers (Bosch, 1995, pp. 36–39; Gallaty, 2015, pp. 33–34).

Because Jesus of Nazareth is the eternal Son of God incarnate, he is the expression of truth and reality and the effective communication of God's fullness and who he desires us to become (Bjork, 2015, pp. 54–61). As such, he is more than the fulfiller of the Old Testament Scriptures. He is also their definitive interpretation (Goldsworthy, 2006, p. 81; Thiselton, 1992, p. 150). Along this line, Goldsworthy (2006, p. 16) correctly asserts that the real link between God as the communicator and us as the receivers is the incarnate God-man. Thus, he writes:

- Jesus is God, the infallible communicator;

---

9 John Stackhouse (2000, pp. 45-46) writes that "the Holy Spirit remains ... a relatively minor, shadowy figure in the New Testament, compared with the centre stage, fully lit person of Jesus." See also Fee (1994); Pinnock (1996).

10 Because of our tendency to think of Jesus primarily as the Saviour, we sometimes understand the Spirit more in terms of empowerment for our mission than as the ongoing presence of Jesus wherever and whenever two or three people are gathered to learn how to obediently follow him (cf. Mt. 18:20; 28:20; Jn. 20:21-22). For an example of how this plays out in our understanding, see Packer (1988, p. 319).

- Jesus is the Word, the infallible message;
- Jesus is the God-man, the infallible receiver.

Goldsworthy further maintains that because Jesus is the ideal and true receiver of the word of God, he is also "the true and faithful responder to the word and proclaimer of that word" (2006, p. 16). This makes Jesus of Nazareth, the incarnate Son, the ultimately authoritative communication from God to the world. This is the affirmation of the Bible: the Word of God is, first and foremost, the God-man Jesus of Nazareth, the Messiah. He is the infallible and ultimate divine revelation. He is also the perfect and trustworthy human response to that communication.

In this sense, we can say that Jesus of Nazareth is the true *imago dei*, or the image (Greek *eikon*) of God (2 Cor. 4:4; Heb. 1:3; Bates, 2017, pp. 156–159; Jipp, 2015, pp. 100–127),[11] but also the true *imago hominis*, or the image of man. What do I mean by that? I mean that the man Jesus of Nazareth lived in total orientation toward and free obedience to the Creator, as we saw in our previous study. He realized what the Creator intended from the very beginning, namely a life of communion with him. Do you want to know what it means to be truly "human"? Look at Jesus of Nazareth. Van der Kooi and van den Brink (2017) state this truth powerfully:

> In his ministry and proclamation Jesus realizes a form of humanity that does not create isolation from God and is not inspired by fear and mistrust. He lives fully on the basis of this relationship with God, and as a result, God's love is revealed in an astounding way in what he does. Jesus crosses boundaries that in his context and culture seemed impossible to transcend. Precisely because he is so intimately connected with God the Father, he can touch sick people who were ceremonially unclean. He was a Jew but was accessible to gentiles. He was a man but related to women in a way of total integrity that did them justice. (pp. 472–473)

In his way of relating to others, Jesus of Nazareth is the true *imago sanctus*—the image of holiness. The atmosphere his life produced was characterized by a holiness that enabled those around him to flourish. His way of making room for people who were estranged from the Father is a pattern of how we should welcome those who are estranged from or even violate the Creator's work and intent (van der Kooi and van den Brink, 2017, p. 473).

But we must not stop there! As we will see in a later chapter, Jesus of Nazareth, the God-man, is also the true *imago fides* (image of faith) in his relationship to his Father and the true *imago pietas* (image of piety). By this I

---

11 The first Christ-followers drew the connection between Jesus of Nazareth as the fullness of the *imago dei*, and as Grenz (2001, p. 147) writes, the *similitudo dei* (likeness of God). Justo Gonzales (1970, p. 165) explains, "This triune God created man according to his image. But man himself is not the image of God; that image is the Son, in whom and by whom man has been created. ... Therefore, the image of God is not something to be found in man, but is rather the direction in which we are to grow."

mean that he demonstrated what it means to love God with all one's heart, soul, and mind (Mt. 22:37), and how to worship him in spirit and truth (Jn. 4:24).

Since Jesus of Nazareth is the God-man, the authority of the Word inscripturate (the written Word) stems from him who is the Word incarnate. Van der Kooi and van den Brink also tie the authority of the Word inscripturate to the Word incarnate, but they narrow it to "God's *saving acts* in Jesus Christ" (2017, p. 566; emphasis added). However, a gospel-centered, biblical theology finds an even more solid basis for the authority of the Bible in its testimony to the *identity* of Jesus of Nazareth, the Word incarnate. In Jesus of Nazareth, we have not only the perfect atonement for our sin; he is also the ultimate example of a flawless alignment of a human being to what the Creator intends us to be (1 Pet. 2:22; 2 Cor. 5:21; Heb. 4:15) and of God's glorious presence (2 Cor. 4:4; Col. 1:15; 2:9). This is what makes him authoritatively superior to the Old Testament revelation of God. As van der Kooi and van den Brink (2017, p. 84) state succinctly, "If ... someone wants to know the Father, he must go to Jesus; he must consider his message, his acts, his death and resurrection. From now on we must recognize that he who has seen Jesus has seen the Father."

This leads me to yet another problem, also tied to our restricted understanding of the gospel, that currently hampers much of our discipleship. We often read the Old Testament as if Jesus never came. I am staggered by how different our reading of the Scriptures is from that of the first Christ-followers! They didn't read the Old Testament with "the same eyes" as they had done before (McKnight, 2011, p. 133). Their new way of interpreting the Scriptures (a hermeneutical shift) happened when they came to understand Jesus, the Christ, as a pre-existent divine agent who was exalted by God after his death and bestowed by God with the divine name (*Yahweh*).[12] This revelation created in the thinking of the early disciples of Jesus what Richard Bauckham has labelled a "Christological monotheism" (and what I call a "Christ-centered trinitarianism"), by convincing them that Jesus the Christ is to be understood in the unique identity of the one God of Israel.[13] In other words, the early disciples in some sense regarded Jesus as on a level with *Yahweh* (Fitzmyer, 1983, p. 203).

While we can affirm wholeheartedly that Jesus is God (i.e., that Jesus of Nazareth is the *imago dei*), we must avoid the trap of thinking that God is Jesus (the eternal Father is incarnate in Jesus of Nazareth) or that Jesus and God are

---

12 Cf. among many others Bauckham (1998) who bluntly states, "There can be no doubt that 'the name that is above every name' (Phil. 2:9) is *YHWH*: it is inconceivable that any Jewish writer could use this phrase for a name other than God's own unique name" (p. 131).
13 For a rather extensive scholarly discussion of this question, see Bauckham (1998); Bruce (1971, p. 80); De Lacey (1982, pp. 191–203); Dunn (1996, p. 180); Hurtado (2015, p. 97); Wright (1993, pp. 128–129); Hagner (1991, pp. 28–29); Richardson (1995, p. 300); Witherington (1994, p. 316); Thiselton (2000, pp. 636–637).

the same (no distinction between the Father and the Son). In this sense, discipleship is all about Jesus of Nazareth, and not about God! We do ultimately live "for God" (Father, Son, and Holy Spirit) or for "the glory of God" (cf. 1 Cor. 10:31), but we do so by conforming to and identifying ourselves with the indwelling Christ (cf. 1 Pet. 4:11; Col. 3:17; Rom. 13:12–14; Gal. 3:27–28).[14] This explains why Paul could so boldly write in his letter to the Corinthians that "for us there is but one God, the Father, from whom all things came and for whom we live; and there is but one Lord, Jesus Christ, through whom all things came and through whom we live" (1 Cor. 8:6). Paul distinguished clearly between God and Jesus reserving the title "Lord" for and explicitly centering his discipleship on Jesus.[15] In fact, he summed up his message as one of "repentance toward God and embodied allegiance[16] to the Lord Jesus" (Ac. 20:21).

Clearly, the risen Lord Jesus was the center not only of Paul's discipleship, but also of that of the early Christians generally. This truth is apparent in several ways. Its adherents were "disciples of the Lord Jesus" (Ac. 9:1); they were baptized "in the name of the Lord Jesus" (Ac. 8:16); they spoke in his name (Ac. 9:28). The last thing Luke tells us about Paul is that in Rome he was "teaching the things about the Lord Jesus Christ" (Ac. 28:31). Throughout his

---

14 God is glorified when we become like Christ who is "our righteousness, sanctification and redemption" (1 Cor. 1:30); for he (Christ) is the radiance of the glory of God and the exact imprint of his nature (Heb. 1:3). In this sense, "giving glory to God" is the same thing as discipleship, or growth in Christ-likeness (cf. 2 Cor. 3:18; Gal. 4:19); for God is remaking us into his image, and he is doing so by conforming us to the One who is that image. This is the only way we truly give glory to God, for the entire divine project is focused on our complete participation in Christ's life, which joins us to the life of our triune God. And when God accomplishes our glorification in Christ, "we will be participants in that one stupendous act of union in which things in heaven and earth will be reconciled to God through Christ, through whom and for whom all things were created" (Johnson, 2013, p. 187; see also Bjork, 2015, pp. 111–128).
15 Paul also refers to God far more often than anyone else in the New Testament. He has more than 40 percent of all the New Testament references to God (548 out of 1,314). But in Paul's writing, God is not some abstract, remote deity; he is the Father of Jesus Christ. Thus he normally begins his letters with a greeting like this one: "Grace to you and peace from God our Father and the Lord Jesus Christ" (Rom. 1:7; 1 Cor. 1:3; 2 Cor. 1:2; Gal. 1:3; Eph. 1:2; Phil. 1:2; 2 Th. 1:2; 1 Tim. 1:2; 2 Tim. 1:2; Tit. 1:4; Phm. 3). Occasionally he links God to Christ in prayer: "May God our Father himself and our Lord Jesus direct our way to you" (1 Th. 3:11; cf. 2 Th. 2:16–17). He can speak of God as "the God and Father of our Lord Jesus Christ" (Rom. 15:6; 2 Cor. 1:3; 11:31; Eph. 1:3; cf. Eph. 1:17; Col. 1:3). With regard to this linking of God to Jesus Christ, Leon Morris (1990, p. 43) suggests that it might be understood in the sense that "we know God only to the extent that Jesus has made him known. He is not some abstract, remote deity, but the Father of Jesus Christ." As a validation of this understanding, Morris adds that it is through Christ that Paul offers thanksgiving to God (Rom. 1:8; 7:25; Eph. 5:20).
16 The Greek word in this text is *pistis*; on its meaning, see chapter 11.

ministry, he argued that all must have "the mind of Christ" (1 Cor. 2:16). And he claimed that he was ready to die "for the name of the Lord Jesus" (Ac. 21:13).

In short, the communication of the first Christ-followers could be summarized by saying that they "preached the Lord Jesus" or simply that they "announced the Good News of Jesus" (e.g., Ac. 8:35; 11:20).[17]

Toward a Full Understanding of the Gospel[18]

The "gospel" that we proclaim today is abridged and too anthropocentric—I have a problem, Jesus died for my sins, now I can change and go to heaven. But what difference might it make in our spirituality, worship, and mission if our understanding of the gospel began not with me and my sin, but with God's creation and his new creation, or with the royalty of Jesus of Nazareth and his cross as the accomplishment of his royal work (Wright, 2012, pp. 178–209)?

The Meaning of the Gospel

To answer these questions, we must reach agreement on the meaning of the gospel. We agree that there is only one gospel (Gal. 1:6–8). But not all Evangelicals give the same answer to the question: "What is the gospel?"

An unbelievable number of books, articles, and blogs in recent years have debated the question of what composes the gospel (e.g., Gilbert, 2010; Chandler & Wilson, 2012; Dixon, 2005; McKnight, 2016; Carson, 2010; Piper, 2011; Wright, 2012). Trevin Wax (2011) even compiled an extensive list of the definitions of the gospel proposed by Christians through the ages.

Even if people admit that the gospel contains elements that are found in the definitions offered by others, they still frequently either emphasize one aspect of the gospel more than the others or completely eliminate an element found in the others. Jackson Wu (2015, pp. 30–31) offers three examples to assist us in understanding each other on this point. First, Matt Chandler says, "The Bible establishes two frames of reference for the same gospel" (Chandler & Wilson, 2012, p. 15). As a first frame, "the gospel on earth" refers to the call presented to individuals to repent and be forgiven for their sins because of Christ's death. Meanwhile, the "gospel in heaven" links "human salvation to cosmic

---

17 John Stackhouse (2000, p. 45) argues that a Christological and Christo-centric reminder should be issued to those who "currently pursue trinitarianism as a sort of key to unlock a wide range of theological puzzles. Can we learn about the one true God, yes, from Old Testament revelation ... but we know what we know ... because of God's revelation in Christ. It was, after all, the disciples' encounter with Christ that led to their worship of him and conceptualizing of him as the divine Lord."

18 In what follows, I draw primarily from Matthew Bates (2017) and Jackson Wu (2015).

restoration," as it is explained in the "meta-narrative of the Bible's story of Redemption" (Chandler & Wilson, 2012, p. 16).

In contrast with this understanding, Greg Gilbert offers a more restricted vision of the gospel. Gilbert (2010) examines three gospels of substitution, maintaining that the fact that Jesus is "Lord" is not the gospel, nor is the frequently expressed paradigm "creation-fall-redemption-consummation" the gospel. Furthermore, "cultural transformation is not the gospel" (Gilbert, 2010, pp. 103–107). Gilbert adds, "It should be obvious by now that to say simply that 'Jesus is Lord' is really not Good News at all if we don't explain how Jesus is not just Lord but also Saviour" (2010, p. 104). "Problematically," writes Wu (2015, p. 30) of Gilbert, "he presumes that those who preach the gospel as Jesus' kingship separate his being Lord from his being Saviour, perhaps even 'making their center something other than the cross.'" However, as we will see, the cross need not necessarily be pitted against the reign of the resurrected Jesus of Nazareth. Nor must it be downplayed when the kingdom is highlighted as the biblical narrative framing the communication of the gospel.

As a third group, Wu mentions those who make the word "gospel" a synonym for "justification." He takes as an example a book titled *The Gospel as Center* (Carson & Keller, 2012) in which the contributors use the words "justification" and "righteousness" at least 385 times. More specifically, a close reading reveals that the words "justify," "justified," and "justification" are found 185 times. The word "righteousness" appears more than 200 times, and the terms "impute(d)" and "imputation" appear about 25 times. Not surprisingly, Romans 3 is cited 25 times in the book.

As I have sought to show up to this point, our understanding of the gospel unavoidably influences our understanding of what it means to follow Jesus of Nazareth. My argument here is that certain understandings of the gospel create an environment that is more conducive to intentional discipleship to Jesus, the Christ,[19] than others. We must deliberately choose the biblical themes we will highlight to frame our understanding of the gospel. Our understanding must be rooted in a biblical theology, not only in a systematic theology. Keeping in mind the overall narrative of the Scriptures, we can better discern the themes that foster a deliberate link to the rabbi Jesus (Wu, 2015, p. 29).

Several scriptural themes or motifs "frame," as it were, a core of unchanging facts that constitute the gospel and that help us to communicate it. The clearest description of those elements is found in three Pauline texts: Rom. 1:1–4, 16–

---

19 With Bates (2019, p. 47), I maintain that we must avoid using "Christ" as if it were the family name of Jesus. "Christ" is a title. It comes from the ancient Greek word *christos*, which signifies "anointed." The Greek word comes from the verb meaning "to anoint." It is parallel to the Hebrew *mashiah*. Neither of these words was a name. They were both in fact honorific titles. Understanding the meaning of the title "Christ" is extremely important because it fixes our attention on what the biblical gospel highlights in the resurrected person of Jesus: his royalty.

17; 1 Cor. 15:1–5; and 2 Tim. 2:8. These texts are important because some of Paul's letters are the oldest books in the New Testament, dating back to within 15 years of Jesus' death.[20] Their explanations of the gospel express the understanding of the earliest Christ-followerships.

The Permanent Elements of the Gospel

Romans 1:1–4 is one of the most important texts of the Bible, but it is very often misunderstood. It is also remarkably ignored, given its preeminence at the beginning of the most famous of Paul's letters. Consider, for instance, that neither Matt Chandler in *The Explicit Gospel* nor Greg Gilbert in *What Is the Gospel?* ever mention this passage (they also completely ignore 2 Tim. 2:8). Let's attentively read this text to learn what others seem to ignore.

Romans 1:1–2

> Paul, a servant of Christ Jesus, called to be an Apostle and set apart for the gospel of God—the gospel he promised beforehand through his prophets in the Holy Scriptures.

Paul begins his letter by clarifying his relationship to Jesus of Nazareth. Even this fact tells us something about the nature of the gospel. Jesus of Nazareth is the Messiah, the Christ. Paul is a *doulos*, a slave of this king (see also Gal. 1:10; Phil. 1:1; 1 Cor. 4:1).[21] By identifying himself in this manner, he signifies that Jesus of Nazareth is his master. In that relationship, Paul's responsibility was to completely obey Jesus and one day to give him an account of his life and activities (Wenham, 1995, pp. 121–122). Paul also saw himself as an emissary, a representative, an ambassador of Christ. For that is what the word "apostle" means. In other words, according to Matthew Bates (2019, pp. 9, 49), even before presenting the elements of the gospel in detail, Paul suggests that the gospel is a "kingly proclamation about Jesus."

Are you not shocked by that suggestion? Typically we jump too quickly to Romans 1:16–17, which describe the gospel as "the power of God for the

---

20 Based on both internal and external evidence, the redaction of the first letter to the Thessalonians is generally dated about 51 CE. Except for the possibility of an early date for Galatians (48-49 CE), 1 Thessalonians is Paul's earliest canonical letter. The redaction of the Epistle to the Romans is generally situated between 56 and 58 CE, and 1 Corinthians one or two years earlier. The gospel of Mark is generally dated in the years 63 to 68 CE.

21 Although Paul never explicitly calls the followers of Jesus of Nazareth "slaves of Christ," Murray Harris (1999) demonstrates why we can reasonably infer such a relationship through an examination of the Pauline texts (see also Glancy, 2006, pp. 99–101; Wenham, 1995, p. 122).

salvation of everyone who believes," without sufficiently taking into account the context given by Paul in verses 1–4 (Jipp, 2015, p. 249).

When Paul claims to be "set apart for the gospel[22] of God" (literally, "in view of the gospel"), he is stressing that God is the source of that Good News and that his life is totally dedicated to that Good News in Christ. For Paul, that dedication encompasses faith, obedience, and the proclamation of that message (Moo, 1966, p. 43).

Note also that Paul does not say "my gospel" here, although he uses that expression elsewhere (cf. Rom. 2:16; 16:25; 2 Tim. 2:8). Since for him there is only one true gospel (cf. Gal. 1:6–7), he speaks in more universal terms, calling it the "gospel of God." That gospel was "promised" beforehand by God through his prophets in the Holy Scriptures.[23] Paul affirms that God *promised* the gospel (which implies an engagement; see also Rom. 4:13–25; 9:4; 15:8) when he could have said God just prophesied or predicted it. This points to the fact that the gospel is the accomplishment of something God committed himself to do, as is confirmed throughout the Scriptures. Scot McKnight sees this divine commitment to keep his own promise in the Father's sending of the Son to establish Jesus as the Messiah (which means King):

> The point of the gospel in Romans 1:1–4, where Paul defines it, is that it is *a narrative about Jesus as King/Messiah and Lord*. ... the gospel was first and foremost for the apostles *the Story of Jesus as the fulfillment of the Story of Israel*. This Jesus is Messiah/King, he is Lord, and he saves as the one who is the perfect image of God, the true and faithful Israelite. In Jesus, God has taken up rule of creation, and those who enter into Jesus' death and resurrection by repentance, faith, and baptism join him in that rule. (McKnight, 2016, p. 80; emphasis in original)

Romans 1:3

Regarding his Son, who as to his human nature was a descendant of David ...

Observe first that the gospel as described here is not centered on man and his pursuit of salvation. It is rather a cosmic meta-narrative concerning the acts of the eternal Son of God. Paul calls Jesus of Nazareth *huios* (son), something he does frequently in his Epistles (17 times) to underscore Jesus' particular relationship with the celestial Father.

---

22 *Euangelion* is a typically Pauline word; 60 of the 76 occurrences of this word in the New Testament are in Paul's letters.
23 This is the only place where Paul writes "Holy Scriptures." He uses the plural *graphai* ("scriptures") four times (Rom. 15:4; 16:26; 1 Cor. 15:3, 4).

The gospel begins with what we call the Incarnation—the point at which the eternal Son, who pre-existed with the Father from all eternity, became a man.[24] We will see in our study of 1 Corinthians 15 that this is indeed cosmic Good News, tied to Adam who also began his earthly existence when he became a man. Jesus of Nazareth, the model and ideal for humanity (*imago hominis*), he who is truly human,[25] corresponds to Adam.

"The gospel ... regarding his Son, who *as to his human nature* was a descendant of David (literally, "according to the flesh"). Paul never uses the word "flesh" (*sarx*) to indicate the soft tissues of the human body. He sometimes uses it to speak of the entire human body (e.g., 1 Cor. 5:5; 6:16; 2 Cor. 7:1; 12; Gal. 4:13; Eph. 5:31), but more often it refers to the entire person (e.g., Rom. 3:20; Gal. 1:16). When Paul uses the word more theologically, it can have a neutral meaning, designating simply human nature or existence (e.g., Rom. 4:1; 8:3; 9:8; 1 Cor. 1:29; 15:50), or take on a much more negative sense indicating human life independent of or in opposition to the spiritual world (Rom. 7:5; 8:8; 13:14; Gal. 5:13–18) (Moo, 1996, p. 47, n. 27; see also Ridderbos, 1978, pp. 64–68, 100–107; Dunn, 1998, pp. 62–73).

"The gospel ... regarding his Son who as to his human nature *was a descendant of David*" (literally, "seed of David"). Here we have the affirmation that this Good News corresponds to the promises of the Old Testament that the Messiah would be a descendant of that king (2 Sam. 7:12–14):

> When your days are over and you rest with your fathers, I will raise up your offspring to succeed you, who will come from your own body, and I will establish his kingdom. He is the one who will build a house for my Name, and I will establish the throne of his kingdom forever. I will be his father, and he will be my son.

This promise became the major preoccupation of messianic hopes in the Old Testament (cf. Isa. 11:1, 10; Jer. 23:5–6; 30:9; 33:14–18; Ez. 34:23–24; 37:24–25). It echoes the promise made to Abraham that through him and his descendants (literally, his seed) all the peoples of the earth would be blessed

---

24 The pre-existence of the Son mentioned in Romans 1:3 is suggested by the use of the verb *ginomai* to highlight that this was no ordinary birth (otherwise the verb *gennao* would be used). It signifies that the incarnation of the eternal Son entailed a change in existence from non-fleshly to fleshly (cf. Gal. 4:4; Phil. 2:7). Romans 8:3 reinforces that interpretation, since God is described as having "sent his own Son in the likeness of sinful man." It is presumed that the Son was first with the Father in a non-carnal state, and that he was then sent to take on a truly human nature (yet without sin) so that he could now condemn sin in man (cf. Gal. 3:13; Rom. 3:25; 1 Pet. 2:24–25).

25 I agree with Emil Brunner (1953, pp. 65-66) who argues that human nature can be understood ultimately only in the light of Christ. But more significant than the epistemological claim is the ontological. Brunner (1939, pp. 94-96) adds that the Word of God constitutes the human person.

(Gen. 12:3; 22:18), a promise that would be repeated to Isaac (Gen. 26:4) and to Jacob (Gen. 28:14).

Bates (2019, p. 52) insists that the phrase "was a descendant of David" should not be translated in that way, nor by "is one of David's descendants." He does not find these translations precise enough. He notes that when Paul speaks of a normal birth, he prefers the word *gennao*, the word commonly used for human procreation (Rom. 9:11; Gal. 4:23, 24, 29). "But," Bates continues, "when a change from preexistence to human existence is in view for God's Son, he opts instead for *ginomai*—as he has done in Romans 1:3." For instance, Paul uses the verb *ginomai* when he writes "God sent his Son, born of a woman" (Gal. 4:4). He uses the same verb when he writes that the eternal Son did not consider his divine equality something to be grasped when "being made in human likeness" (Phil. 2:7). For this reason, Bates argues that we should translate Romans 1:3 with the words "he came into being" rather than "descended" or "was born."

However, the gospel is not only about the promises made to David. It also includes the resurrection. The most concise articulation of the gospel anywhere in Paul's letters clearly demonstrates this: "Remember Jesus Christ, raised from the dead, descended from (literally, "from the seed") of David. This is my gospel" (2 Tim. 2:8).

Romans 1:4

And who through the Spirit of holiness *was declared with power* to be the Son of God by his resurrection from the dead: Jesus Christ our Lord.

If the first movement in the cosmic narrative is the eternal Son's "coming into being" as a man, the second movement is the enthronement of Jesus of Nazareth as resurrected from the dead. Based on his resurrection, Jesus was installed in a new position of authority. He was "declared with power to be the Son of God," which may properly be understood as an informal description of the position in which the Son was installed (Bates, 2017, p. 34). That installation of the bodily resurrected Jesus of Nazareth at the right hand of the Father demonstrates God's absolute acceptance of the work of the incarnate Son. As Goldsworthy (2006, p. 305) states, "The resurrection shows that Jesus is the one true human who has merited life with the Father." Van der Kooi and van den Brink (2017, p. 435) flesh this idea out further: "By raising him from the dead and clothing him with divine glory, God, as it were, positioned himself beside Jesus and said: 'This man belongs with me'." Jesus of Nazareth is the *imago sanctus*!

The fact that the resurrection demonstrates the divinity of Jesus of Nazareth is not the only thing that makes it so important. Nor is the importance of his resurrection limited to its function as a prototype of our own resurrection (Rom. 8:11; 1 Cor. 15:35–57; Phil. 3:10–11). Jesus of Nazareth represents us before the Father not only in the atonement, but also in the fact that in the God-man we have someone who is human, just as we are, and in whom God's covenant is a reality (van der Kooi & van den Brink, 2017, p. 484). When we add that Jesus of Nazareth, resurrected, enthroned, and glorified, intercedes for us (1 Jn. 2:1–2; Rom. 8:34), we still haven't exhausted the major significance of his resurrection. On top of all this, the resurrection and enthronement of Jesus of Nazareth indicate that he reigns now over all of creation.

The phrase "through the Spirit of holiness" in Romans 1:4 contains the term *hagiōsunē,* which is never used in the New Testament to designate the Holy Spirit (Moo, 1996, p. 50). Bates (2019, p. 53), however, points out that most biblical scholars recognize it as corresponding to a Hebrew way of signifying the Holy Spirit. He concludes that the term undoubtedly refers to the domain of the presence and activity of the Holy Spirit. This would be a way of indicating that the reign of Jesus corresponds to the presence and activity of the Holy Spirit. We will come back to this in another study.

The word translated "declared" (*horizō*) did not have that meaning in the first century after Jesus Christ (Moo, 1996, p. 47). In its other uses in the New Testament, it is translated by "delimited," "designated," or "established" (cf. Lk. 22:22; Ac. 2:23; 10:42; 11:29; 17:26, 31; Heb. 4:7). We should therefore conclude that its meaning here is that the Son was "designated" or "established" the Son of God by God the Father when he was resurrected (see also Ac. 13:33; Heb. 1:5).

What is the function of the phrase "declared with power to be the Son of God" (NIV) or "appointed the Son of God in power" (KJV)? Paul is affirming that the preexisting Son, who entered into the experience of being human as the promised Messiah, was established by his resurrection in a more powerful and authoritative position in relationship to this world (Moo, 1996, pp. 47–48). Joshua Jipp (2015) explains how this phrase and the surrounding verses form the context of the gospel of which Paul was not ashamed, and which reveals the righteousness of God by faith from first to last (Rom. 1:16–17):

> In addition to sharing the common word *euangelion* (1:1b, 16a; cf. 1:9),[26] the confession speaks of the Messiah as "son of God *in power*" (*huiou theou en endynamei;* 1:4), whereas the gospel as "God's power (*dynamei ... theou*) for salvation" (1:16). This divine power for salvation is related to the Messiah's resurrection in 1:4 and is of one piece with Paul's frequent deployment of *dynamis* to describe resurrection elsewhere in his letters.[27] Thus "the power of God for salvation" (1:16a) would appear to be dependent upon God's installation of his son to a position of power. God's resurrected and enthroned Son is invested with divine power, and therefore the association in 1:16 between gospel and

---

26 Some significant Greek manuscripts read *ta dynamis Christou* in Romans 1:16, and this would seem to connect Rom. 1:16–17 to Rom. 1:1–4 even more explicitly.
27 For a few examples, see 1 Cor. 6:14; 15:43; 2 Cor. 4:7; 12:9; 13:4; Eph. 1:19, 21; 3:16; Phil. 3:10.

God's power further attests to the closest connection between Christ's resurrection and God's righteousness in 1:17. (pp. 248–249)

Based on his exegesis of this text (Rom. 1:4) and of Paul's epistle to the Colossians, Peter O'Brien (1982, p. 163) affirms that Jesus of Nazareth resurrected and exalted "is in a position of supreme authority." This means that the resurrected Jesus now shares with the Father supremacy over all creation. Bates (2017) explains the progression we see expressed in Romans 1:3–4:

> Previously he was the Son of God; now he is the Son-of-God-in-Power, actively reigning until all his enemies are made a footstool for his feet (1 Cor. 15:25). In other words, in his earthly life Jesus was the anointed one, the one chosen as the royal Davidic Messiah (the Christ), but during his earthly sojourn he had not yet received his throne, he had not yet begun to reign as king. But the resurrection (and ascension) changed all this, as Jesus has now been enthroned at the right hand of God and is reigning as the Lord of heaven and earth. (p. 34)

Paul refers to this "Son-of-God-in-Power" as "Jesus Christ our Lord" (Rom. 1:4). Thomas Torrance (1996, pp. 46–47) describes the resurrection as "the solution to the enigmatic identity of Jesus." His resurrection and his exaltation "reveal and give access" to the hidden identity of Jesus of Nazareth. He is coequal with God the Father. He is Lord and must be worshipped. And although this identity is intimately tied to his *function* as mediator between the deity (Father, Son, and Spirit) and humans in his expiatory death, we would be wise to recognize that his *ontological* identity as God-man is primary. He is, first and foremost, the Lord and the Christ! The saving rule of God is actively made present through the enthronement of Jesus of Nazareth crucified and resurrected, the Lord and the Messiah.

Let us pause a moment to measure the importance of this fact! Ever since the resurrection, the Father has glorified the Son (see Jn. 17:5) by giving him the name which is above every name (Phil. 2:9). This name can be no other than the name of the deity. And we must not be fooled on this point! It is not sufficient to imagine that we can use the word "God" to refer at the same time to the Father, to the Son, and to the Spirit and be consistent with biblical theology. The biblical text is explicit on this point! At the resurrection, God the Father gave Jesus of Nazareth a mandate and full authority in heaven and on earth (Mt. 28:18) and welcomed him into his heavenly glory (Lk. 24:51; Eph. 1:20; 4:10). From that moment on, the Father has placed the Son "under the projectors," as van der Kooi and van den Brink (2017) forcefully state:

> Just as the Son had always pointed to the Father, so the Father now consistently points to the Son. Everything in the New Testament is now about Jesus. Nobody is asked to remain silent anymore about his being the Messiah. On the contrary, now the entire house of Israel, says Peter, may know that God made him Lord (*kyrios*—the Greek rendering of the divine name YHWH) and Messiah (Ac.

2:36). In the proclamation of the Good News about God, as the disciples now took over the preaching from Jesus, the core is now the key position that Jesus now occupies. For just as consistently as the Son had distinguished himself from and had pointed the people to the Father, the Father now distinguishes himself from and points to the Son. (p. 84)

The resurrection of Jesus of Nazareth, and his enthronement as the messianic King are correctly recognized in Evangelical circles as the sign that a new eschatological reality has arrived: "The rule of the Lord Jesus Christ begins with the resurrection and ends with the defeat of death on the last day" (Schreiner, 2001, p. 165). With Schreiner, we appropriately affirm that his resurrection validates the acknowledgment that Jesus of Nazareth is Lord (Rom. 10:9). And we find it reasonable to believe that since Jesus conquered the grave, our victory over the world and over the forces of evil is assured. We even acknowledge that since he has been enthroned at the right hand of the Father, he reigns over all angelic powers (Eph. 1:20–22). But it is somehow difficult for us to admit that he should be at the heart of our theology, our worship, and our spirituality and our hermeneutical key for understanding the biblical texts. We direct people to Jesus of Nazareth for the salvation of their souls. But we point them to "God" for everything else.

By His Resurrection Jesus Was Declared with Power to Be the Son of God through the Spirit of Holiness

Paul writes that the enthronement of Jesus of Nazareth crucified and resurrected took place "through the Spirit of holiness." Based on Old Testament passages (*ruach quodesh* in Ps. 51:11; Isa. 63:10–11) and texts from Qumran, the phrase "Spirit of holiness" was a Hebrew way of designating the Holy Spirit (Bates, 2019, p. 53). At this point in our study, we can draw two conclusions. First, this indicates that the actual reign of the Lord Jesus, the Christ is co-extensive with the presence of the Holy Spirit. And second, we can conclude that even in the realm of the Spirit, Jesus is the Son of God with power who reigns and brings life (cf. Rom. 1:16). We will come back to this point in another study. But I want to make one further observation here.

Sometimes we fool ourselves into thinking that since Jesus of Nazareth is no longer among us, the Holy Spirit has taken over the baton and is in the center of the divine project. According to this dispensationalist thinking, God the Father, in his relationship to Israel, was in the spotlight in the Old Testament. Then it was God the Son, during the time of the life and death of Jesus of Nazareth. Now, it is the Holy Spirit during the church age (Ryrie, 1997). John F. Walvoord (2011, pp. 3–4), who succeeded Lewis Sperry Chafer as the head of Dallas Theological Seminary, expressed this view in the following way: "The primary goal of God is the manifestation of his own glory. Toward that end, each dispensation, each successive revelation of the plan of God through the centuries, his way of treating the elect and the non-elect … unites to manifest the divine glory."

This understanding incorrectly minimizes the fact that the Father continues even today to place Jesus of Nazareth, the Christ, in the spotlight by the Spirit. We have ample confirmation in the New Testament that it was by the Spirit that Jesus of Nazareth was conceived, inspired, and equipped for his work (Mt. 1:18–20; 3:16; 12:28; Mk. 1:10; Lk. 1:35; 3:22; 4:14, 18–19; Jn. 1:32–33; 3:34). In fact, the Spirit has now been unambiguously sent into the world to ensure that the Son remains in the center of our theology, worship, and mission. As van der Kooi and van den Brink (2017, p. 85) argue, insisting that Jesus of Nazareth was baptized with the Holy Spirit (Mt. 3:11) for the benefit of those who belong to him by receiving that Spirit (Lk. 11:13; Jn. 7:39). It is the Spirit who "gives life" (Jn. 6:63), and Jesus of Nazareth is "the Life" (Jn. 14:6). It is the resurrected Messiah who gives the Spirit. For it is only after his exaltation that the "living water" begins to flow (Jn. 7:38–39) (Lindars, 2010, pp. 301–302; Keener, 2003, pp. 729–730). Scottish theologian Andrew Murray (1908) concludes that precisely for that reason the Spirit of God is called the "Holy Spirit" in the New Testament. Murray writes:

> At Pentecost the Holy Spirit was sent as the Spirit of the glorified Jesus, the Spirit of the incarnate Christ, crucified and ascended to heaven to bring and communicate to us the divine life. Not a life coming directly from God, but a life mixed with the human nature which Jesus Christ had lived on earth. It is at that time that he received the name Holy Spirit, for it is in dwelling in us that God reveals his holiness. It is therefore literally true to say that the Spirit who dwelt in Jesus-man, and who later would dwell in us: the "Holy Spirit" did not yet exist. (pp. 23-24)

Summary

Bates (2019, p. 54) summarizes in the following way the manner in which Paul details the gospel in Romans 1:1–4. When Paul thinks of the gospel, he has two activities in mind: first, the coming of the eternal Son, who left his divine preexistence to enter into a divine-human existence in the person of Jesus of Nazareth; second, his royal elevation to the right hand of the Father. Other elements of the biblical narrative that support this understanding of the Good News are the royal Davidic bloodline, the resurrection from the dead, and the way in which the reign of Jesus corresponds to the presence of the Holy Spirit. Here, the gospel treats primarily the ancient promises of *Yahweh* that are accomplished in the *incarnation* and *enthronement* of the Son. This understanding of the gospel should be at the heart of and direct any theology that seeks to be evangelical.

Romans 1:1–4 shows that the primary fact of the gospel is that Jesus has become the sovereign king of the universe. Paul highlights this in four ways:

(1) his own identity as the slave and Apostle of this king; (2) his use of the title "Christ;" (3) his way of highlighting the enthronement of Jesus as the Son of God with power; and (4) his declaration that this Son is "Jesus Christ our Lord." Bates maintains for this reason that the gospel is in fact a royal proclamation.[28]

This information that Paul gives us about the gospel allows us to understand discipleship as growth in obedience to Jesus, who has been established in his position of authority by his resurrection from the dead. We also see this in the fact that immediately following his presentation of the elements of the gospel, Paul affirms that the Lord Jesus had commissioned him along with the other Apostles to communicate the gospel in such a way that it calls people "from among all the Gentiles to the obedience that comes from faith"—to the glory of Jesus' name (see also Rom. 16:26).

We could ask why the Apostle does not say here that the gospel has the aim of bringing men and women to faith (without adding obedience). In his second letter to the Corinthians, Paul affirms that we "take every thought captive to make it obedient to Christ" (2 Cor. 10:5). John the Baptist understood too that faith must produce obedience. He proclaimed, "Whoever believes in the Son has eternal life, but whoever *does not obey* the Son will not see life, for God's wrath remains on him" (Jn. 3:36). These words remind us of the words of Jesus himself, who testified that it is not enough to call him Lord:

> Not everyone who says to me, "Lord, Lord," will enter the kingdom of heaven, but only the one who does the will of my Father who is in heaven. Many will say to me on that day, "Lord, Lord, did we not prophesy in your name and in your name drive out demons and in your name perform many miracles?" Then I will tell them plainly, "I never knew you. Away from me, you evil doers!" (Mt. 7:21–23)

If we correctly understood the nature of the gospel, we would not even ask about its relationship to discipleship! That is the main point of this study. The crucified, resurrected, and enthroned Jesus, the Christ is himself the Good News (gospel) we embrace and communicate! A recognition of this person, who as to his earthly life was a descendant of David but whom we know by his resurrection from the dead to be the enthroned and reigning ruler in the eternal kingdom he announced, should naturally place us in a position of learning how to live out obedient allegiance to him. This logic is neatly summed up by Dean Gilliland (1983, p. 47): "The phrase *Jesus is Lord* means that life has a new center of loyalty, a fixed point to which everything must now conform. Jesus is the new Head and he will have his preeminence in everything."

---

28 There is a broad consensus that the notion of "gospel," from the biblical perspective and historically, refers to an "announcement concerning the king, or of a royal victory" (Dickson, 2005).

Questions to Think About

1. I state that the ontological question related to the incarnation is eminently important for our justification, for our worship and for our mission. How might keeping in mind the two natures of Jesus of Nazareth, the God-man function as a corrective to imperfect models of discipleship and Christian growth?

2. I argue that we often reduce the gospel to Jesus' death on the cross to the atonement for our sins, and I quote a couple of other scholars who describe us as "salvationists" or "vampire Christians" rather than Evangelicals. How does your local congregation or your denomination define the gospel?

3. Why is it important for our spiritual lives and for our mission to keep in mind that the God-man Jesus of Nazareth is both the infallible and ultimate divine revelation and also the perfect and trustworthy human response to that communication? How does this truth influence your understanding of the gospel and of discipleship?

4. What are the components of the gospel as presented in Romans 1:1–4? How do these relate to Paul's declaration in Romans 10:9–10?

5. In the last paragraph of this chapter, I claim that the Lord Jesus is himself the Good News we embrace and communicate! How well would you say your church emphasizes this? How could you contribute to improvement where the church's performance is weak?

8. The Good News of Jesus, the King

Historians tell us that the word "gospel" was primarily a political or royal word, not a religious concept. A gospel was the public announcement of an enthronement, birth, or victory of a king. That was the meaning of the word "gospel" in the Greek culture at the time of the writing of the New Testament (Dickson, 2010, pp. 111–140). This observation should warn us about our way of understanding the gospel as the Good News of salvation in an almost exclusively religious sense. Recognizing how the word "gospel" was understood at that time also introduces us to the idea that the royalty of Jesus is the most essential fact of the Good News (Bates, 2019, p. 47).

Three Biblical Narratives that Always Frame the Unchanging Elements of the Gospel

In our previous study, we saw that the Good News as announced by Paul describes two activities. First, it declares the coming of the eternal Son who left his divine pre-existence to take on a divine/human existence in the person of Jesus of Nazareth. Second, the gospel underscores his elevation and enthronement as king at the right hand of his Father. Other elements of that description of the Good News are his royal heritage in the line of David, his resurrection from the dead, and the way in which the reign of Jesus corresponds to the presence of the Holy Spirit. Here we see the ancient meaning of the word "gospel," since it describes the accomplishment of the earliest promises made by the Almighty (*Yahweh*) in the incarnation and enthronement of the Son.

Jackson Wu maintains that these elements constitute the unchangeable core of the gospel, and that these unalterable components are always communicated in the Bible within one or another of three narrative "frames." He writes, "These framework themes are creation, covenant, and kingdom. Without exception, biblical writers always use one or more of these ideas in passages that explicitly reference the 'gospel'" (Wu, 2015, p. 40). N. T. Wright (2015, pp. 71–73, 98) proposes the same three themes, except that he uses "coronation" instead of "kingdom."

Wu summarizes the relationship between these themes and how they frame the gospel:

Because God is the Creator of the world, he is the King over all nations. However, humanity has acted as usurpers, creating idolatrous kingdoms to rival God's rule as the Creator-King. God therefore enacted a plan to rectify the world. Beginning with Abraham in Genesis 12, God established a covenant according to which he would bless all nations. Through a series of covenants that would follow (such as the covenants with Moses and David), God explains how he will set his creation right, overthrowing those who rebel against his reign. (2015, p. 41)

In this process of re-establishing his reign, Jesus of Nazareth, the God-man, plays the central role. He demonstrates and proclaims the divine project and initiates his kingdom. The resistance he encounters demonstrates the point at which humanity has estranged itself from this plan. Because of his love for mankind and according to the will of the Father (Mk. 14:36), he took on himself that fault and obtained our forgiveness. In this act of reconciliation, the power of death is overcome, and our estrangement and rebellion against our Creator are judged and emptied of their definitive character. And as van der Kooi and van den Brink (2017, pp. 450–451) so apply point out, in the realization of this entire project the royalty of Jesus of Nazareth plays the main role:

This is not just the case after his resurrection but also applies very clearly during his earthly life, not only when his kingship is announced (Lk. 1:32–33) and acknowledged (Jn. 1:50), but also when people attach all kinds of concrete expectations to it (Mt. 20:20–21; Jn. 6:15). In the end, Jesus enters Jerusalem as a messianic aspirant to the throne, not on a horse but on a donkey (Mt. 21:6–11 and pars.)—a sign of humility and servanthood and in response to Jewish expectations of Israel's restoration (see Zec. 9:9). From then on, the controversy around Jesus finds its center in the question of the nature of his kingship (Lk. 23:2–3; Jn. 18:36–37; 19:14–15), until he is ultimately mocked as "the king of the Jews" (Jn. 19:2–3) and crucified (Jn. 19:19). Only after the resurrection does the true nature of Christ's kingship become clear. In the emerging kingdom of God, Jesus Christ, who reigns on God's behalf (1 Cor. 15:25–27), who will be the judge and to whom has been given all power in heaven and on earth (Mt. 28:28). He is the Messiah who was anointed with God's Spirit and who announces, realizes, and maintains a new mode of existence.

From the beginning to the end of his summary of this internal logic of the Bible, Wu underscores the reign of God. Wu's argument is that by understanding that logic, we can communicate the gospel message in a more coherent and comprehensive way.

I will take up this subject from another angle. I think the New Testament narratives that frame the gospel seek to answer four essential questions. They explain (1) who Jesus of Nazareth is, (2) what he did, (3) why what he did is important, and (4) how we should respond to his call. My thesis is that the three themes of creation, covenant and kingdom, which frame the unchangeable core of the gospel, embody different responses to these four questions. The kingdom theme, more than the other two, establishes and maintains an environment in which intentional discipleship to Christ is considered the norm for all the faithful. Therefore, the kingdom theme is at the heart of a gospel-driven theology of discipleship. Table 1 summarizes the three thematic frameworks and how each one answers the four questions concerning the person and work of Jesus of Nazareth and our appropriate response to him.

	The Theme of **Creation**	The Theme of **Covenant**	The Theme of **Kingdom**
Who is Jesus of Nazareth?	He is the last Adam who gives life (1 Cor. 15:45), the firstborn over all creation (Col. 1:15).	He is the Saviour (Lk. 19:10; 1 Tim. 1:15; Ac. 4:12; 1 Jn. 4:14), the mediator of the New Covenant.	He is the Christ, the Lord who actively reigns over the universe (Lk. 2:11; Rom. 10:9; Col. 3:17; 1 Pet. 3:15; 1 Cor. 8:6; Phil. 3:20).
What did Jesus of Nazareth do?	He was tempted in every way just as we are, yet without sin (Mt. 4:1–11; Heb. 4:15). He has destroyed death and brought life and immortality (1 Cor. 15:24–26; 2 Tim. 1:10). And he has destroyed the dividing wall of hostility (Eph. 2:11–22).	He accomplished all the covenants made since creation (Ac. 13:32–34; Rom. 1:1, 2: cf. 1 Cor. 15:3, 4). He is the mediator of the New Covenant, the High Priest who offers himself as the Paschal Lamb (Mt. 20:28; Heb. 9:11–10:18).	He did not consider equality with God something to be grasped but was made in human likeness. He became obedient to death (Phil. 2:6–8). In him we have access to the kingdom (Col. 1:13–14; 2 Pet. 1:11).
Why is Jesus of Nazareth important?	Just as sin entered the world through the first Adam, bringing sin and death to all men, so also through the obedience of Jesus the many will be made righteous (Rom. 5:12–19). He tasted death for everyone (Heb. 2:9) and reconciles us to the Creator in the new creation (2	The New Covenant prophetically announced by Jeremiah has come in Jesus. That covenant is eternal and accomplishes all the other covenants made by God since creation (Ezek. 34:24–25; Isa. 11:1, 6-9; Gal. 3:14, 16–19, 21, 22, 29).	God was pleased to have all his fullness (his attributes and essential nature) dwell in him (Col. 1:19; 2:9), and it is in Christ that God reigns over his creation (Col. 1:15–20; 1 Cor. 8:6). God has placed all things under the feet of Jesus (Eph. 1:22; 1 Cor. 15:25–27). In this way, the

	Cor. 5:17–21).		Creator reconciles all things with himself (Col. 1:20; 1 Cor. 5:18).
How should we respond to the call of Jesus of Nazareth?	We must belong to him (1 Cor. 15:23), be in him (Rom. 8:1, 2; 2 Cor. 5:17) and work for reconciliation (2 Cor. 5:18–20).	We must believe in him (Jn. 3:16–18) and receive him (Jn. 1:12; 1 Jn. 5:11–12).	We must follow him, incarnating a life of believing allegiance and obedience (Lk. 9:23-25).

Table 1: Biblical Frameworks and Gospel Answers

Obviously, the frontiers between these biblical themes are not impermeable, and we find elements of one theme mixed with another. Nevertheless, I believe that the elements of the kingdom theme must be allowed to dominate the others in our understanding of the person and work of Jesus of Nazareth and our response to him.

Not all interpreters have arrived at this conclusion. For example, Thomas Schreiner, Professor of New Testament at Southern Baptist Theological Seminary in his important and comprehensive (more than 500 pages) book on the theology of the Apostle Paul, notes that all biblical scholars recognize the "gospel" (*euangelion*) as the crucial element in Pauline theology (Schreiner, 2001, p. 48). Then he proceeds to link Paul's understanding of the gospel to Isaiah 40:9 and 52:7 to highlight the themes of salvation and the divine kingdom. In this way, Schreiner develops the elements that compose the gospel within the framework of adamic Christology. But the few references he makes to the kingdom are almost always from the angle of soteriology; that is, they are tied to the idea of entering the kingdom, rather than living in the kingdom.

Trevin Wax (2011, pp. 87–107) also attempts to incorporate the theme of the kingdom in his presentation of the inalterable message of the gospel. But his language communicates the conviction that Jesus of Nazareth remains eternally submitted to God the Father. He affirms that "in the person of Jesus Christ, God himself comes to restore the world and save his people" (p. 37), and he correctly maintains that "the resurrection of Jesus" is a major element of the gospel (p. 88). However, his presentation of the heart of the gospel does not include either the exaltation or the enthronement of the resurrected Jesus. He writes, "The work of Christ consists primarily in reconciling us to God and thereby restoring the *Shalom* which our sin had destroyed" (p. 92).

Let me reaffirm that the three narratives that frame the unchangeable core of the apostolic Good News are all equally legitimate. Each one highlights in its own way some of the unsearchable mystery of the glory of God as manifested in Jesus of Nazareth. Each one helps us to penetrate more fully the depths of his love and grace. But among these three narratives, the message of the kingdom of God is the one that sustains an environment in which intentional discipleship to the Christ develops and continues. For this reason, I am convinced that a theology of the kingdom of God is an essential element of a theology of discipleship.

Toward a Theology of the Kingdom of God

George Eldon Ladd (2000) affirms that two verses from the gospel of Matthew contain the essential theology of the kingdom of God. These verses are Matthew 12:28–29: "But if it is by the Spirit of God that I drive out demons, then the kingdom of God has come upon you. Or again, how can anyone enter a strong man's house and carry off his possessions unless he first ties up the strong man? Then he can plunder his house." Ladd (2000, p. 74) comments:

> These two verses contain the essence of the theology of the Kingdom of God. Rather than wait for the end of the world to reveal his royal power and destroy satanic evil, Jesus declares that God acts in his royal power to overcome the power of Satan. In other words, the Kingdom of God taught by Jesus manifests itself in two ways: at the end of time to destroy Satan, and in Jesus' mission to bind him. Before the final destruction of Satan, men can already be delivered from his power.

Diverse Understandings of the Kingdom of God

How we understand the other two themes (creation or covenant) colours our understanding of the Kingdom theme. To see this, we can look at how the Reformed theologians Meredith Kline (2006), Jeong Koo Jeon (2017), and Peter Gentry and Stephen Wellum (2012) tie the theme of covenant to that of the Kingdom of God. These authors do not emphasize discipleship enough because they see everything through covenant. This is also the case of Richard (1982, p. 153), who affirms that the essence of the Christian message is the message of salvation even though he affirms that the kingdom theme "is not only a Christian symbol among many others." To construct a solid theology of discipleship to Christ we must incorporate a good theology of the Kingdom, and that undoubtedly means an alteration of our way of thinking about the other biblical themes.

Though I do not agree fully with the way he handles the kingdom theme in his writing, Thomas Schreiner (2013) does rightly affirm that this kind of modification can be done successfully if we are flexible enough to comprehend the other biblical themes in a way that summarizes the fundamental message of the Bible. He argues that the Kingdom of God, if that term is defined with sufficient flexibility, "fits well as a central theme of the entire Bible" (pp. xii - xiii). He explains his meaning further:

Such a thesis does not rely on a word study approach, for it is quite obvious that the kingdom of God cannot be a central theme if we count up how many times the words "king," "kingdom," or "rule," "reign" appear, for in many books of the Bible they do not appear at all. Instead, the contention here is that the phrase "kingdom of God" thematically captures, from a biblical theology standpoint, the message of Scripture. (Schreiner, 2013, p. xiii)

What, then, is the biblical, gospel-driven relationship between the theme of the kingdom of God and the atoning death of the Christ on the cross? The answer lies ultimately in the identity of the God-man Jesus of Nazareth, the long-awaited, crucified, then resurrected and enthroned king, as properly understood within the story and logic of the reestablishment of God's kingdom on earth.

The Biblical Narrative of the Kingdom of God

Many books on the cross of Christ written from the interpretive perspective of the covenants barely mention the message of the kingdom, although it is widely acknowledged as the primary theme of Jesus' teaching and preaching. Perhaps some of the understandings of the kingdom I sketched in the previous section of this chapter account for this omission. After all, some of the theologians I mentioned above make the opposite error, advocating for the kingdom of God to the exclusion of the cross. Others see it as a uniquely future reality. Our own understanding of the cross solely as a means of personal salvation has certainly also contributed to this divide between the kingdom of God and the Christ's atoning death on the cross. Russell Moore (2004) has provided an excellent historical survey of these debates.

Contrary to those who *separate* the cross of the Christ from the Kingdom of God, some scholars argue that the kingdom is the *unifying* motif of the Bible (Bright, 1957; Treat, 2014). Some theologians emphasize that the kingdom entails the fulfillment of all the promises of God for salvation. Others, myself included, believe that the kingdom of God is first and foremost a statement about God the Father and his eternal Son incarnate in the man Jesus of Nazareth (the Father's crucified and resurrected kingdom-bringer), who they are together, and what they do together (reign).

This is the unifying vision of the entire biblical narrative. It begins, as Jeremy Treat correctly argues, with Genesis 1–2, which presents the Creator's intention to reign through his image-bearing servant-kings. This is the aim, or *telos*, of creation. Treat (2014, p. 42) explains, "God's reign over and through his servant-kings requires a realm. In Genesis 1-2, the realm of God's rule is Eden, but the eschatological goal is for God's reign to be over all the earth."

After the first image-bearing servant-kings were deceived into sinful rebellion, the Evil One began to reign over this earth. Yet the promise of the Creator to the fallen image-bearing servant-kings, declared in Genesis 3:15, is that the offspring of Eve will crush the head of the serpent—which typologically prefigures the birth and victory of Jesus the *imago dei* and *imago hominis*. For this reason, Jesus of Nazareth, "in whom we have redemption, the forgiveness of sins" (Col. 1:14), is the central focus of the biblical narrative. He is the one in whom the Creator (Father, Son, and Spirit) has chosen to reconcile with himself "all things [that] were created, in heaven and on earth" (Col. 1:14, 16, 20). Even in his death on the cross, Jesus of Nazareth, the perfect *imago hominis*, persevered in his dedication and submission to the Creator's royal authority (Lk. 23:46). In this unfailing allegiance and faithfulness, Jesus of Nazareth is empowered by the Spirit. Hebrews 9:14 affirms that the power of the Spirit enabled Jesus to persevere in his dedication to the Father. In this process, Jesus of Nazareth, the eternal Son incarnate, has occupied the place where the powers of rebellion and disintegration dominate, thereby making our restoration as servant-kings possible.

For this reason, the coming of the kingdom to earth (once again) is inseparably linked to the cross. Emil Brunner (1955, p. 306) stated, "We cannot speak rightly about atonement without at the same time thinking of redemption, as the overcoming of resistance and the restoration of the rule of God." Herman Ridderbos (1978, pp. 169–174) asserts correctly that the kingdom cannot be understood apart from the cross, nor the cross without the kingdom. Scot McKnight (2005, pp. 82-84) rightly claims that Jesus' kingdom vision and atonement are related and an integral part of the early Christian kerygma.

But the restorative power of Jesus' obedient faithfulness does not end with Good Friday and Easter. His resurrection, exaltation and enthronement mean that he is sharing in the Father's reign (which is exactly what "sitting at God's right hand" means; cf. Lk. 22:69; Rom. 8:34; Col. 3:2; Heb. 1:3; 10:12; 1 Pet. 3:22; Rev. 3:21). Seated at the Father's right hand, Jesus exercises all power in heaven and earth, and he secures for us a glory and blessing that exceed all expectations. That eschatological glory as his restored image-bearing servant-kings will be greater than its prototype (1 Cor. 15:46–47; cf. Rom. 8:16–21; Col. 3:4). Thus, Jesus of Nazareth, the Messiah, is the Alpha and Omega, the beginning and the end of world history (Rev. 22:13).

The Understanding of the Kingdom of God in the Old Testament

When Mark summarizes the beginning of the public ministry of Jesus of Nazareth by saying that he "proclaimed the Good News of [the kingdom] of God" (Mk. 1:14), he is explaining something that was not surprising to his fellow Israelites. The expression is absent from the Old Testament, and only nine texts refer to the kingdom that *Yahweh* rules (Beasley-Murray, 1986, p. 17). In contrast, the term "King" is applied to *Yahweh* 41 times in the Old Testament. This observation leads the Old Testament scholar L. Köhler (1953, p. 30) to claim, "The one fundamental statement in the theology of the Old Testament is this: God is the ruling Lord." Similarly, Martin Buber (1968, p. 58) affirms, "The realization of the all-embracing rulership of God is the

Proton and *Eschaton* of Israel." The affirmation of the Old Testament is that the reign of *Yahweh* is genuinely Good News.

Take for instance Isaiah 52:7 (quoted by Paul in Romans 10:15):

> How beautiful on the mountains are the feet of those who bring Good News (LXX *euangeliomenou*), who proclaim peace, who bring good tidings (LXX *euangeliomenou*), who proclaim salvation, who say to Zion, "Your God reigns!"

Isaiah 40:9 makes a similar declaration:

> You who bring Good News (LXX *euangeliozomenos*), to Zion, go up on a high mountain. You who bring Good News (LXX *euangeliozomenos*), to Jerusalem, lift up your voice with a shout, lift it up, do not be afraid; say to the towns of Judah, "Here is your God!"

Jackson Wu (2015, p. 41) observes that this appears in the context of a prophetic proclamation that the Lord *Yahweh* reigns as Creator over the earth. We can therefore conclude that the affirmation that "*Yahweh* reigns" (Ps. 93:1) is just as absolute as the affirmation that "*Yahweh* is God" (Ps. 100:3) and that this is Good News (gospel).

The Good News (Gospel) of *Yahweh* Who Reigns

As we begin to look in more detail at this subject, we are not straying from our quest to identify the important elements of a gospel-driven theology of discipleship. Rather, I am following the lead of Joshua Jipp (2015), who maintains that the first followers of Jesus of Nazareth re-ordered their ultimate allegiances and social relations in ways they would not have foreseen previously because they now understood themselves to have become the subjects of Christ the King. Jipp's basic argument in his comprehensively researched book is that Paul used and applied ancient conceptions of the good king—both Greco-Roman and Jewish—to Christ so as to establish a "totalizing alternative scenario to any other competing claim to supreme rule and power" (2015, pp. 9, 16).

We can find a link between the reign of *Yahweh* and the Good News (gospel) in the ancient term *melek* (king), which Beasley-Murray (1986, p. 17) shows to be the foundation of Semitic thinking. Contrary to modern thinking about kings and kingdoms, the Semitic people considered their gods to be kings. And for them, royalty connoted much more than being at the head of a monarchical state. It also meant "prince" or "counsellor." Along this line, Buber (1967, pp. 2–23) maintains that from the beginning, the meaning of *melek* in Israel was shaped by the presence of nomadic tribes. He explains that the *melek* was the god who accompanied the people through unknown regions to places of "green pastures" and who protected them from their enemies. If that reading is correct (and I find no reason to doubt it), from the time of the patriarchs *Yahweh* was seen in this way, although the events of the Exodus, the revelation at Sinai, and the pilgrimage through the desert nuanced that understanding (Buber, 1967, pp. 95, 99). In spite of the possible ambivalence and even occasional opposition that Israel exhibited toward monarchy; Israel's royal ideology saw the king as a benefactor, one who imitates God in the dispensation of justice and provides a model for people to imitate, thereby producing harmony and justice (Smith, 2011, pp. 37–47).

Beasley-Murray (1986) adds to this list the importance of "divine acts" in the Hebrews' history. He maintains that these acts added an eschatological aspect to their understanding of the reign of *Yahweh* which contributed to its being perceived as "Good News." He writes:

> Thus it became a fundamental element of Israel's understanding that the nation had been founded through a succession of acts of God for their salvation, forming a God-controlled continuity, a history, and that this history was moving forward to a future according to God's will. Israel's eschatology was the end product of its consciousness of God in history. (1986, p. 19)

Beasley-Murray concludes, as does Buber (1967), that the ancient Hebrews had a "theo-political" understanding. This coincides with the conclusions of H. D. Wegland (1938) that the Israelites had a "theo-teleological" understanding. This is important for our study because it indicates that as surely as the content of Israel's hope was *Yahweh* in his words and deeds (political), their real hope was *Yahweh* himself (theo-teleological). This is another way of saying that in the Old Testament, hope in the coming kingdom is hope in the coming of *Yahweh*. This observation parallels what we have seen in our previous studies, which have shown that the identity, words and deeds of Jesus of Nazareth, the God-man, are the content of the gospel we have been commissioned to communicate to our world.

The Good News (Gospel) of the Reign of Yahweh and of His Messiah

Without entering the debate surrounding the role of the Messiah in the Good News of the ultimate reign of *Yahweh* (the theo-teleological understanding mentioned above), it is evident that a number of texts highlight his place in the Kingdom, whereas others do not mention it (Beasley-Murray, 1986, pp. 20–22). I agree with Beasley-Murray, for whom the important messianic pericopes of the Old Testament communicate the Good News that the forces of evil in the world, along with all nations, will one day be submitted to God. In this process, the establishment of the new regime of salvation is the work of *Yahweh*, and the government of that Kingdom is given to his Messiah. This is the clear teaching of the prophetic passages concerning the Messiah and his reign (i.e., Isa. 9:1–7; 11:1–9; Mic. 5 :1–4; Jer. 23:5–6; Ezek. 34:22–24).

Jipp (2015, pp. 31–41) skillfully traces how the Torah and other ancient Hebrew writings bear the marks of a broad royal ideology that centers upon God's agenda being worked out through a coming king from the line of Judah. This theme can be clearly seen in Genesis 17:6, 16; 49:10 and Numbers 24:17, which cite God's promise that "kings would come from Abraham." It shows up again in the prayer of Hannah (1 Sam. 2:10) and the hymn of David (2 Sam. 22:1–50). Pointing to these and other relevant passages, Jipp (2015) writes:

> Throughout 1–2 Samuel, then David is: elected by God to rule on God's behalf (1 Sam. 2:10, 35; 24:7–11; 26:9–16; 2 Sam. 1:14, 16; 19:22), endowed with God's Spirit (1 Sam. 10:1–13; 16:1–13; 24:6), promised to have God's presence with him (1 Sam. 16:17–18; 18:12, 14, 28; 2 Sam. 5:10; 7:6, 11, 13), and designated as God's son (2 Sam. 7:14). So too he is said to rule the people as God's shepherd (2 Sam. 5:2; 7:7), represent God's people (1 Sam. 18:3; 2 Sam. 21:17), and fight God's battles. (p. 32)

This theme also gives a "royal shape" to the Psalter, even after the downfall of the Davidic monarchy. One way in which this occurs is through the installation of the king by means of anointing such that he received the title and office of "Messiah," which, as Jipp (2015, p. 33) points out, marked him "not merely as 'the Messiah' but 'the Messiah of *Yahweh*'." He adds:

> The important point here is that the royal figure is the subordinated vicegerent of God, whose job it is to rule and act on God's behalf by bestowing divine benefits to God's subjects. He is the royal agent who shares in God's rule and acts as the channel through whom God acts. (p. 34)

Like Beasley-Murray (1986), Jipp (2015, pp. 37–38) finds in Israel's prophets a wealth of information regarding this Davidic king who will establish God's saving rule over the people. For instance, the prophet Isaiah highlights the Davidic ancestry of the coming ruler (Isa. 9:7; 11:1; cf. 11:10). Jeremiah looks toward the day when *Yahweh* will "raise up for David a righteous branch" (Jer. 23:5; cf. 33:15, 17, 21–22). Ezekiel links this coming ruler to *Yahweh's* "servant David" (Ezek. 34:23–24; cf. 17:22), and Haggai declares that when Israel returns to *Yahweh* the Hebrews will also seek "David their king" (3:5). And the prophet Amos speaks of Israel's restoration as the time when God will raise up the booth of David that is fallen" (Amos 9:11). Zechariah refers to the coming king who will, through his victorious battles, bring peace to the nations (Zech. 9:9–10).

Beasley-Murray underscores the similarities in structure between this last passage and the announcement of the coming of *Yahweh* in Isaiah 40:9–10. He concludes that this similarity is not coincidental but points intentionally to the fact that if victory belongs to *Yahweh*, then the reign of the Messiah-king is the gift he gives to his people (Beasley-Murray, 1986, p. 22). He adds, "One thing is indisputable: in the Old Testament prophetic teaching *the Messiah* is *uniquely related* to *God and man, and as the representative of Yahweh he* is *the instrument of his rule*" (1986, p. 23; emphasis added). Beasley-Murray quotes H. H. Wolff, who goes even further in connecting Zechariah 9:9 and Isaiah 40:9-10 when he claims that "the Messiah is the form, or the appearance of *Yahweh*, the Lord" (Beasley-Murray, 1986, p. 23).

These observations should remind us of the importance of understanding Jesus of Nazareth in his ontological identity, as I stressed in our last study. They should also help us to comprehend the gospel message's insistence on the Davidic lineage of Jesus of Nazareth, which we saw so clearly indicated in Romans 1:3. This lineage identifies Jesus the Christ as the fulfillment of *Yahweh's* covenant promises concerning the seed of David, as the Apostle Paul states specifically in Romans 15:8.

Unfortunately, we can easily fall into the trap of thinking that the title "Messiah" simply sets Jesus of Nazareth apart in reference to *Yahweh's* covenant faithfulness. Sometimes we link the title primarily to Israel's long wait for the coming of this promised one, who would bring the nation back under *Yahweh's* rule and usher in a time of justice and peace. Or we tie the title "Messiah" to our own eschatological hope of a future kingdom. Or we take it as a sign that in Jesus of Nazareth, the Messiah, a new era in redemptive history began. Indeed, the title includes all these elements, but it carries even greater significance. It also indicates that the Good News has everything to do with the kingdom and kingship of Jesus of Nazareth, the *imago hominis* who makes our own restoration as human beings possible.

The title "Messiah" or "Christ" points to Jesus of Nazareth's identity as the one "who belongs to God in such a special way that we can say that his origin is with God, that he is part of the life of God himself" (van der Kooi & van den Brink, 2017, p. 425). He is the promised Davidic king who, as God's son, rules in God's stead (1 Chron. 17; Jer. 33:14–22; Zech. 6:12–13). For this reason, Psalm 2 states that, in response to the "the kings of the earth and the rulers" who "take their stand against *Yahweh* and against his anointed one (or son)," God institutes the king as ruler: "*Yahweh* said to me, 'You are my Son, today I have become your Father'" (Ps. 2:7).

Thus, the title of "Christ/Messiah" underscores and links together two core dimensions of the identity of Jesus of Nazareth: he belongs to God in a very special way, being of the same kind as God, and he is also the perfect human being who has been commissioned to rule on God's behalf. Jesus' ontological core is his identity as the incarnate, eternal Son.

Some people with whom I have shared these ideas have wondered if I am not making too much ado about nothing. They insist that they already believe that Jesus is the God-man, the Messiah, and they do not understand why I am making such a big issue of our ontological understanding of Jesus. I acknowledge that Christians generally profess that Jesus is the God-man and Messiah, but we do not put these truths together in the way that the Scriptures do.

A friend of mine offers a useful analogy. If you learned to drive on the right side of the road but then move to the United Kingdom or a British-influenced nation where people drive on the left, you will be in for a rude discovery. Although in both instances you are driving, you must now change many of your spontaneous driving habits. When you come to an intersection of a roundabout, you must learn to look in the opposite direction to see oncoming vehicles. When you think that you are in the passing lane on the highway, you are actually in the slow lane. Similarly, we have learned a way of understanding Jesus of Nazareth that highlights his role or function as Saviour. This has led us to confuse the gospel with a "plan of salvation" and has moved Jesus out of the center of our theology and our spirituality.

When we begin to understand the identity of Jesus of Nazareth as the eternal Son incarnate, the Son of David, we begin to apprehend the royal associations of his title as the "Messiah" or "Christ." He is the Father-appointed and Spirit-equipped implementer of the divine project to bring creation back to the liberating rule of the Creator God. Note that Jesus of Nazareth did not ask people what they thought he had come from his Father to accomplish. He did not ask, for example, whether people thought he had come to seek and save the lost, or if they understood that he had come to die for their sins. Instead, Mark tells us how Jesus approached the topic of his identity:

> On the way [Jesus] asked his disciples, "Who do men say that I am?" And they told him, "John the Baptist; and others say, Elijah; and others one of the prophets." And he asked them, "But who do you say that I am?" Peter answered him, "You are the Christ." And he charged them to tell no one about him. (Mk. 8:27–30)

The images and expectations that the Jews of Jesus' day usually connected with the title of "Messiah" had to be drastically revised before they could understand the true nature of Jesus' messiahship. And this is perhaps true of us in a different way.

The Kingdom of God is Near

In the prologue to his gospel, Mark summarizes the message of Jesus of Nazareth with the words, "The time has come. The kingdom of God is near. Repent and believe the Good News!" (Mk. 1:15). Scholars have devoted much discussion to the meaning of this text. The general consensus is that in the person of Jesus of Nazareth, there is an initiation of the sovereign action of *Yahweh* that brings salvation and will result in the transformation of the universe (Beasley-Murray, 1986, p. 74).

Therefore, the proclamation of Jesus of Nazareth encompasses a declaration that the dynamic activity of *Yahweh* was operative in and through his person (see for instance Mk. 4:11; Mt. 11:25; 12:28). This corresponds to the testimony of the Old Testament indicating that the Messiah would be the instrument of the reign of *Yahweh*. For this reason, as Matthew Bates writes, Jesus of Nazareth proclaimed that in him the favorable moment was at hand and that the reign of *Yahweh* had arrived. Bates (2019) adds:

> Perhaps the most important thing to notice, however, is that Jesus himself is at the center of his own message—doubly so. As we read Mark, we discover that Jesus is the one bringing about the fullness of time through his climactic ministry. He is also the anointed king who will one day rule. (p. 42)

Jeremy Treat (2014, pp. 42–43) agrees: "Jesus' proclamation of the kingdom was radical not because of its content, but because he announced its fulfillment in himself." I agree with Treat that Jesus is the appointed "king" through whom God reestablishes his reign over all the created order. However, I argue that the resurrected Jesus of Nazareth is more precisely the human being in whom God currently reigns over his kingdom. During his earthly life, the eternal Son of God, incarnated in the person of Jesus of Nazareth, was in the process of becoming fully king. This is the central theme of the gospels, even though not all commentators recognize this fact. N. T. Wright finds it tragic that today's church has lost the importance of the gospel message that in Jesus of Nazareth, the living God has become the king of the whole world. Note that for Wright, it is *in* and not *through* Jesus of Nazareth that God has (already) become king. Similarly, Matthew Bates (2019, p. 47) sees in Jesus' death on the cross the dramatic and theological *center* of the gospel, but sees in the proclamation that Jesus of Nazareth is the king the climactic *summit* of the gospel.

These authors' affirmation of the royal sovereignty of Jesus of Nazareth is reinforced by the first thing we learn about him in Luke's gospel (1:32–33): "He will be great and will be called the Son of the Most High. And the Lord God will give him the throne of his father David, and he will reign over the house of Jacob forever, and of his kingdom there will be no end." Jesus' demonstrations of victory over demonic forces constitute one proof, among others, that in him the reign of the deity is present (cf. Mt. 12:28). Thomas Manson (2012, p. 89) insists that in contrast to the ancient Greek world, where exorcism prepared contact with the deity, in Matthew 12 the reverse occurs: contact with the deity expels the demon.

As I have noted in a previous study, even though Paul rarely refers to Jesus as reigning, New Testament scholar David Wenham argues that his use of the title "Christ" shows that Paul "does not see Jesus just as Saviour of the world" (1995, pp. 120–121). And as we saw in our study of the description of the core elements of the gospel as detailed in Romans 1:1–5, Paul and the first followers of Jesus of Nazareth linked the Messiah's humanity and resurrection to his royal enthronement.

When John the Baptist sent two of his disciples to ask Jesus of Nazareth if he was "the one who was to come," he was trying to know if Jesus is the one *Yahweh* had anointed to reign in his kingdom (Mt. 11:2–3; Lk. 7:18–20). Jesus' response corresponds to many of his teachings concerning the kingdom of God, in that it is direct yet hidden in the sovereign acts of *Yahweh*: "The blind receive sight, the lame walk, those who have leprosy are cured, the deaf hear, the dead are raised, and the Good News is preached to the poor" (Mt. 11:4-6; Lk. 7:22-23).

I find it significant that John the Baptist had no difficulty identifying Jesus of Nazareth in his *function* as "the Lamb of God who takes away the sin of the world" (cf. Jn. 1:29, 36) but struggled to understand him in his *ontological* identity as the Messiah. I argued in our last study that this seems to be a major difficulty for us as well. This study offers a solution: framing our understanding of the gospel with the biblical theme of the kingdom may help us to better promote intentional discipleship to Jesus.

The Good News of the Treasure and the Pearl

Jesus teaches clearly that his reign is good, and that the possibility of living under his rule is truly Good News. The parables of the treasure hidden in a field (Mt. 13:44) and of the pearl of great value (Mt. 13:45) highlight this. Both parables express the incomparable joy in the heart of the one who finds such a valuable treasure. For the characters in the parables, it is the discovery of a lifetime, something that completely changes their lives.

John Dominic Crossan (1973, pp. 34–39) argues that the presence of the kingdom of *Yahweh* in the person of Jesus of Nazareth does the same thing in the life of the person who discovers it. The kingdom shakes the recipient's world to its roots, reversing its course and empowering him or her for action. The projects of the labourer who worked the field were changed by the discovery of the treasure. The discovery motivated him to abandon his past achievements and sell everything he had to buy the field. This exchange allowed him to act differently than he ever had before. Here we see a firm link between Jesus of Nazareth, the Messiah, who reigns in the kingdom of his Father, and discipleship. As Rudolf Otto (2009) rightly emphasizes, the reality of the reign of the Messiah is Good News:

> The thing of which the parables were meant to treat is the kingdom neither as a constraining power, nor as claim to sovereignty, nor as realm of power, nor even as concrete supramundane condition, but as the blessing of salvation, the blessing pure and simple, and purely and simply a blessing. (p. 128)

The powerful acts of Jesus of Nazareth, his words of forgiveness, and his welcome into the kingdom over which he now reigns signify a new beginning of the sovereign reign of *Yahweh* over the earth. The second Adam, the eternal Son, made in human likeness, humbles himself in obedience even to death on the cross and thereby "picks up the thread where Adam dropped it" (van der Kooi & van den Brink, 2017, p. 474).[1] Jesus of Nazareth is the human being who perseveres in obedient faith where Adam failed and gave in to distrust. He is the new man, the last Adam, who does right what Adam did wrong (1 Cor. 15:20–22). Van der Kooi and van den Brink powerfully summarize the transformative power of life under his reign:

> The new humanity Jesus brings in as the Messiah is not fed by fear or distrust but is confident and untouched by cynicism. In the sphere of royal freedom Jesus's humanity flourishes, and what was crooked becomes straight. The powers that enslave or destroy human life are now placed under the authority of a new regime; they are bypassed and finally placed in the service of God's love. (2017, p. 475)

Even the demands of life under the reign of Jesus of Nazareth "set us free" (cf. Jn. 8:32). The teaching of Jesus, which goes against everything we see as "normal," is the new normal for those who follow him. In and around him, the contours of what it means to participate in the new creation become visible. Discipleship is learning how to live as new creations—in conformity to our Lord Jesus the Messiah, empowered by his Spirit, and faithful in our witness to him. Jesus the Messiah is the human being who incarnates the Torah through his perfect embodiment of Leviticus 19:18, and he achieves the transformation of his subjects by empowering them to love one another and "so fulfil the law or Christ" (Gal. 6:2). He is our highest authority, to whom all power has been given in heaven and on earth (Mt. 28:19). And he sets the pattern to be imitated by his subjects (Jipp, 2015, p. 70). He is the one who gives meaning to our understanding of the biblical texts about our heavenly citizenship (Eph. 2:19; Phil. 3:20; Col. 1:13). Jipp explains:

> Christ functions as the supreme example of the one who bore his neighbour's burdens, as called for by Lev. 19:18, and pursued his neighbour's good even at the cost of pleasing himself (Rom. 15:1b). Earlier in the epistle Paul has spoken of Christ as the one who even died for "we who are weak" (5:6; cf. 15:1). This ... is reminiscent of Galatians, where "the law of Christ" (6:2) is fulfilled through bearing another's burdens by imitating Christ who brought the Torah to completion *and reconfigured* it through his love for neighbour (Gal. 5:14). (2015, p. 72; emphasis mine)

Jesus of Nazareth, the Messiah, is both the gospel and the "living law" of the kingdom of God. This explains why the third-century theologian Origen

---

1 See the helpful study of Romans 5:12-8:39 by Joshua Jipp (2015, pp. 179–197), who shows that this section of Romans is filled with kingship discourse played out in a cosmic manner.

went so far as to picture Jesus of Nazareth, the Messiah, as the *autobasileia*, the kingdom of God in person (O'Collins, 2008, p. 34).

Questions to Think About

1. I argue in this chapter that the kingdom theme is at the heart of a gospel-driven theology of discipleship, then I refer to a couple of scholars who mention the kingdom theme but prefer to highlight entrance into the kingdom (soteriology) over life in the kingdom (sanctification). What does your local congregation or your denomination do to ensure that life in the kingdom is kept in view? Or conversely, do you see ways in which your church or denomination is held back from emphasizing discipleship by over-emphasizing covenantal theology?

2. Why is it important for our spiritual lives to keep in mind that we cannot speak rightly about atonement without at the same time thinking about the overcoming of resistance and the restoration of the rule of the Creator?

3. How does the Old Testament gospel of the reign of *Yahweh* and of his Messiah help us to understand the meaning and importance of discipleship to the Lord Jesus?

4. Why is it important for discipleship to keep in mind that although the kingdom belongs to God the Father, at this time the human being Jesus of Nazareth, resurrected and exalted, reigns as his vice-regent over the kingdom?

5. The last section of this chapter presents the fact that Jesus of Nazareth is the human being who incarnates the Torah and sets the pattern to be imitated by his subjects in the kingdom of God. How should this reality affect our lives, both individually and in our interaction with other believers?

9. The Good News of the Son of Man

We began this collection of studies by claiming that an evangelical and biblical theology of discipleship is grounded in the identity of Jesus of Nazareth. We then looked at the surprising authority that Jewish teacher claimed for himself, even over the inspired Law given through Moses. That study showed us that we are not speaking of someone who was disconnected from his historical and cultural context. Rather, he was a Jew and a rabbi who respected the practices of ancient Judaism. Yet he gave himself the freedom to amend the prayer that is at the heart of the Jewish religion.

In chapter 3, we were introduced to the concept and practice of discipleship as presented in the gospel of Matthew. In that study, we saw that Matthew highlights the disciples' response to the authority of Jesus and his teaching. They did more than just follow this man from Nazareth; they submitted themselves totally to him and worshipped him. They recognized that he has received all authority in heaven and on earth. And they acknowledged that because he is at the center of the Creator's plan, he can legitimately call for our complete and ultimate allegiance.

In chapter 4, we looked at two possible ways of understanding our relationship to God the Father: *in* and *through* Jesus of Nazareth. That study was based on Jesus' conversation with Thomas and Philip as recorded in John 14. We observed how the widespread understanding that we come to God *through* Jesus gives the impression that his primary identity is that of Saviour. I argued that the perspective of encountering God *in* Jesus of Nazareth is more akin to that of his first followers and fosters an environment more conducive to intentional discipleship to him.

This led us back to the question of Jesus' full humanity, which we considered in chapter 5. I placed that study there to remind us that Jesus of Nazareth was a real person—a son, a neighbor, a friend, and a rabbi. We saw how in many ways Jesus of Nazareth acted and taught like the other rabbis of his time. We also saw that the disciples mirrored in many ways the practices and attitudes of the disciples of other rabbis. Yet, the discipleship of Jesus' apprentices differed in some significant ways from that of other disciples. Jesus' centring of discipleship on himself, rather than on the Torah, steered us once again to acknowledge his unique authority. Reconsidering his authority brought us to examine briefly the three phases of the existence of the eternal

Son of God, and the claim made by the resurrected Jesus of Nazareth that he had come into full possession of that authority.

In chapter 6, we took up the question of the divine authority of the resurrected Jesus of Nazareth as revealed in the gospel of John. In that study, we followed the pattern set by the Fourth Gospel as expressed in Jesus' words to his first disciples: "As the Father has sent me, I am sending you" (Jn. 20:21). My purpose was to show that it is Jesus of Nazareth, the eternal Son incarnate, who sends us, not God nor the Father. Therefore, we are to glorify him, do his will, testify to him, represent him faithfully, and maintain an intimate relationship with him. This is yet another key element of a gospel-driven theology of discipleship. To be true to the witness of Scripture and to the testimony of Jesus of Nazareth, our discipleship must be intentionally centered on him.

In chapter 7, we examined how an ontological view of Jesus of Nazareth as the God-man links him more logically to discipleship than does a more functional understanding of his primary identity as the mediator between God and humanity. We were also reminded of the negative results of building our theology and discipleship practice on a truncated understanding of the gospel that sees it as some sort of Plan of Salvation. This led us to examine how the Apostle Paul details the gospel in Romans 1:1–5. My argument in that study was that Jesus of Nazareth crucified, resurrected, and enthroned is himself the gospel we embrace and communicate. This correct comprehension organically links the gospel to discipleship.

In our last study (chapter 8), we looked in some detail at how the biblical theme of the kingdom of God coherently frames the gospel in its presentation in the Scriptures. I demonstrated that the motif of the kingdom of God announces the reign of *Yahweh* and his Messiah in the Old Testament, and that this leads to the New Testament recognition of the Lord Jesus of Nazareth, the Messiah. It is Good News because the life-giving reign of *Yahweh* over the whole earth has been begun anew in the second Adam—the rabbi from Nazareth, the Lord Jesus, the Messiah. Through the faithful obedience of that man, the eternal Son of God made in human likeness, we can be restored to mirroring the Creator's original intent. In our conformity to our Lord Jesus, the Messiah, who perfectly embodied obedience to the Law of *Yahweh*, and through the empowerment of his Spirit we already participate in the new creation.

In this study, we will look at what the Scriptures have to say about a claim some New Testament scholars have made during the last century. I refer to the idea that Jesus of Nazareth neither was nor wanted to be the Messiah, and that only later did people make him into their Messiah.[1] However, before we move

---

1 Recent scholarship provides evidence that the worship of Jesus of Nazareth as Messiah and Lord had very early Judeo-Palestinian roots and was not a later development. See for example the important studies of Larry Hurtado (1988, 2003),

further in our reflection, we must establish a clear understanding of what basic elements compose the gospel.

The Gospel: An Outline

According to an oft-quoted study by C. H. Dodd (1964), seven elements constitute the gospel. The eternal Son of God:

1. pre-existed with God the Father (Jn. 1:1, 18; 8:56–58);
2. assumed our human nature, and in so doing accomplished the divine promises made to David (Mt. 1:1, 6, 17; Lk. 3:31);
3. died for our sins according to the Scriptures (Mt. 20:28; Mk. 10:45; Jn. 1:29);
4. was buried (Mt. 27:57–61; Mk. 15:42–47; Lk. 23:50–56; Jn. 19:38–42);
5. was raised from the dead on the third day according to the Scriptures (cf. Mt. 27:62–66; Lk. 24:12; Jn. 20:3–9);
6. appeared to many people (Mt. 28:9; Jn. 20:14–17; Mk. 16:12–13; Lk. 24:33–34; Jn. 20:19–28; 1 Cor. 15:6–7; Ac. 9:3–9; 22:6–11; 26:12–18);
7. is seated at the right of the Father where he reigns as Lord (cf. Mk. 12:35–37).

This last point—the reign of Jesus, the Messiah—is the most important one for the present study. Through his resurrection, Jesus of Nazareth, the Son incarnate, was exalted by the Father and enthroned at his right hand. This is metaphorical language, of course, using the image of an Eastern ruler on his throne as described in Psalm 110. It clearly indicates that Jesus now shares in the rule of his Father. Matthew Bates (2017, p. 67) offers two reasons why this element of the gospel is of extreme importance:

1. When the gospel is presented today by a preacher or teacher, most of the time this "Jesus reigns" portion of the gospel is either entirely absent or mentioned as an aside. The cross and resurrection get central billing, but Jesus' kingship is tucked away off-stage.
2. Jesus reigns right now. Jesus' reign corresponds to the present epoch of world history that we find ourselves in now. The first six stages of the gospel refer to events in the past with respect to Jesus' life story—for example, [the eternal Son of God][2] has already taken on human flesh, died for our sins, and been raised from the dead. But if Jesus has been raised from the dead, then where is he now? And what is he doing? It should not surprise us if the answer proves to be fundamental to all aspects of Christian life today. Jesus is currently the enthroned king, Lord

---

which discuss early devotional practices among his followers to prove that the worship of Jesus as divine must have been caused by an early "explosion" (Easter?) and not by some gradual development.

2 Here Bates uses the name "Jesus" which I have replaced with "the eternal Son of God."

of heaven and earth, and he is actively ruling until, as Paul puts it in 1 Corinthians, "he has put all his enemies under his feet" (15:25). ... Satan may be called "the god of this age" (2 Cor. 4:4), but his power is limited because it has been decisively broken through the cross and resurrection; the new age of Jesus's kingly rule is currently overwhelming the old age (Col. 1:13–14).

Bates also adds an eighth central component of the gospel that Dodd did not include in his list, even though it is contained in the Apostles' Creed: Jesus of Nazareth is coming again as judge (Mt. 23:32–39; 25:31–32; Mk. 13:26–27).

When the reigning Son of God incarnate has put all his enemies under his feet, the majesty and glory of the triune Creator will again be the determining element in all his creation (1 Cor. 15:28; Phil. 3:21; Rev. 22).

Figure 3 represents my attempt to present this schema visually.

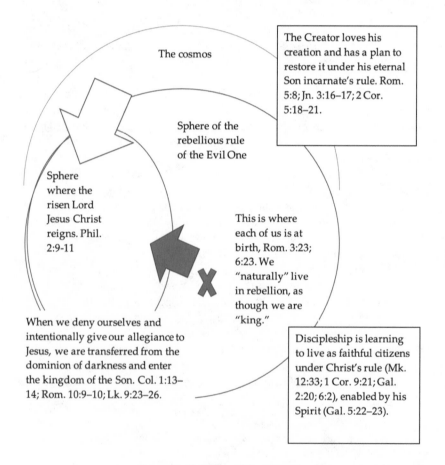

Figure 3: Schema of the Gospel

Did Jesus of Nazareth See Himself as the Divinely Appointed King?

When Jesus announced the Good News that the kingdom of God was near (Mk. 1:14–15), did he see himself as the divinely appointed king, the Messiah? Or was this rather a post-Easter understanding that grew among his first followers?[3] The evidence in the gospels that Jesus saw himself as the messianic king seems rather meager. Others speak of him in those terms occasionally, but Jesus of Nazareth appears to show little enthusiasm for the idea (Wenham, 1995, p. 106). In Mark 8:29, for instance, when Peter confesses Jesus as Messiah, Jesus responds with no evident enthusiasm. In his discussion with the scribes whether the Messiah is the son of David, he makes no direct claim.

Just how important is the messianic identity of Jesus of Nazareth to the development of a gospel-driven theology of discipleship? Bates obviously thinks it is very important, claiming, "That Jesus will become king is the primary theme of the Gospels" (2019, p. 42). He explains further:

> Jesus' death on the cross for our sins is a nonnegotiable gospel fact alongside other gospel facts. Arguably, the cross is the *dramatic* center of the gospel story, with the resurrection as the denouement. The cross is essential to the gospel and is theologically central. Yet the gospel climax, the theological point that receives the most emphasis in the Bible's own descriptions of the gospel, is that *Jesus is the Christ, the king.* (2019, p. 40, emphasis mine)

In this study, we will look at the unique way in which Jesus of Nazareth highlighted his identity as the one anointed by God the Father to reign over his kingdom.

Who Is the Son of Man?

Any attentive reader of the gospels quickly recognizes that Jesus of Nazareth often referred to himself as "the Son of Man" (*ho huios tou anthropou*). In the gospels, the expression "Son of Man" is the phrase the most often used (other than the name "Jesus") to designate Jesus of Nazareth; it is used 69 times in the Synoptics, 13 times in John. And it is used exclusively on the lips of Jesus of Nazareth! We can therefore reasonably assume that the evangelists retained in this title one of Jesus' typical self-designations.

The question of the role of Jesus of Nazareth in the kingdom of God is largely tied to the interpretation of the teachings in which Jesus calls himself the Son of Man. These teachings can be grouped into three categories. First,

---

3 Thus Adela Yarbro Collins writes, "Most New Testament scholars would still agree with Bultmann's judgment that the creation of the 'idea of a suffering, dying, rising Messiah or Son of Man' was not done by Jesus himself but by his followers '*ex eventu*,' that is, after the fact of the crucifixion and the experiences of Jesus as risen" (2011, p. 97). In this, she is entirely representative of the dominant scholarly tradition today about the Son of Man and the exalted status of Jesus, the Christ.

some of them speak of the work of the Son of Man in his current historical and cultural context in Palestine (notably Mk. 2:10, 28; Mt. 8:20; 11:19; Lk. 19:10). Second, there are teachings about the suffering, death, and resurrection of the Son of Man (notably the predictions of his passion in Mk. 8:31; 10:32–45; 14:21, 41). And finally, there are teachings about the *parousia* (or second coming) of the Son of Man at the end of time (especially Mk. 8:38; 13:26; 14:62; Mt. 10:23; 24:44; Lk. 17:24).

Why Does Jesus Identify Himself as the Son of Man?

Contemporary New Testament scholars have disagreed for some time as to why Jesus of Nazareth identified himself using this title (Casey, 2009; Burkett, 2004). Some have claimed that "Son of Man" referred to the Messiah (Christ) only during the time of his exaltation in heaven. In Mark 14:61–62, the high priest asks Jesus, "Are you the Christ [the Messiah], the Son of the Blessed One?" Jesus responds, "I am, and you will see the Son of Man sitting at the right hand of the Mighty One and coming on the clouds of heaven." It would be easy to conclude from these verses that "Son of Man" refers only to the moment when he will be seen coming on the clouds of heaven. After all, if the Son of Man is the Christ sitting at the right hand of the Mighty One and then coming on the clouds, how could Jesus use the term to refer to his earthly existence (Boyarin, 2013, p. 48)?

Other scholars argue that the title refers to the human nature of Jesus (Bird, 2013, p. 46). David Wenham (1995, p. 109) points out that this understanding is widespread. Still others claim that the title should be understood as a mere statement that Jesus of Nazareth is the "son of man," meaning that he is fully human, rooted into the descendance of a particular family, having friends, trade skills, and a village. Understood in this way, we could read Mark 2:10 to be saying, "That you may know that *the human being* has authority on earth to forgive sins." Again, if the title refers to the humanity of Jesus of Nazareth, then Mark 8:31 would be stating, "*The human being* must suffer many things," and Mark 8:38 would mean, "Whoever is ashamed of me … , of him will *the human being* be ashamed when he comes in the glory of his Father."

The discussion between Jesus and the high priest (Mk. 14:62–63) is in fact the only teaching of Jesus of Nazareth in which there is no ambiguity about his identity. The context of this conversation is unique, and its clarity is exceptional. Jesus stands before the Sanhedrin during his passion. He is silent in front of his accusers who testified falsely about him (Mk. 14:55–60). But as I just referred to, when the high priest asks him, "Are you the Messiah" he responds using the title "the Son of Man."

This dialogue furnishes us with several key elements to guide us as we read the Son of Man texts in the gospels. First, we see that "Messiah" is equivalent to "the Son of Man" for Jesus of Nazareth. Second, pretending to be "the Son of Man" was considered blasphemous by the high priest. Therefore, it expressed not just a messianic pretension but a claim to be divine. Boyarin (2013, p. 162) points out that the response by Jesus, "I am" (Mk. 14:62), is precisely how *Yahweh* identifies himself when Moses asks him for his name (Ex. 3:14).

When Jesus of Nazareth identifies himself as "the Son of Man," the high priest does not respond by asking, "What exactly is the Son of Man?" No, everyone present that day understood exactly what that title meant, even if they didn't agree that Jesus of Nazareth deserved the title. And their response to his claim was both violent and absolute. They understood his self-designation as "the Son of Man" to be blasphemy,[4] and as a result "They all condemned him as worthy of death" (Mk. 14:64). "Then some began to spit at him; they blindfolded him, struck him with their fists … and beat him" (Mk. 14:65).

The Son of Man and the Kingdom of God

One of Jesus' statements about the Son of Man allows us to interpret all the others with confidence (Beasley-Murray, 1986, p. 224). It is Luke 12:8–9 (with a parallel in Mt. 10:32–33):

> I tell you, whoever acknowledges me before men, the Son of Man will also acknowledge him before the angels of God. But he who disowns me before men will be disowned before the angels of God.

These words of Jesus of Nazareth inform us that a declaration in his favor before men is at the same time a confession of the Son of Man before God. And in like manner, the denial of Jesus of Nazareth before men is equivalent to denying the Son of Man before God. This teaching also indicates that the Son of Man plays a decisive role in determining who enters or is kept out of the kingdom of God. And it underscores the importance of listening to the words of Jesus, in whom the reign of God the Father is present. H. Tödt summarizes the significance of this teaching:

> He by no means appears as the lowly one, the sufferer, but demands with supreme authority that allegiance which detaches the disciple from this generation. In demanding this, Jesus utters an unsurpassable claim. No prophet in Israel ever claimed that men should confess him. (1965, p. 43)

---

4 The renowned Talmudic scholar Daniel Boyarin writes, "Blasphemy consists of imputing divine status to oneself or to another human. … Even if *ego eimi* is innocent, Jesus' further allusion to himself as the Son of Man and coming with the clouds of heaven certainly, according to the high priest's reaction, constitutes blasphemy and thus a claim to divine status. … Since stoning is the biblically ordained punishment for blasphemy, the people seek to stone him. This is precisely the same blasphemy for which Stephen was stoned according to Acts 7:56, although there the blasphemy consisted in implying the divine status of Jesus, not, of course, his own (Boyarin, 2012, pp. 138–139, note 9).

Matthew Bates (2019, p. 99) observes that the word translated by "acknowledge" (*homologēsē*) in this text refers to a verbal confession and is a fitting way to describe swearing allegiance to Jesus as King of kings. Paul uses the same word in Romans 10:9 when he says that anyone who believes and confesses that Jesus is Lord will be saved.

In sum, Jesus of Nazareth demands this kind of allegiance because he is divinely sovereign and exercises the authority of the Father who sent him. To confess him is to swear allegiance to him and identify oneself with the fellowship of those who are apprenticed to him. This also implies that when Jesus acknowledges before the angels the individual who has sworn allegiance to him, that person enters the communion of the Son of Man in the kingdom of God.

Remember, the foundational element in Jesus' teaching concerning the kingdom of God is that that the kingdom is present in his person and in his work. He could, therefore, legitimately demand total allegiance to himself by virtue of his authority as the representative and mediator of the reign of God over his creation. The kingdom of God, in its present and future dimensions, is present in Jesus of Nazareth. The kingdom that has arrived in Jesus is the same one as the kingdom promised for the end of time. This is the theme of his parables of the kingdom, as Beasley-Murray explains:

> However difficult it may have been for some of his contemporaries to believe, Jesus was proclaiming that the promised saving sovereignty of God was operative even as he spoke. He was thereby proclaiming himself to be the representative and mediator of the kingdom of God. (1986, p. 227)

It could be argued that the expression "Son of Man" was, as I. Howard Marshall (1966, pp. 350–351) contends, a perfect vehicle for Jesus' proclamation of the message of the kingdom of God. It is a term with associations of divine glory that preserves "the secrecy of self-revelation from those who had blinded their eyes and closed their ears to it." This understanding corresponds with the obscurity of Jesus of Nazareth as representative of the divine sovereignty, and also with the hiddenness of the kingdom that is to give way to manifest splendor at the revelation of the Son of Man. And it finds support in the occasions when people asked, as they heard Jesus refer to the present service and future exaltation of the Son of Man, "Who is this Son of Man?" (Jn. 12:34).

The Image of the Son of Man in the Prophecy of Daniel

The seventh chapter of the book of Daniel, written around 161 BCE, furnishes a remarkable apocalyptic vision:

As I looked, thrones were set in place, and the Ancient of Days took his seat. His clothing was as white as snow; the hair of his head was white like wool. His throne was flaming with fire, and its wheels were all ablaze. A river of fire was flowing, coming out from before him. Thousands upon thousands attended him, ten thousand times ten thousand stood before him. The court was seated, and the books were opened. Then I continued to watch … As I watched I looked and there before me was one like a son of man [i.e., a human being] coming with the clouds of heaven. He approached the Ancient of Days and was led into his presence. He was given authority, glory and sovereign power; all peoples, nations and men of every language worshipped him. His dominion is an everlasting dominion that will not pass away, and his kingdom is one that will never be destroyed. (Daniel 7:9–11a, 13–14)

Daniel Boyarin, Taubman Professor of Talmudic Culture and rhetoric at the University of California, Berkeley, succinctly summarizes the significance of this passage:

In this remarkable text, we find the prophet Daniel having a vision in which there are two divine figures, one who is depicted as an old man, an Ancient of Days, sitting on the throne. We have been told, however, that there is more than one throne there, and sure enough a second divine figure, in form "like a human being," is brought on the clouds of heaven and invested by the Ancient of Days in a ceremony very much like the passing of the torch from elder king to younger in ancient Near Eastern royal ceremonial. (2012, pp. 31-32)

We can see from Daniel's vision that the second person to whom an everlasting dominion over the whole earth is given has certain characteristics:

• He is divine.
• He is in human form.
• He can be described as a divine being who appears younger than the Ancient of Days.
• He will be enthroned on high.
• He will receive authority, dominion, and even sovereignty on earth.

These are all characteristics of Jesus of Nazareth, the Messiah! Boyarin explains that the title "Son of Man" as a name for a specific figure is unintelligible in Hebrew and Aramaic. And he adds that in Greek it indicates, at best, somebody's child. The context in Mark's gospel, however, does not allow us to interpret Jesus' use of the term as meaning just a human being. Moreover, the term "Son of Man" as used in Mark did not refer only to Jesus' coming on the clouds at the *parousia*. It was the living, breathing, Jesus of Nazareth, not the already exalted, resurrected, or returning-to-earth Messiah, who referred to himself as the Son of Man. This means that the title does not represent a particular stage in the Messiah narrative but refers to all these stages. "If Jesus believed that he was the Son of Man, he was from beginning to end of the story, not just at one moment within it" (Boyarin, 2012, p. 38).

The fact that in Daniel's vision the Son of Man comes "on the clouds of heaven" is significant, since this attribute is habitually connected to appearances of the deity in the Bible (Emerton, 1958, p. 231). This observation reinforces the notion that in Daniel's vision we have two divinities: the Ancient of Days and the Son of Man. Boyarin (2012, pp. 40–41, n. 3) stresses this point and quotes two rabbis, Rabbi Aquiva and Rabbi Yosé the Galilean, who understand this passage as referring to two divine figures in heaven, God the Father and a King (David).

Beasley-Murray (1986) has a similar understanding. He concludes that the teaching of Jesus of Nazareth about the kingdom is tied to his own role in the kingdom, and that the recognition of his role in the kingdom is tied to a confession of allegiance to him. He writes:

> Disciples of Jesus will almost certainly perceive who is meant [by the title Son of Man with which Jesus identifies himself] and receive the message of the saying; others may divine the implication [of the title] and be offended by it; still others may be in the dark as to who the "son of man" is and yet perceive the claim being made about the importance of a decision about the word of Jesus. (pp. 228–229)

The Ministry of the Son of Man

Jesus of Nazareth called men and women to change their mind[5] about him and give him their allegiance, declaring that in his person the reign of God had drawn near to them (cf. Mk. 1:15). Jesus the Messiah used many images to reassure them and convince them that God the Father was ready to release them from their bondage and bring them into a new reality. It is in Jesus' identity as "crown prince" and mediator of the new reality of the kingdom that he delivers others from the powers of evil (see e.g. Mk. 1:21–28; 5:1–20). Wherever Jesus of Nazareth appears and makes the kingdom a present reality, the powers of evil must recede. Moreover, as members of the kingdom, we are called to actively participate in the Messiah's liberating reign. Hence, Jesus of Nazareth taught his disciples to pray for deliverance from evil, after their requests for the coming of the kingdom, and the hallowing of God's name (cf. Mt. 6:9–13).

It is also as crown prince of the kingdom of God the Father that Jesus of Nazareth called people to begin to live in communion with himself and with others. In Jesus of Nazareth the messianic promises are fulfilled, and people who have become estranged from the Creator, from themselves, and from others can now participate in the new eschatological community which he

---

5 I use the notion of conversion (*metanoia* in Greek) to denote a change in attitude or mentality that results in a new allegiance, way of life, system of belief, and mode of relating to the Almighty, to reality, and to others (Hill, 1986; Gillespie, 1991; Rambo, 1993; Packer, 1994; Taylor, 1999).

announced and initiated (Jer. 31:31-34). In this context, Jesus identified himself as the Son of Man who has come to seek and to save what was lost (Lk. 19:10).

The Son of Man Who Seeks and Saves

We can logically associate that image of the Son of Man who has come to seek and to save what was lost with the words of Ezekiel about the unfaithful shepherds (Ezek. 34:1–16). In that passage, *Yahweh* declares that he will do what those treacherous shepherds failed to do. In Ezekiel 34:16, *Yahweh* affirms, "I will search for the lost and bring back the strays. I will bind up the injured and strengthen the weak." The implications are clear: Jesus of Nazareth, the Messiah, the Son of Man, realizes the promise of *Yahweh*. In the context of Luke 19, Jesus of Nazareth makes that declaration as his reason for associating with tax collectors and outcasts. This is a divine activity linked to the role of the Son of Man in the kingdom of God.

The Suffering of the Son of Man

In the gospel of Mark, we find three predictions of the passion of Jesus of Nazareth: Mark 8:31, 9:31, and 10:32. Despite their differences, these three predictions share the same contents. In all three cases, the Son of Man is the subject of the prediction, and it is said of him that he will be killed, and that after three days he will rise again. As we have already noted, the enigmatic and sometimes shocking declarations of Jesus of Nazareth about his identity and authority can be illuminated by a careful reading of the passage from Daniel about the Son of Man. Boyarin (2012) maintains that Jews of Jesus' day searched the Scriptures and interpreted each detail, seeking to understand what the Messiah would look like and what could be expected when he arrived. He argues that Jesus' contemporaries saw, in the figure of the Son of Man of Daniel 7:25–27, the suffering of the Messiah (Boyarin, 2012, pp. 129–145, see also Kim, 1983, pp. 81–86). Here are the relevant verses from Daniel:

> He [another king] will speak against the Most High and oppress his saints and try to change the set times and the laws. The saints will be handed over to him for a time, times and half a time. But the court will sit, and his power will be taken away and completely destroyed forever. Then the sovereignty, power and greatness of the kingdoms under the whole heaven will be handed over to the saints, the people of the Most High. His kingdom will be an everlasting kingdom, and all rulers will worship and obey him. (Dan. 7:25–27)

The Jews of the second Temple period believed that the destiny of the Son of Man, as revealed in this passage in Daniel, entailed being oppressed for a time, two times, and half a time before being triumphantly exalted. And it is precisely in association with the title "Son of Man" that Jesus of Nazareth predicts his passion:

The Jews were expecting a Redeemer in the time of Jesus. Their own sufferings under Roman domination seemed so great, and this Redeemer had been predicted for them. Reading the Book of Daniel closely, at least some Jews—those behind the first-century Similitudes of Enoch and those with Jesus—had concluded that the Redeemer would be a divine figure named the Son of Man who would come to earth as a human, save the Jews from oppression, and rule the world as its sovereign. (Boyarin, 2012, p. 142)

The first disciples of Jesus understood that the "saints" mentioned in verse 25 of Daniel 7 represent the Son of Man who is mentioned earlier in the chapter, in verses 13–14 (see Casey, 2009, pp. 85–86). For this reason, they could come to understand that consistent with this prophecy, their rabbi Jesus of Nazareth, the Messiah, had been handed over to the Gentiles for a fixed time, called here a time, two times, and half a time. If these "times" are understood as days, then Jesus would rise after a day, two more days, and part of a day—that is, after the third day (Boyarin, 2012, pp. 144–145).

The Son of Man and the Eternal Son of God

The title "Son of Man" is found 13 times in the gospel of John, where it is associated with the image of the *Logos* (Hamerton-Kelly, 1973, p. 225). Hamerton-Kelly (1973, p. 198) notes that John's gospel is distinguished from the Synoptics by its presentation of the divine glory of Jesus of Nazareth, the Messiah. His detailed study of the Son of Man in that gospel shows that Jesus is revealed as clearly existing in heaven before being revealed on earth. We see this in the words spoken by Jesus to Nathanael: "I tell you the truth, you shall see heaven open, and the angels of God ascending and descending on the Son of Man" (Jn. 1:51). Interpreted in the light of John 1:18, these words of Jesus indicate that as the Son of Man, he is the place where the divine activities become visible (Hamerton-Kelly, 1973, p. 228). This is true because he, the Son of Man, is the one who "came from heaven" (Jn. 3:13).

When did the Son of Man "come from heaven"? This took place when the eternal Son of God, the *Logos*, became flesh in Jesus of Nazareth (cf. Jn. 1:14). And when did the eternal Son of God, the *Logos*, the Son of Man, return to the status he had before becoming flesh in Jesus of Nazareth? This answer is also found in Jesus' teaching: "Just as Moses lifted up the snake in the desert, so the Son of Man must be lifted up" (Jn. 3:14). Jesus is referring here to his death on the cross. These words of Jesus highlight the soteriological importance of his death, but they also show the importance of his exaltation. Hamerton-Kelly ties these two notions together, asserting, "This is a way of affirming that he who believes in the exalted one has eternal life" (1973, p. 232).

The exaltation of the Son of Man is not just soteriologically significant. It also confirms the return of the *Logos* to the divine place he occupied for all eternity before becoming flesh in Jesus of Nazareth. Higgins (1980, pp. 177–178) similarly links the exaltation of the crucified and risen Son of Man to the prophecy of Daniel 7. According to that prophecy, it is when Jesus of Nazareth, the Messiah, the Son of Man, was given "glory and sovereign power" that "all peoples, nations and men of every language" would begin to "worship him." His dominion is an everlasting dominion that will not pass away, and his kingdom will never be destroyed (Dan. 7:14).

The exaltation of the Son of Man who had come from heaven is a key and permanent element in the tradition of his first followers. In Acts 2:33–35 and 5:31, Jesus of Nazareth, the Messiah crucified and risen from the dead, is exalted to the right hand of God. From that exalted position, he will reign until all his enemies have been made his footstool (Ac. 2:34–35). In Philippians 2:9, he is exalted by the Father to the "highest place." Admittedly, his kingship is hidden for us, even as it was for his first disciples. Like them, although in faith we understand that he has been crowned with glory and honor, "at present we do not see everything subject to him" (Heb. 2:8–9). This fact did not prevent those first disciples, however, from centering their theology and their practice on him. In fact, Jesus' exaltation was central to their message even though it could not yet be perceived on earth. "For we preach not ourselves," Paul insists, "but Jesus Christ as Lord" (2 Cor. 4:5). By this, the Christ-followers were not simply affirming the absolute supremacy of Jesus of Nazareth, the Messiah, over the physical and moral universe (Mt. 28:18; 1 Pet. 3:22). Nor were they making simply a blanket statement of his ultimate authority over human history (Rom. 9:5) and all human beings (Ac. 10:36; Rom. 10:12), whether living or dead (Rom. 14:9). We would also be wrong to think that such statements referred only to the believers living at that time (Eph. 1:22). Rather, they were indicating that Jesus of Nazareth, the reigning king in the Father's kingdom, is also the sovereign Lord over our own lives as his willing slaves.

Jesus, the Son of Man, Is the Sovereign Lord and We Are His Slaves
The Apostle Paul, who called himself a "slave of Christ Jesus" (Rom. 1:1) and described all of Jesus' followers, whether slave or free, as slaves of the Christ (1 Cor. 7:22; Eph. 6:6), affirms that those who have been brought under the reign of the Son (Col. 1:13) have not received "the spirit of slavery' (*pneuma douleias*) or "the spirit of a slave" that would prompt a return to fear (Rom. 8:15).

Murray Harris meticulously unpacks the nature of slavery in the Greco-Roman world and skillfully unfolds the New Testament's use of slavery as a metaphor for total devotion to the Christ in his book *Slave of Christ* (1999). He concludes that in its description of figurative slavery to Christ, "the New Testament has eradicated those negative features that attached to the notion of slavery, so that the metaphor has become a wholly positive image depicting the believer's exclusive devotion to the Lord Christ" (1999, p. 142). Harris highlights the fact that slaves of Christ have a master who is peerless in status (Mt. 28:18; Phil. 2:9) and meek and gentle in character (Mt. 11:29; 2 Cor.

10:1), provides for them generously (2 Pet. 1:3; Phil. 4:12–13), protects them jealously (2 Th. 3:3), and rewards them handsomely (Eph. 6:8; cf. 2 Cor. 5:10; Col. 3:24). Moreover, Harris demonstrates why the relationship of the Lord Jesus of Nazareth, the Christ to those who live under his reign cannot be properly described as "domination" or the follower's relation to the Christ as "submission":

> In the Christian transformation of the metaphor, while the notion of voluntary submission to the divine will remains intact, the idea of domination finds no place—if by "domination" we mean not simply a way or a state of being ruled, but the imposition of one person's will on another who is either unwilling or reluctant to accept that imposition. (Harris, 1999, p. 151)

Given this situation, as Christians we should never think that we are free from slavery! For one of the paradoxes of the Good News of our freedom from slavery to sin is our entry into a new, permanent slavery to Jesus of Nazareth, the Father-appointed reigning king. "Indeed," Harris (1999, p. 153) appropriately writes, "the one slavery is terminated precisely in order to allow the other slavery to begin." Hence Paul twice issues the command, "Give a slave's service to the Lord [Christ]" (Rom. 12:11; Col. 3:24).

This correlation between the lordship of the risen and exalted Jesus of Nazareth, the Messiah, and our enslavement to him is evident in many New Testament passages. Consider, for example, the following statements where the two terms *kyrios* (lord) and *doulos* (slave) are used together to describe our relationship to Jesus as his followers:

> A *mathētēs* (disciple/student) is not above his teacher, nor a *doulos* above his *kyrion*. It is enough for the student to be like his teacher, and the *doulos* like his *kyrios*. (Mt. 10:24–25)

> His *kyrios* replied, "Well done, good and faithful *doule!*" (Mt. 25:21, 23)

> I tell you the truth, no *doulos* is greater than his *kyriou*, nor is a messenger greater than the one who sent him. (Jn. 13:16)

> I no longer call you *doulous* [the plural of *doulos*] because a *doulos* does not know his *kyrios*'s business. (Jn. 15:15)

> We do not proclaim ourselves, but Jesus Christ as *kyrios*, and ourselves as your *doulous* for Jesus' sake (2 Cor. 4:5).

> The *doulos* of the *kyrios* must not be quarrelsome. (2 Tim. 2:24)

> James, a *doulos* of God and of the *kyrios* Jesus Christ. (Jas. 1:1)

Because the crucified, risen, and exalted Jesus of Nazareth is enthroned and reigning over the kingdom into which we have been transferred by the Father (Col. 1:13), we are in his service and our devotion is entirely to him. Harris

(1999, p. 143) details three elements included in this absolute devotion to the Christ:

1. Humble submission to the person of Christ. This involves an acknowledgment that as supreme Lord, he has absolute and exclusive rights to our will, affections, and energy, now and forever. It is a matter of complete devotion for all of one's life.
2. Unquestioning obedience to the Master's will. Slavery involves subjection to another's will, whether voluntarily or involuntarily. The faithful slave is the obedient slave, just as the first requirement for commendable military service is compliance with commands.
3. An exclusive preoccupation with pleasing Christ. Believers give satisfaction to their Master not only by obeying him, but also by devising innovative ways to please him. "We make it our ambition," says Paul, "to be constantly pleasing to him" (2 Cor. 5:9). This was Paul's magnificent obsession, an obsession that had the effect of expelling inferior—albeit legitimate—pursuits.

In chapter 6, when we studied the sending of the disciples in John's gospel, I maintained that because the risen Jesus of Nazareth is the one who sends us on mission, and not "God" or even "God the Father," he is the one we must seek to honor, obey, represent, and relate to. These attitudes of devotion and obedience to the Lord Jesus are reinforced by our study of the title "Son of Man" and, indeed, throughout the New Testament. As C. F. D. Moule (1962, p. 9; cf. p. 211) proposes in discussing the unity and variety of New Testament teaching, "The common factor holding all together is devotion to the person of Jesus Christ—the historical Jesus acknowledged as Messiah and Lord."

Discipleship means learning how to better serve the Lord Jesus of Nazareth, the reigning King, totally and unconditionally—"all of life for the whole of life" (Harris, 1999, p. 154). This is so because, as we saw in chapter 4, we serve and interact with the entire Godhead (Father, Son, and Spirit) in our obedient service to Jesus of Nazareth. Under the reign of the Lord Jesus, the Son of Man in Daniel's vision, we participate in the life intended for us by the Creator with an enthusiasm generated by Christ's Spirit. In Romans 12:11, immediately after saying, "Be aglow with the Spirit," Paul adds that we should "serve the Lord as his slave," as if to suggest that the "real proof of the presence of this fire of the Spirit would be not effervescent religious excitement but renewed energy and determination in the humble and obedient service of the Lord Jesus" (Cranfield, 1979, Vol. 2, p. 635).

Questions to Think About

1. In the introduction to this chapter, I quote a scholar who claims that when the gospel is presented today the "Jesus reigns" portion of the gospel is either entirely absent or mentioned as an aside. How can the Jesus' self-designation as the Son of Man function as a corrective to this practice?

2. Review Luke 12:8–9. What is the significance of Jesus' reference to himself as the Son of Man in this passage? How could a proper understanding of these verses help us to interpret all the other statements about the Son of Man with confidence?

3. This chapter presents a detailed interpretation of Daniel 7:9–14. What are the implications of this passage for developing a gospel-driven theology of discipleship? How would such a theology be useful in developing maturity in Christian discipleship?

4. The last section of this chapter argues that we are the "slaves" of Jesus of Nazareth and follows the thinking of another scholar who details three elements that are included in that absolute devotion to the Christ. How might each of these elements be fostered and strengthened in your own life, and in your local church?

10. The Apostolic Good News

I concluded chapter 9 with a claim that the Good News is about our freedom from slavery to sin and our entry into a new permanent slavery to Jesus of Nazareth. In that study, I have shown that Jesus of Nazareth deliberately used the title "Son of Man" to express his "hidden" identity. I have demonstrated that this self-designation of Jesus did not need to be explained to his friends and followers or to his enemies. It embodied Jesus' claim, linked to the vision of Daniel 7, to be the King of all kings—the one who demands absolute service and devotion because he is divinely sovereign and exercises the authority of the Father who had sent him. Based on that observation, I have argued that one of the paradoxes of the gospel is that it proclaims both our freedom and our slavery. It tells us that freedom from our sin means permanent slavery to Jesus of Nazareth, whom the Father appointed as king and whom we serve in the renewed energy of his indwelling Spirit.

This realization led the first followers of Jesus of Nazareth to a succinct but shocking confession: *Kyrios Iēsus*, "Jesus is Lord." Paul expresses this conviction in 1 Corinthians 12:3 in a form that had apparently already become common among Jewish followers of Jesus (van der Kooi & van den Brink, 2017, p. 371):

> For although there may be so-called gods in heaven or on earth—as indeed there are many "gods" and many "lords"—yet for us there is one God, the Father, from whom are all things and for whom we exist, and one Lord, Jesus Christ, through whom are all things and through whom we exist. (1 Cor. 8:5–6)

Here Paul clearly recognizes a differentiation in the concept of God: Jesus of Nazareth, the eternal Son incarnate, shares the Father's power to create and to rule. Here Jesus of Nazareth, the God-man, is the goal of all things including the aim of redemptive history. He embraces in his person *all* of reality, namely God and the realm of creation. Graeme Goldsworthy (2006, p. 249) puts this in another way:

> Jesus is God incarnate—that is, he is fully God and fully human. But to be human is to be made from the created dust of the earth while being given life by the breath of God. In the God-man we thus have all of reality present in a representative way that involves no dislocation of relationships. Jesus is thus the

representative of the new creation. If reality consists of God-Humanity-Universe, Jesus is the perfect representative of all three dimensions in which all relate perfectly. Christology in the New Testament shows Jesus to be the comprehensive expression of reality in the purpose of God.[1]

Thus, the confession that Jesus is Lord is our way of attributing to him the highest honor. It singles him out as the one toward whom all the former revelation of God is leading, and in whom it is fulfilled and given meaning. This is demonstrated by what his followers do in the name of the "Lord Jesus" (Col. 3:17) and their willingness to suffer for his name (1 Pet. 4:14). According to Larry Hurtado (2003, p. 117), the attribution of the title of Lord to Jesus of Nazareth proves (1) Jesus' absolute authoritative status, (2) Jesus's future role as the one who will come to judge, and (3) Jesus' place in the devotion of his earliest followers.

When Did, or Will, the Reign of Jesus the Messiah Begin?

I contend that the reign of Jesus the Messiah began after his crucifixion and resurrection. In contrast, many teach that it has yet to begin, and will happen only at some time in the future, after the "Day of the Lord." Have the kingdom, judgment, and rule already been transferred to Jesus of Nazareth? Or is it more appropriate to assume, as Johannes Weiss (1985, p. 130) maintains, that only when he establishes the kingdom "God will raise him to the office of 'Son of Man' (Jn. 3:14), to which he is entitled (Jn. 5:27), and will make him Lord and Messiah (Ac. 2:36)"?

Scripture may support both viewpoints. For instance, 1 Corinthians 15:24–25 can be interpreted at least in three ways. The text reads:

> Then the end will come, when he [the Christ] hands over the kingdom to God the Father after he has destroyed all dominion, authority and power. For he must reign until he has put all his enemies under his feet.

Should we understand this text as indicating that one future day the God-man will rule over all the members of the coming kingdom of God because he humbled himself, and that after a certain period of ruling, perhaps a thousand years (Rev. 20:4), the *basileia* (kingdom) will be given back to the Father? Or does it affirm that the resurrected Jesus reigns now as the head of a fellowship of restored humanity while reinstating the Creator's sovereignty as before? The text may also indicate that there is a joint governorship between the Son and the Father (Rev. 3:21; 7:15, 17).

The question of when Jesus has begun or will begin to reign may seem relatively unimportant, as Weiss (1985, p. 128) suggests. I disagree because

---

1 By "Universe" Goldsworthy means everything in creation that is not human.

this issue can decisively foster or diminish intentional allegiance to Jesus of Nazareth, the Christ. I do not mean to imply that people who answer this question differently are not intentionally loyal followers of Jesus. However, I find that much of our preaching and teaching shifts the center of interest away from obedient service to the risen and enthroned Lord Jesus and toward an overemphasis on the salvation of the individual human being. In so doing, it creates too rigid a distinction between the identity of the God-man in his humble service of the divine sovereignty and his present authority over all of creation. Jeremy Treat (2014, pp. 250–251) rightly states that this results in "the overcategorization commonly employed in the doctrines of the two states of Christ (humiliation and exaltation) and the three offices of Christ (prophet, priest, and king)." Treat laments that this reasoning makes "impossible any connection between the kingdom and the cross" (2014, p. 251). I agree with him that one's understanding of the kingdom of God is bound to affect one's view of the Messiah in the kingdom, as well as our relationship to the crucified Jesus of Nazareth.

Support for the View that Jesus' Reign Has Not Yet Begun

Some argue that the kingdom of God will be ushered in by the coming of the resurrected Jesus and the Day of the Lord, which will entail the overthrow of evil powers and the establishment of the kingdom of God in this world (Beasley-Murray, 1962, p. 46). George Ladd (2000) expresses the sentiment of many who hold this position. Ladd sees the kingdom of God as his defeating of his enemies and bringing men and women into the enjoyment of the blessings of his reign, all of which will be accomplished in three acts or stages. Working backwards chronologically, the third and final victory occurs at the end of the Millennium when death, Satan, and sin are finally destroyed and all people are sent to either heaven or hell. The second phase occurs at the beginning of that thousand-year reign of Jesus as king over Israel as well as all over the nations of the world (Isa. 2:4; 42:1). The initial manifestation of God's kingdom is found in the person and work of the Christ.

According to this view, until Jesus returns in glory and begins to reign, this evil age will prevail and intensify. "Subtle, deceitful influences will seek to turn men away from Christ. False religions, deceptive messiahs will lead many astray. Wars will continue; there will be famines and earthquakes. Persecution and martyrdom will plague the Church" (Ladd, 2000, p. 74). However, the kingdom of God has already entered this evil age:

> Satan has been defeated. The Kingdom of God, in Christ, has created the Church, and the Kingdom of God works in the world through the Church to accomplish the divine purposes of extending His Kingdom in the world. We are caught up in a great struggle—the conflict of the ages. God's Kingdom works in this world through the power of the Gospel. "And this gospel of the kingdom will be

preached throughout the whole world, as a testimony to all nations; and then the end will come [Mt. 24:14]." (Ladd, 2000, p. 74)

Although Jesus the Messiah has already achieved a great initial and decisive victory over Satan and his evil power, he will finish his work only when he begins to reign over a physical kingdom from Jerusalem, after his glorious return.

Support for the View That Jesus' Reign Began at the Resurrection

I have argued throughout that according to a biblical perspective, sin is rebellion against the triune Creator. I further maintain that the Creator chose to resolve this cosmic rebellion by entering his creation in the person of Jesus of Nazareth, the eternal Son made flesh. This implies that the Christ and Son of Man must enter the world as God-man to defeat the cosmic rebellion. Thus, this was accomplished when he obeyed his Father even through death on the cross, then was resurrected and "installed" over the kingdom as "Son of God in power" (Rom. 1:4a), as I argued in chapter 7. A good number of contemporary theologians disagree here and maintain that sin is better understood as individual human beings having enmity with God, entailing both divine wrath and human guilt. This is the heart of the problem according to these theologians. I agree with Jeremy Treat (2014, p. 194) that both positions have solid biblical support. Treat concludes from his observation that sin is both multifaceted in its essence and its effects, and that at its core it is against God. With Treat, John Murray (1978, p. 50) rightly states, "We must view sin and evil in its larger proportions as a kingdom that embraces the subtility, craft, ingenuity, power, and unremitting activity of Satan and his legions."

As I showed in chapter 6, Jesus of Nazareth did not undertake his work or proclaim his word on his own authority but on the authority of God the Father, who sent him as representative for the Creator's redemptive plan. This authority underpins the sovereign command Jesus gives to follow him, as expressed in such passages as Matthew 10:34–38, Mark 8:34, and Luke 9:57–62, as well as the imperious words about the importance of hearing his teaching as stated in such passages as Matthew 7:24ff. and Luke 8:31–32, and the importance of heeding his works as expressed in such passages as Matthew 11:20–24. As Beasley-Murray (1962, p. 228) correctly states, "The recognition of his [Jesus'] function in the kingdom is bound up with our confession of allegiance to him."

We give Jesus of Nazareth our allegiance not to repay him for his act of self-sacrifice, but because of who he is. I have argued in chapter 7 that we must reexamine our presuppositions about the primary identity and role of Jesus of Nazareth. My goal is not to introduce a separation between the "functional" and "ontic" categories for Christ. On the contrary, I recognize that his identity as the God-man is expressed in all his actions and accomplishments, and that his role as the Lamb of God who died for our sins on the cross is not his primary identity. I have also argued that the focus of Scripture is on his identity as the centre and core of the Creator's plan and as the goal of our transformation and that of all creation.

In the last two studies, we saw that Jesus of Nazareth not only proclaimed the kingdom but also identified himself with it. He went about doing good (Ac. 10:38) and claiming that those acts proved his embodiment of the presence and reign of the Father (Mt. 12:28). After liberating a demonized man from his oppression, Jesus declared, "If I drive out demons by the finger of God, then the kingdom of God has come to you" (Lk. 11:20). Even prior to his resurrection and enthronement, Jesus of Nazareth, the Son of Man, was "he who has to accomplish the coming of the kingdom and to carry out the divine judgment, and in whose hands, therefore, all authority has been placed" (Ridderbos, 1978, p. 31). Jürgen Moltmann (1989, pp. 98–99) writes:

> When Jesus expels demons and heals the sick, he is driving out of creation the powers of destruction, and is healing and restoring created beings who are hurt and sick. The lordship of God to which the healings witness, restores sick creation to health. Jesus' healings are not supernatural miracles in a natural world. They are the only truly 'natural' things in a world that is unnatural, demonized and wounded.

In various places the gospels refer to Jesus of Nazareth as king.[2] Moreover, as we saw in chapter 8, "kingdom of God" or, as in Matthew, "kingdom of heaven" is the central concept in Jesus' teaching. Though these phrases are less frequent in the rest of the New Testament, we will see that the content and meaning of "the kingdom" were at the heart of apostolic preaching.

For instance, Beth Stovell (2012, p. 308) notes that although John's gospel does not use the word "kingdom" as frequently as the Synoptic Gospels do, John is "concerned with representing Jesus as king as one of the important elements of Jesus' overall identity." Stovell (2012, p. 217) and Robert Hodgson (1987, p. 165) argue convincingly that the proprietorship of the kingdom shifts from God to Jesus, and from a theologically apocalyptic image to a Christological one, between John 3 and John 18. And Tom Wright (1996, p. 267) notes that the idea evoked by the phrase "kingdom of God" is present in John's gospel, though the phrase itself is absent. N. T. Wright correctly notes, "Any attempt to separate out a Johannine redemption theology from the equally Johannine theology of God's kingdom and the new creation is doomed to failure" (2011, p. 231). He further states, "We should not imagine that 'forgiveness of sins' here is a purely individualistic thing. ... Jesus' followers

---

2 "King of the Jews" in Mt. 2:2; 27:11, 29, 37; Mk. 15:2, 9, 12, 18, 26; Lk. 23:3, 37ff; Jn. 18:33, 37, 39; 19:3, 14–21); "King of Israel" in Mt. 27:42; Mk. 15:32; Jn. 1:49; 12:13; and simply "king" in Mt. 1:5; 25:34, 40; Lk. 19:38; Jn. 12:15.

were thereby commissioned and then empowered by the Spirit to announce to the world there was a different way to be human" (Wright, 2011, p. 233).

In our previous study, we saw that the followers of the resurrected and enthroned Jesus of Nazareth systematically identified him as "Lord." Wright (2011, p. 37) contends that this title is a recognition that in and through Jesus of Nazareth "a new state of affairs has been brought into existence. A door has been opened that nobody can shut. Jesus is now the world's rightful Lord, and all other lords are to fall at his feet." Wright convincingly and meticulously argues that this is not an eschatological message in the sense that it heralds the end of the world, but an "inaugurated eschatological message." By this he means that this is something that "has indeed happened in and through Jesus and does not look like what people might have imagined" (Wright, 2011, pp. 37–38).

One of the things we wrongly imagine, says Wright (2011, pp. 42–46), is that Jesus came to teach people how to go to heaven. He finds this problem to be present principally in the Western churches that "have assumed that the whole point of Christian faith is to 'go to heaven'" (2011, p. 42). Wright links this faulty understanding to a poor interpretation of the phrase "kingdom of heaven" that goes all the way back to the fourth century (2011, p. 43). When we read the gospels (especially the gospel of Matthew) with that idea in mind we "are almost bound to see the 'kingdom of heaven' as a place from which believers might have been barred because of sin, but to which now, through the death of Jesus, they have access" (2011, p. 43). Wright also argues that this understanding has led us to think wrongly that the gospels are there to "tell us how to go to heaven" (2011, p. 44). This prominent Bible scholar argues convincingly that in Jesus' Jewish world, *everlasting* or *eternal life* referred to the "age to come" that would arrive to "bring God's justice, peace, and healing to the world as it groaned and toiled within the 'present age'" (2011, pp. 44–54).

Among the various results of our reduced understanding of the nature of salvation is that we have misread the gospels and "made them ordinary." Wright (2011) explains further:

> We have cut them down to size, have allowed them only to speak about the few concerns that happened to occupy our minds already, rather than setting them free to generate an entire world of meaning in all directions, a new world in which we would discover not only new life, but new vocation. (p. 158)

He explains that our truncated view of salvation is only one of many habitual ways of unbalanced thinking and of practicing our faith "that are so engrained that we do not realize they are there" (2011, p. 158).

A truly gospel-driven theology of discipleship should seek to recover the full apostolic understanding that bondage to sin is not only a question of individual choice. It is also the consequence of humankind's rejection of the

Creator's reign. In like fashion, salvation entails far more than rescuing individual human souls from damnation, as important as that is. It entails the restoration of the Creator's original intent for his creation. The eternal Son incarnate proclaimed the reign of the triune Creator God over his creation and performed the deeds necessary for its inauguration. All through the long history of sin and grace and sin again, the whole purpose was salvation—that is, restoration and repair of the effects of humankind's choice not to submit to the reign of the Creator. In his *The Way of Jesus Christ*, Moltmann (1989) at times proposes to translate "the kingdom of God" by "new Creation" because, he argues:

> The lordship of God whose efficacy already reaches into this history of injustice and death, is accordingly to be understood as the newly creating, life-giving activity of God … . With the resurrection of Christ, the new creation begins, *pars pro toto*, with the crucified one. (pp. 64, 98–99)

Adrio König (1988) affirms the same idea:

> That Christ is the alpha and omega means that there is a special relationship between Christ and the *entire history* of the world. … Christ as the "end" *(telos)* involves the ideas of both *terminus* and *goal* and amounts to the same thing as pronouncements, which depict Christ as the *goal* of creation. Christ as the 'last' emphasizes his decisive meaning for creation. (pp. 33–34; emphasis in original)

From the beginning, the triune Creator reigns over all of creation. Both Satan (a fallen angel) and humankind rebelled against him, and death entered the world. The triune Creator initiated a redemptive counterattack by becoming human as Jesus of Nazareth through the incarnation of the eternal Son. In him, the Creator came to set right what Adam set wrong, recapitulating in himself the story of Adam and Israel but keeping the covenant where it was previously broken. The evil one continually thwarts God's plan through temptation, deception, and accusation. The Lord Jesus, who is the Son of Man, the Messiah, and the God-man, is "the servant-king who rules through obedience, truth, and suffering—resulting in life" (Treat, 2014, p. 209). This same perspective is evident and rich in Apostle Paul's description of the saving grace of Jesus of Nazareth, the Lord and Christ.

Sharing in the Restorative Kingship of Jesus the Christ: Romans 5:12–8:39

Joshua Jipp (2015, p. 179) grasps that Romans 5:12–8:39 is filled with kingship discourse as played out in a cosmic manner. For example, he observes that Adam and the Christ both share in dominions (5:12–21), sin and death are overlords (6:9, 12, 14), humanity awaits either judgment or vindication (8:1, 33–34), humanity is liberated through sharing in Christ's regal-filial status

(8:15, 29), and "echoes of enthronement to lordship through resurrection abound (8:9–17)" (Jipp, 2015, pp. 33–34).

Douglas Campbell has also shown that underlying Romans chapter 8 is "a story of ascent through resurrection to glorification and heavenly enthronement" (2002, p. 116). In other words, according to this text humanity shares in the identity and resulting consequences of either Adam or the Christ—both of whom are portrayed as kings with dominions that exert lordship over humanity (Jipp, 2015, p. 197).[3]

Jipp (2015, p. 180) suggests that Paul has taken into account here the unchangeable gospel elements described in Romans 1:3–4 and worked out the soteriological significance of Jesus of Nazareth's regal identity as set forth in those introductory verses. He summarizes his thinking as follows:

> Thus, Christ's messianic identity as seed of David who shares in human flesh, his installation as God's powerful Son, resurrection from the dead, his resurrected state as marked by God's Spirit, and enthronement to a position of lordship over the nations are cosmically reworked by Paul as royal events in which humanity participates. (Jipp, 2015, p. 180)

He also rightly insists that Paul is using political and royal terms when he describes the Messiah's deliverance of humanity from evil powers in the first eleven verses of chapter 5 (Jipp, 2015, p. 181). Based on numerous Jewish texts portraying Adam as a ruler, and on the work of Daniel Kirk (2008, p. 105) and Constantine Campbell (2012, p. 345), Jipp (2015) writes:

> Adam's humanity and primal kingship allow Paul to invoke "Adam as the one who unleashed a worldwide reign of sin and death." Apart from Christ's liberating work, these evil overlords exert their dominion by taking root in the very body and flesh of unredeemed humanity and thereby bringing death and judgment. ... Paul repeatedly uses regal and military language, more specifically the language used to describe a powerful enslaving tyrant, to speak of the "kingly reign" (Rom. 5:13, 17, 21; 6:12), "lordship" (Rom. 6:6, 9, 14), "enslavement"

---

3 This reading by Jipp differs from that of many New Testament scholars who regard "reconciliation" as the centre of Paul's theology, or at least of his soteriology (i.e. Martin, 1981; Schreiner, 2001, pp. 152–154; Marshall, 2004, pp. 440–442, 719–720). For systematic theologians who approach this text from the covenantal perspective, the doctrine of reconciliation is the label for the entire field of soteriology itself (Dennay, 2010). Reading Romans 5:12–8:39 from this perspective, we find that the contrast between Adam and Christ emphasizes that Adam introduced a breakdown in the relationship between humankind and God, bringing death and judgment into the world, but that Christ's work of restoring that relationship to a friendly status is even greater. In contrast, Jipp (2015 p. 187), sees in this text Paul's conceptualization of human salvation as "participation in the constituent events of Christ's rule, namely, his sonship, resurrection life, receipt of the Spirit, and cosmic inheritance."

(Rom. 6:15–22), and "waging of war and imprisonment" (Rom. 7:23) of the powers of Sin and Death. (p. 182)

I cannot give Jipp's careful exegetical work the detailed attention it deserves. I will only touch on a few of his major points, which link the gospel description of Romans 1:1–5 to Romans 5–8. I would encourage you to consult Jipp (2015, pp. 179–197) for a thorough examination.

First, Jipp highlights humanity's situation, including that of Israel, of enslavement to hostile cosmic powers, all of which are introduced in the Adam-Christ antithesis in Rom. 5:12–21 (pp. 181–186). Second, not only does Christ's crucifixion enable humanity to be freed from the tyrannical reign of sin and death, but "his installation as God's resurrected Son who now has God's *pneuma* (Spirit) functions as the catalyst for inaugurating his messianic reign over his people" (p. 186). Flowing from this point, Jipp writes that it is precisely because Christ-followers have the same *pneuma* as their reigning Lord Jesus that "they belong to him and his royal family" (p. 188).

We will look in detail at this important association of the person of the Spirit with the person of the eternal Son in chapter 14. Jipp also sees a link between Romans 1:3–4 and 5:12–8:39 in that in both passages, our adoptive sonship into Christ's royal family enables us to experience the reversal of God's curses (Gen. 3:17–19) and "something like a return to the Garden of Eden and its peaceful and fertile conditions" (p. 193). He writes, "It is likely ... that the Messiah's inheritance (Ps. 2:7–8; Rom. 4:13; 8:17) is his rule over the entire world and its eschatological renewal (Rom. 8:18–25)" (p. 194). Jipp (2015) further affirms:

God's intention for humanity to reign over creation as God's vicegerents (Gen. 1:26–28; Ps. 8:4–9), an intention that was corrupted by Adam's unleashing of a dominion of sin, death, and corruption of the cosmos (Rom. 5:12–21), is brought to fruition through the Messiah's cosmic rule and his extension of this rule to his people. (pp. 194–195)

In the gospel presentation we are about to look at, Paul reminds the Christ-followers in Corinth that they have been called by God the Father for the purpose of "fellowship with his son Jesus Christ our Lord" (1 Cor. 1:9). One of the ways he conceptualizes this "fellowship" is through sharing in the Messiah's divine lordship over all things by virtue of sharing his spirit. This idea is expressed in a short text which, along with Romans 1:1–5, is without doubt one of the oldest expressions of the gospel to which we have access. It summarizes the apostolic tradition (cf. 1 Cor. 11:2; 2 Th. 2:15; 2 Tim. 2:2) that existed before the four New Testament gospels were compiled.[4]

---

4 Even if some scholars contest these dates, we can reasonably estimate that 1 Corinthians was written about 55 CE, Mark and Matthew toward the end of the 50s or

The Gospel Elements according to 1 Corinthians 15:1–5

First Corinthians 15 is the classic presentation of the doctrine of the resurrection. In this chapter, as in the text in Romans that we looked at in chapter 7, Paul once again contrasts Adam, the man of dust (Gen. 2:7), and Jesus of Nazareth, the man from heaven who was raised from the dead and who will allow his followers to participate in his cosmic rule (1 Cor. 15:20–23). Paul's argument here is different from that of Romans 5:12 to 8:36, however.

Paul's Two Arguments about the Contrast between Adam and the Christ

In Romans, the contrast between Adam and the Christ highlights the "Adamic role" of Jesus of Nazareth, who undid what Adam had done through his faithful obedience to his Father to the point of death on the cross for our rebellion (Horton, 2011, p. 703). The argument in Romans is that had Adam been faithful in his role as the triune Creator's servant-coregent over creation, all of us in Adam would have "entered triumphantly into the 'seventh day' of everlasting Sabbath. In other words, glorification (at once individual and cosmic, spiritual and bodily) would immediately have followed" (Horton, 2011, p. 703). This, however, did not happen. Adam failed to extend the Creator's righteous dominion over creation and instead unleashed the "death-dealing rule over creation by God's enemies" (Jipp, 2015, p. 207). The man Jesus of Nazareth, who descended from Adam (Lk. 3:23–38), overcame temptation where Adam failed (Mk. 1:12–13). It was in his *human nature* that the eternal Son incarnate *learned* obedience from the things he suffered (Heb. 2:10–18; 5:8–10). John Murray (2015, pp. 18–19) underscores the importance of this fact:

> The heart and mind and will of our Lord had been molded—shall we not say forged?—in the furnace of temptation and suffering. And it was in virtue of what he had learned in that experience of temptation and suffering that he was able, at the climactic point fixed by the arrangements of infallible wisdom and everlasting love, to be obedient unto death, even the death of the cross. … It was through this course of obedience and of learning obedience that he was made perfect as Saviour, that is to say, became fully equipped so as to be constituted a perfect Saviour.

In this sense, Jesus of Nazareth is the first human being to be authentically human. As Bird (2013, p. 480) states, "The universe at last beholds a human being who glorifies God." The late Bishop Stephen Neil (1960, p. 37) puts it this way:

---

the beginning of the 60s, Luke between 59 and 63 CE, and John toward the end of the 80s or a little later (Gundry, 1994, pp. 481–482).

When Jesus died, something happened that had never happened before in the whole history of the world. A man had lived the whole of his life in perfect and complete obedience to God. Death really is an end. It marks the end of the chapter. Nothing can now change what has gone before. ... At last we have seen a man.

The Contrast between Adam and the Christ in the Epistle to the Corinthians

Although Paul's contrast between Adam and the Christ in 1 Corinthians 15 has the important purpose of refuting any teaching that denies the future bodily resurrection of believers (Schreiner, 2001, pp. 456–459), we often overlook the fact that he is also using this contrast to speak of "the sphere of Christ's power and saving work" (Wenham, 1995, p. 184). Jipp (2015, pp. 208–209) prefers to speak of the "dominion" of Christ here, contending that the words used in 1 Corinthians 15 address Adam's kingly role and the events that inaugurated the Messiah's royal enthronement and elevation to a place of divine power.

Here is the text from 1 Corinthians 15:1–5:

Now, brothers, I want to remind you of the gospel I preached to you, which you received and on which you have taken your stand. By this gospel you are saved, if you hold firmly to the word I preached to you. Otherwise you have believed in vain. For what I received I passed on to you as of first importance: that Christ died for our sins according to the Scriptures, that he was buried, that he was raised on the third day according to the Scriptures, and that he appeared to Peter, and then to the Twelve.

With the introductory words of verse 1, Paul announces the importance of the unchangeable gospel elements he is about to present. He underscores the centrality of what he is about to detail in verse 3, saying that it is "of first importance" (Campbell, 2009, p. 18). This is precisely the gospel that he himself had preached to the Christ-followers in Corinth.

In fact, to be more precise, Paul does not say that he "preached" that gospel at all. Scott McKnight (2016, p. 48) points out that Paul uses a specific Greek phrase: *to euangelion ho euengelisamen,* which he translates by "the gospel I gospelled." The Darby translation is the only English translation that proposes a translation other than "preached to you," reading, "which I announced to you as the glad tidings." I suggest that *euengelisamen* might indicate one or both of the following things. First, this specific referral to "gospelling" the gospel may be Paul's way of saying that even his *manner* of communication reflects the *contents* of that message. If this is what he is saying, that might be a way to alert his readers that what follows is his essential message, or what would have commonly been called a *kerygma*[5]—the announcement on the public square of a military victory or a new city ordinance. The first readers of Paul's letter would have thus been expecting something like the kind of major political or governmental proclamation that is presented at an official press conference.

Moreover, and this is my second proposition, perhaps Paul is stressing that the elements he is about to detail are "Good News." In the process of asserting the absolute necessity of the resurrection in 1 Corinthians 15:14, Paul refers to "our *kerygma*" as the *euangelion* (Good News) he defines in the opening verses of the chapter. The interchangeability of *kerygma* and *euangelion* in this passage indicates unmistakably that the content of what is being proclaimed is Good News. McKnight (2016, p. 50) puts this all together by writing, "To gospel for Paul was to tell, announce, declare, and shout aloud the Story of Jesus Christ as the saving news of God."

The words of verse 2, "By this gospel you are being saved,[6] if you hold firmly to the word I preached to you. Otherwise, you have believed in vain," are significant. Paul's use of the notion of embracing ("believe in") the Good News of the story of Jesus indicates that more than intellectual assent or a one-time decision is required. A certain amount of tenacity in adhering to the contents of the gospel is also needed (Bates, 2019, p. 92). Nijay Gupta (2020, pp. 96–114) concurs, stating that "resurrection is not just about the reanimation of the body, but the nature of discipleship and the Christian life itself" according to Paul's argument. Remember that Paul was writing to people who were trying to embrace the Christ while still holding on to pre-conversion social and cultural values that were blocking their spiritual growth.[7] In response to this problem, Paul declares that the resurrection is the validation of the transfiguration of perception and action, and of the tenaciousness needed to adhere to the proclaimed message. Thus, Paul writes in verse 14 that if Christ has not been raised, our tenacity in adhering to the gospel is useless.

1 Corinthians 15:3–5

For what I received I passed on to you as of first importance: that Christ died for our sins according to the Scriptures, that he was buried, that he was raised on the

---

5 The word *kerygma* is used once in Matthew (12:41), once in Luke (11:32), and six times in Paul's letters (Rom. 16:25; 1 Cor. 1:21; 2:4; 15:14; 2 Tim. 4:17; Tit. 1:3). In all these New Testament occurrences, the word refers to what is being proclaimed.

6 The Greek verb *sōzō* (saved) is in the present tense, which indicates that the action is ongoing (cf. Rom. 5:9; Acts 2:47; 1 Cor. 2:15; 1 Th. 5:9–10; see also Barrett, 1968, p. 336; Fee, 1987, p. 720).

7 Anthony Thieselton (2011, p. 9) notes three traits that hindered their spiritual growth: (1) a drive toward competitiveness, self-achievement, and self-promotion; (2) an attitude of self-sufficiency, self-congratulation, autonomy and entitlement to indulge freedoms; and (3) the tendency to overvalue gifts of knowledge, wisdom, and freedom over and above more basic gifts in everyday life such as love and respect for others.

third day according to the Scriptures, and that he appeared to Peter, and then to the Twelve.

Not only do these verses summarize the apostolic tradition, but they also substantiate the official description of the gospel that Paul received from the first disciples of the Christ.[8] Such an official nature of the gospel description assures us that Paul neither invented or modified it, nor did he receive a different version from the original position (Leon-Dufour, 1963, p. 297).

Thomas Schreiner (2001, p. 427) claims that this summary of the tradition in the opening verses of chapter 15 presupposes that the Corinthians were already familiar with it via oral instruction. David Wenham (1995, p. 392) thinks that we can see signs throughout 1 Corinthians that the recipients of the letter were familiar with the traditions of Jesus but were using them in ways that "Paul strongly disagreed with" (with some of them justifying their immorality while others advocated Christian celibacy). Paul had taught some of these traditions in Corinth himself, as he explicitly notes, for example, about the last supper and the resurrection (1 Cor. 11:23 and 15:3).

The difference between this and other Jesus traditions can be seen in the fact that here Paul employs the language of tradition (*paredoka* = "I delivered"; *parelabon* = "I received") to underscore that here he is passing on to the Corinthians the story of the crucial events in the life of Jesus of Nazareth, the Christ, as he had received it. This use of tradition language is troubling to some people who are also familiar with Paul's words to the Christ-followers in Galatia: "I want you to know, brothers, that the gospel I preached is not something I made up. I did not receive it from any man, nor was I taught it; rather, I received it by revelation from Jesus Christ" (Gal. 1:11–12). I agree with David Wenham that Paul's statement in Galatians does not call into question the notion that Paul received the gospel from the Christ-followers who preceded him. Wenham (1995, p. 396) states that, given the opportunities Paul had before, at, and after his conversion to learn from others about the Jesus tradition, Paul is probably saying in Galatians that the essence of his gospel of grace for all, including the Gentiles, was given to him at his conversion on the Damascus road. Wenham explains:

> After his conversion he was, according to Acts, with the Christians of Damascus for some time, including, notably, Ananias (Ac. 9:10–23). Scholars have questioned the Acts story of Ananias ministering to Paul, arguing (among other things) that Paul says in Gal. 1:17 that after his conversion, "I did not confer with any human being." But to take Paul's words to mean that he had no significant contact with any Christian after his conversion is to press them much too far. He means that he had no official consultation or briefing with any of the apostles (or

8 On the official nature of this description, see Fitzmyer (2008, p. 545); McKnight (2011, p. 49); Congar (1969, p. 9).

anyone equivalent), not that he lived somehow in isolation from the Christian community in Damascus. There is every likelihood that he was instructed as a new convert and took every opportunity to learn of Jesus from his fellow Christians. (1995, p. 397)

Scot McKnight suggests that we might need to pause and remind ourselves again of what Paul is actually claiming: "He is saying that the gospel he gospelled and passed on is the authentic, reliable gospel of the Apostles—he both received that gospel and passed it on. He is no innovator when it comes to the gospel" (2016, p. 49). And this authentic gospel was what connected Paul to the Christ-followers in Corinth (1 Cor. 15:1).

The apostolic gospel that Paul passed on can be broken into four phrases, each of which is introduced by the Greek word *hoti*, "that" (Fitzmyer, 2008, p. 541):

(a) *hoti* Christos apethanen	*that* Christ died
hyper ton hamartion hēmōn	for our sins
kata tas graphas	according to the Scriptures
(a^2) *kai hoti* etaphē	*that* he was buried
(b) kai *hoti egégertai tē hémera tē trite*	*that* he was raised on the third day
kata tas graphas	according to the Scriptures
(b^2) *kai hoti* ōphthē Kēpha.	*that* he appeared to Peter

Let us look now in more detail at these four elements that construct this apostolic Good News.

Christ Died for Our Sins

The composition of the gospel begins with the affirmation that Jesus of Nazareth died "for the sake of" or "because of" our sins. The Scriptures offer a multitude of metaphors and images to express what the death of Jesus of Nazareth for our sins signifies, and I cannot fully unpack that constellation of meaning here. He reconciled us to himself (2 Cor. 5:18) when he became a ransom for us (Mk. 10:45), gave his life for us (Lk. 22:19), died for us (Rom. 5:8), justified us as in a court of law (Rom. 3:24–25), made himself an offering (Heb. 10:10), delivered us from slavery (Rom. 8:15), and made us children of God (Rom. 8:21). And this list is far from exhaustive.

Jeremy Treat recognizes that fitting these metaphors together is difficult and requires more than attempting to meld their meanings into a single whole. He writes, "'There must be a particular ordering' as Paul's words indicate, 'For what I received I passed on to you as *of first importance*'" (Treat, 2014, p. 186; emphasis in original). Treat (2014, pp. 193–246) places at the top of his list two themes: penal substitution and *Christus victor*,[9] following the lead of the Reformers who understood these words as demonstrating that certain doctrines that have more theological significance than others.[10] After examining these two metaphors through both the Old and New Testaments, Treat rightly concludes, "Since the kingdom and the cross are held together by the Christ, the doctrines of Christology, atonement, and kingdom must be properly understood, especially as they mutually inform each other" (2014, p. 250).

Attempting to summarize the superabundance of scriptural metaphors that describe what Christ's death for our sins accomplished, Michael Bird writes, "We can say that the atonement brings God's people into God's place under God's reign to share in God's holy, loving glory on account of the love demonstrated in the cross and the justice satisfied on the cross" (2013, p. 421). I follow this emphasis on the identity of Jesus of Nazareth as Messiah as central to the Apostles' message. He is the God-man who, by the "blood of his cross" (Col. 1:20), offered his reconciling life to the Father in heaven, followed by his resurrection (Heb. 9:14), and realized the promise of cosmic reconciliation (Col. 1:15–20) under his rule over "the kingdom of light" (Col. 1:12–14). Hebrews 2:1–10 specifically says that the message the apostles transmitted was that Jesus of Nazareth, the eternal Son incarnate "tasted death for everyone" (2:3) and thereby regained our "crown of glory and honor" (cf. 2:9–10) through his death on the cross.

The royal implication of the cross can be seen in the observation that when Paul speaks of the significance of Jesus' death and resurrection, he repeatedly uses the title *christos* (e.g. Rom. 5:5–6; 14:9, 15; 1 Cor. 5:7; 8:11; 15:20; Gal. 2:21; 3:13).[11] As already noted, *christos* has royal associations. The Messiah is the son of David, the *Yahweh*-appointed and Spirit-equipped implementer, who "brings the people back to the liberating rule of God" (van der Kooi & van den Brink, 2017, p. 423). This idea follows the logic of the gospel narrative as well. Jesus of Nazareth was declared king at his birth (Mt. 2:2); anointed as king and empowered by the Holy Spirit for his kingly mission at his baptism (Mt. 3:13–17); recognized as king in his ministry by his first disciples (Jn. 1:49; 6:15), his enemies (Jn. 19:14), and himself (Lk. 23:2); and ultimately entered Jerusalem to die on the cross with the acclamation, "Your king is coming to you" (Mt. 21:5). During his trial, Jesus spoke of "my kingdom" (Jn. 18:36); received a

---

9 Aulén Gustaf (1969, p. 20) offers the following basic definition of *Christus Victor*: "*Christus Victor*—fights against and triumphs over the evil powers of the world, the 'tyrants' under which mankind is in bondage and suffering, and in Him God reconciles the world to Himself."

10 The Reformers understood the concept of "theological rank" and therefore made a threefold distinction between *articuli fundamentals* ("fundamental articles"), *articuli fundamentals secundarii* ("secondary fundamental articles"), and *articuli non-fundamentales* ("non-fundamental articles") (Muller, 1985, pp. 45–46).

11 See Hurtado (2003, pp. 100–101).

"crown" of thorns (Jn. 19:2); and was identified at his crucifixion with the announcement, "Behold your king!" (Jn. 19:14). Although he was mocked by the soldiers and Pharisees, the sign above his head denoted him as "King of the Jews" (Mk. 15:26). The cross is undoubtedly the decisive moment when Jesus finalized the initiation of the Father's kingdom on earth "through suffering" (Treat, 2014, p. 151).

According to the Scriptures

In 1 Corinthians 15:3–5, the Apostle twice affirms that the events of the Jesus story are "according to the Scriptures" (verses 3 and 4). This says that the story of the God-man as set forth in the gospel describes the prophetically foreordained action of the Creator in human history in such a way that its meaning and purpose are revealed. In this way, the gospel narrative maintains that the cross is not an unfortunate accident of history but the key to the triune Creator's plan for the salvation of all his creation from its enslavement under an illegitimate ruler. The life, death, resurrection, and enthronement of Jesus of Nazareth, the eternal Son incarnate, define all history from the beginning.

The repeated reference to the Scriptures also signifies that the gospel event is the hermeneutical norm of Scripture: "We can say that, while not all Scripture is the gospel, all Scripture is related to the gospel that is its centre" (Goldsworthy, 2006, p. 63). And because the gospel event is the heart of Scripture, Paul Althaus can write, "All Scripture points to Christ alone. Because Christ is the incarnate Word, the Bible can only be the Word of God if it deals with Christ." He adds, "Christ is Lord of the Scripture" (Althaus, 1966, pp. 74–81).

He Was Buried

In a New Testament letter to Christ-followers who appear to have had Jewish origins, we read an important statement concerning the death of Jesus of Nazareth: "Jesus who was made a little lower than the angels, is now crowned with glory and honour." This is so "because he suffered death, so that by the grace of God he might taste death for everyone" (Heb. 2:9). The confession that Jesus was buried is not a secondary element of the gospel. The burial of the body of the Christ highlights the fact that in the flesh and blood of Jesus of Nazareth, the eternal Son existentially experienced something that neither the other members of the Godhead nor the angelic spirits could. His incarnation through the grave to resurrection assures that our own body of blood and flesh is included in his rule on the heavenly throne (Moffitt, 2011, p. 50, n. 7).

Moreover, since you cannot bury a spirit, and since Scripture (Ps. 104:4) in particular, identifies angels as spirits—flames of fire—who are ministers,[12] the burial of the body of Jesus of Nazareth highlights the ontological contrast between the God-man and the angels (Ellingworth, 1993, pp. 144–145; Johnson, 2006, p. 899; Lane, 1991, pp. 1–8, 43–45; Peeler, 2014, pp. 74–75). This fact further buttresses my claim that the ontological identity of Jesus of Nazareth as the God-man sets him apart as the centre, measure, and goal of all that we are called to be and do as his followers. Fudge (1973, p. 13) rightly states:

> In him [Jesus], God found a man who gave what He had always wanted from man but which no man had ever given—a human life fully and always dedicated to pleasing God. In Christ, man's glorified potential was fully realized. This glory was not even planned for angels. It was not intended for other heavenly beings, earthly creatures or occupants of the subterranean depths. It was the Creator's original intention for man. And now one man is in that position. One man has a foothold in glory! And because He is a representative man, acting on behalf of all mankind, His people will one day enjoy the same position of glory.

The burial also highlights that Jesus of Nazareth in his humanity is the "pioneer" or the "model of faith" (Heb. 2:10) and not only the "basis of our faith." It emphasizes the importance of the rabbi Jesus of Nazareth as the "model" or "greatest exemplar" of our humanity (Heb. 12:2).

Hebrews 12:2 says that we are to "fix our gaze" on Jesus. We sometimes think that this means learning to focus on who God is rather than on ourselves and our problems. But that is not what the verse says. It urges us to keep our eyes focused on *Jesus*, who was selected from and elevated above his peers (Heb. 1:9; 2:6) and above the angels to the throne at the Father's right hand. In this way he has "been ushered into the promised inheritance [of Psalm 8] and placed at the pinnacle of God's creation, so too will those who are sanctified be (cf. Heb. 2:10–11; 12:2)" (Moffitt, 2011, p. 128). Moffitt claims that this argument hints at the presence and importance of Jesus' human body for the ultimate possession of our own inheritance. The human Jesus of Nazareth continues to be the focus and model of everything for those whom he has called. He is the only legitimate pattern and aim of our discipleship. In this sense, we Christians are not simply theologians. We are Jesus-centred theologians. We are not theists (believers in one God), we are Jesus-centered theists. We do not seek simply to love a vague, distant God with all our heart and soul and strength and mind; we love God the Father of our Lord Jesus of Nazareth, the Messiah in that complete way. And in so doing we bring glory and honour to the triune Creator and to Jesus of Nazareth, the flesh-and-blood eternal Son.

---

12 Heb 1:14 specifically states that angels are ministering spirits sent to serve.

He Was Raised on the Third Day

The testimony of Jesus' resurrection naturally belongs to the core of the apostolic message. "God raised Jesus from the dead" is the recurrent formula (Rom. 4:24; 10:9; 1 Cor. 6:14; 15:4; see also Ac. 2:24, 30, 32; 4:10). The resurrection provided the proof and confirmation of Jesus' messiahship and uniqueness:

> God has affirmed him as the Messiah and has rehabilitated him. He made him a Kyrios and a Christos, a Lord and an Anointed One (Ac. 2:36). By raising him from the dead and clothing him with divine glory, God, as it were, positioned himself beside Jesus and said: "This man belongs with me" (see Rom. 1:4). (van der Kooi & van den Brink, 2017, p. 435)

As David Moffitt convincingly argues, the writer of Hebrews identifies Jesus' death as the moment that sets in motion the sequence of events that ultimately results in his exaltation to the throne at the Father's right hand. These subsequent events are the resurrection of Jesus' human body, his atoning offering—that is, his very life—and his enthronement:

> Because Jesus' human body rose to indestructible life, he is able to present his blood (which in a biblically informed, sacrificial context is language for life, not language that symbolizes death), his body, and himself in the very place where the author [of Heb. 9:14] says he presented these things—before God *in heaven*. Jesus' atoning offering occurred precisely where the author depicts it occurring—in heaven, not on the cross. (Moffitt, 2011, p. 42; emphasis in original)

Moffitt's affirmation is based on a detailed reading of how Jesus' blood functions metaphorically in the letter to the Hebrews, which is driven by the logic of the two great moments of Yom Kippur (also known as the Day of Atonement, described in Lev. 16:1–34; 23:27–28). Those two central moments in the once-a-year sacrifice are the death of the sacrificial animal and the offering of its blood sprinkled on the ark of the covenant. The texts in Leviticus fully agree with Moffitt on this important point, confirming why Jesus' blood shed on the cross is crucial to our salvation. The apostolic gospel, however, does not stop there. It highlights the second great focal point of our salvation, that moment when the God-man presented his own life—that is, his blood—before God in the holy of holies in heaven after his resurrection (Heb. 9:11–14). Moffitt writes, "The point is that in and of itself the death or slaughter of the victim, while necessary to procure the blood/life that is offered, has no particular atoning significance" (2011, p. 271). The two moments can neither be separated, nor should they be conflated. In the same vein, Moffitt admonishes us that we should not "spiritualize" or "take as a metaphor" the language of Jesus' offering in heaven. Instead, we should understand it literally:

After his death and resurrection, Jesus ascended into heaven, entered that tabernacle, and went into the inner sanctum where God's throne is. There he presented himself before God, alive and in his glorified, human body. Jesus' living, human presence was pleasing to God and accepted by God for atonement. … There, once the offering of his life was accepted, he was invited to take the throne and status promised by God to humanity. Thus, Jesus is the first human being to dwell fully in God's presence *qua* human being. (Moffitt, 2011, p. 296)

Paul applies the words of Psalm 110:1 to the resurrected Jesus of Nazareth in 1 Corinthians 15:25 and proclaims that he must reign until he has put everything under his feet. We often insist that this affirmation points to Jesus as "the image of God" (*imago dei*) but fail to mention that it also reveals him as the image of being human (*imago hominis*). I agree with Treat (2014, p. 158) who writes that "the fact that the kingship of Jesus of Nazareth, the Christ, is attributed primarily to his humanity is often over-looked" (see also van der Kooi & van den Brink, 2017, pp. 435–436).

He Appeared to Peter

Based on 1 Cor. 15:3 and 15:17, "And if Christ has not been raised, your faith is futile; you are still in your sins," most scholars stress that together with the sacrifice of Jesus of Nazareth on the cross, the resurrection is of first importance in the gospel (e.g., Horton, 2011, p. 496). There is, however, a clear connection between the argument of 1 Corinthians 15 and the restoration of the Creator's intended rule over the order of creation by the resurrected Jesus of Nazareth. The presence of death in 1 Cor. 15:21, which came through Adam, is counteracted by the resurrection of the risen Jesus of Nazareth, the eternal Son incarnate, in 1 Cor. 15:22. In her detailed study of Paul's theology of glory in Romans, Haley Goranson-Jacob convincingly argues that Paul's contrast between Adam and the "man of heaven is *a*, if not, *the* foundation for his anthropology, hamartiology, and soteriology in Romans" (2018, p. 80). Goranson-Jacob rightly claims that the death and resurrection of Jesus of Nazareth together make possible our own transfer from the powers of the old dominion to participation with Christ, the new Adam, as redeemed humanity (2018, p. 138). The messiahship of Jesus of Nazareth is not "showcased by the sheer presence of his body" following the resurrection, but "by what he does *with* the body":

The Son of God was raised with an incorruptible body, but … the body is only an indication of the fact that the Messiah now reigns over the powers of sin and death. Paul's point is that the Son reigns in glory over his inheritance with his new body, and believers, with their renewed bodies, will do the same. (Goranson-Jacob, 2018, pp. 252–253)

Multiple accounts in the gospels describe persons seeing, hearing, and touching the resurrected Jesus. Evidently, the writers not only believed that those people had really seen Jesus alive and physically present, but they also realized that his resurrection signified that a new creation had begun.

In 2 Corinthians, Paul declares that the very Good News about Jesus' death and resurrection means that his followers should "no longer live for themselves" (2 Cor. 5:15). They should change their outlook and especially learn to do things differently in their relationship with others. Life in the new creation means that everything has changed, because people who are in the new Adam no longer think the same way (2 Cor. 5:16). Because we are being recreated into the image of the God-man, we live with the passion expressed by Paul: "Not I, but Christ" (Gal. 2:20). This is, as Larry Richards (1998, p. 125) states, "the grandest single theme in all the Bible. In the beginning God created; God is presently recreating human lives; and God will soon create again, a new heaven and a new earth (Rev. 21:1–5)."

This same scheme can be seen in Colossians, where participation with Christ occurs through a person's dying with Christ (Col. 2:20), being buried with the Son, and being raised with him in baptism (Col. 2:12; 3:1). Paul's theological anthropology is firmly rooted in Christ, the firstborn from the dead who reigns in his kingdom in glory as the perfect human. Wright (1986, p. 138) fittingly describes the "new man" as "the solidarity of those who are incorporated into, and hence patterned on, the Messiah who is himself the true Man. ... At last, in Christ, human beings can be what God intended them to be." This description climaxes in Col. 3:5, where Paul transitions from articulating the believer's position in Christ's kingdom to their lived expression of that fact.

This concept inseparably unites salvation to intentional discipleship to the Christ. Salvation means entrance into the new sphere of creation where Jesus of Nazareth reigns. Such is the apostolic Good News! Life can and should be radically different. Progressive transformation in conformity to the *imago hominis* is the goal of our salvation. We are called to be stamped by the characteristics of what Grentz (2001, p. 236) has labeled the *imago Christi*. This is our destiny as those who belong to the new humanity he has inaugurated. In the next chapter, I will look specifically at what it means to be a "believer" and to "live by faith" (Hab. 2:4; Rom. 1:17; Gal. 2:20; 3:11–12; Heb. 10:38) under the reign of the Christ.

Questions to Think About

1. I argue in this chapter that Jesus of Nazareth embraces in his person all of reality, namely God and the realm of creation, and I quote another scholar who insists that the attribution of the title of Lord to Jesus of Nazareth is our way of attributing to him the highest honor. How can

using the title "Lord" only when referring to Jesus function as a corrective to imperfect models of discipleship and Christian growth?

2. This chapter presents two possible interpretations of when the reign of Jesus the Messiah begins. Which one do you believe represents the best reading of the Scriptures? What are the implications of this for the understanding of the goal of salvation and of discipleship?

3. I propose that in Romans 5:12–8:39, Paul describes the saving grace of the Lord Jesus of Nazareth as entrance into his restorative kingship. Do you agree? If so, what might the implications be for sharing the gospel and for developing maturity in Christian discipleship?

4. Review 1 Corinthians 15:3–5. What are the four elements that form the apostolic Good News? Which ones would you say your church is good or not so good at highlighting and communicating? How could you contribute to improvement where the church's performance is weak?

11. Faith, the Link between the Gospel and Discipleship

Why is faith so important to Christians? Many of us would answer by pointing to Hebrews 11:6, which affirms that without faith it is impossible to please God. Even for theologians, the centrality of faith is so obvious that its meaning tends to be taken for granted. But what is faith? As with many of our key words, an adequate response is difficult to construct. According to Paul Tillich, few religious words are more exposed to misunderstandings, distortions, and problematic definitions than faith, despite the fact that it is irreplaceable (Seckler & Berchtold, 1988, p. 261). Teresa Morgan (2017, p. 17) makes a similar observation:

> If one thing is clear from the wealth of scholarship in the last century alone, it is that no one study or approach can do full justice to the meanings which can be elicited from *pistis* (faith) language in the New Testament, let alone in later Christian tradition. Nor will any one approach satisfy everyone, or perhaps anyone: the subject is too large, too significant, and too much pondered.

In the Old Testament, for instance, there is no expression that is used consistently to refer to the nature of a person's faith. To describe the attitude that we might call faith, the Old Testament uses derivatives of several root words, such as *aman* (solid, certain, reliable), *batah* (confidence), *quiwwah* (hope), *hikkah* (wait), and *hasah* (shelter). Nijay Gupta (2020, pp. 5–6) writes that this multiplicity of concepts led the people who translated the Hebrew Scriptures into the Greek Septuagint to focus on three Hebrew words in particular. The first is *batach*, used in the sense of "trust" or "reliability." The second, *emun* or *emunah*, found primarily in contexts related to human relationships, often refers to people who, in Gupta's words, "have the capacity to remain stable (i.e. faithful) amid the unsettling circumstances of life" (2020, p. 6). The third term, *eminot*, can be translated as faithfulness or dependability.

In the New Testament, as in the Hebrew Scriptures, faith must characterize people's fundamental attitude toward God. The frequent use of the noun *pistis* (240 times), the verb *pisteuō*, and the adjective *pistos* (67 times) signals that faith is a central concept of the New Testament. *Pistis* is the short formulation of a complex reality that carries a wide range of meaning. It can be used to refer to an individual who wrongly believes in incorrect eschatological understandings (as in Mk. 13:21), or to one who responds correctly to the preaching of John the Baptist (Mt. 21:32; Mk. 11:30). It can describe an individual who believes the testimony of Scripture (Jn. 2:22), the prophets (Ac. 24:14; Lk. 24:25), or the words of Jesus of Nazareth (Jn. 2:22; 8:45).

In linguistic terms, we would say that *pistis* is polysemic—i.e., that this word can have several possible meanings. Teresa Morgan's in-depth study of this word and its Latin equivalent *fides*, as used within the early Roman Empire and among the first followers of Jesus of Nazareth, is among the most complete of such examinations to date. Morgan observes how easily scholars in distinct disciplines bring different assumptions to the study of *pistis* in the New Testament:

> One thing that almost all studies of New Testament *pistis*, and Christian faith have in common is that they are deeply influenced by … Augustine's division of faith into *fides quae creditor* and *fides qua creditor*, 'the faith which is believed' (the propositional content of faith) and 'the faith by which it is believed' (that which takes place in the heart and mind of the believer). (Morgan, 2017, pp. 11–12)

Morgan (2017, p. 13) concludes that as a result most biblical and theological explorations of *pistis* "focus on 'trust,' 'faithfulness,' 'propositional belief,' and related meanings." However, she writes, "some have seen other ranges of meaning as equally important." In this regard, she cites James Kinneavy (1987), who maintains that *pistis* carries more the connotation of persuasion, and notes its meaning as "evidence" or "grounds of belief." These authors correctly demonstrate the importance of taking into careful consideration the historical, cultural, and literary context in determining the precise meaning of *pistis*, rather than projecting our unexamined presuppositions on this most important biblical notion. In other words, we must look synchronically at the notion of faith within the total semantic field in which *pistis* and its associated words appear in the New Testament. Morgan (2017, p. 23) rightly claims that this context that gives meaning to the word *pistis* "is as culturally unique, definitive, and distinctive as a fingerprint."

Morgan (2017, p. 24) observes, however, that "the extensive literature on belief … typically focuses on propositional belief rather than on relationships involving both belief and trust." Even when we do link the two together, in our attempts to avoid falling into "salvation by works" we stress that in this relationship between belief and trust, God is active in our justification and we are passive. "Grace gives, and faith gratefully receives—and even faith must itself be seen as a gracious gift of God," Martin Luther said (Pelikan & Lehmann, 1972, p. 34). Old Testament scholar Walter Kaiser (1998, p. 54) exemplifies this understanding of *pistis* as non-meritorious acceptance of God's grace when he contemplates the exemplary faith of Abraham:

God does the accounting; God does the reckoning; God does the crediting; God does the justifying—the declaring of this man to be just. Abraham does nothing. God gave the promise which Abraham had only to receive. Sometimes the question is asked, is believing a work in itself? Do we have "faith in faith"? Can we pull ourselves up by our own bootstraps? The answer, of course, is that faith is passive. It is a passive act. It is like receiving a Christmas present: we put out our hands to take, to accept, to receive. There is nothing more than a passive act here. We don't earn our Christmas presents. The same is true with faith.

Matthew Bates (2017) agrees that the language of faith does, as Kaiser claims, often include the passive element of believing that something is true or trustworthy, as in "I believe that God exists" or "I believe that Jesus died for my sins." However, he also correctly recognizes that *pisteuō* and its associated terms also carry more active meanings (see also Wallis, 1995, p. 7). In this regard, Morgan (2017, p. 31) writes, "We might assume that active and passive meanings cannot be in play at the same time, but in practice they often are."

In his recent work on Paul and mission, Michael Gorman (2015, pp. 90–91) argues for translating *pistis* as "faithfulness," "believing allegiance," "faithful allegiance," or "trusting loyalty." He correctly defines this attitude as "a posture of both heartfelt devotion and concrete commitment." Bates (2017, p. 5) prefers the active notion of "allegiance," which he affirms "captures what is most vital for salvation—mental assent, sworn fidelity, and embodied loyalty." Gupta (2020) objects vigorously to viewing *pistis* as only a kind of passive reliance on Christ. Rather, based on a survey of the use of the term and its derivatives in ancient non-Jewish and Jewish literature, the gospels, and Paul's letters, he argues that it carries a relational dynamic that has often been too toned down in our current understanding.

Our understanding of *pistis* as trust or belief in what is promised and as a passive "receiving and resting in Christ" (Horton, 2011, p. 581) is too limited. So is seeing it only as "recognition of the royal power of the cross" (Treat, 2014, p. 230). Perceiving it as believing and professing the right things (Bird, 2013, pp. 56–57) is also insufficient. So is describing *pistis* only as "a trusting commitment to God that is accompanied by a sense of wonder, respect, and love" (van der Kooi & van den Brink, 2017, p. 50). As good as these definitions are, each one must be expanded if we are to be true to the biblical use of the term.

"Faith" and "belief" are not inspired words. Their use to translate *pistis* is often appropriate, but sometimes it isn't. Moreover, the applied meaning of those two words today is "frequently distant from the real meaning of *pistis* and *pisteuō* in the Bible" (Bates, 2019, p. 60). I find sufficient warrant to translate *pistis* by "allegiance" when the surrounding context is presenting the appropriate response to the gospel. For that reason, the remainder of this study concentrates on this more active understanding of *pistis*.

Reasons to Translate *Pistis* as Allegiance

Bates (2017) proposes several reasons why we should translate the Greek word *pistis* as allegiance[1] more often that we do. First, he maintains that even if the word does not *always* or even *usually* mean allegiance, it does carry that meaning from time to time in the New Testament. Second, Bates stresses that because of Paul's view of Jesus of Nazareth primarily as the king (Messiah, Christ) and as Lord, it would be natural for him to use *pistis* in the sense of allegiance to explain how the people of God should respond to Christ's call. Bates further argues that translating *pistis* by allegiance makes some "difficult" New Testament texts such as Romans 1:3–5 and 16:25–26 more understandable. He also cites the use of *pistis* within the Roman empire as another reason to prefer this particular meaning.

We will consider these arguments in more detail below, but first I want to restate, as Bates also does, that *pistis* does *not always* signify allegiance! When we see people place their faith in Jesus for healing, for instance, allegiance is not in view here, but rather a certainty of heart and mind (for example Mt. 8:10; 9:2, 22, 29; 14:31; 15:28; 16:8). When Jesus states that a person who has faith the size of a mustard seed can "move a mountain" (Mt. 17:20–21), allegiance is not the most appropriate translation for *pistis*. Or when Jesus asks blind men if they believe that he can heal them (Mt. 9:28), he is certainly not asking them to pledge allegiance to his ability to do that miraculous act.

But in other cases, a call for allegiance is manifestly present. In 2 Thessalonians 1:4, Paul writes, "Therefore among God's churches we boast about your perseverance and *pistis* in all the persecutions and trials you are enduring." Given the immediate connection with perseverance, Paul seems to be using *pistis* here more in the sense of loyalty, faithfulness, or allegiance than mental assent (Bates, 2019, pp. 61-62). Paul is saying, "I am proud of you because of your perseverance and loyalty." Bates explains the importance of attaching this particular meaning to the word *pistis* here:

> This informs our understanding of the relationship between *pistis* and the gospel. The presence or absence of loyalty (*pistis*) during these trials (2 Th. 1:4) is specifically the criterion for whether one is helped or harmed by the Lord Jesus's judgment when these difficulties continue (v. 7). The Lord Jesus will be revealed from heaven and will take "vengeance on those who do not know God and on those who do not *obey the gospel* of our Lord Jesus" (v. 8). Contextually, loyalty (*pistis*) *to the Lord Jesus* when experiencing difficulties has been equated with *obedience to the gospel*. (Bates, 2019, p. 62; emphasis in original)

---

1 Allegiance can be understood as faithfulness, reliability, fidelity, and commitment (Danker, 1969, pp. 818–820). Bates (2019, p. 208) writes, "Allegiance does not exclude inward trust in Jesus's atonement. Yet it refocuses faith's aim. Allegiance stresses that saving faith (*pistis*) in the Bible is above all outward facing, embodied, and relationally directed toward a crucified, risen, ruling *king*."

There are many New Testament examples of texts where the word *pistis* might more appropriately be translated by loyalty or faithfulness or allegiance than by faith. This observation is of utmost importance for a gospel-driven theology of discipleship, because *pistis* is the proper response to the Lord Jesus, the Christ. For instance, when Paul tells the Philippian jailer, "*Pisteuson* on the Lord Jesus and you will be saved, both you and your household" (Ac. 16:31), is he saying "place your trust" in the Lord Jesus?[2] Or might the context indicate that Paul is urging the jailer to make an embodied switch in his loyalty from the emperor's magistrates to Jesus as the ultimate sovereign? This latter interpretation would indicate that *pistis* was, for the primitive followers of the Lord Jesus of Nazareth, a fundamentally relational concept and practice centring on trust, trustworthiness, and loyal allegiance (Morgan, 2015, p. 503). This observation brings us to the first of the four reasons given by Bates to translate *pistis* by allegiance more often than we do.

Pistis *Often Means Relational Allegiance in First-Century (BCE) Texts*

The first example proposed by Bates (2015, p. 4) to support the claim that we should translate *pistis* by allegiance more often than we do is a text written in Greek approximately 150 years before the death of Jesus of Nazareth. This text contains a letter written by a king named Demetrius, who was concerned that his rival, Alexander might have already formed an alliance with the Jewish people. In seeking to persuade the Jews to support him, Demetrius wrote:

> King Demetrius to the nation of the Jews, greetings. Since you have kept your agreement with us and have continued your friendship with us, and have not sided with our enemies, we have heard of it and rejoiced. Now continue still to keep faith (*pistis*) with us, and we will repay you with good for what you do for us. (1 Macc. 10:25–27)

Here Demetrius is asking the Jews to continue to show *pistis*—loyalty or allegiance—to him rather than to his rival. Bates (2017, p. 4) asks:

> Could it be that when Paul and others talk about salvation by "faith," not by works, they intend something close to what Demetrius means by *pistis*—so that we should translate, "It is by grace you have been saved through allegiance" (Eph. 2:8)?

Bates offers many other examples to support his position which reviews many ancient texts, not just Demetrius, focusing on the meaning of *pistis* in relation to salvation; my main interest is in the overall relational aspects of *pistis* in our bond to the Lord Jesus of Nazareth. Morgan (2015, p. 117) furnishes many examples from ancient Jewish, Greek, and Roman societies to

---

2 This meaning of "place your trust" is apparent in Acts 2:44 and 26:18.

illustrate this relational feature. She concludes that *pistis* "is one of the few qualities which are equally at home in the domestic and public spheres: in the family, the marketplace, the council chamber, the temple, the palace, and the battlefield." Morgan shows that this is a key quality that characterizes the ideal relationships of wives and husbands, parents and children, master and slaves, patrons and clients, subjects and rulers, armies and commanders, friends, allies, fellow human beings, and gods and their worshippers.

Pistis *in Pauline Letters*

Gupta (2020, pp. 56–57) warns us that as we approach Pauline texts that use *pistis*, we often do so with the popular misunderstanding that the Apostle is using primarily religious language, or that he is attempting to oppose faith language to some people's theology of works. Instead, Gupta rightly asserts that we should reconsider Paul's use of *pistis* as discussing a new type of relationship with the Creator that occurs via the Christ-relation.

The work of Douglas Campbell (2005) on *pistis* moves in the same direction. In his *Quest for Paul's Gospel*, Campbell explains that Paul uses *pistis* often in the sense of "faithfulness" because this corresponds to the predominant meaning of the word in both the Septuagint and other ancient Greek texts:

> This dominance is probably because faithfulness is such a ubiquitous feature of human relationships, and especially in the context of a hierarchical and highly status-conscious society like the one Paul inhabited. Ideally, patrons and clients act faithfully towards one another, as should ideal families, marriages, political associations, religious and covenantal associations, and so on. The partners in these relationships should be reliable, trustworthy and faithful to one another. (p. 186)[3]

Campbell further maintains that the semantic domain of *pistis* includes notions of obedience as well as endurance, loyalty, and trustworthiness:

> A faithful servant is also an obedient servant. And hence we find *pistis*, when used in this basic sense, sometimes placed alongside notions of submission and obedience in Paul, which were often denoted in Greek by *hupakoē*, or the verbs *hupakouō* and *hupotassō*. Obedience as a theme *per se* is of course readily apparent in Paul. And even Christ is explicitly described as obedient to God in certain important texts. (Campbell, 2005, p. 187)

---

3 To substantiate this claim, Campbell points to numerous Pauline passages where *pistis* carries the meaning of faithfulness, such as Rom. 1:5, 8, 12; 16:26; 2 Cor. 5:7; arguably Gal. 5:5, 6, 22; Phil. 1:25, 27; Phm. 5, 6, cf. Eph. 1:15; 6:16, 23; Col. 1:4, 23; 2:5, 7, 12; 2 Th. 1:3, 4, 11.

Flowing from these observations concerning this very commonplace use of *pistis* in Paul's world and that of his first readers, Bates looks at how Romans 3:3 has been translated:

> What if some did not have faith (*ēpistēsan*)? Will their lack of faith (*apistia*) nullify God's faithfulness (*pistin*)?

As Bates points out, all New Testament scholars agree that *pistis* in this verse does not refer to merely believing in something. Instead, it refers to God's faithfulness toward his people.

Of course, Paul clearly expects followers of the Christ to *believe* that certain things are true, and he writes with great earnestness to correct people who seem to believe other things (1 Cor. 15:1–17; Rom. 6:8; 2 Cor. 10:15; Gal. 2:16; 1 Th. 4:13–14). In all his epistles, Paul attaches great importance to right thinking and correct beliefs. As Campbell (2005, p. 183) states, "The Pauline corpus is nothing less than an extended 'battle for belief.'" Moreover, a certain priority of beliefs, with some being more central than others, can be perceived in Paul's preaching and teaching:

> We tend to designate these "the gospel" … These beliefs are linked to the fact of Christ's resurrection and heavenly enthronement. The *locus classicus* for this is Rom. 10:9–10, but the point is widely attested; see, in addition, Rom. 4:24–25; 6:8; 1 Cor. 1:1–17; 2 Cor. 4:14; and 1 Th. 4:14. (Campbell, 2005, p. 183)

This statement is consistent with my overarching theme that the gospel (properly understood) should drive all our theology and practice. But as these scholars also point out, *pistis* is quasi-exclusively understood as certainty of heart, or an attitude of confidence toward God and his words. However, the intended meaning of *pistis* is often most appropriately understood as embodied loyalty, submissive service, and obedient faithfulness. For instance, Bates's proposed translation of Romans 3:21–25 reflects the Pauline logic of the surrounding verses:

> But now the righteousness of God has been manifested apart from the law, although the Law and the Prophets bear witness to it—the righteousness of God through the *allegiance* of Jesus the Christ[4] for all who *give allegiance*. For there is no distinction: for all have sinned and fall short of the glory of God, and are justified by his grace as a gift, through the redemption that is in the Christ Jesus, whom God put forward as a propitiation by his blood, through his *allegiance*.[5] (Bates, 2017, pp. 81–82)

---

4 Or "through *allegiance* to Jesus the Christ." See the subsequent discussion regarding the translation options.
5 Or "to be received by allegiance."

I could cite many relevant passages from Paul, and both Campbell and Bates offer several in their discussions,[6] but I will narrow the field of view to two texts in 1 Corinthians:

> For since, in the wisdom of God, the world did not know God through wisdom, God was pleased through the folly of the proclamation [of a crucified king] to save those who *give allegiance*. (1 Cor. 1:21, as translated by Bates, 2017, p. 83)

> Now, brothers and sisters, I bring to your attention the gospel that I gospelled to you, which you received, on which you stand, and through which also you are being saved-that is, if you hold fast to the word that I gospelled to you, unless you have *given allegiance* in vain. (1 Cor. 15:1–2, as translated by Bates, 2017, p. 83)

Considering that the notion of allegiance includes mental assent and a promise of faithfulness, loyal acts, obedience, and submission, the use of that word seems appropriate in these and arguably in many other texts. This might help to explain the absolute permanence of *pistis* alongside hope and love in 1 Corinthians 13:13: "And now these three things remain: *pistis*, hope and love." Scholars have questioned how faith can be permanent when it ought to be replaced by sight (cf. 2 Cor. 5:7, see for instance Houghton, 1996; Fee, 1987, pp. 650–651; Fitzmyer, 1983, pp. 501–502). It is arguably true that some aspects of *pistis*—for example, being persuaded by things we do not see (cf. Heb. 1:1) or the anticipation of things hoped for—will no longer be needed in the heavenly state. But when *pistis* is understood in its fuller sense as embodied allegiance to our Lord Jesus of Nazareth, who is the firstborn from the dead and the ruler of the kings of the earth (cf. Rev. 1:5), then we can correctly say that faith is eternal.

Other scholars have concluded that Paul probably had the dimension of allegiance in mind quite often when he used *pistis* in his epistles. For example, N. T. Wright (2015, p. 14) states, "For Paul, *pistis* is personal allegiance to God who is now known as 'the God who resurrected Jesus from the dead'; a personal confession that 'Jesus is Lord.'" Along the same line, Michael Gorman (2004, p. 92) writes:

> Since for Paul faith is not only the initial response of a person to the gospel message, but also a person's ongoing posture of devotion and commitment, the word "faithfulness"—meaning "trusting faithfulness" or "believing allegiance"—is a better rendering of *pistis* and its cognates than is "faith."

In *Paul and the Gift*, John Barclay (2015), often links faith and allegiance: "What now counts for worth is only one's status in Christ, and the consistency of one's allegiance to him" (pp. 397–398). In fact, Barclay uses "allegiance" 34

---

6 In passing, Bates (2017, pp. 81–82) offers these examples: Rom. 1:5, 8, 12; 5:1; Gal. 2:16, 20; 5:4–6; Phil. 3:8–11; 1 Pet. 1:5–9; Rev. 2:13; 14:12.

times in his book, such as in this statement: "Paul's allegiance is now exclusively to Christ, the source of his new life in faith" (2015, pp. 397–398).

Obedience of Faith and Law of the Christ

Translating *pistis* by "allegiance" rather than by "faith" might also help us to make sense of some puzzling texts in his letters (Bates, 2017, pp. 85–87). For example, Paul twice speaks of his gospel as aiming to produce what has traditionally termed "the obedience of faith":

> The gospel concerning his Son ... through whom we have received grace and apostleship to bring about the obedience of faith in behalf of his name among all the nations. (Rom. 1:3, 5)

> Now to him who is able to strengthen you according to my gospel and the proclamation of Jesus the Christ, according to the mystery kept secret for long ages but now disclosed and through the prophetic writings, having been made known according to the command of the eternal God in order to bring about the obedience of faith among all the nations. (Rom. 16:25–26)

These exhortations to the "obedience of faith" (*hypakoēn pisteōs*) have been seen by some scholars as smacking of external performance. The ordinary solution seems to fall back on the notion that "the obedience of faith" is an equivalent of the obedience "required by faith" (Cranfield, 1975, p. 20). Others prefer to place the emphasis on post-conversion commitment, or the "obedience that springs from faith" (Davies, 2015). A few scholars have suggested that faith in this instance denotes a body of doctrine that one is to obey or to preach: "to promote obedience to the faith." Others take faith here as a definition of obedience: "the obedience which consists in faith" (Murray, 1964). Recognizing that the meaning is not entirely clear, Stanley Porter (2011, pp. 183–184) proposes that it may be either the faith of those who are obedient or a call for obedience that results in faith. Käsemann (1994) finds here an obedience that includes acceptance of the message of salvation. Schreiner (1998, p. 42) insists, however, that it is unlikely that "the obedience of faith" should be confined to a single act of obedience that occurred when the gospel was first believed, or that faith and obedience should be separated, as if a believer could have the former without the latter. All these scholars are attempting to avoid confusing works and faith. Bates argues that there is a better solution to this problem:

> If we recognize that the climax of the gospel is Jesus's enthronement and that *pistis* is predominately allegiance, then Paul's point is lucid: the gospel is purposed toward bringing about *the practical obedience characteristic of allegiance to a king*—what I have termed *enacted allegiance*. (2017, p. 86; emphasis in original)

This understanding of *pistis* as enacted allegiance also helps make sense of the positive place of the "law of Christ" in Pauline epistles:

> Carry each other's burdens, and in this way you will fulfill *the law of Christ*. (Gal. 6:2; cf. Gal. 5:14; Rom. 13:9)

> To those not having the law I became like one not having the law (though I am not free from God's law but am under *Christ's law*) so as to win those not having the law. (1 Cor. 9:21)

> ... because through Christ Jesus the *law of the Spirit* of life set me free from the law of sin and death. (Rom. 8:2)

If faith in the Christ is understood as enacted allegiance to "king Jesus" of Nazareth, as Bates proposes, the reasons why his followers saw the law of Christ as something positive become evident. This was not an attempt to establish their righteousness through obedience, but the position of a faithful slave in relationship to his or her benevolent lord. In this way, *pistis* is not fundamentally opposed to every law. Instead, faith in the Lord Jesus of Nazareth, the Christ, is above all enacted allegiance to the reigning king.

Joshua Jipp (2015) correctly expands on what fulfilling the law of Christ entails in terms of enacted allegiance:

> Participation in the person and pattern of Christ supports the notion that to "fulfill the law of Christ" (Gal. 6:2) is to reenact the same patten of Christ's fulfillment of Torah in his self-giving love for others (Gal. 5:14) and that the empowerment to do so derives not only from Christ's providing the perfect paradigm and embodiment of neighbor-love but also by means of uniting his people to himself and sharing his transformative presence with them such that they are incorporated into his cruciform pattern of love for the other. (p. 67)

This conviction is foundational to any gospel-driven theology of discipleship and disciple-making.

Allegiance, Gospel, and Empire

Not only was *pistis* widely used to describe faithfulness and loyalty in all kinds of hierarchical relationships in the world of Jesus and his first followers, but it was also highlighted in the "fundamental gospel of the Caesar-religion" (Georgi, 1997, p. 149). This observation emphasizes the probable allegiance overtones of Paul's constant use of the titles "Lord" and "Christ" to refer to Jesus of Nazareth. It also points to the fact that in his letters Paul used language that was central to imperial claims of his time.

For instance, the goddess *Fides*, loyalty or faithfulness, was understood to be active through the empire's rulers. Augustus, the emperor who reigned during the life of Jesus of Nazareth (from 31 BCE to 14 CE), saw himself as the embodiment of Rome's loyalty or faithfulness to treaties and alliances

(Livius, 2020, pp. 31–34). In the text *Augustus, Res Gestae*, which describes Rome's universal friendship with foreign powers and rulers, one finds the summary statement that under the principate of Augustus many previously un-befriended peoples "discovered the *pistis* of the Roman people" (Livius, 2020). Beginning in the time of Augustus, *fides,* the Latin synonym of *pistis,* was reassessed and assumed weightier dimensions (Georgi, 1997, p. 149). The Caesar represented the *fides* of Rome in the sense of loyalty, faithfulness to treaty obligations, uprightness, truthfulness, honesty, confidence, and conviction—all, as it were, understood as a Roman monopoly. The ancient cult of the goddess *Fides* was revived under Augustus, and the word *fides* appeared frequently on coins.

This use of *pistis* in the imperial rhetoric within the Greco-Roman world of Paul's day is the last reason Bates offers to justify translating the word as allegiance rather than as faith in some important New Testament verses. Warren-Carter (2006, pp. 89–91) also argues that many words, though "religious" from our point of view as well as in the first century, were also profoundly "political." By using such loaded terms as *euangelion,*[7] *pistis, dikaiosynēn* (righteousness, justice), and *eirēnēn* (peace) as central concepts in his epistles, Paul evokes their association with Roman political theology. N. T. Wright (2000, p. 172) makes the same claim:

> Paul's declaration that the gospel of King Jesus reveals God's *dikaiosynēn* must also be read as a deliberate laying down of a challenge to the imperial pretension. If justice is wanted, it will be found not in the *euangelion* that announces Caesar as Lord but in the *euangelion* of Jesus.

Pistis and *fides*, in Greek and Roman thinking, are understood as powerfully functional and transformative. *Pistis* is an allegiance that makes possible new relationships and communities (Morgan, 2015, pp. 174–175).

The Dimensions of Allegiance

According to Bates (2017, pp. 92–99), when we look at the ways in which *pistis* was used to indicate enacted allegiance during the New Testament era, we find that it included three dimensions (although not in every context or instance): *intellectual agreement* that the elements of the gospel of King Jesus correspond to reality; a *confession of loyalty* to Jesus in recognition of his universal reign; and an *embodied fidelity* as a citizen of his realm. Bates recognizes that he is proposing a distinct alternative to the classic definitions of faith, but he justifies his proposal by contending that the goal of faith has often been slightly misaimed toward the forgiveness of sin in the dominant

---

7 On the Roman imperial connotations of the "gospel," see Jipp (2015, pp. 77–138) and Elliott (2000, pp. 17–39).

understanding. Contrary to this widely believed goal of faith, Bates rightly maintains that *pistis* has as much to do with recognizing the ontological identity of Jesus of Nazareth as with his death on the cross. Bates also insists that the dominant understanding of *pistis* inappropriately imposes a dimension of interiority that is foreign to the Greco-Roman understanding. In other words, he argues that the incomplete understanding of the goal of faith as personal salvation does not sufficiently maintain in the foreground the lived reality of embodied fidelity (or what I call intentional discipleship to Jesus of Nazareth). Let's look a little more closely at these facets of *pistis*.

Intellectual Agreement

Paul affirms the importance of intellectual assent in the process of placing one's faith in the Christ (cf. Rom. 10:14). Similarly, the author of John's gospel writes so that we may come to believe (*pisteuēte*) that Jesus is the Messiah, the Son of God, and that through believing (*pisteuontes*) we may have life in his name (Jn. 20:30–31). Embracing the Jesus story as true is of utmost importance, as John's use of *pistis* frequently emphasizes (Jn. 1:7, 50; 2:22–23; and many other passages).

However as necessary as it is, intellectual assent is not enough. Much of the logic of the gospel of John appears in one compressed statement in which John explains why Jesus performed his miraculous water-to-wine sign during the wedding in Cana: "This, the first of his signs, Jesus did at Cana in Galilee, and manifested his glory. And his disciples put their *pistis* (*episteusan*) in him" (Jn. 2:11). This goal of intellectual assent to the Jesus story, leading to faithfulness embodied in obedient action, can also be seen in John 3:36: "Whoever believes (*pisteoun*) in the Son has eternal life, but whoever is not obeying (*apeithōn*, present active participle) the Son will not see life, for God's wrath remains on him."

Confession of Loyalty

Bates argues that allegiance starts with intellectual agreement but that more is required. He points to Romans 10:9, "If you confess with your mouth that Jesus is Lord and you *pistis* (*pisteusēs*) in your heart that God raised him from the dead, you will be saved." The significance of this short Pauline confession of faith is revealed when it is situated within the reasoning Paul develops throughout this letter.

In Romans 9:30–33, the Apostle laments that Israel approached the law wrongly, as a matter of observance rather than trust in *Yahweh*. When he testifies regarding Israel's misinformed "zeal" (Rom. 10:2), he knows from personal experience that this is true (Gal. 1:14; Phil. 3:6). He comments that his fellow Jews seek to embody *dikaiosynēn* (righteousness) through their heritage as sons of Abraham, the covenants, the receiving of the Torah, the temple worship, and the promises (Rom. 9:4–5). And the Apostle argues that their failure to "submit themselves" to *Yahweh's* righteousness was to be expected, insofar as mere human effort cannot submit to God's law from the heart (Rom. 8:7).

Thus, Paul argues, Jesus of Nazareth, the second Adam (Rom. 5:12–19), is the "end" (*telos*) of the law for righteousness, replacing it in his own being with the reign of righteousness (Rom. 9:4; cf. Rom. 5:17). Throughout the epistle to the Romans, there is a clear semantic relationship between the righteous obedience of Jesus of Nazareth to his Father, even to the point of embracing death on the cross (cf. Phil. 2:6–8; Heb. 5:7–8), and the establishing of his people in righteousness. In both Rom. 1:17 and 5:18, for instance, the Christ is righteous and his righteousness results in life.[8] When Paul claims that the resurrected Jesus of Nazareth, the Christ is the "end" of the law, the Greek word can properly be interpreted as either the "goal" or the "termination." Either way, Paul argues that recognizing the reality of who Jesus of Nazareth is in his perfect allegiance to his Father (*pistis*) should finish off all attempts to establish our own righteousness through obedience to the Torah.

Paul does not argue that the followers of Jesus should believe passively, in opposition to the active attempts by the Jews to obey the Torah! The heart of his argument derives from Dt. 30:12–14. The point in Deuteronomy was that the Torah was not too difficult for Israel (Dt. 30:11), provided that it directed the seat of the inner life, of feeling and thought (Dt. 5:29; 10:16; 30:6). Craig Keener (2009, p. 105) offers a helpful comparison of the argument in Dt. 30:12–14 and Paul's application in Rom. 10:6-10, which I modify here (Table 3).

Dt. 30:12–14	Paul's application in Rom. 10:6–10
Do not say, "Who will ascend to heaven?"[9] (to bring down the Torah, *Yahweh's* perfect gift, 30:12)	Do not say, "Who will ascend to heaven?" (to bring down Christ the perfect king, the Father's gift, 10:6)
Do not say, "Who will descend into the deep?" (to experience redemption again, crossing the "sea," 30:13)[10]	Do not say, "Who will descend into the deep?" (to bring Christ the perfect human up from the dead, 10:7)

---

8 In the New Testament writings, the designation "Righteous One" often functions to portray the Messiah as someone who, in spite of his righteousness, has suffered at the hands of the unrighteous (Matt. 27:19; Acts 3:14–15; 7:52; James 5:6; 1 Pet. 3:18; 1 Jn. 2:1–2). Luke's passion narrative has the Roman centurion proclaim that "truly this man was righteous" (23:47) at the moment of Jesus' last breath and his David-like entrusting of himself to his Father (Lk. 23:46; cf. Ps. 31:6).

9 Jewish traditions viewed Moses as having ascended to heaven to receive the Torah (Ginzberg, 2021), though in Scripture he ascended only Mount Sinai.

10 In the Septuagint, one could speak of the depths of the sea as an "abyss" (e.g., Job 28:14; 38:16, 30; Ps. 33:7), even in contrast to heaven, as done here (Ps. 107:26; perhaps also Ge. 7:11; 8:2; Dt. 33:13; Ps. 135:6). Most relevant for Paul's usage here are texts about *Yahweh* bringing his people through the *abyssos* of the sea in the exodus (the point of Dt. 30): Ps. 106:9, where *Yahweh* "saved" them (106:8–10) despite their

The Word (inscripturate) is near you (the Torah, 30:14)	The Word (incarnate) is near you (the message of embodied allegiance [*pistis*] we now proclaim, 10:8)
It is in your mouth and in your heart (30:14), as the Torah was to be recited continually (Dt. 6:6–7)	He is in your mouth and in your heart: Confess with the mouth that Jesus of Nazareth is Lord, and believe with the heart that he has been enthroned by the Father in power to rule and judge through his resurrection from the dead (10:9–10)

Table 2: Paul's Application of Dt. 30 in Rom. 10

We must remember that in the Greco-Roman world, the best governance was not one in which the laws rule supreme, but one in which the virtuous king submits himself to the laws and acts as an embodiment of the law:[11]

It is only through this royal "living law," whereby the king's subjects imitate the king who provides the perfect pattern for their own character, that they are able to fulfill the demands of the law. The results of the people's imitation of the royal living law are harmony, friendship, and the eradication of dissension among the king's subjects. (Jipp, 2015, p. 45)

Jesus of Nazareth, his disciples, and all the New Testament writers lived in the social environment of the Roman empire, in which loyalty and allegiance to Caesar were both understood and enforced by the Roman army.[12] Caesar who

---

rebellion (106:7); and Isa. 51:10, emphasizing *Yahweh's* "righteousness" and "salvation" (Isa. 51:8). Additional texts include Ps. 77:16; Isa. 63:13; and possibly a new exodus in Isa. 44:27. Shifting terms might allow Paul to play on the image's associations with death (Ezek. 31:15).

11 This was also true of the Old Testament writings, which often evaluate Israel's kings and rulers according to Deuteronomy's standard of internalization of the Torah, as Jipp points out. He adds, "Nowhere does Deuteronomy speak of the people as writing out the Torah" (2015, p. 56, n. 50). Referring to the book of Chronicles in support of this argument, Jipp (2015, p. 58) writes, "The Chronicler does not depart from this model of evaluating Israel's kings according to their taking the lead in obedience to the Torah (1 Chron. 22:13; 28:7; 2 Chron. 6:16; 14:4; 33:8). David is held up as the model king who walked before the Lord and did all that the Lord commanded through his laws and ordinances (2 Chron. 7:17-18). The depiction of the Torah-observant kings is inextricably related to the harmonious and unified people of God."

12 Lance Richey (2007, pp. 55–57) argues convincingly that even when there was no legal sanction against those members of society who did not comply with the emperor cult, the social pressure to do so was inescapable. This was because systematic avoidance of the many "festivals" would be noticeable: "The 'official' character of these ceremonies made any public resistance to them appear as anti-social and a potential threat to the public order deserving the notice of the Roman authorities. ... It was not by accident that willingness to perform sacrifice came to be used as a key test of Christians

embodied peace and justice to the whole world. He was therefore to be hailed as Lord and trusted as Saviour.[13] This is the world in which the first followers of Jesus were to "confess with their mouths" that Jesus of Nazareth, crucified by the Romans, was the true king. His embodied *dikaiosynēn* (righteousness) must be read as not only a challenge to works-righteousness, but also a challenge to the imperial pretension. If we want justice or righteousness, we will find it not in the *euangelion* that announces Caesar as Lord but in the *euangelion* of Jesus as Lord:

> If Rom. 3:21–4:25 concludes that God has been faithful to the covenant with Abraham, Romans 5–8 concludes that God has thereby been true to the implicit covenant with the whole of creation. It is in 8:18–27 (more or less ignored, significantly enough, in much standard Pauline theology) that Paul finally shows how what God has done in Jesus the Messiah, in fulfillment of the covenant with Abraham, has addressed and in principle solved the problem of the whole world. God's covenant faithfulness has put the world to rights. Nothing Augustus or his successors could do, bringing their much-vaunted *Pax Romana* wherever they went, could compete with that; this is real justice, justice flowing from the throne of Jesus to the whole world. (Wright, 2000, p. 172)

Paul's answer to Caesar's empire is the empire of Jesus and life under his rule. Paul presents Jesus of Nazareth as the perfect human being who has become the embodiment of a new and authentic humanity. In this new humanity, righteousness means being incorporated into his saving rule by sharing the same *pneuma* (spirit) that the Christ received when he was raised from the dead (Jipp, 2015, p. 167). This claim that God's action to make things right for all people, "to the Jew first and also to the Greek," is underway in Jesus of Nazareth[14] opposed the empire's false promise to create wholeness or

---

during the persecutions of the second and third centuries. ... The position of the emperor within the empire made it a central element in the Augustian ideology. ... Given this context, it is not surprising that rejection of the Imperial cult was seen not as a private decision but as a public and political act of rebellion against Rome."

13 When Paul identifies "the Lord Jesus Christ" as the "saviour" (e.g., Phil. 3:20), he uses the term *soter* that was widely used for the emperor. By using it for Jesus, Paul indicates, among other things, that he does not think Rome and its emperors have saved the world from anything. Warren Carter (2006, p. 89) explains, "Rome's claim to have brought security and safety, to have effected deliverance from danger (*soteria*) is false. Rather God saves the world from Rome and its false claims. At Jesus' coming, in a vision that imitates imperial triumphs, 'every ruler and every authority and power' are destroyed; 'all his enemies' are 'put under his feet' and subjected to God's reign (1 Cor. 15:23–28; Phil. 2:5–11)."

14 Romans 10:12 underscores, as do many other passages in Romans, the equal footing given to both Jews and Gentiles by the gospel of *pistis* in Jesus of Nazareth. As there is no distinction between the two groups of people in sin and judgment (3:23), so there is also no distinction between them with regard to the Lord who rules over them. Earlier in the letter, Paul has shown that the confession that there is only one God leads naturally

well-being for all people through enacted allegiance (*pistis*) to Caesar. Thus the importance of the verbal confession that Jesus (not Caesar) is Lord.

Faith as Embodied

Public verbal confession of Jesus as Lord is not sufficient. To demonstrate this, we need look only at how the Apostle Paul describes the wayward elders in the Christ-followerships of Ephesus in his first letter to Timothy. He says that these people have "wandered from the faith" (1 Tim 6:10, Greek *tēs pisteōs*). These were good men who had emerged as leaders in the *ekklēsia* of Ephesus but had allowed themselves to be ensnared by the Evil One (1 Tim. 6:3–9). "They apparently became enamored of new ideas, fell in love with speculative interpretations, or made themselves look good by appealing to an ascetic ideal. ... But underneath they had come to love money, and it did them in" (Fee, 1987, p. 146).

Responding to this sad situation in his final exhortation to Timothy, as in two other instances (1 Tim. 1:3–7; 4:1–3), Paul appeals to Timothy's spiritual beginnings (1:18–19; 4:6–16; 6:12) to encourage him to resist these false teachers. Fee (1987, p. 148) observes that Paul is telling Timothy to keep his calling and confession before him as he "fights the good fight of faith" (6:12; i.e., carrying on the present struggle of *pistis*). Although it is not altogether clear whether Paul refers to contending for the gospel itself (thus referring back to verses 3–10) or in a broader way to the fact that all of life as a Christ-follower requires discipline and purpose (in light of verse 11), I prefer the latter because of the immediate context of this passage. Paul is exhorting Timothy to persevere in his call to obedient faithfulness and verbal confession of loyalty to the Lord Jesus: "Fight the good fight of the faith. Take hold of the eternal life to which you were called when you made your good confession in the presence of many witnesses" (1 Tim. 6:12).[15]

Timothy is receiving this command, as Paul reminds him, in the presence of Christ Jesus who made a good confession before Pontius Pilate (6:14). The perfect obedience of the second Adam, Jesus of Nazareth, as a specific historical act becomes the basis on which Paul exhorts Timothy to faithfulness, in contrast to the unfaithful teachers. Timothy is charged to keep the command without spot or blame until the manifestation of our Lord Jesus Christ. For the purpose of our discussion, it is significant to note that instead of using the more common term for our Lord Jesus' appearing (*parousia*), Paul chooses *epiphaneia* here. Paul uses *epiphaneia* or its cognate verb several times in the

---

to the conclusion that God must rule over both Jews and Gentiles (3:23-30). He insists that "the same Lord is Lord of all" (Greek *ho gar autos kyrios pantōn*).

15 Paul uses the "confession" word group (*homologeō* and *homologias*) rarely. In 1 Tim. 6:12–13, confession is a public attestation of one's *pistis* (cf. also Tit. 1:16, where the confession is verbal only); in 2 Cor. 9:13, the confession is linked to the person's obedient service.

letters to Timothy and Titus (2 Tim. 1:10; 4:1, 8; Tit. 2:11, 13; 3:4). *Epiphaneia* is the same word that was used for the appearance of the Roman emperor. By applying this term to our Lord Jesus, the Christ, Paul is making a direct assault on the call to allegiance to the emperor.

Paul's exhortation to Timothy to continue to demonstrate faithful and obedient allegiance to the Lord Jesus until he appears reminds us of some of the most terrifying words of the New Testament, uttered by Jesus of Nazareth himself:

> Not everyone who says to me "Lord, Lord," will enter the kingdom of heaven, but only he who does the will of my Father who is in heaven. Many will say to me on that day, "Lord, Lord, did we not prophesy in your name, and in our name drive out demons and perform many miracles?" Then I will tell them plainly, "I never knew you. Away from me, you evildoers!" (Mt. 7:21–23)

However we interpret these chilling words, it is clear that simply calling Jesus of Nazareth "Lord" is not enough. France (2007, p. 300) comments that there are good people who claim to follow Jesus as "Lord," do good works, and think they are doing them in Jesus' name but who are nonetheless on the broad road (Mt. 7:13). He observes that a professed allegiance to Jesus that is not embodied in a living relationship to him, and to others falls short, even when the individual does the enthusiastic performance of charismatic activities "in his name."

Jesus' absolute Lordship calls for a *pistis* that is anything but lip service or religious activity. Paul stresses that a complete shift of life-altering allegiance is the appropriate response to the gospel: "For none of us lives to himself, and none of us dies to himself. For if we live, we live to the Lord, and if we die, we die to the Lord. So whether we live or die, we are the Lord's" (Rom. 14:7–8). As we will see in our next couple of studies, Paul believes that in the *ekklēsia* of the people who embody *pistis* to Jesus as their Lord there is (or should be) better socio-political justice, freedom, peace, and relationships with each other than in the society of the people who live under the *ekklēsia* of Caesar. I do not believe that Paul's goal is to pit Rome and its ideology directly against the Christ.[16] The important facet here is that the people to whom the gospel of the slain, risen, and enthroned Lord Jesus was first delivered understood the notion of *faith* in a fullness that helps us to understand the foundational importance of intentional discipleship to the Christ.

---

16 It has been correctly observed that the letter to the Romans has no explicit argument about the inadequacy of the Roman *dikaiosynēn*, *sōtēria*, *eirēnēn*, or *eueutheria* (freedom). And even that the 13th chapter of that epistle contains positive statements about the Roman authorities as keepers of justice and order (Kim, 2008, p. 20). This observation is, in my opinion, not in contradiction to Paul's use of these words, and their usage in Roman society, to accurately point to enacted *pistis* toward the Lord Jesus of Nazareth.

Thus, we might say that just as the atonement of Jesus of Nazareth is regarded in the Scriptures as absolute and encompassing the sin of all humankind (Rom 3:23–24; Eph. 2:8–9), so his lordship is regarded as absolute and all-encompassing (1 Cor. 8:6; Phil. 2:9–11; Col. 1:18). Bates (2017, p. 210) states the indivisible yet often missing link between salvation and life under Christ's rule in this way:

> Discipleship and salvation are not separable categories. Why is this of practical import for the church? The church must not think of evangelism or mission (traditionally, "getting people saved") and discipleship (traditionally, "growing people in Christ") as separate or even separable tasks—and church programming needs to be reconfigured accordingly. Evangelism programmes are only accurate and compelling when they are not merely an invitation to forgiveness but an invitation to full-orbed discipleship. Programmes for discipleship are only accurate and compelling when discipleship is understood to be absolutely required for the allegiant outworking of salvation.

Questions to Think About

1. I argue in this chapter that the Greek word *pistis* should sometimes be better translated as embodied or enacted allegiance than as believing faith, and I quote other scholars who describe *pistis* as both passive believing and concrete commitment. How can this truth function as a corrective to imperfect models of conversion and discipleship?

2. Which of the reasons offered by Bates for sometimes translating the Greek word *pistis* as "enacted allegiance" rather than as "believing faith" do you find most compelling? Why is this important for our spiritual lives?

3. This chapter discusses two puzzling expressions found in Pauline texts: "obedience of faith" and "law of Christ." What do you believe represents Paul's intended meaning of these expressions and what are the implications for overcoming the seemingly uncommitted believers in our local churches?

4. Review Romans 10:6–10. What is Paul's purpose in paralleling Deuteronomy 30:12–14 in this passage? What tendencies—in his own day and in ours—does the passage counteract?

12. Rooted in the Christ

In our last study, we examined the importance of the cultural and semantic background of Paul's uses of *pistis* and related words. We considered how readers within the ancient Mediterranean world would have understood his uses of this terminology. We particularly noted how language functioned within Paul's response to the politically sensitive issues of his day. We do not know whether Paul's vision of the relationship between God, Christ and humanity drew consciously on contemporary Greco-Roman models, but it clearly resonated with a wide range of common applications of *pistis* and *fides* in the world around him, and so it may have been intuitively easy for first-century listeners, whether Greek, Roman, or Jewish, to understand (Morgan, 2015).

New Testament scholars agree that the prescribed responses to the gospel are repentance and *pistis*. Paul summarized his message to the Ephesian elders: "I have declared to both Jews and Greeks that they must turn toward God in repentance and *pistis* towards Christ" (Ac. 20:21).[1] Typically this has been understood as an initial changing of one's verdict about Jesus, expressing contrition for one's sins that are an offence to God,[2] and entrusting oneself to the faithfulness of God (Horton, 2011, pp. 580–582; Bird, 2013, p. 51). Understood in this sense, *pistis* implies not only believing that God was in Christ reconciling the world to himself, but also a sure trust and confidence that Jesus of Nazareth died for my sins, that he loved me and gave himself for me. When repentant sinners believe this, God pardons them. This is an event of such extraordinary proportions that it is sometimes referred to as a new birth (Jn. 3:3, 1 Pet. 1:3, 23).

Unfortunately, in all but the rarest of occasions, too often we assume that *pistis* means only believing in and relying passively on the work that Jesus of Nazareth has done for us on the cross, as in this example:

---

1 Morgan observes that at least 27 of the 52 occurrences of *pistis* language in Acts make some reference to conversion (2017, p. 382, n. 115).

2 Michael Horton (2011, p. 580) writes that biblical repentance involves the turning of the whole self both "from self-trust and from the autonomy that demands final say as to what one will believe, whom one will trust, and how one will live."

Saving faith relies on God to fulfill his promises and entrusts the future to him. …
Believers … trust that sins are forgiven in the death and resurrection of Jesus
(Rom. 4:23–25) and therefore believe that the promise of the resurrection will
become theirs on the day of the Lord. (Schreiner, 2001, p. 249)

However, Ninjay Gupta (2020, pp. 186–187) rightly maintains that as
convenient as such a formulation might be for understanding Paul's thought,
there are enough nuances and complexities in Paul to make this view
untenable. He concludes:

We cannot discount the way *pistis* functions for Paul anthropologically,
epistemologically, and socially as the *way* believers relate to God through the
Christ-relation, which is necessarily thoughtful and participatory (socially,
volitionally, existentially, etc.). (Gupta, 2020, p. 189)

In this study, I will examine more closely how *pistis* functioned for Paul,
and how it should function for us, in constructing and maintaining a theology in
which thoughtful relationship to God and to others in the Christ-relation
flourishes. To do this, I will look first at Paul's use of the notion that by *pistis*
the Colossians were "transferred into the kingdom of [God's] beloved Son"
(Col. 1:13), and what it means to share in the Lord Jesus' sovereign rule. After
that, I will describe Haley Goranson Jacob's (2018) excellent biblical
examination of the phrase used by many to capture the end goal of the
Christian life: conformity to Christ (cf. Rom. 8:29). My goal is to highlight the
central role of the reigning Lord Jesus of Nazareth, the perfect God-man, not
only in our redemption but also in our present re-creation into the pre-Fall
image of humanity (i.e., our glorification).

Participating Today in the True King's Rule

After presenting Timothy and himself to the "holy" and "faithful" (*pistos*)
brothers and sisters in Christ[3] living in the region of Colossae, Paul uses the
word *pistis* three more times (Col. 1:4, 5, 7) before commencing his
introductory description of Jesus of Nazareth. The Apostle describes the Christ
as the one through whom the Creator God rules, bringing freedom from evil
and the forgiveness of sins: "For he [the Father] has rescued us from the
dominion of darkness and brought us into the kingdom of the Son he loves, in
whom we have redemption, the forgiveness of sins" (Col. 1:13–14).

Before being "rescued" by the Father, the *pistos*—the "faithful," or those
who by the Father's grace have believed and changed their allegiance (cf. Eph.

---

3 As Moo (2008, p. 79) remarks, although calling his readers "holy" is typical for Paul,
addressing them as "*pistos*" is not. He concludes that Paul chooses this unusual word to
remind his readers of their need to continue to maintain "allegiance to the gospel
tradition that they have been taught."

2:8–9)—lived in a power structure characterized by the forces of chaos, evil, and judgment.[4] Some scholars consider that the coming of the kingdom is in the future,[5] but the emphasis of verse 14 is clearly in the present.

The glorification of the reconciling Creator God in the present reign of the Son he loves is clearly seen throughout the letter. It is summarized in the central command to "continue to live your lives in Christ Jesus as Lord" (Col. 2:6). Moo (2008, p. 176) affirms that this clause succinctly restates "the key theological argument of the letter to this point: Jesus the Christ is Lord, and we have entered into his Lordship." According to James Dunn (1996, pp. 136–137), Paul's central argument in this letter is that the starting point of *pistis* toward Jesus the Christ (who is the ideal king) provides the pattern for all that happens afterwards in the life of the *pistos* (believer).

The ongoing fruits of *pistis* in the life of the *pistos* are spelled out in 2:7, where Paul lists four characteristics of what it means "to live in [the Lord Jesus]" (2:6). Each characteristic is expressed with a participle. The first participle ("rooted") appears in the perfect tense (expressing the continuing results of an action completed in the past); the next three ("being built up," "being strengthened," and "overflowing") are in the present tense. Bird (2009, pp. 70–71) argues as much when he writes that Paul is returning to the metaphor of 1:10 ("walk worthily of the Lord"), which "is equivalent to remaining loyal to and grounded in the faith they were first taught." Paul links together the initial *pistis* of these Christ-followers and their current social identity and behavior. Since they now live under his rule, their conduct must be consistent with the character and conduct of the one they recognize as the risen Lord Jesus Christ. He has become their "paradigm of value" (Talbert, 2007, p. 210).

This can be seen when Paul exhorts them to continue to live out their *pistis* to Christ alone (2:6) and, because of that allegiance to him, to change their way of relating to others (i.e., "strengthened in *pistis*," 2:7). He does this first by highlighting the person of Jesus of Nazareth, the Christ, as the ruler of both the old creation and the new creation (1:15–20), the substance of the "mystery" of the Creator's plan for human history (1:27; 2:2), and the repository of all wisdom and knowledge (2:3). Next, he reminds the Colossians that they must learn to reflect this new Lord of the universe through the transformation of their human relationships (1:5–8, 21–23). Paul says this is so important that they must "see to it" (2:8) that they "do not let anyone judge you" (2:16). Many more imperatives follow: "Do not let anyone ... disqualify you" (2:18); "set your hearts on things above" (3:1); "Set your minds on things above" (3:2); "Put to death" (3:5); "you must ... rid yourselves" (3:8); "Do not lie to each other" (3:9); "clothe yourselves" (3:12); "Bear with each other" (3:13);

---

4 Paul labels this the "dominion" (*exousias*) of darkness.
5 For instance, Lohse (1971, pp. 37–38) claims that "whenever Paul mentions the 'rule of God' in his letters, the futuristic meaning of the concept is presupposed."

"forgive one another" (3:13); "put on love" (3:14); "let the peace of Christ rule in your hearts" (3:15); "be thankful" (3:15); "Let the message of Christ dwell among you richly" (3:16); "do it all" (3:17); "Wives, submit yourselves to your own husbands" (3:18); "Husbands, love your wives" (3:19); "Children, obey your parents" (3:20); "Fathers, do not embitter your children" (3:21); "Slaves, obey your earthly masters" (3:22); "work at it with all your heart" (3:23); "Masters, provide your slaves with what is right and fair" (4:1); "Devote yourselves to prayer" (4:2); "pray for us, too" (4:3); "Be wise" (4:5); "Let your conversation be always full of grace" (4:6).

Present Everyone Perfect in the Christ

Several things should be evident from this list of things that the *pistos* (believers) must "see to." First, these are not often the things that come to mind when we define "discipleship," "Christian maturity," or "faith in Christ." The constant use of "action verbs" also indicates that the necessary changes in how we relate to others do not happen automatically nor are they things that God does for us. We must "set our hearts," "rid ourselves," "put to death," "clothe ourselves," and "work at it with all our hearts." Fortunately, as Paul explicitly states (when talking about his own ministry), the power of the resurrected and enthroned Jesus of Nazareth, the force that results from one's indwelling in him, carries out this work together with him: "We proclaim him (the Christ), admonishing and teaching everyone with all wisdom, so that we may present everyone perfect in Christ. To this end I labour, struggling with all his energy, which so powerfully works in me" (Col. 1:28–29).

This short description of the goal of Paul's entire ministry is significant. His focus is on the Christ, whom he identifies in verse 27 as "Christ in you, the hope of glory." And he claims to be tirelessly pursuing the aim of "presenting [presumably to either the Father or the Christ, or perhaps to both], everyone perfect in Christ." It is helpful to clarify the meaning of three notions in these verses as they are used by the Apostle in this letter to the Colossians: "Christ in you," "hope of glory," and "perfect in Christ."

The two expressions "Christ in you" and "perfect in Christ" share the common denominator of a reciprocity of identity that reflects the shared identity of the eternal Son incarnate and his Father (Jn. 14:10, cf. 5:19; 10:38). The expression "Christ in you" is a classic distinctive of Pauline theology, occurring more than eighty times in the Pauline letters, but elsewhere in the New Testament only in 1 Peter.[6] It has already occurred seven times in this epistle. Paul describes "Christ in you" and "[you] in Christ" as a great and

---

6 This is a conservative figure. Marcus P. Johnson (2013, p. 19) estimates that in combination with "in Christ Jesus," "in the Lord," and "in him," it occurs approximately 164 times in Paul's letters. Bruce Demarest (1997, p. 313) has estimated that the number of occurrences of "union with Christ" terminology in Paul's letters alone exceeds two hundred.

profound *mysterion* that lies at the heart of the gospel (cf. also Eph. 5:31–32). Explaining this "mystery," O'Brien (1999, pp. 111–112) writes, "Christ is the one *in whom* God chooses to sum up the cosmos, the one in whom he restores harmony to the universe. He is the focal point, not simply the means, the instrument, or the functionary through whom all this occurs." O'Brien highlights the words "*in whom*" because this idea is so foreign to much of our "*through* Christ" thinking.[7]

I agree with O'Brien that for Paul the life-altering *mysterion* is the realization that the enigmatic God-man, the crucified yet now reigning king, is the one who, in and through us in the person of his Spirit, is renewing the old creation to its pre-fall condition. This is the *mysterion* of the gospel for which Paul saw himself to be an ambassador in chains (Col. 4:3; cf. Eph. 3:7; Rom. 16:25). For this reason, Paul implores the *pistos* of Colossae to pray for us, "that God may open a door for our message, so that we may proclaim *the mystery of Christ*, ... Pray that I may proclaim it clearly" (Col. 4:3–4).

Lest I be accused of reductionism, I admit that we would be wrong to overlook the complex multidimensionality of the Good News of our mysterious union with Christ in Paul's thought. Marcus Peter Johnson (2013, pp. 19–20) offers this helpful overview:

> His [Paul's] letters include references to believers being created in Christ (Eph. 2:10), crucified with him (Gal. 2:20), buried with him (Col. 2:12), baptized into Christ and his death (Rom. 6:3), united with him in his resurrection (Rom. 6:5), and seated with him in the heavenly places (Eph. 2:6); Christ being formed in believers (Gal. 4:19) and dwelling in our hearts (Eph. 3:17); the church as members—limbs and organs—of Christ's body (1 Cor. 6:15; 12:27); Christ in us (2 Cor. 13:5) and us in him (1 Cor. 1:30); the church as one flesh with Christ (Eph. 5:31–32); and believers gaining Christ/being found in him (Phil. 3:8–9).

Yet the thrust of Paul's argument in Colossians centres on the centrality of the Lord Jesus as both the model and the aim of *pistis* for all people (*panta anthropon*, which is repeated three times in Col. 1:28). About this "mystery of the gospel" that is for all people, Johnson (2013, p. 50) observes that our union with the eternal Son of God does not have the goal of "making us other than human, but to heal our sin-disfigured humanity." In other words, the Christ (reigning vice-regent with the Father, the man as he was intended to be from the beginning), united with us through repentance and *pistis*, works today in the person of the Holy Spirit, allowing us the possibility of becoming truly human.[8]

---

7 For instance, see Charles Talbert (2007, p. 2002), who understands "*in* Christ" "instrumentally" and therefore translates the expression "through Christ."
8 In this I follow J. G. Herder's famous statement, "We are not yet, but are daily trying to become, human beings" (Grenz, 2001, p. 180). However, unlike Grenz (2001) and Pannenberg (1970), who attempt to tie this to our being made in the image of God, I

This vision of the eternal Son who in every moment of his human existence gave faithful allegiance to his Father, and whose *pistis* embraces every person in the process, is highlighted in Colossians.

The Centrality of the Christ

Paul pleads with the Colossian *pistos* to continue to learn in their relationships with others how to enact (put into practice) their initial *pistis* (belief in) and ongoing *pistis* (allegiance to) the reigning Lord Jesus. He is the pattern for the life of all who live in the kingdom. Paul's argument is precise. We often fail to see the coherence of his thought because our insistence on the divinity of Jesus and our justification by faith obscures it. My argument is that the "Christ hymn" of Colossians 1:15–20, while expressing the identity of the person of the Christ in uniquely exalted terms (creator, ruler, sustainer), places the emphasis elsewhere, given the context of the letter.

With Moo (2008, pp. 167–182), I maintain that Paul uses this hymn to center the theology, devotion, worship, and daily living of the *pistos* intentionally and explicitly on the humanity of the Lord Jesus of Nazareth, the Messiah, and our participation in him. Along with Philippians 2:6–11, this text is one of the most important for a gospel-driven theology of discipleship:

> He [the Son] is the image of the invisible God, the firstborn over all creation. For by him all things were created: things in heaven and on earth, visible and invisible, whether thrones or powers or rulers or authorities; all things were created by him and for him. He is before all things, and in him all things hold together. And he is the head of the body, the church; he is the beginning and the firstborn from among the dead, so that in everything he might have the supremacy. For God was pleased to have all his fullness dwell in him, and through him to reconcile to himself all things whether things on earth or things in heaven, by making peace through his blood, shed on the cross. (Col. 1:15–20)

This is one of the most studied and quoted texts written by Paul. It also contains many elements that biblical scholars continue to debate.[9] In my own examination, I will underscore what I find to be most helpful concerning the person of the Lord Jesus, the God-man, in the formulation of a gospel-driven theology of discipleship.[10]

---

find it more reasonable to link it to Jesus of Nazareth as the *imago hominis*, the one who is the prototype of humanity as the Creator designed us to be.

9 For a survey of most of the diverse interpretations of this text, see DeMaris (1994).

10 My endeavour is greatly influenced and guided by the work of Joshua Jipp (2015, pp. 100–126).

Jesus the King Is God's Son and God's Image

This text is undoubtedly a hymn or poem about Jesus of Nazareth, the Messiah (Bird, 2009, pp. 47–48). It corresponds to the hymnic features of ancient prose written to bestow praise on the human messianic King, who was seen as God's vice-regent, creator and sustainer over creation, and peacemaker among those under his rule (Jipp, 2015, p. 100).[11]

The origin of the hymn is debated. Some scholars postulate that it comes from a gnostic background, but this view has been increasingly abandoned because Gnosticism didn't reach its peak of importance until the second century. It is more probable that its antecedents are in the ancient Jewish traditions of wisdom and creation (Moule, 1957, pp. 63–64). Just as Wisdom was with *Yahweh* "at the beginning of his activity" (Pr. 8:22–31), so also the eternal Son is represented as having been given by the Father what the ancient Near East considered to be the preeminently kingly task: the act of creation (Jipp, 2015, p. 109). This idea is reinforced by Paul's identification of the Christ as the wisdom of God in Col. 2:3.

Paul's dependence on the Jewish creation traditions is highlighted in the first phrase of the poem, which identifies the incarnate Son, Jesus of Nazareth, as the "image of the invisible God." This phrase recalls Genesis 1:26–27, where Adam is created in the image and likeness of God. Thomas Schreiner (2001, p. 174) appropriately rejects the notion that this likeness should be limited to Jesus' humanity, for the simple reason that the preeminence given to him as the image of God clearly surpasses that of Adam who is "in the image" of God.[12] The man born of the virgin is the visible face of the triune, invisible God (Col. 1:15; cf. Jn. 1:18; 1 Tim. 1:15) who is spirit (Jn. 4:24), and therefore the prototype of humankind.

Adam was commissioned to subdue and rule over the earth as the Creator's sovereign representative (Gen. 1:26, 28), maintaining and expanding the divine

---

11 N. T. Wright (1992, p. 104) explains clearly and convincingly the structure of the hymn. Verse 17 is the centre of Paul's argument and summarizes the entire text: "He is before all things and in him all things hold together." The poem has a chiastic structure, highlighting the importance of this affirmation at its centre.

12 This is clearly different from the Christology of the proponents of the "word of faith movement," for whom man was originally created to be like God. In his doctoral thesis, Genis Pieterse (2016) summarizes this incorrect understanding:

This likeness, or image, is contextualized along the lines of two arguments; the first is that man has become a living soul, "just like God," and the second that man possessed "dominion and authority over everything in the earth, as God did." Dollar (2006, p. 104) views man as having restored righteousness, which means that when man stands before God he has "rights" and "equality." Other Word of faith ministers such as Copeland, Benny Hinn, Eddie Long, Earl Pink, Paul Crouch and Morris Cerullo—who states that "when we stand up here, brother, you're not looking at Morris Cerullo; you are looking at God. You're looking at Jesus"—all express the same erroneous principle of man having equality with God (p. 78).

order of creation. As Gerhard Von Rad (1962, p. 146) states, "God set man in the world as the sign of his own sovereign authority, in order that man should uphold and enforce his—God's claims as Lord."

Not surprisingly, when Adam is named in Paul's epistles he appears in explicitly royal contexts (Rom. 5:12–21; 1 Cor. 15:20–28), as Jipp (2015, p. 106) observes:

> In Rom. 5:12–21 the language of "rule" and "dominion" are [sic] spoken of in relation to Adam and Christ. And in 1 Cor. 15:20–28 Adam is spoken of in antithesis to Christ, who hands the kingdom over to God the Father (v. 24), pacifies God's enemies (vv. 24b–27), and who is the subject of the royal Psalms 8 and 110.

The observation that the Lord Jesus of Nazareth *is* the image of God, and that we have been made *in* the image of God, is important for discipleship. It highlights his role as the archetypical one in whose image we are to be formed even now as his subjects. He is the realization of the Creator's intention for humanity whom the *pistos* (believers) are to "put on" (Col. 3:10; Eph. 4:24), whereas they must "take off" the "old man" (Col. 3:9; Eph. 4:22).[13] The fact that Paul is addressing those who are already *pistos* (believers) is significant. It highlights the fact that a person must still learn to "put on" Jesus of Nazareth, even after that person is "in Christ" (Col. 3:1; 1 Cor. 1:30).

Jesus the King Creates and Rules

In verse 15, to the honorific title of "image of God," Paul adds "firstborn over all creation." The word "firstborn" certainly recalls the place of Israel (also called "firstborn" in Exodus 4:22) as the one who exercises sovereignty over his younger siblings.[14] As such, the ancient Hebrews were the people chosen by *Yahweh* to extend his rule throughout the world (Heil, 2010, p. 65, n. 4).

To understand Paul's description of Jesus of Nazareth, the Messiah, as "firstborn over all creation," we must consider Psalm 89:28, which refers to *Yahweh's* covenant with David: "I will make him the firstborn, the highest of the kings of the earth" (Bruce, 1984, p. 59; Jipp, 2015, p. 108). Explaining the

---

13 There has been considerable debate as to what exactly the apostle means by the designations "old and new human in Colossians and in Ephesians 4:22-24. Some see it as the old-new self, others the old-new humanity, and others still Adam-Christ. I agree with Grenz who feels that these three views are not necessarily mutually exclusive. Yet from the perspective of the New Testament writers (2001, p. 255), Grenz convincingly argues that Paul uses the imagery as "two frames of reference from which participants in each realm gain their identity, and out of which, on the basis of which, or in keeping with which they conduct their lives." This entails learning with and from others what is appropriate to life in the new community under Jesus' reign.

14 The exceptions to this rule, Jacob and Esau and Manasseh and Ephraim, are notable precisely because they are contrary to custom (Gen. 27:18–46; 48:8–22; Rom. 9:10–13).

parallelism between Col. 1:15 and Ps. 89:28, Schreiner (2001, p. 175) writes, "David was not the firstborn in the sense that he was the oldest in his family, nor was he the first legitimate king in Israel. The term firstborn indicates that he was appointed to rule."

The reign of the Lord Jesus the Christ over the world even today (not just at some future time) is not surprising, since he is the one "in whom all things have been created" (Col. 1:16; Heb. 1:2) and the one "through whom and for whom all things have been created" (1:16). John's gospel declares, "Through him all things were made; without him nothing was made that has been made" (Jn. 1:3).

The Greek word *panta* (meaning all, or all things) appears eight times in this text, highlighting the Lord Jesus' dominion aver creation and his identity as the one "in whom all things have been created" (1:16) and "through whom and for whom all things have been created" (1:16). In other words, Jesus is the most exalted of all the kings of the earth (cf. Ps 88:28). Commenting on verse 16, Jipp (2015, p. 109) points out that the incarnate Son "not only rules but even creates the lesser rulers." He observes that regardless of the exact identity of the lesser rulers, the language used to describe them is political. These are the same "rulers and authorities" whom Jesus disarmed at the cross, and whom he shamed and led in an imperial triumph (Col. 2:15).

When the hymn arrives at verse 17, the heart of the chiasm, the primacy of the eternal Son incarnate in Jesus of Nazareth is highlighted. Douglas Moo (2008, p. 121) summarizes the thought of this poem concerning the supremacy of the God-man over creation, saying that the entire creative work of the triune God took place "in terms of" or "in reference to" the Messiah. The eternal Son incarnate in Jesus of Nazareth is the goal, the reference point, and reigning Lord of all creation! This fact is fundamental in a gospel-driven theology of discipleship, as it calls for acknowledging him in every part of salvation history. This point is driven home in verse 17, where we read that "he is before all things." This affirmation can refer to both the preexistence and the preeminence of the eternal Son.

The superiority of Jesus of Nazareth over Adam is evident. Adam was a creature within the cosmos; the risen Lord Jesus is the one in whom the cosmos "holds together." The physical cosmos would lose its order, cohesion, meaning. and even its very existence without the sovereign reign of him who is the perfect *imago dei* and the perfect *imago hominis*.[15]

---

15 We have seen that praise of Augustus' rule often centred on his production of cosmic stability and order. This theme can also be seen in the Davidic Psalms (Ps. 2; 45; 72; 89; 110).

Jesus the King Rules over His People

Paul states that the Lord Jesus, the Christ, is "the head of the body of the assembly" (*autos estin hē kephalē tou sōmatos tēs ekklēsias*; Col. 1:18). Paul's use of *kephalē* (head) has spawned an enormous amount of literature, with some scholars seeing connotations of authority and preeminence while others find connotations of source and origins.

Based on the context of this verse, I do not think Paul is suggesting here that the eternal Son incarnate is only the source or origin of the *ekklēsias* (assembly, congregation). In using the word *kephalē*, I believe, Paul is describing the God-man in his regal authority or, as Jipp (2015, p. 113) puts it, "as the heavenly enthroned ruler over his body politick much as Caesar or David was spoken of as the head of the empire/Israel." I am convinced of this view first because the verses preceding and forming this hymn are full of messianic, kingly metaphors: the kingdom of the Son (1:13), the image of God (1:15), the firstborn over all creation (1:17).[16] Another reason why I think Paul sees the crucified and risen Jesus of Nazareth in his regal authority over the *ekklēsias*, not as its source, is his description of the Christ as the *kephalē* over "every power and authority" (Col. 2:10). Paul says the worship of angels should be unthinkable for the members of the Christ-followerships in Colossae, who apparently were tempted to give in to that temptation (Schreiner, 2001, p. 177). How could they worship other powers and authorities if Jesus reigns supreme?

The supremacy of the eternal Son, who became man in Jesus the Christ, over the network of *ekklēsiae* is highlighted by the fact that he is its beginning not only in terms of rank, but also in temporal terms. Both readings find plausible justification in the hymn (Jipp, 2015, p. 116). In the next line, Paul celebrates Jesus of Nazareth as "firstborn from the dead" (1:18). which results in his preeminence over everything. Besides affirming Jesus as the universal ruler, this acclamation emphasizes that the people of God are no longer defined in relationship to the Hebrew people, but in relationship to Jesus of Nazareth. The history of the saving presence of *Yahweh* in the world has taken a decisive turn with the coming of the eternal Son incarnate, since he is the firstborn (*prōtotokos*) from among the dead.

In Genesis 49:3, the words "first" and "firstborn" are used to describe Reuben, because he is the beginning of the twelve tribes. The phrase "firstborn from among the dead" (Col. 1:18) signifies that the age to come has penetrated the present age, since the resurrection from among the dead has already become a reality in and by Jesus of Nazareth. Israel awaited the resurrection as an indicator of the coming age. Paul maintains that since the Lord Jesus is the

---

16 See also the parallel text of Eph. 1:20–23, where Paul refers to the Christ as "head over all things with respect to the assembly" (*kephalēn hyper panta tē ekklēsia*). The context of this passage indicates that the Father, through raising Jesus of Nazareth, the Messiah, from the dead and "seating him at his right hand in the heavenly realm," has placed him "above every rule, authority, power and lord."

initiator of a humanity renewed in his image, he is the one who is first in everything (*prōteuōn*).

This conviction is important for a gospel-driven theology of discipleship. The disciple of the Lord Jesus of Nazareth is recognizable not because he practises spiritual disciplines such as Bible study or faithfulness in attending church, fasting, prayer, or witnessing (as important as these are). The most distinguishing feature of a disciple is that he gives Jesus of Nazareth, the Christ, preeminence in everything, even in his personal relationship to God. The Apostle Paul oriented his theology and everything else in this sense. He considered everything else "a loss" compared to the "surpassing greatness" of knowing Christ Jesus his Lord (Phil. 3:7–8). He directed all his energy and "strained" toward that objective, not being satisfied with what he had already obtained (Phil. 3:12–14) and pressing on to "know Christ" and "become like him" (Phil. 3:10).

Paul's desire to become like Jesus of Nazareth even included the area of *pistis*! In other words, Paul was not satisfied with believing *in* Jesus; he wanted to believe *like* Jesus. I have been referring to the "believers" in Colossae as the *pistos* (Col. 1:2) to underscore that Jesus of Nazareth was himself a *pistos* (in a very special way, according to Hebrews 12:2). In the context that I have just sketched, it becomes very meaningful to see Jesus in this way. Particularly in the Pauline writings, we find more allusions to this idea than has often been acknowledged; many contemporary exegetes believe that the Greek genitive constructions *pistis Iēsou* and *pistis Cristou* in Romans 3:22, 26; Philippians 3:9, and Galatians 2:16, 20 probably denote "the faith of Jesus/Christ" and not "faith in Jesus/Christ," as has often been translated.[17] Simply put, we enter into the obedient confidence and enacted allegiance (*pistis*) *of* Jesus of Nazareth to his heavenly Father (Phil. 2:8, cf. Mt. 20:28; Jn. 10:18; Heb. 5:8) as we confidently obey and learn to enact allegiance (*pistis*) *to* the Lord Jesus of Nazareth, the Messiah (Rom. 14:7–9, cf. Gal. 2:20; Mt. 10:38; Lk. 9:23; 14:27).

The *pistos* of Colossae share in the supremacy of the exalted Messiah by way of sharing in his resurrection and heavenly exaltation: "you have been raised together in him" (Col. 2:12). He is all things for them, as for Paul (Col. 2:12). This is not for the Christ's own benefit but for the nourishment, growth, and good of those who participate in his sonship through *pistis*. Hence Paul makes the remarkable claim that the Colossian *pistos* are "being filled up in him" (2:10), where the prepositional phrase refers to the one in whom "all the fullness of deity dwells bodily" (2:9). This is so because the *pistos* constitute

---

17 See for instance, Allen (2009, pp. 268–273, 288–305); Campbell (1992; 1994, pp. 58–69); Dodd (1995); Dunn (1997; 1998, p. 642); Hays (1997; 2002); Hooker (1989); Horrell (1997); Hultgren (1980); Johnson (1982); Longenecker (1993; 1996); Martyn (1997, pp. 150–151); Matlock (2000; 2003); Stowers (1989); Stubbs (2008); Taylor (2004); Williams (1980, pp. 274–275; 1987; 1989); Wright (1996, p. 259).

those "who were formerly alienated and enemies" (Col. 1:21), but who now share in the Messiah's cosmic reconciling work (1:21–22).

Conformed to the Image of His Son

Romans 8:28–30 is considered by many to be the "golden chain of salvation,"[18] a precious description of biblical truth concerning God's will for his people. The short affirmation in verse 28 that "we know that in all things God works for the good of those who love him" is often clung to in situations of anxiety and stress. Those words remind us that behind history, the God of the Bible is sovereignly orchestrating good for his people and his glory (cf. Gen. 50:20; Eph. 1:11). This statement that it does not matter who or what attempts to thwart God's plan—because no one and nothing can—is probably one of the most quoted and claimed verses of the Bible.

Although verse 28 contains one of the most quoted phrases of Scripture, verse 29 offers one of the phrases most neglected by scholars: "conformed to the likeness of his son" (*symmorphous tēs eikonos tou huiou autou*).[19] In her landmark study of this familiar text, Haley Jacob (2018) argues that we will properly understand what Paul is saying only when we come to grips with the meaning of "glory" as he uses that notion in Romans. She maintains that practical theologians, biblical theologians, systematic theologians, missionary theologians, pastors, preachers, Bible teachers, and laity all make the same mistake. Our tendency to focus our attention on justification and salvation as ends in themselves, whether for the benefit of the individual or of the corporate body of Christ, has kept us from correctly understanding these key notions.

Wrong Understandings of Glory

Jacob (2018, p. 2) explains that for centuries terms such as "glory" and "glorify" have been used within Christian jargon basically without question. Unfortunately, these terms are often understood, on the basis of lexical definitions of glory, as splendour or radiance of God manifested in light phenomena (Jacob, 2018, p. 64). Jacob declares that such definitions are not adequate. The words "splendour" or "radiance," even as representing the visible presence of God (though these conceptions may exist in the background), are not Paul's concern here. We will come back to this point, because the significance of the correct understanding of "glory" (*doxa*) and "glorify" (*doxazō*), as Paul uses these words, cannot be overstated. It influences

---

18 Theologians refer to this as the *ordo salutis*, the order of salvation: "Those he predestined he also called, and those whom he called he also justified, and those whom he justified he also glorified."

19 In her excellent treatment of this expression, including a thorough survey of existing studies, Jacob (2018) found only four articles and no monographs analyzing this expression exegetically.

our interpretation of the phrase "conformity to the image of Christ" and thus our understanding of discipleship to him. This can be seen in some of the ambiguous and incorrect ways we use Romans 8:29.

The first mistake we often make is to gather and synthesize all the other verses in which themes such as glory and vocation, sanctification and suffering, suffering and glory, or glory and body[20] appear throughout the Pauline corpus. Although several of these categories unquestionably are related to one another, Jacob maintains that they do not really help us to understand Paul's thinking in Romans.

A second mistake identified by Jacob is to see conformity to Christ as spiritual or moral conformity, or sanctification. Jacob's review of the existing literature on the subject leads her to believe that this is the most common assumed interpretation of the word "conformed" (*symmorphous*). Some authors she quotes (2018, p. 5) differentiate this as a present, spiritual conformity, in contrast to those who see it as a future, physical conformity. Their argument is that if this gradual sanctification is not what Paul had in mind, then a very important link in the "golden chain" of salvation is missing. The prominence of understanding "conformed to the image of his Son" as spiritual formation or sanctification can be seen in popular Christianity.

Some scholars attempt to avoid the present–future paradox by reading "conformity" in the context of the suffering and death of the Christ. Most who suggest that Romans 8:29 refers to suffering see it as the first part of a two-part process that consists of suffering and resurrection. Jacob (2018, p. 7) gives the example of C. K. Barrett (1991, p. 170), who writes, "At present we are conformed (*symmorphizomenos*) to his death (Phil. 3:10); we shall be conformed (*symmorphon*) to the *body of his glory* (Phil. 3:21)." Jacob (2018, p. 8) observes that most scholars who suggest suffering with Christ or sharing in Christ's sufferings as an explanation for conformity are primarily dependent on Romans 8:17, where suffering with Christ is deemed a prerequisite for being glorified with Christ. Jacob recognizes the connection between these verses but argues that there are some significant problems with this interpretation of Romans 8:29.

The most common view among Pauline scholars is that Paul refers to conformity to Christ's glory.[21] Douglas Moo (1996, pp. 534–536) offers an excellent example:[22]

---

20 For instance, 1 Cor. 15:49; 2 Cor. 3:18; Phil. 3:10, 21; Col. 1:15, 18.
21 See Dodd (1932, pp. 141–142); Black (1981, p. 125); Cranfield (1975, p. 432); Wanamaker (1987, p. 187); Dunn (1988, pp. 483–484); Ziesler (1989, p. 227); Scott (1992, pp. 245–247); Moo (1996, pp. 534–535); Gorman (2001, p. 35; 2009, p. 169); Witherington (2001, p. 230).
22 See for instance Dunn (1988); Jewett & Kotansky (2007); Schreiner (1998); Byrne (2007); Wright (2004).

Paul may think of the believer as destined from his conversion onward to "conform" to Christ's pattern of *suffering followed by glory*. ... But the closest parallels, Phil. 3:21 and 1 Cor. 15:49, are both eschatological; and eschatology is Paul's focus in this paragraph. ... It is as Christians have their *bodies resurrected* and transformed that they *join Christ in his glory* and that the purpose of God, to make Christ the "firstborn" of many to follow, is accomplished.

This brings us back to the importance of properly understanding glory (*doxa*) and glorification (*doxazō*) in Paul's thought in Romans 8. Contrary to Moo and the many other scholars who hold a similar interpretation, Jacob (2018, p. 10) forcefully states, "I will argue ... that Romans 8:29b refers to believer's eschatological glory only if *glory* is understood as something *other than* splendour/radiance or the visible, manifest presence of God." I was surprised by those words because they express a position I held before I read Jacob's study (Bjork, 2015, pp. 114-128).

Finally, Jacob (2018, p. 11) mentions another suggestion which, she claims, some others have hinted at "almost in passing" and which she adapts, expands, and most importantly substantiates exegetically. She examines what she has labeled "vocational participation" with Christ which we just reviewed, looking in detail at the six Greek words that make up the goal of salvation given in Romans 8:29. She defines that goal, which she labels "the believers' vocational[23] participation with Christ," as the "believers' active share in the resurrection life and glory of Christ as redeemed humans in him" (Jacob, 2018, p. 15).

Our Glorious Participation with the Christ

That short definition of "vocational participation with Christ" is meticulously unpacked through a detailed exegesis, which begins with the motifs of glory and glorification in Romans as well as establishing the motif of vocational participation throughout Paul's letters (Jacob, 2018, pp. 21–172). Then Jacob (2018, pp. 173–266) focuses on Romans 8:17-30 and examines three key elements of the passage: the phrase "image of [God's] Son," the believer's participation in the Son's glory, and the implicit notion of believers' present glorification. In the following discussion, I will present only those elements that are most helpful in illuminating Jacob's conclusions.

---

23 Jacob (2018, p. 123, n. 2) explains that the word "vocational" should not be taken to imply "functional." Rather, it implies only an ontological reality expressed as a lived reality (being and act held inseparably). In other words, believers are not divine like the eternal Son incarnate in the Christ, but the depth of their humanity is shaped by his humanity as they embody his same human experience. "Participation in Christ does not blur the ever-present distinction between God in Christ and believers in Christ. The glory in which believers participate is not innate to themselves; it originates in God alone and is received only as a gift from God in union with Christ" (pp. 134–135).

Humanity's Glorification

In Jacob's (2018) exegetical analysis of the words "glory" (*doxa*) and "glorify" (*doxazō*) on pages 21–32, she draws three conclusions regarding the term's function in reference to humanity:

> First, *glory* (and its cognates) primarily bears its denotative meaning of status/honour associated with power, authority, character, or riches. In nearly every instance it is a reference to the exalted status or honour the person possesses or in which they exist, rather than a visible splendor after the likeness of God's theophanic splendor. Second, humanity's glory and glorification as exalted status or possessed honour is often associated with the person's status as king, ruler, or person of authority. Third, glorification of a person is never indicative of the transformation of a person's sanctity. (p. 256)

Having established the basic use of the notion of glory, Jacob (2018, pp. 55–63) shows that this was indeed the use of the word in the Old Testament book of Daniel, and she concludes with a significant observation:

> Other than Moses' face reflecting the splendour of God, at no point is it unequivocally the case that a human is given glory or glorified such that the human's body is made to shine due to being in the presence of God. Rather, it is almost entirely the case that the glory given to a person (or a person's glorification) either constitutes or is closely related to the honour, power, wealth, or authority associated with an exalted status of rule. (pp. 62–63)

Jacob (2018, p. 64) regrets that our incorrect notion of glory as the presence of God manifested in light phenomena has so widely "affected the message of redemption in Romans and thereby also the meaning of 'conformed to the image of [God's] Son' in Romans 8:29b." She also laments the fact that Paul's frequent use of *doxa* and *doxazō* is so neglected in current New Testament scholarship.[24] This is troublesome since, as she demonstrates, Romans 8:29b can be understood only when the motif of glory is properly grasped in its surrounding context (especially Romans 5:2; 8:17, 18, 21, 30). In this context, the glory for which all God's people hope (Rom. 5:2) is "humanity's renewed status of honour associated with its created purpose of having dominion over creation, then creation's renewal as a result of humanity's restored *doxa*" (Jacob, 2018, p. 120). This was made possible through Jesus of Nazareth the eternal Son incarnate, who undid "what Adam did, condemn[ed] sin in the flesh

---

24 Jacob (2018, p. 65, n. 2) offers the following list of the 61 occurrences of *doxa* within the Pauline canon: Rom. 1:23; 2:7, 10; 3:7, 23; 4:20; 5:2; 6:4; 8:18, 21; 9:4, 23 [2x]; 11:36; 15:7; 16:27); 1 Cor. 2:7, 8; 10:31; 11:7 [2x], 15; 15:40, 41 [4x], 43); 2 Cor. 1:20; 3:7 [2x], 8, 9 [2x], 10, 11 [2x], 18 [3x]; 4:4, 6, 15, 17; 6:8; 8:19, 23; and relatively speaking, in Eph. 1:6, 12, 14, 17, 18; 3:13, 16, 21 and Phil. 1:11; 2:11; 3:19, 21; 4:19, 20. The verb *doxazō* appears 12 times: Rom. 1:21; 8:30; 11:13; 15:6, 9; 1 Cor. 6:20; 12:26; 2 Cor. 3:10 [2x]; 9:13; Gal. 1:24; 2 Th. 3:1.

(Rom. 8:3), and restore[d] humanity's crown of glory." Jacob (2018, p. 121) writes that "understanding glory as humanity's honourable position associated with its dominion over the created order as God's vicegerent" is fundamental to understanding the phrase "conformed to the image of [God's] Son."

Participation with the Christ

Jacob (2018, pp. 122–169) also presents a detailed study of Paul's "incorporative language," in which he refers to believers sharing in fellowship with the Christ to the extent that what is true of the Christ becomes true of them also. Jacob demonstrates how Paul articulates in Romans 5–8 in general, and in Romans 8:29 in particular, a vocational participation in which the participation of the *pistos* in the resurrection life and glory of Jesus of Nazareth fulfils their intended vocation as the Creator's earthly representatives. She does this by focusing on Romans 6:4–8, where Paul says believers are transferred in baptism from their identity in Adam to their new identity in the Christ. Being united with the Christ, believers participate in the resurrection life of Jesus of Nazareth and actively share in his new Adamic reign.

Skilfully integrating the participation of the *pistos* in the inheritance of the eternal Son incarnate, their participation in his glory (Rom. 8:17), and their own glorification as adopted children of God (Rom. 8:30), Jacob (2018, p. 264) concludes:

> The depiction of humanity being crowned with glory and honor and established with dominion over creation in Psalm 8 is now again a reality, both through the Firstborn Son of God and those who participate in his exalted status, that is, his glory. This is the heart of Romans 8:17–30 and Romans 8:29b and is thus the heart of my argument: as children of God, believers are coheirs with the Son of God and thus share in his glory: they are conformed to the image of the Son, who rules as God's Firstborn and as humanity's representative. (2018, p. 264)

Jacob maintains that participation in the firstborn Son's exalted position over creation is the calling and purpose of all *pistos*, in the present as well as the future. As we participate now by *pistis* in the life of Jesus of Nazareth, reflecting him as the perfect *imago hominis*, our humanity is redeemed to fulfil the Creator's purposes, and this is the hope of all creation (Rom. 8:19–22). As Jacob (2018, p. 241), quoting Hahne (2006, p. 215), notes, "The futility of nature will be removed *so that* it fulfils the purpose for which it was created" (emphasis hers). She suggests that, though we do not yet fully possess our inheritance in the perfect God-man, we are nevertheless called by the Creator with the purpose of cooperating with him to restore his creation in the present (Jacob, 2018, p. 242).

Jacob (2018, p. 266) sums up her answer to one of the key questions of her study—what is the goal of salvation?—with these meaningful words:

For too long, scholars and laymen alike have myopically viewed justification and salvation as ends in themselves, whether for the benefit of the individual or of the incorporative body of Christ. The goal of salvation is believers' conformity to the Son of God—their participation in his rule over creation as God's eschatological family and as renewed humanity—but only and always with the purpose of extending God's hand of mercy, love, and care to his wider creation. This was humanity's job in the beginning; it will be the believers' responsibility and honor in the future; it is God's purpose in calling his people in the present.

Concluding Thoughts

As far as I can ascertain, Haley Jacob had no knowledge of the work of Joshua Jipp (2015) when she conducted her careful study of Romans 8:29. Jipp's name does not appear anywhere in her work. The two scholars do not examine the same biblical themes or motifs, nor are they attempting to answer the same questions.

However, the similarity between the results of their research is striking. Both authors highlight the importance of our participation in the eternal Son's rule over creation as the goal of our salvation. And like Jacob, Jipp ties this to our conformity to the image of the Son (2015, pp. 194–195) writing:

> God's intention for humanity to reign over creation as God's vicegerents (Gen. 1:26–28; Ps. 8:4–6), an intention that was corrupted by Adam's unleashing of sin, death, and corruption of the cosmos (Rom. 5:12–21), is brought to fruition through the Messiah's cosmic rule and his extension of this rule to his people. ... The references to believers' future "glorification" (8:17), the coming "glory that will be revealed for us" (8:18), and "the freedom of glory for God's children (8:21b) is precisely the pristine glory meant for Adam, eschatologically restored to redeemed humanity by virtue of the resurrected-enthroned Messiah's new bodily existence (cf. "the image of his son"; 8:29).

I have not presented in this chapter a framework or context for understanding all the metaphors Paul uses to describe the transformation of status and/or identity of those who by *pistis* are "rooted in the Christ." Entering into debates about justification and union or participation with the Christ, which often arise in current exegetical discourse, would not advance my argument. My purpose is to highlight the central role of the reigning Lord Jesus of Nazareth, the perfect God-man, not only in our redemption but also in our present re-creation into the pre-Fall image of humanity (i.e., our glorification). This perspective is central to a gospel-driven theology of discipleship.

In chapter 13, we will look at the role of the person of the Holy Spirit in the process of our re-creation or glorification in union with the God/man and our participation in his restorative reign.

Questions to Think About

1. The first part of this study examines faith (*pistis*) in the life of the faithful (*pistos*) as they participate in the "kingdom of the Son he [God] loves" (Col. 1:13–14). What is Paul's purpose in highlighting our transfer into the kingdom of the Son in this passage? What are the implications of this passage, for those believers and for us?

2. I propose that the thrust of Paul's argument in Colossians centres on Lord Jesus as both the model and the aim of *pistis* for all people. Do you agree? If so, what might the implications be for developing maturity in Christian discipleship?

3. In the section of this chapter entitled, "Jesus the king is God's Son and God's Image" I state that a person must still learn to "put on" the likeness of Jesus of Nazareth, even after that person is "in Christ," and I quote another scholar who states that the goal of our salvation is conformity to the Son of God. How can this truth function as a corrective to imperfect models of discipleship and Christian growth?

4. The last section of this chapter presents the claim that the goal of our salvation is participation in the rule of the crucified, resurrected, and enthroned eternal Son incarnate over a redeemed and restored creation. How should this reality affect our lives individually, collectively, and in our interaction with the world around us?

13. Enacting Allegiance, Empowered by the Spirit

In chapter 12, we examined how the Apostle Paul explained the goal of his life and ministry in his letter to the Colossians. His objective was to "present everyone perfect in Christ" because, as he put it, that is our "hope of glory" (Col. 1:28). In his letter to the Romans, when Paul says that the Father's goal is to "conform us to the likeness of his Son" (Rom. 8:29), he again ties this process to our "hope of glory." This is not the only similarity between these two important Pauline texts. In Colossians, Paul connects the process of "perfecting everyone" (Col. 1:28) in order to present them perfect in Christ with "his [God's] energy which so powerfully works in me" (Col. 1:29). In Romans, Paul is more explicit, tying our hope to the "Spirit of adoption" (Rom. 8:22–24), who "helps us in our weakness" (Rom. 8:26–27).

In this study, we look at the Spirit, the third member of the triune God, and the vital role he plays in our apprenticeship to the Lord Jesus. We recognize from the start that it is impossible to have a relationship with Jesus of Nazareth that has not been prepared and mediated by the Spirit. In the person of the Spirit, the Creator draws us toward the God-man in repentance and *pistis*. Moreover, the Spirit connects us with the Son who, the Father loves, leading and empowering us to enact our allegiance to him. Furthermore, the Spirit binds us with one another in the community of Christ-followers, both locally and globally.

This study does not pretend to be comprehensive. It would be impossible to examine the many facets of the Spirit's work in this short chapter. For instance, I will not look at the Spirit's action in the creative work of the Godhead. Nor will I trace the Spirit's work in empowering Israel's leaders. Neither will I address the Spirit's role in revealing the Word in Scripture, and I will not engage in the debate about whether all believers are "filled with the Spirit." I will not discuss the role of the Spirit in spiritual gifts and ministerial offices, or the Spirit's empowerment of the individual Christ-follower in all its dimensions. Many good resources are available for those who wish to pursue these (and other) important questions.

Instead, I will focus on the Spirit's role in our lives under the reign of the Lord Jesus. In our study of Colossians, we saw that the Christ must clearly have the preeminence in everything (Col. 1:18). Because Jesus of Nazareth, the incarnate Son, is at the center of the overall project of the Creator, we must resist the error of separating the Spirit from Jesus. Just as it can be legitimately argued that without the Spirit, Jesus of Nazareth could never have become the Christ (van der Kooi & van den Brink, 2017, p. 411), we can also reason that the Spirit, if disassociated from Jesus of Nazareth, the Christ, would not energize our restoration to the Edenic state, which is the Creator's purpose for us. This is so because Jesus of Nazareth is the prototype of that Edenic state, and the Creator purposes that we be "conformed to his image" (Rom. 8:28). This is the heart of the biblical image of our salvation as "participation with Christ," metaphorically expressed in terms of belonging to a family, political or military solidarity with Christ, participation in the *ekklēsia*, or living within the Christ story (Jipp, 2015, p. 280).

The Spirit's association with the eternal Son incarnate is evident in the biblical portrait of the Christ, as van der Kooi & van den Brink (2017, p. 498) note: "The Spirit precedes Jesus, rests upon him, and is handed on through him. Or to reverse the angle: Jesus proceeds from the Spirit, bears the Spirit, and is the exalted Lord of God's Spirit." New Testament scholars and theologians recognize that the followers of the Christ must understand the identity and work of both Jesus of Nazareth and the Spirit, and how they fit together in the Creator's restorative purposes. This is the subject we will examine in this chapter.

We will begin by looking at the character or inner disposition of the Spirit. My argument is that the Spirit cannot be properly understood if we ignore or minimize his[1] personality. Next, we will study the inseparability of the resurrected and reigning Jesus of Nazareth and the Spirit. Having established that it is biblically impossible ever to separate the Christ and the Spirit, we will see why it is also biblically inconceivable to live under the reign of Christ without the empowering of the Spirit.

The Personality of the Spirit

There is only one God, who exists from all eternity and who is fully present in three "persons," "personalities," or (as Karl Barth preferred) "modes" (Johnson, 2013, p. 44). Each member of the Trinity is coequal in divinity. Each is God from all eternity, and each is fully God. There are not three gods, but three entities of one God (Giles, 2012, pp. 263–264). Drawing from the

---

1 Although the Hebrew Scriptures characterize the work of the Spirit primarily as a creative, liberating, and prophetic power, from Pentecost on this power acquires stronger personal traits. Opinions differ about whether the Spirit must be regarded as a person. Many theologians have opted for an alternative term such as "personality" or "mode of existence." Others, based on descriptions of the Spirit as "Comforter" (Jn. 14:16) and "Helper" (Jn. 14:26; 15:26; 16:7–8), prefer to label the Spirit as "her." I will use "him" to underscore the Spirit's close association with the Christ (1 Cor. 15:45; 2 Cor. 3:17).

principle of "simplicity" in God developed by Augustine, Dennis Jowers (2012, pp. 375–400) demonstrates why each characteristic of God is identical to what he is intrinsically, and that there can be no differentiation in him. Therefore, the Spirit is fully God, yet the Spirit is not the only divine being. The Spirit exists eternally with the Father and the Son, who possess the same divine nature. What distinguishes the Spirit from the Father and the eternal Son is his particular role in relationship to theirs.

And the role of the Spirit mirrors his own disposition and work in the Creator's project. Bruce Ware (2005, p. 104) affirms that only to the extent that we understand and respect the desire of the Spirit to honor the Son, to the glory of the Father, do we properly understand his activity. Ware (2005, p. 104) writes:

> It is nothing short of remarkable that the Spirit clearly embraces and in no respect resents the fact that he has, eternally, what might be called "the background position" in the Trinity. ... The Holy Spirit embraces eternally the backstage position in relation to the Father and the Son. ... Even when the Spirit has the role of authority over the incarnate Son, his whole purpose in this work of empowerment and anointing is to advance the work of the Son, to the glory of the Father. ... In creation, redemption, and consummation, he willingly accepts the role of supporter, helper, sustainer, and equipper, and in all these respects he forsakes the spotlight.

Because it is his character, nature and choice, the Spirit is the "environment" (Carr, 1975, p. 506) or the "sphere" in which growth in Christ-likeness happens. He is never the goal of discipleship (Gunton, 2003, p. 180). Furthermore, just as eternal Son is no longer the same after the Incarnation, neither is the Spirit. Today, the Spirit is always active with a Christological or filiological dimension. Along this line, James Dunn (1997, p. 322) affirms that "the Spirit not only creates the character of Christ in believers, but also the Spirit has himself taken on the character of Christ." In short, it is wrong to detach the Spirit from Jesus of Nazareth in our thinking or practice. Making the power, fullness, or charisms of the Spirit the center of our attention is inappropriate. We are not called to be disciples of the Spirit. Our purpose is not to become more "charismatic" in that sense. The Spirit empowers us as we seek to learn more about Jesus of Nazareth, the Christ, and conform our lives to him. We cannot have the Spirit by himself. In fact, since the Spirit seeks always and only to point away from himself to the Son and, through him, to the Father, the best way to honor the Spirit is bringing glory to Jesus of Nazareth (Jn. 16:12–14).

The Spirit Is the Spirit of Jesus

The fact that the Spirit who works in us is the Spirit of Jesus of Nazareth, our reigning Lord, helping us to progress in our conformity to his image can be seen in the way Paul identifies the Spirit as "the Spirit of Christ" (Rom. 8:9), "the Spirit of his [God's] Son," (Gal. 4:6), and "the Spirit of Jesus Christ" (Phil. 1:19).

Jesus of Nazareth Is Above; the Spirit Is Below

Admittedly, the perfect God-man, the reigning Christ, is intimately linked to the Spirit, but they are also distinct. This distinction is reflected in the fact that the Spirit, not the Christ, personally indwells his followers.[2] Paul explicitly tells the Colossian believers that Christ is "above" and "seated at the right hand of God" (Col. 3:1, see also Ac. 2:33–34; Eph. 1:20–23; Heb. 1:13). As Horton (2011, p. 601) states, "Christ does not dwell in our hearts immediately, but through the indwelling of the Spirit. Furthermore, the Spirit's ministry is always to point us outside of ourselves to Christ's person and work."

Paul expresses the relationship between Jesus of Nazareth who is in heaven and the Spirit who is among us with a sort of equation: "So it is written: 'the first man Adam became a living being': the last Adam became a life-giving spirit" (1 Cor. 15:45). Some understand this formula as an illustration of the totalizing effect of the human condition as sin and death, and as "flesh opposed to the Spirit." Others see it as a sort of affirmation certifying the future resurrection of the followers of Jesus of Nazareth, the last Adam (Schreiner, 2001, p. 153). Evidently, Paul is referring to the resurrected Jesus of Nazareth. However, describing the risen Jesus of Nazareth as "life-giving" carries yet another important meaning, as Luke Timothy Johnson (2013, p. 286) says: "In the case of Christ, resurrection means exaltation into the presence and power of God, since God alone is the giver of life."

These preliminary observations about Jesus of Nazareth and the Spirit remind us that we must avoid the tendency to confuse one with the other in our attempts to solve the mystery of their relationship and connection to the Father. We must, as the Creed of Athanasius reminds us, consider the Father, eternal Son, and Spirit simultaneously in their unity and distinction.[3] The Scriptures

---

2 I have heard many times the evangelical appeal to "ask Jesus into your heart." Although this wording may seek legitimacy in the New Testament notions of "Christ in you, the hope of glory" (Col. 1:27), "Christ dwelling "in your hearts through faith" (Eph. 3:17), or believers having "received Christ Jesus the Lord" (Col. 2:6), it downplays the clear fact that Christ dwells in or among his people by his Spirit, for the bodily, risen Jesus is in heaven.

3 The popular tendency to pray "Dear Lord Jesus" or "Come, Holy Spirit" is conspicuously absent from the New Testament. Although prayer is talking to God, and although both the God-man and the Spirit are truly divine, Scriptural reasons for praying to anyone but the Father are scant. There are a few prayers directed toward the Lord

indicate that it was the Father who installed Jesus of Nazareth, the eternal Son, above all other kings (Rom. 8:29). As a result, Jesus of Nazareth's royal identity, reign, and destiny are shared with his followers through their reception of the life-giving "Spirit of adoption" (Rom. 8:15). Each member of the Trinity is, and has always been, active in the accomplishment of the Creator's redemptive project.

Returning to 1 Corinthians 15:45, it is clear that when Paul uses the title "last Adam" he is referring to the resurrected Jesus of Nazareth. In this sense, Jesus of Nazareth is the beginning of a new race, the firstborn of a new family. Just as the first Adam became a living being through the breath (Heb. *ruach*) of the Creator (Gen. 2:7), in the same way Jesus of Nazareth became a "life-giving breath" by his resurrection. Dunn (1997, p. 322) explains: "The 'life-giving Spirit' is that power which believers experienced as new life, liberating life, life from the dead." Dunn warns that we should not think that Paul is saying that the eternal Son abandoned his human body and became as he was before the incarnation. Instead, Paul is affirming that by his resurrection, insofar as the religious experience of his followers is concerned, Jesus of Nazareth and the Spirit are inseparable. Although Jesus is above and the Spirit is below, any religious experience the character and effect of which are not in conformity to Jesus of Nazareth's reign does not derive from the life-giving Spirit.

The Pauline parallel between the first and the last Adam is also highlighted in 1 Corinthians 15:49: "Just as we have borne the likeness of the earthly man, so shall we bear the likeness of the man from heaven." Kline (1999, p. 82) notes that the birth of Seth in Adam's image (Gen. 5:1–3) seems to confirm that "the image of God and son of God" are "twin concepts." For this reason, Kline concludes that the eternal Son incarnate is the archetypal pattern—the true human—according to which the Spirit recreates human beings as ectypal (i.e., reproduced as a molding or cast) copies. It is no wonder, then, that the eternal Son, the glorified new Adam, returns as the life-giving Spirit to inaugurate the renewed or restored creation.

Jesus (Acts 7:59–60; 1 Cor. 16:22; Rev. 22:20; Heb. 7:25). There are no prayers directed toward the Holy Spirit in the Bible. The instructions of both the Lord Jesus (Matt. 6:9) and the Apostle Paul (Eph. 2:18; 3:14) indicate that prayer is addressed to the Father, through the mediation of the Son, enabled by the Spirit. This "trinitarian" form of prayer is vitally important. Much Christian praying today is effectively unitarian: "Dear Lord … Amen." This ambiguous use of the title "Lord," without signifying whether it intends to designate the Father (*Yahweh*, the Almighty) or the risen Christ, is a deviation from the norm established by the New Testament to address our prayers specifically to the Father.

We Experience Jesus Only by the Spirit

Until he returns to judge the world (Rev. 19:11–21) and complete the Creator's plan of restoration of the cosmos (Rev. 21–22), the risen and reigning Jesus of Nazareth can be experienced only through the Spirit. This observation reflects the promise given by Jesus to his first disciples shortly before his crucifixion:

> If you love me, you will obey what I command. And I will ask the Father, and he will give you another Counsellor to be with you forever—the Spirit of truth. The world cannot accept him, because it neither sees him nor knows him; But you know him, for he lives with you and will be in you. I will not leave you as orphans; I will come to you. (Jn. 14:15–18)

Some scholars think that the "return" Jesus of Nazareth is promising here is the Parousia, or his second coming. However, if Jesus had been speaking of that event that will occur at the final judgment of the world, then it would follow that his disciples have been "orphans" ever since he ascended to heaven (Ac. 1:2, 9). Therefore, the only reasonable interpretation of this promise to "come back" to his disciples is that this took place when, in the Spirit, he came to "be with us forever" (Jn. 14:16–17, 23).[4] The "other Comforter" is the agent in whom the presence and the life of Jesus of Nazareth are communicated to the disciples. This is how they "see" or "perceive" him and participate in his reign (Bennema, 2002, pp. 222–223). We find the same affirmation in 1 John, which proclaims that the followers of the Lord Jesus are in communion with the Father and the Son, and that the Father and the Son live in them by the Spirit (1 Jn. 1:3; 2:28; 3:24; 4:13). It is precisely this relationship with the Father and the Son by the Spirit that frees and empowers those who have lived under the hostile lords of darkness (Col. 1:13), enabling them to "put on the new self" (Col. 3:5, 8–9, 12).

I realize that the relationship between the Spirit and Jesus of Nazareth continues to be debated by scholars and missiologists. Much of contemporary evangelical theology attaches the salvific merits of Christ's life and death that are imputed to us by grace through faith (i.e., the doctrines of atonement, salvation, and justification) to the person of Jesus, whereas it attributes our ensuing growth in holiness (the doctrine of sanctification) to the work of the Holy Spirit. It is customary to think of Jesus as the Saviour and the Spirit as the sanctifier. But I fully agree with Marcus Johnson's (2013, p. 126) claim that this view needs serious revision, "lest we begin to imagine that the work of the Spirit in some way eclipses or replaces the work of Christ" in our growth in discipleship. Johnson continues, "Jesus does not send the Spirit to the church in order that she might become holy in Jesus's absence. Rather, Jesus sends the Spirit in order that he, through the Spirit, *might be present as her holiness*" (p.

---

4 See Bennema (2002, p. 223); Brown (1971, pp. 645–646); Dunn (1997, pp. 350–351); Ladd (1993, pp. 330, 339); Turner (1992, p. 81).

126; emphasis in original). Drawing from 2 Corinthians 13:5, Galatians 2:20, Colossians 1:27, and Ephesians 3:16f, Dunn (1997, p. 323) conclusively summarizes this truth: "The distinctive mark of the Christian is experience of the Spirit as the life of Christ" (see also Hamilton, 1957, pp. 10–11).

This understanding of the Spirit goes far beyond that of the Old Testament concerning the Spirit of God. Through his resurrection and enthronement at the right hand of the Father, Jesus of Nazareth, who lived his life "under the influence of the Spirit" (Greek *kata pneuma*; Rom. 1:4), became the most visible and distinct expression of the Spirit. The life of the incarnate Son was so empowered by the Spirit that his relationships and actions became the most distinct and perfect reflection of what it means to be a Spirit-filled human (cf. Lk. 1:15; 4:1). The gospel we announce declares that Jesus of Nazareth was a man determined by the Spirit, and that he lived in such a way that he himself became the perfect expression of the *karpos* (fruit) of the Spirit (Gal. 5:22). He was and continues to be the true "spiritual person" (1 Cor. 2:15; Greek *pneumatikos*). For this reason, we can say that he is the one who makes the invisible Spirit "visible."

A gospel-driven theology of discipleship is therefore profoundly trinitarian and anchored in our vocational participation in the God-man, the Christ. It is evident that insofar as Paul was concerned, those who by *pistis* become followers of the Messiah enter into a dual relationship—to God as Father and to Jesus of Nazareth as Lord. This relationship and the awareness of it was attributed by them to the Spirit, as Jipp (2015, p. 188) notes: "Christ's people belong to him and his royal family, then, precisely because they have the same *pneuma* as Christ." In other words, the first followers of the Christ understood the Spirit as the one by whom they belong to the Father, in service to the Lord Jesus.

Notice that the eternal Son incarnate rarely gives "credit," as it were, to the Spirit for the work and ministry he performs. One example where he does so is instructive. In Matthew 12, after casting a demon out of a blind and mute man so that he could see and speak (Mt. 12:22), Jesus explained his power to do so as follows: "But if it is by the Spirit of God that I cast out demons, then the kingdom of God has come upon you" (v. 28). Bruce Ware (2005, p. 106) observes that although this text is helpful in indicating the true source of Jesus' miraculous power to cast out demons, his reference to the Spirit was probably intended to call attention to his own identity as the Spirit-anointed Messiah who was bringing the kingdom. Ware thus concludes that Jesus' reference to the Spirit was to establish his own identity.

The Spirit and Our Conformity to the Christ

In chapter 12, we examined the notions of being "glorified" and "conformed" to the image of "God's Son" as they interact in the epistle to the Romans.

Another key text that links these notions to the work of the Spirit is 2 Corinthians 3:17–18:

> Now the Lord [Jesus] is the Spirit, and where the Spirit of the Lord is, there is freedom. And we, who with unveiled faces all reflect the Lord's glory, are being transformed into his likeness with ever-increasing glory, which comes from the Lord, who is the Spirit.

There is a broad consensus among scholars that Paul wrote 2 Corinthians to defend himself against Christ-followers who were questioning his apostleship (2 Cor. 3:1), sincerity (2 Cor. 1:12), appearance, simplicity of speech (2 Cor. 10:10) and even his sanity (2 Cor. 5:13). In 2 Corinthians 3:7–18, Paul addresses yet another problem. There was apparently a group of people, probably from a Jewish background, who overestimated the continuity between Judaism and discipleship to Jesus of Nazareth, the Christ. They seem to have held that the revelation given to Moses, the Law, continued to apply to Christ-followers (2 Cor. 3:3–6).

Paul responds to this incorrect understanding by alluding to two biblical promises that he regards as fulfilled in his day (cf. 2 Cor. 1:20). First, Ezekiel 36:26 (cf. 11:19) indicates that *Yahweh's* Spirit would give his people hearts of flesh instead of hearts of stone, so that they would keep his commandments (36:27; cf. 11:20). Whereas *Yahweh's* finger had written the law in stone tablets (Ex. 31:18; 34:1, 4), the Spirit had now inscribed divine life in their hearts (2 Cor. 3:2). The life referred to here is that of the life-giving Spirit. He is the one, who communicates regarding Jesus of Nazareth in whom the entire law was "fulfilled" or "brought to completion." We will come back to this topic later in this chapter.

Second, Paul alludes to Jeremiah, stating that in contrast to the disobedience of God's people in history (Jer. 31:32–33), participation in the life of the Christ, the living law who has brought the law to fulfilment in his self-giving death, enables people to obey the Torah (2 Cor. 3:9; cf. Jer. 31:31–34; Ezek. 36:24–28; Dt. 30:6, 8). Here we immediately note that Paul speaks of this as the "new covenant," of which he is a minister[5] (2 Cor. 3:6). The "letter," or

---

5 This is the only place in the NT where the phrase "minister of a new covenant" (*diakonous kainēs diathēkēs*) appears. The *diakon* word group alludes to the obligations of the followers of the Christ within the metaphor of slavery. The lordship of the crucified, resurrected, and reigning Jesus of Nazareth is the heart of the gospel, and thus in 2 Cor. 4:5 Paul writes, "It is not ourselves that we proclaim, but Jesus Christ as Lord, *and therefore* ourselves as your slaves." There is a natural sequence from lordship to lowly, unquestioning service to one's fellow believers. There were, however, two important differences between these two relationships (i.e., to Christ as Lord and to fellow Christians as servants) of which Paul speaks. First, the Corinthians were not Paul's lord any more than he was their lord (cf. 2 Cor. 1:24). His service to them was "for Jesus' sake," and only Jesus of Nazareth is Lord. Thus Paul can refer to himself and

what is merely written on stone or with ink (cf. 3:3; Rom. 7:6), cannot give life, but can only sentence transgressors to death (cf. Rom. 7:5, 10; 8:2; 1 Cor. 15:56; Gal. 3:21). The law written on human hearts (vocational participation with Christ) by the life-giving Spirit enables them to obey the law of Christ.[6]

In 2 Cor. 3:7–11, Paul infers logically that the "glory" of this gospel-driven new covenant ministry he describes in Rom. 1:5 and 16:26 (cf. Rom. 15:7–12) is that of securing "the obedience of *pistis*" among the nations, and that it exceeds that of Moses' day. Jipp (2015, p. 178) observes:

> Remembering that God's decree in Psalm 2, echoed in Rom. 1:4, has promised the "nations as an inheritance for you" (Ps. 2:8) to the enthroned Son, it seems likely that Paul views his apostolic task as securing the inheritance of God's Son through his apostolic ministry.

Paul dwells on the surpassing glory of this new covenant ministry at some length. He contends first that it is only reasonable to believe that the life-giving Spirit would reveal greater glory than the law does. It is noteworthy that although glory (*doxa*) in 2 Corinthians 3 does clearly refer to *Yahweh's* visible splendour as it was revealed on Moses' face, Paul's point is not to emphasize God's presence. Paul is using this reference as background to describe the authority and power of the Spirit's Christ-communicating ministry as superior to that of the law. As such, this glorious manifestation of divine power is not limited to the superiority of "the ministry of justification" as compared to the "ministry of condemnation" (Newman, 1992, p. 235). Nor does it refer simply to a "manifestation of (divine) power," "divine presence," or "divine nature" (Thrall, 1994, p. 246). Neither is the greater glory of this second covenant ministry due primarily to the fact that this glory is more "permanent" than that of the first covenant (Keener, 2005, p. 168; Hughes, 2006, pp. 77–78). Although these elements are present in the background, I believe Paul is using the notion of glory here to signify that our lived–out loyalty to the "law of Christ" makes any attempts to obey the Torah ridiculous.

Paul develops his argument from the lesser to the greater, which was a well-known principle of biblical interpretation (Collins, 2013, p. 83). The reader of 2 Cor. 3:8 might have expected the ministry of death to be contrasted with the ministry of life, but Paul speaks of the latter as the ministry of the Spirit. Whereas some glory belonged to the old slavery or service to the law of Moses,

---

his fellow Apostles as "slaves of God" (2 Cor. 6:4) or "slaves of Christ" (2 Cor. 11:23; cf. 1 Cor. 12:5) In his earlier correspondence with the Corinthians, Paul asked the question "Who are we?" with regard to himself and Apollos and answered, "Slaves through whom you came to believe" (1 Cor. 3:5). Second, Paul was not obliged always and everywhere to obey and please the Corinthians as he was obliged to serve his heavenly Lord (Harris, 1999, p. 103).

6 Thus, in 1 Cor. 9:21, Paul refers to himself as "not being without God's law but in the law of Christ" (*ennomos Christou*).

an abundance of glory belongs to the new Spirit-empowered obedience to the law of Christ. Paul drives home his point by stressing that "what was glorious" has no glory now, because it has been surpassed (3:10). Previously, Paul has written about the transient radiance on Moses' face, which was now passing away (3:7). The transient glory on his face symbolized the entire dispensation affiliated with Moses, the old covenant (sometimes called the Sinai covenant) between *Yahweh* and his people Israel. According to this Mosaic covenant, the people were responsible for following the Law, and in return God promised to abundantly bless and protect Israel (Ex. 19:5–8). That too has disappeared, along with its glory, for followers of the Christ. What remains with the ministry of the life-giving Spirit is our empowerment to live out the law of Christ (righteousness). The focus is on Spirit-led ethical conformity to the Christ by virtue of their incorporation into Him, not on compliance with the Old Testament law. This is the case because Christ Jesus is "our righteousness, holiness and redemption" (1 Cor. 1:30) and the one in whom we should "boast" (1 Cor. 1:31).

Paul pursues his argument further by claiming that since we have "such a hope, we are very bold" (3:12).[7] We learn from 1 Corinthians that the so-called "spiritual persons" (1 Cor. 2:15; 3:1) made bold and boisterous claims about their rights and freedoms (1 Cor. 6:12; 8:9; 10:23). Paul's own boldness is produced by hope and grounded in a "freedom" (from the law of Moses) that derives from Spirit-enabled conformity to the Lord Jesus of Nazareth (2 Cor. 3:17–18).

Paul develops this argument by contrasting himself with Moses, the most revered figure after Abraham in Jewish history (3:13). Moses was not unknown in the Gentile world (see Collins, 2013, p. 85). Paul's intent is not to disparage Moses in his comparisons and contrasts (3:7–11), but to highlight the supremacy of Spirit-enabled conformity to the last Adam over obedience to the Torah in our everyday existence. Paul contrasts himself with Moses, pointing out that he spoke openly whereas Moses put a veil on his face so that the children of Israel would not gaze intently at it while his radiance was passing away (3:13). The negative comparison in verse 13 refers to Exodus 34:33–35, allowing Paul to continue his commentary on the Hebrew Scriptures that he began in verse 7. Once again, Paul introduces the thought of something passing

---

7 The term "boldness" was well known in the Hellenistic world. Speaking boldly was a right of citizens, and a quality attributed to great speakers. But Paul may have had something else in mind as well. In the biblical tradition, boldness is a quality of prophetic speech (Collins, 2013, p. 86). Interestingly, in his eulogy at the time of Moses' death, Joshua said, "But since then there has not arisen in Israel a prophet like Moses, whom *Yahweh* knew face to face, in all the signs and wonders which *Yahweh* sent him to do in the land of Egypt, before Pharaoh, before all his servants, and in all his land, and by all that mighty power and all the great terror which Moses performed in the sight of all Israel" (Dt. 34:10–12).

away and speaks of its end. On this all scholars agree. What they do not agree on, is exactly what it is that has passed away.

Based on his continued use of the veiling and unveiling metaphor in association with transformation into "the likeness of the Lord Jesus of Nazareth" in his perfect humanity (3:18; 4:3–4, 6), I propose that Paul is alluding to his own example and experience in reflecting the likeness of the God-man. A typical feature of Midrashic exposition[8] of biblical texts is the application of the text to the author's present circumstances. Paul does this: "Even to this day when Moses is read, a veil covers their hearts" (2 Cor. 3:15). The veil introduced in verse 13 is thus reintroduced into Paul's exposition with a contemporary application. It serves as the motif around which Paul develops his argument. This is the only use of this metaphor in Paul's letters. His purpose is to emphasize our inability to reflect the will of the Creator by following the Torah.

Collins (2013, p. 87) points out that Paul is evoking the scene when the Torah is read publicly in the synagogue. He explains:

Here 3:14 contains the oldest known use of the expression "old covenant" (*tēs palaias diathēkēs*, "Old Testament") in reference to a text. The terminology does not appear elsewhere in the NT. It appears here in contrast with "new covenant" (*kainēs diathēkēs*, 3:6), but the word "covenant" has a different connotation in each of the two cases.

Up to this day, Paul says, attempts to actualize the pre-Adamic intent of the Creator by mirroring the Scriptures have fallen short. A veil has fallen over the understanding, and it needs to be destroyed. Here Paul is alluding to a similar phrase that occurs in the citation of Dt. 29:4 in Rom. 11:8. In each case, there is a sort of hardening of hearts whenever Moses is read (2 Cor. 3:15).

How is the veil removed? Without asking the question, Paul introduces another passage of Scripture to give an answer. "Whenever anyone turns to the Lord [Jesus], the veil is removed" (3:16). The passage cited here is Exodus 34:34, "Whenever Moses went in before the Lord to speak with him, he would take the veil off," but Paul's actualizing exegesis of the text leads him to adopt some modification. He applies the text to anyone rather than just to Moses. He uses "turn to," suggesting "turning from," rather than "went in before." And he says that the "veil is removed," as if by the Creator, whereas the biblical text says that Moses removed the veil.

We miss Paul's point when we interpret this "turning to Christ" as a "conversion" from Judaism to Christianity. That is not what Paul wishes to communicate. His letter is written to those who have already experienced

---

8 Midrashic exposition can be understood as a homily on an Old Testament passage derived by traditional Jewish exegetical methods and consisting of interpretation of or commentary on the text.

"conversion" to Christ. Rather, his argument is that each time Christ-followers turn back to the Old Testament to find guidelines for their growth in Christ–likeness, the veil falls back over their understanding. However, whenever they turn to the Lord Jesus (and to the obedience of *pistis*), the veil is taken away. This is not to say that Christ-followers should not read the OT. Only to highlight that this reading must be "filtered" or "guided" by the life and teaching of the Lord Jesus.

Once again, Paul affirms a dynamic equivalence between the Christ and the Spirit in verse 17.[9] This repeats the pneumatological focus that characterizes his writing about the new covenant (see Col. 3:3, 6, 8, 18). Paul writes that where the Spirit of Christ is, there is freedom (3:17). This is the only place in 2 Corinthians where he mentions freedom.[10] This freedom is not only freedom from the restrictive aspects of the old covenant. It is freedom for true life transformation that comes from reflecting the "glory of the Lord" Jesus.

Returning to the theme of the removal of the veil (see vv. 14, 16), Paul brings his argument to its conclusion: "And we, who with unveiled faces all reflect the Lord's glory, are being transformed into his likeness with ever-increasing glory, which comes from the Lord, who is the Spirit" (3:18). The word translated "reflect" (*katoptrizomenoi*) is a rare word, found neither in the Greek Septuagint translation of the OT nor elsewhere in the NT. Paul uses it to describe the singular experience of those Christ-followers who metaphorically "keep their vision" focused on Jesus of Nazareth, which results in them being transformed[11] into the same image (cf. Rom. 8:29).

"His likeness" (3:18) is undoubtedly that of Jesus of Nazareth, the Christ. Many commentators equate this to the Christ as the image of God, in connection with 2 Cor. 4:4. However, they fail to make the connection to the

---

9 Both the title "Lord" and the noun "Spirit" in the phrase "Lord is the Spirit" (v. 17) lack a qualifying article, resulting in an expression the sense of which is difficult to determine precisely. This ambiguity is apparent in the differing translations that appear in published English versions of the text and the works of commentators. Among these translations are the following: the Spirit of the Lord; the Lord of the Spirit; the Lord who is Spirit; the Lord who is the Spirit; the Lord, the Spirit; the Spirit who is the Lord, and the Spirit of the Lord. Each of these translations demonstrates the close connection between the incarnate Son seated on high and the Spirit below.

10 Freedom is a major theme of Paul's letter to the Galatians who seem to have struggled with the same temptation to believe that following the Old Testament Scriptures makes a person a better follower of the Christ (Gal. 2:4; 5:1, 13, cf. Rom 6:18).

11 To speak of the transformation of the followers of Jesus of Nazareth, the last Adam and reigning Lord of creation, Paul uses the verb "transform" (*metamorphoomai*). Paul uses this verb only one other time (in Rom. 12:2), and it appears only four times altogether in the NT. In Romans 12:2, Paul says it is the Creator's perfect and pleasing will that we no longer follow and participate in the narrative and identity of the first Adam, but rather that we be changed to the pattern established by the narrative and identity of the Christ.

first humans, made in the image of God, and our recreation or restoration as we are remade in the image of the second Adam. As we saw at the beginning of this chapter, the second Adam, Jesus of Nazareth, is the true image of God (the human prototype). The fall of the human race into rebellion against the Creator caused humans even to destroy their own humanity which was made according to the Creator's perfect pattern (i.e., the incarnate Son). The Creator's plan now is to restore the prototype's image in us from "glory to glory," as Paul says (2 Cor. 3:18). This progressive transformation into the image of the Lord Jesus who is reigning above is enabled by "the Spirit of the Lord Jesus" who is below.

Those Who Don't "Get It" (4:1–4)

Paul began his argument with an exposition of the exodus story, and, referring to what he had written in 3:7–11, he wrote, "Therefore, since we have such a hope, we are very bold" (3:12).[12] In 4:1, he says that this ministry of making the Christ known and accompanying people from among the nations in their progressive transformation into his image is an act of mercy on the Creator's part. Since he (and his coworkers) are beneficiaries of God's graciousness, Paul says that "we do not lose heart" (2 Cor. 4:16).

Rather than being discouraged, Paul says that in his ministry he did not use deception or distort the word of God (4:2). On the contrary, he says that he fully disclosed the truth. And since he communicates the truth in this way, Paul commends himself to everyone. Paul first raised the issue of self-commendation in 3:1 and cited his own conscience as a witness to his integrity (1:12). Now he calls upon the conscience of his readers to attest to the quality of his lifestyle.

Paul had previously invited his readers to examine his way of life in Christ Jesus in 1 Corinthians 4:17, as a visible proof that he was not acting deviously in what he taught. In fact, in that argument based upon his Christ-like attitudes, he urged the Corinthian Christ-followers to imitate him (1 Cor. 4:16). He repeated the same message later in that letter: "Follow my example, as I follow the example of Christ" (1 Cor. 11:1, see also Phil. 3:17; 1 Th. 1:6; 2 Th. 3:7, 9). The last verse of 1 Corinthians 10 alludes to the example of Lord Jesus of Nazareth, the living law of those who live in the kingdom (cf. Col. 1:13), whose every action embodies the one law of Leviticus 19:18, thereby bringing to completion the entirety of the Torah. Paul's argument is that since he has begun to pattern his life after the one who embodied perfect obedience to the Creator in his vicarious giving of himself for humanity, they should imitate him in making the Christ the focal point (cf. 1 Cor. 9:19–23).

---

12 Here Paul continues to use the first-person plural but seems to use it now to refer to his own ministry, the integrity of which he defended in 2:14–3:6.

If we are to intentionally imitate the Lord Jesus of Nazareth, the incarnate Son, then we might be surprised to read the Pauline exhortation of Ephesians 5:1, which tells us to "be imitators of God" rather than imitators of Christ. This is the only explicit reference in either the OT or the NT to "imitating God." Lest we be confused here, Eph. 5:1 should be linked to the admonitions of 4:25–32, which address the "putting off" of the former way of life and the "putting on" of the new self, created to be like God in true righteousness and holiness" (vv. 22–23). Paul refers to this as "the truth that is in Jesus" (v. 21). The imitation of God in Eph. 5:1 should also be understood in relationship to the final clause of the verse: "Just as Christ loved us and gave himself for us." This logical link to the final verses of chapter 4 is seen in the word "therefore" in 5:1. And the words "as dearly loved children" in 5:1—"Be imitators of God, therefore, as dearly loved children"—underscores the idea of reproducing the family likeness, since we have been "adopted as his sons through Jesus Christ" (Eph. 1:4–6; see also Gal. 3:26–28; 4:4–7; Heb. 2:10–11; 1 Jn. 3:1). No one better expresses that family likeness than the perfect God/man, Jesus of Nazareth. He provides the pattern the Corinthians should imitate as they embody the "mind of Christ" (1 Cor. 2:16).

Paul claims that the "truth" he is setting forth clearly (2 Cor. 4:2) is "the gospel" (4:3). In other references to the truth in this letter, he calls it "the truth of Christ" (*alētheia Christou*), as in 2 Cor. 11:10. In his short prayer closing the letter (13:7–9) the Apostle says that we cannot do anything against the truth, and in 6:7 he links truth to doing what is good and avoiding evil, just as he models.

To address those who do not accept his message, Paul again takes up the image of the veil: "And even if our gospel is veiled, it is veiled to those who are perishing" (4:3; cf. 2:15). Paul is certainly referring to those who refuse to adhere to Christ by *pistis*. On this all commentators agree. However, in the context of Paul's overall argument, I suggest that he is also referring to those in the Christ-followerships of Corinth who do not understand that spiritual growth and holiness depend on our relationship to Jesus, who is both the second Adam and the face of God (4:4, 6).

Thomas Schreiner (2001, pp. 137–138) poignantly describes this spiritual blindness: "Unbelievers ... are blinded from perceiving and sensing that Christ is glorious and full of splendor. ... The god of this age obstructs their vision so that they do not perceive Christ as beautiful, lovely and the source of all happiness." We often assume that Paul is describing the unrepentant and unconverted people who cannot perceive the Christ in all his beauty and fullness because the "god of this age" has blinded their eyes. And this is certainly true. However, Paul's use of the metaphor of light shining in darkness could also refer to the creation story (Gen. 1:3). In that Old Testament text, light shining in darkness is used along with references to the "image of God" and to Adam as the head of the old humanity (Barnett, 1997, pp. 225–226; Minor, 2009, p. 82). Understanding Paul to be alluding to the creation story fits more appropriately into the argument he is developing that those who return to the Old Testament Scriptures to determine how to best follow Christ are not seeing clearly. In this sense, they too are "unbelieving" and have been blinded to the beauty and fullness of the God-man.

This second reading, in which some of the Christ-followers have been "blinded," is reinforced by 4:5: "For we preach not ourselves, but Jesus Christ as Lord, and ourselves as your slaves (*doulous*) for Jesus' sake." There is also clearly a precise parallelism between "Jesus Christ as Lord" and "ourselves as your slaves," which suggests that acknowledgement of the lordship of Jesus leads naturally and inevitably to unquestioning service to others (Harris, 1999, p. 103). This once again places the spotlight on our calling to embody the Creator's intent in the person of Jesus of Nazareth, our reigning Lord.

Spirit and Word

Paul's reference to "light shining in our hearts to give us the knowledge of the glory of God in the face of Christ" (2 Cor. 4:6) parallels 2 Peter 1:19: "And we have the word of the prophets made more certain, and you will do well to pay attention to it, as to a light shining in a dark place, until the day dawns and the morning star rises in your hearts." Peter goes on to explain that the word of the prophets did not come from their own initiative but was produced as "they were carried along by the Holy Spirit" (1:20–21).

The difficulties experienced by the Christ-followers in Corinth lead me to address the difficult question of the proper role of the Scriptures in the life of those who adhere to Jesus of Nazareth. I think we would all agree that the Spirit's inspiration and illumination of the Scriptures are related to knowing the Christ who is above and to the restoration of our existence enabled by his Spirit who is below. That is why appropriate biblical interpretation must be seen as the spiritual struggle that it is. As Goldsworthy (2006, p. 315) writes, "Gospel-centred hermeneutics is above all the endeavour to understand the meaning of any aspect of reality, including the Bible, in light of him who is the Light of the World." This is part of the process of putting to death what is "earthly" in us (Col. 3:5) and letting "the word of Christ" dwell in us richly (Col. 3:16).

Though we might agree in general with what has just been stated, it is probably more difficult to reach a consensus on how exactly this is done, or on the roles of both the Word and the Spirit in the process. In the following pages, I will trace what I consider to be the guiding principles of a gospel-driven answer to the important question of the relationship of the Spirit to the Scriptures in the life of a Christ-follower. My observations are based on two fundamental beliefs. First, I am convinced that the Scriptures, produced through the inspiration of the Spirit, reflect his personality and purpose in the Creator's project. Second, although all Scripture is "God-breathed and useful" (cf. 2 Tim. 3:16) its usefulness is not automatic. In other words, the Scriptures can also be used wrongly, and their inappropriate use can be and often is damaging even among well-intended "Bible-believers."

The Scriptures Reflect the Personality and Work of the Spirit

The Spirit is discreet in that his activities are determined by the Creator's project, which is centred on the Lord Jesus of Nazareth the Christ. If the Creator has indeed summed up all things in the Lord Jesus (Eph. 1:10), if the Christ is the locus of the new creation (2 Cor. 5:17), and if the goal of the person and work of the eternal Son incarnate is the new heavens and new earth (Isa. 65:17; 2 Pet. 3:13), then all of Scripture is the Spirit's testimony to him (Goldsworthy, 2012, p. 189). Just as the Spirit and the eternal Son are "Christomorphed" (metamorphosed in the Creator's project of restoration), so are the Scriptures.

For this reason, a gospel-driven understanding of the Spirit and the Scriptures is guided by the conviction that the divine project of the incarnation of the eternal Son, who is the centre and aim of all of creation, stands prior to the biblical text and its historic and cultural contexts. This is the first presupposition of a gospel-centred hermeneutics, as Goldsworthy (2006, p. 58) maintains: "For hermeneutics to be gospel-centred, it must be based on the person of Jesus Christ." To center our understanding of the Spirit and the Scriptures on God and his love for humans is not precise enough. Neither are the popular notions of "being saved" and the aim of "getting to know God." We must go beyond demolishing "arguments and every pretension that sets itself up against the knowledge of God" (2 Cor. 10:5a) in our relationship to the "world." We must also discipline ourselves as followers of Jesus of Nazareth to "take captive every thought" (even biblically based ones) and make it "obedient to Christ" (2 Cor. 10:5b).

Second, a gospel-driven understanding of the Spirit and the Scriptures is guided by the conviction that the living Word, the pre-existent *Logos* (Jn. 1:1) incarnate in Jesus of Nazareth (Jn. 1:14), has authoritative priority over the Scriptures. The Creator has spoken through the Prophets, but he has spoken authoritatively and definitively in the incarnate Son, "heir of all things and through whom he made the universe" (Heb. 1:1–2). In other words, Jesus of Nazareth, the Christ, mediates the meaning of all the Creator's communication to us (Goldsworthy, 2006, p. 62). This is so because all reality was created by the Christ, through the Christ and for the Christ (Col. 1:15–16). The Creator's plan is to sum up all things in the Christ (Eph. 1:9–10). In him are all the treasures of wisdom and understanding (Col. 2:2–3). The renewing of the universe to be the perfect new creation, as it was before the fall, is foreshadowed in Jesus of Nazareth, the Christ. Hence, "the ultimate interpretation of the meaning of everything is found only in Christ. This includes every text of the Bible" (Goldsworthy, 2006, p. 63).

When Jesus of Nazareth amended the heart of the Torah, he was not lightly setting the Scriptures aside, like a false prophet urging people to abandon their ancient loyalties, lifestyles, and understandings of Scripture and embrace new ones. Nor was he blaspheming against Moses, an offense that, according to Josephus, could have carried the death penalty (Wright, 1996b, p. 646). He was, however, establishing himself and his teaching by word and example (what Paul referrers to as the "law of Christ") as the norm by which loyalty to him, to Israel's God, and to a correct understanding and application of the Torah is to be measured. Whatever authority the Scriptures carry emanates from the Christ. Jesus of Nazareth, the Christ, is the "wisdom of God" (1 Cor. 1:24) and also "our wisdom" (1:30).

Wright (1996b, p. 432) points out the significance of this "redefinition of the Torah":

> Torah defined Israel: specifically, the works of Torah functioned as symbolic praxis, as the set of badges which demonstrated both to observant Jews and to their neighbours that they were indeed the people of the covenant. For Jesus, the symbolic praxis that would mark out his followers, and which therefore can be classified as, in that sense, redefined Torah, is set out in such places as the Sermon on the Mount.

This observation helps us make sense of Jesus of Nazareth's affirmation to the Jews who had believed in him: "If you hold to *my* teaching, you are really my disciples" (Jn. 8:31; emphasis added).

Spirit and Scripture in the Renewal of the Heart

One of the great scriptural promises to which Paul alludes in 2 Corinthians 3:3 is the restoration or renewal of the heart (Dt. 30:6–10; Jer. 31:33; cf. 24:7). This promise was stated by the Psalmist: "The Law of his God is in his [the righteous, faithful and just person's] heart, his feet do not slip" (Ps. 37:31). The prophet Isaiah proclaimed that such people, those with *Yahweh's* "law in the heart," are the ones who "know what is right" and need not fear the reproach of men (Isa. 51:7). And through the Prophet Jeremiah, *Yahweh* promised that upon the return of the Jews from exile, those he has gathered would "be my people, and I will be their God. I will give them one heart and one way, that they may fear me for all time. ... I will make an everlasting covenant with them, never to draw back from doing good to them; and I will put the fear of me in their hearts, so that they may not turn from me" (Jer. 32:38–40).

In other words, renewal of the covenant and renewal of heart go together. Wright (1996b, p. 283) affirms that the distinction being made in these passages is not between outward and inward renewal, or between earning grace and expressing it. Instead, these texts are promising that renewal of the heart would characterize the restored followers of *Yahweh*. Wright adds, "Jesus would call into being 'a graced discipleship' in which 'your hardness of heart' (Mark 10:5) would be cured." Jesus of Nazareth said, "If anyone loves me, he will obey my teaching. ... He who does not love me will not obey my teaching" (Jn. 14:23–24). And this love-conditioned obedience to Jesus, the Christ, is directly linked to the Spirit, sent from the Father, who would teach his followers "all things" and remind them of "everything I have said to you" (Jn. 14:26).

This restoration of the heart and leading of the Spirit in understanding the Scriptures is also conformed to his personality and work. Jesus said that the "Spirit of truth" would "guide us into all truth", and that he "will only speak what he hears" (16:13). This does not free us from our responsibility to apply ourselves by studying and working to understand the Scriptures correctly (2 Tim. 2:15). For everything written in the Scriptures "was written to teach us, so that through endurance and the encouragement of the Scriptures we might have hope" (Rom. 15:4). But we need the Spirit to enable us to overcome the effects of sin on our rational processes. He makes it possible for the Christ-follower to use our faculties to properly discern and apply scriptural truth (1 Cor. 2:2; 2 Cor. 4:4–15; Eph. 1:17–19; Phil. 1:9–11; Col. 1:9–13). But the presence of the Spirit does not guarantee that we will do so. Neither does he guarantee that we will do so appropriately.

The Spirit, called the *Parakletos*—which is often translated "Comforter" (KJV), "Helper" (NASB), "Advocate" (NRSV), or "Counsellor" (NIV), or someone who is called or sent to assist another—is the one who "leads us into all truth" (Mounce, 1993, p. 353). The Spirit of truth leads or guides; he does not overwhelm or overpower us with truth. The word for guiding here is *hodēgēsei*, which is often used literally, such as for leading the blind. However, the word is also frequently used metaphorically—for instance, to speak of the Spirit guiding Moses' mind to truth, or of wisdom "leading" the righteous (Keener, 2003, p. 1036). Paul uses this same word to speak of followers of Jesus being led by the Spirit (Rom. 8:14; cf. also Gal. 5:18).

The Spirit not only continues Jesus' presence below; he also expounds the teachings of the Christ, bringing things to our mind and helping us to understand them. This does not mean that individual Christ–followers, or even any particular Christian tradition, has been or is being led into "all truth," whereas the others have wrongly interpreted or applied the Scriptures. Faithful to his personality, the Spirit comes alongside all who are followers of the Christ, in an approach that emboldens them to look deeply *into* and *through* the Scriptures and the events of their lives to discern their past and present conformity to the image of the Son. He does not ignore or overlook incorrect interpretations and applications of Scripture, or the sinful twists and turns of our traditions. The Spirit does continuously bring to remembrance the teaching and works of Jesus of Nazareth, and he helps his followers to understand them and the way they "fulfil" the Scriptures (Jn. 2:2; cf. Lk. 22:61) and know how to apply them (Jn. 16:4; cf. Rev. 2:5). But even as he leads the followers of the

Christ into all truth (Jn. 16:13), he does so with the compassion and patience of a Comforter, Helper and Counsellor.

To put it in practical terms: we Christians are renewed by the Spirit who will lead us into all truth, but we haven't discovered all truth; on the contrary, we Christians disagree with each other on almost everything imaginable. Why is this and what can we do about it? My point is that the Spirit's guiding does not guarantee that we get everything right. In the next chapter, we will look at some of the ways we help each other to grow in our conformity to the Christ. How we can learn together how we can reduce our frequency of falling into error, or how others can help us identify our blind spots.

Questions to Think About

1. I state that the Spirit is never the goal of discipleship, and I quote another scholar who describes the Spirit as always in "the background position." How can these truths function as a corrective to imperfect models of discipleship and Christian growth?
2. Why is it important for our spiritual lives to keep in mind that the Spirit—not Jesus—indwells us?
3. Review 2 Corinthians 3. What is Paul's purpose in highlighting the role of the Spirit in this passage? What tendencies—in his own day and in ours—does the passage counteract?
4. I propose that in 2 Corinthians 4:1–6, Paul is referring not only to unbelievers as "blinded," but also to some believers. Do you agree? If so, what might the implications be for developing maturity in Christian discipleship?
5. The last section of this chapter presents a dilemma: all Christians have the Spirit, yet Christians disagree in their interpretation of Scripture. How should this reality affect our lives, both individually and in our interaction with other believers?

14. Learning to Enact Allegiance to the Lord Jesus with Others

I began this collection of studies with the claim that the identity of Jesus of Nazareth, and the meaning of the titles "Lord" and "Christ" given to him by his first followers are of utmost importance. Throughout this set of studies, my underlying emphasis has been that reflecting on the identity of Jesus of Nazareth is the key to the entire project of theology. This is so because Christ's identity is foundational to understanding the triune Creator's project of restoration. It is Jesus' identity that makes him the "Good News." His death, resurrection, and enthronement are fully appreciated only as we begin to measure his significance as the perfect God-man. Jesus of Nazareth is the person in whom the fullness of the Godhead chose to dwell in bodily form, and he is the flesh-and-blood person in whom the fullness of our humanity can be restored as we live under his reign through *pistis*.

At the end of the previous study, I affirmed that although the Spirit is leading us into all truth about Jesus of Nazareth, the Christ, none of us individually, or even collectively in our particular Christian traditions, fully understands the biblical witness to him. Nor does any one of our various Christian faith traditions by itself express fully what it means to be led by the Spirit in our conformity to the Christ's example and teaching. Being led by the Spirit into the truth of Jesus does not mean that we all should look alike, as Luke Timothy Johnson (1999, p. 199) observes:

> There is a very real diversity of witness to and interpretations of Jesus. One could almost say that there is a different portrait of Jesus in each of the New Testament scriptures. The portrait of Jesus painted by Paul and that of the book of Revelation each possesses distinctive features. The Jesus of the Epistle to the Hebrews is not in every point the same as the picture of Jesus that we find in the Epistle attributed to James. Mark and John do not witness to Jesus in exactly the same way. The interpretations of Jesus that we find in Matthew are dissimilar to those of John. Every effort on our part to eliminate or diminish that diversity in order to simplify our understanding of Jesus' identity would be a violation of the texts that witness to Him. In all these portraits, however, the humanity of Jesus is seen as the measure of the life of the disciple. His words are the injunctions that His disciples seek to obey. And above all, whatever be their particular experience of His presence, His character remains the norm for all His disciples.

In our previous study, we looked at the solid tie between the Spirit and the incarnate Son. Paul stressed this close association when he summarized the gospel in Romans 1:4. There he wrote that Jesus of Nazareth was declared to be the Son of God with power, and he identified the source of that power as "the Spirit of holiness." In other words, the reign of the Lord Jesus is coextensive with the enabling presence of the Spirit in the disciples' lives (Bates, 2019, p. 101). This undoubtedly explains Paul's claim: "Our gospel came to you not simply with words, but also with power, with the Holy Spirit and with deep conviction" (1 Th. 1:5; cf. Eph. 1:13). Again, it is important to recognize that the Spirit of power is always associated with the glory of the Christ. He always exercises his power to honor the Christ. And the glory of the Christ is clearly seen when those under his reign learn to live out his amended *Shema* (see chapter 2 of this book) in their daily relationships. This is what Paul was urging the followers of Jesus in Philippi to do when he claimed that their attitude should be the same as that of Christ Jesus (Phil. 2:5) and then explained what that looks like (Phil. 2:6–8).

We must not lose sight of the relationship between the identity of the Lord Jesus of Nazareth and ecclesiology. If we do not want the *ekklēsia*[1] to lose sight of its goal, we must be sure that its *vocation* is not dominated by its *institutional character*. Theologically stated, *Christology* must determine *ecclesiology*, and not the other way around. When the latter happens, we end up "doing church" without really functioning as an *ekklēsia*. We have deviated

---

1 The English word "church" is a translation of the Greek word *ekklēsia* which signifies "called out from" (from the Greek *ek*, meaning "out," and the verb *kaleō*, signifying "call"). As E. W. Bullinger (1995, p. 72) writes, this word was used in relationship to "an assembly, and more particularly of citizens, or of a segment from among them, 'middle-class people.'" In the New Testament the word is used 115 times, 3 of which are translated by "assembly" and 112 times where the translators have opted for the word "church." The occasions when the word is translated by "assembly" demonstrate that it was not used exclusively to refer to groups of Christ-followers (i.e., Acts 19:32, 35, 39–40). In this text, the word is used to designate a group of people who opposed the Christ-followers!

This general meaning of *ekklēsia* as an assembly or congregation is also evident in its use in the Septuagint. In that Greek version of the O.T. it appears 71 times, all translating the Hebrew word *qahal*, which signifies "a group, a gathering, an assembly, a congregation, a meeting, and in a larger sense any assembly or multitude of men, of troops, of nations, of the wicked, of the righteous, etc." (Wilson, 1987, p. 92). J. P. Lewis (1980) says that even if that assembly often occurs with a religious motive, it can also have an ignoble goal (Ge. 49:6; Ps. 26:5), a political one (I Ki. 2:3; Pr. 5:14; 26:26; Job 30:28), or even a violent one (Nu. 22:4; Jdg. 20:2). Wayne Grudem (1994, p. 854, note 2) reminds us that the Septuagint was the Bible the New Testament authors used and that they could not have been ignorant of the various natures of the assemblies the word *ekklēsia* designated. Contrary to the opinion of Overman (1990, p. 152) *ekklēsia* was never used to designate a building or edifice that housed an assembly!

from our vocation, and our efficacy in learning together how to live under the Christ's reign is diminished.

This study looks at the context in which those who live under the reign of the Christ, enabled by his Spirit, learn together how to practise his words and conform their daily relationships to his "law." I find too imprecise the common affirmation that the church's function is to "glorify God" (e.g., Schreiner, 2001, p. 34). The Apostle Paul, who uses the word *ekklēsia* more frequently than any other New Testament writer, uses it in a Christ-centered way, describing the Christ-followerships as deriving from the reign of the resurrected king (Jipp, 2015).[2] For instance, the metaphor of the *ekklēsia* as the body of Christ in Ephesians 4:1–16 is founded on the understanding that the members of the body have received the *pneuma* (Spirit) of the resurrected king (Gombis, 2010; Talbert, 2007, pp. 53–75).[3]

Significantly, in the middle of this clearest and most powerful description of the proper function of the *ekklēsia*, we find the only New Testament use of the word "pastor"[4] to describe leaders of the Christ-followers (Earley & Dempsey, 2013, p. 40). Ephesians 4:7–16 is a concentrated piece of deeply foundational Pauline ecclesiology, and one that deals more specifically and authoritatively with the nature of Christ-followerships than any other New Testament passage. I will begin by examining the nature of the Christ-followerships in Ephesus. Next, I will look at the particular role of the "pastor" in assisting the "saints" in their growth in Christ-likeness. Finally, I will argue that laypeople—general, non-ordained Christ–followers—should be actively involved in the process of helping others to progress in obedience to their common Lord Jesus.

I do not attempt in this chapter to provide an all-encompassing explanation of the role of the pastor or the pastorate. Neither do I examine the pastor's role in the governance of a local community of believers. Much of our modern understanding of pastors and their roles has been a self-embracing

---

2 By the time Pliny (23/24–79 CE) had come into contact with Christ-followers, most of them had adopted the term *ekklēsia* to refer to their assemblies, whether they were speaking of the local gathering in a particular city or town or to the network of Christ-followers scattered throughout the Mediterranean world. Robert Louis Wilken (2003, p. 33) states that "in common usage in Greek and Latin *ecclesia* referred to the political assembly of the people of a city, as contrasted with the smaller group of elected officials who comprised the council (*boule*)."

3 In this regard, Jipp (2015, p. 276) writes, "Ephesians conceptualizes the church's participation in the Messiah's heavenly rule through the royal imagery of 'head' and 'body.' This relationship is one between king and subjects as the church participates in the king's lordship, given that God makes the Messiah "head over all things" by means of his royal enthronement (Eph. 1:20–2:10)."

4 The noun "pastor" only occurs four times in the New Testament. Three times it refers to Christ as "shepherd" of the *ekklēsia*—twice in emphasized fashion ("great Shepherd of the flock," Heb. 13:20; "Chief Shepherd," 1 Pet. 5:4). The fourth usage is in Ephesians 4:11.

ecclesiological discourse. We have defined pastoral duties in ways that legitimize and reinforce a particular vision of the church. We have seen the pastor as the primary leader of the churchgoers, responsible for most of the preaching, and governing along with the elders, who are the elected representatives of the congregation.[5] This hierarchical understanding, with a chain-of-command, pyramid-like structure within a divinely commissioned organization, makes the pastor the director of the congregation as it grows spiritually, numerically, and financially. This model is assumed to be the one that Paul used as he spent some time in an area, establishing the assembly of Christ-followers and serving as their first senior pastor, and then moving on to another area after appointing his successor.

This understanding is largely a projection of our own experience and history onto the life of the early Christ-followers. We read the New Testament subjectively, and our ecclesiastical understandings re-present, re-package, and re-image the experience of the first Christ–followers. This allows us to justify, consciously or not, our current practices. Unfortunately, this tendency also fosters what Larry Osborne (2008, p. 49) has labelled the "Holy Man Myth," which implies that pastors and clergy somehow have a more direct line to God than ordinary believers and therefore assigns them tasks that are quite divorced from their scriptural duties (Fee & Stuart, 1993, pp. 13–14; Kennison, 2010, p. 61).[6] It also cripples the lay followers of Christ and keeps them from entering fully into the blessing of life transformation, and spiritual reproduction. To better comprehend the role of the pastor in disciple making, it seems appropriate to examine how Paul first described that function.

The Nature of the Christ-Followerships in Ephesus

Much can be learned about the characteristics of the Christ-followerships in Ephesus from the ambiguity of the letter regarding its audience. Paul addresses

---

5 This view of proper church order can be observed in the *Ecclesiastical Ordinance* adopted by the Geneva City Council under John Calvin's direction: "There are four orders of offices that our Lord instituted for the government of his church: first the pastors, then the teachers, after them the elders, and fourthly the deacons. Therefore, if one would have the church well-ordered and maintained in its entirety, we must observe that form of rule."

6 Marshall Shelly (2017), director of the Doctor of Ministry programme at Denver Seminary, traces the broadening role of the pastor from the New Testament period, through the Reformation emphasis on the pastor as the "teacher of God's Word," to the present day. He highlights the contribution of the Puritans who stressed the pastor's role as "physician of the soul"; the Methodist awakening in the 1700s within which the pastor was an overseer of small groups for the purpose of nurturing believers; the twentieth-century emphasis on the pastor as the person who recruits, motivates, and administers programmes, along with playing a lead role in evangelism and outreach and, more recently, working for justice and compassion in the name of Christ.

this letter to the saints (Greek *hagiōn*,[7] the ordinary Christ-followers, whose only distinction is that they are chosen by God (Eph. 1:4–10), claimed by Jesus Christ (Eph. 1:11–12), and gathered by the Holy Spirit in Christ-followerships (Eph. 1:13–14). The label "saints" does not mean that these people were sinless, or that they had attained moral perfection. Rather, it is the label most often used in the New Testament to speak of the believers who would later be called the laity (Beckwith, 1988, p. 609). It has nothing to do with the person's value in the faith community. It does not depend on the person's capacities, background, education, sex, or social status. They are called saints not because they share the same profession (work or occupation), but because they have the same vocation (calling, ministry). Without exception or exclusion, each of them has been set apart for the mission of God in our world – to make disciples of Jesus.

It is significant that Paul did not write this letter to the leaders of an easily identifiable gathering of believers with firm structures and institutions (like our present-day churches) but, rather, to an informal network of clusters of common Christ-followers. The burgeoning movement[8] of Christ-followerships in Ephesus was made up of ordinary, largely illiterate people, including women, slaves, and people of different races, classes, and socioeconomic status. For this reason, matters of identity and the meaning of being a Christ-follower are at the heart of this letter (Shkul, 2009, p. 4, note 5).[9] Although the followers of Christ come from all racial, socioeconomic, and gender groups, they are bound together as a movement by their self-understanding that they have been empowered with the same spirit God used to raise Jesus back to life (Eph. 1:19–22). They see themselves as Christ's body and fullness (Eph. 1:23; 5:30), whom he nourishes and cares for (Eph. 5:25–30) so that it would be transformed to reflect its divine head (Eph. 4:15–16). It is very unlikely that the informal network of Christ-followerships in and around Ephesus had firm structures or institutions (Heil, 2007, p. 8). What held them together was the ultimate goal of fellowship with and participation in the Christ.

---

7 Paul addresses other letters to the "saints" (Rom. 1:7; 1 Cor. 1:2; 2 Cor. 1:1; Phil. 1:1; Col. 1:2), a term used sixty-two times in the New Testament and never in the singular.
8 Following Gerlach and Hine (1970, p. xvii), I use "movement" to refer to a segmented, usually polycephalous, cellular network composed of individuals who share a common ideology or vision.
9 This perhaps explains why, instead of positioning his readers in the synagogues, temples, marketplaces, or some other actual social setting, Paul places them in the "heavenly realms in Jesus Christ" (Eph. 2:6). This is because the Christ, the one under whose feet God has placed all things (Eph. 1:10, 20–22), and their relationship to him constitute their primary self-identification, which defines them as a group and thus provides them with distinctiveness and communality (Shkul, 2009, p. 29). Appropriately, Paul prays that Christ may dwell in the hearts of these individuals through *pistis* (Eph. 3:17).

Later I will trace the logic developed by Paul in the first three chapters of Ephesians. However, in 4:1–6, which immediately precedes the pericope dealing with the leaders, the Apostle exhorts the members of the Christ-followerships to "live a life worthy of the calling" they had received (Eph. 4:1; cf. Phil. 1:27; 1 Th. 2:12). In his writings, Paul always uses "calling" to refer to the call to follow Christ (Talbert, 2007, p. 108). We know that Jesus called disciples to follow him. And although Jesus was no longer physically present, as he once was in Galilee, it was understood that he continues to call ordinary people in the same way.[10] So even if discipleship could no longer be accomplished by a literal walking with Jesus, the growing movement held fast to the basic similarity and its members saw themselves as belonging to "the Way" of Jesus (Ac. 9:2, 9, 23; 22:4; 24:14, 22; cf. 16:17; 18:25, 26; Jn. 14:6).

Adepts of the Way

Belonging to "the Way" was, it appears, not only an identity marker; it also referred to the behavior of these first Christ-followers. This can be seen in Paul's use of the metaphor of "walking" as a synonym for discipleship in this letter. The Greek verb *peripatōn*, rendered "walk" in the English Bible, is found eight times in Ephesians. Christ-followers are to abandon the life in which they once walked (2:2); they are not to walk as Gentiles do, with a vain mind (4:17); nor in an unwise fashion (5:15); in contrast, they are required to walk worthily of the high calling they have accepted (4:1–3), to walk in love (5:2) as children of the light (5:8), and to walk carefully as those who are wise (5:15). This is discipleship! It is not only believing in Christ for salvation but conforming to his life and teaching in one's inner being and external relationships. Just "belonging to the Way," or becoming a "Christ-follower" was not sufficient one was also expected to become increasingly like the Master.

Learning to "walk" through life, following the pattern of Jesus and empowered by his Spirit, is what the Christ-followership is all about. It is also what "ministry" is all about. For that reason, Paul described ministry as "building up the body of Christ" (Eph. 4:12) and equipping others to assist each other in "growing up into him who is the Head, that is Christ" (Eph. 4:15). The early Reformers made this very clear. See the strong language in article 28 of the Belgic Confession:

> But all people are obliged to join and unite with it, keeping the unity of the church by submitting to its instruction and discipline, by bending their necks under the yoke of Jesus Christ, and by serving to build up one another, according to the gifts God has given them as members of each other in the same body.

---

10 The words used by Jesus to call his first followers, "*Lech Ahari*" (Matt. 4:19), translated "Walk after me," were a standard phrase in Hebrew for designating a disciple (Blizzard & Bivin, 2013).

Limits of the Reformation

And yet, right from the start, people such as Johann Arndt and Philipp Jakob Spener insisted that the Reformation did not go far enough. These men and others like them contended that whereas the original Protestant reformers had concentrated mainly on doctrine and polity, the reform principle had to be extended to how laypeople actually lived out their faith (Atwood, 2004, p. 28). This argument was renewed some 60 years ago when Elton Trueblood wrote two influential and prophetic volumes: *Your Other Vocation* (1952), on the role of laity in the workplace, and *The Incendiary Fellowship* (1967), where he argued that the first Reformation, which succeeded in placing the Bible in the hands of ordinary believers, was in a very significant way unsuccessful. Trueblood contended that the Reformation had failed to effectively give the ministry back to the common Christ-follower. He maintained that we need a second Reformation, one that goes beyond simply stating the priesthood of all believers and actually enables the body of Christ to function as though this were true. Along the same lines, Hendrik Kraemer (2005, p. 62), in his often-referenced *A Theology of the Laity*, wrote:

His [Luther's] attack, fully justified, implied the abolition of all clericalism, and the most emphatic vindication or rehabilitation of the laity ever uttered. And yet it must frankly be stated that neither this new conception of the church nor this strong vindication of the laity ever became dominant. To this present day it rather fulfils the role of a flag than of an energizing, vital principle.

On a more popular level, Ray Stedman reasoned convincingly in *Body Life* (1995 [1972]) that neither the Apostles and Prophets nor the evangelists and pastor-teachers mentioned in Ephesians 4, are expected to do the work of the ministry, or even to build up the body of Christ. These tasks are to be done only by the people, the ordinary Christ-followers. Writing around the same time, Hendrik Hart (1972, p. 30) claimed:

Even though the leaders of the Protestant Reformation sincerely intended to break with the traditional Roman Catholic conception of the church, nevertheless the tradition arising from the Reformation did not succeed in making the break.

In *I Believe in the Church*, David Watson (1978) observed:

Most Protestant denominations have been as priest-ridden as the Roman Catholics. It is the minister, vicar, or pastor who has dominated the whole proceedings. In other words, the clergy-laity divisions have continued in much the same way as in pre-Reformation times, and the doctrine of spiritual gifts and body ministry have been largely ignored. (p. 253)

In *Layman, Look Up: God Has a Place for You*, Henrichse and Garrison (1983) complained that despite the Reformation, the role of ordinary believers continues to be limited to regularly attending church functions, contributing financially, and maintaining the status quo. More recently, Greg Ogden (2010) has demonstrated ways in which the Reformation never fully delivered on its promise to liberate the Church from a hierarchical priesthood.[11] He claims that the church today is sick partly because we have so exalted the clergy and preaching that no other gift can match that level of importance.

Alan Hirsch maintains in *The Forgotten Ways: Reactivating the Missional Church* (2006) and *Fast Forward to Mission: Frameworks for a Life of Impact* (2011) that activating the entire people of God is absolutely essential to achieve any lasting missional impact. He identifies the lingering false distinction between ordinary Christ-followers and the so-called religious professionals as one of the major hurdles we must still overcome so as to activate Jesus' people. In *The Permanent Revolution* (2012), written with Tim Catchim, he picks up the same theme as they urge readers to move beyond the current post-Reformation reduction of "ministry" to the preaching-teaching role of the pastor, so as to rediscover the multifaceted ministry of the ordinary Christ-followers.

This understanding of the ministry is what Paul had in mind when he referred to "becoming mature, attaining to the whole measure of the fullness of Christ" (Eph. 4:13). We will come back to this point later.

Who Does the Ministry?

Ephesians 4:11–12 is one lengthy Greek sentence in which Paul mentions people who are in effect gifts to the Christ-followerships: Apostles, Prophets, evangelists, pastors, and teachers.[12] This sentence has been interpreted in various ways. It is composed of three clauses, each introduced by a preposition: for (*pros*) the perfecting of the saints, for (*eis*) the work of the ministry, for (*eis*) the edifying of the body of Christ (KJV). The key question concerns how these three clauses are related to each other, and the underlying issue is to whom the ministry belongs. The King James translation, with two commas, communicates the idea that the Apostles, Prophets, evangelists, and pastors-teachers were given by the ascended Christ for three purposes: perfecting or

---

11 Martin Luther described the status and role of the pastor five centuries ago:
A Christian preacher is a minister of God who is set apart, yea, he is an angel of God, a very bishop sent by God, a saviour of many people, a king and a prince in the Kingdom of Christ and among the people of God, a teacher, a light of the world. There is nothing more precious or nobler on earth and in this life than a true, faithful parson or preacher (Niebuhr & Williams, 1983, p. 115).
12 Hochner (2002, p. 539) makes a strong argument that these are not offices but people who serve as gifts to the Christ-followers. The early Christian offices, he argues, were bishops, elders, and deacons. The roles mentioned here are rather gifts from the victorious, ascended Christ.

equipping of the saints, doing the work of the ministry, and edifying the body of Christ. This understanding of who does the ministry can be illustrated in Figure 4.

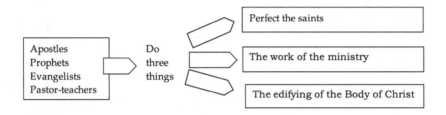

Figure 1: Eph. 4:11-12 Understood as the Leaders Who Do the Ministry

This reading of the text supports the notion that the person who has gone into the ministry (i.e., the Apostle, Prophet, evangelist or pastor-teacher) does the work of the ministry (Kitchen, 1994, p. 75). We distinguish these individuals with titles such as "reverend" or "ministers of the gospel" as if they are set apart into a spiritual realm unattainable by ordinary Christ-followers. This is true even in the Protestant tradition, in which the ministers, because of their office and ordination, are seen as somehow having better access to Jesus or being nearer to him than ordinary believers are. Greg Ogden (2010) has observed that this perspective unduly limits the role of lay believers:

> The laity are often viewed as those who supplement the ministry of pastors because, after all, they cannot do it all. Under this theology, the people of God are at best adjuncts to the true ministers and have no real ministry identity of their own. This restrictive view of ministry seen through the lens of institutionalism leads directly to two peoples of God (clergy and laity) and two ministries (the ministry for first-class Christians, and what's left for second-class Christians). (Kindle locations 1208–1211)

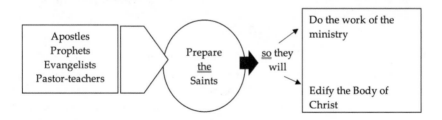

Figure 2: Eph. 4:11-12 Understood as the Laity Who Do the Ministry

In other translations, like the New International Version, the phrase is divided with one or no commas. According to this reading, the purpose of these individuals is to "prepare" ("train" or "equip") the saints for the work of ministry, resulting in the building up of the body of Christ. Figure 5 represents this understanding.

In the first interpretation of the text, the ministry belongs to a few; in the second, the ministry belongs to all the Christ-followers to whom the necessary grace has been given. Which reading is to be preferred?

Some scholars prefer the first interpretation based on the argument that the shift in prepositions (*pros ... eis ... eis*) indicates that the first two prepositional phrases are not coordinate (Gordon, 1994; Hamann, 1988; MacDonald, 2000, p. 292). Others prefer the second reading, arguing that the combining of prepositional phrases, all dependent on the main verb and coordinate with each other, is common to the writer's style (Aletti, 2001, pp. 219–221; Heil, 2007, p. 177; Larkin, 2009, pp. 78–79; Lincoln, 1990, p. 253; Thielman, 2010, p. 279; Wood, 1978, p. 58; Wuest, 1953, p. 101). In his detailed examination of this text Charles Talbert points to other examples of this kind of sequencing of prepositional phrases in Ephesians to demonstrate that both readings are possible. Talbert (2007, p. 114) concludes that "ultimately the larger context is determinative," and he translates the text in a way that places the ministry solidly with all Christ-followers: "for the training of the saints for the work of ministry, for the building up of the body of Christ." Peter O'Brien (1999, p. 264) also looks at the wider context for guidance in which interpretation to prefer:

> The letter as a whole has emphasized Christ's riches being received by *all* the saints (1:3–19; 3:20), while the immediate context of vv. 7–16 is framed by an insistence at the beginning of the paragraph that each believer was given 'grace' (v. 7), and at its conclusion that the *whole* body is growing from the head as *each part* (v. 16) does its work. If it is only the leaders of v. 11 who perfect the saints, do the work of ministry, and edify the body of Christ, then this is a departure from Paul's usual insistence that every member is equipped for ministry. It is better, therefore, to regard those enumerated in v. 11 as helping and directing other members of the church so that all may carry out their several ministries for the good of the whole. (emphasis in the original)

I agree with this understanding and contend that the complementary roles of the people mentioned in verse 11 were designed by the Lord Jesus to lead all his followers to grow as disciple makers (since each of them has received the same mandate from Matthew 28:19–20, and the same grace as stated in Ephesians 4:7). I do not agree with those who equate the "grace" received by each Christ-follower with the spiritual gifts mentioned in 1 Corinthians 12 (Ogden, 2010, Kindle location 686; Talbert, 2007, p. 109). The ministry of accompanying others toward maturity in Christ, which has been given to each of his followers, is not according to the spiritual gift (*charisma*) they have been assigned but corresponds to the grace (*charis*) each has received (Wood, 1978, p. 57). To best appreciate this, we must look briefly at the various ways in which Paul uses *charis*.

To Each of Us Grace Has Been Given

At times in this letter, the Apostle uses *charis* as a prayer-wish that grace would come to his readers (Eph. 1:2; 6:24). As Evangelicals, we are also very aware of Paul's understanding of saving grace, which saves sinners and is accorded to all who believe (Eph. 2:5–8). In Ephesians 1:7, he claims that God did not merely show Christ-followers grace when he forgave them at such great cost to himself; he also caused grace to "abound" toward them or "lavished" it on them. And again in 1:9, he claims that God showed his abundant grace to his people by revealing to them "the mystery of his will." He planned to do this in Christ and took pleasure in it (Thielman, 2010, p. 57). In Ephesians 4:29, Paul uses *charis* in yet another way. In this verse, it describes the kind of speech that builds others up and enables them to accomplish the task God has given them. This resembles Paul's use of the word in the text we are considering.

When Paul writes that grace has been given to each believer according to the measure of the gift of Christ, he is using the same terms he employed to express his personal role as a communicator of the gospel to the Gentiles (Eph. 3:2, 7, 9). He called this role "the grace (*charis*) that God gave me" and said that he received it according to the effect of God's power (Eph. 3:7–8). Paul had already spoken of that grace for service when, at the beginning of chapter 3, he wrote, "Surely you have heard about the administration of God's grace that was given me for you" (v. 2). In this text, Paul speaks of the "administration" of divine grace. The expression signifies the organizing of a work or labour (Col. 1:25). Paul is referring to the "equipping" he had received that enabled him to carry out his mission (Wood, 1978, p. 45). With this background, he writes, "But to each one of us grace has been given as Christ apportioned it."

Paul's particular ministry may be historically unique, but here he is claiming that just as God graciously gave him that role (3:2, 7, 8) and the power to carry it out (3:7), so also the ministry of mutual edification has been given "to each of us" (Thielman, 2010, p. 263). In like fashion, Paul writes to Timothy that he should be "strong in the grace that is in Christ Jesus," just before he exhorts him to pass on to others what he had himself received from the Apostle (2 Tim. 2:1). As Simpson & Bruce (1957, p. 95) so aptly put it, "In the theocracy of grace there is in fact no laity." In that respect, all Christ-followers are "ministers" (i.e., servants) of God (2 Cor. 6:4; 1 Th. 3:2), of Christ (2 Cor. 11:23; Col. 1:7; 1 Tim. 4:6), of the gospel (Eph. 3:7; Col. 1:23), and of the new covenant (2 Cor 3:6).

Some people might fear that this understanding is a relatively recent innovation that is suspiciously supportive of the egalitarian and populist spirit of our day (Gordon, 1994, p. 77; Lincoln, 1990, p. 253; Muddiman, 2001, p. 200). However, this is simply not the case. Westcott's (1998, p. 3) remarks are particularly instructive. "However foreign the idea of the spiritual ministry of all 'the saints' is to our mode of thinking," he says, "it was the life of the apostolic church" (see also Aletti, 2001, pp. 219–221; Best, 1998, pp. 395–399; Bruce, 1984, p. 213; Hochner, 2002, pp. 547–549; O'Brien, 1999, pp. 301–305).

If the ordinary Christ-followers are the people who minister to each other and to those around them, then what is the role of the pastor? Paul writes that the risen and exalted Christ has given "some to be apostles, some to be prophets, some to be evangelists, and some to be pastors and teachers, to prepare God's people for works of service, so that the body of Christ may be built up" (Eph. 4:11–12). The goal of these ministers is clearly spelled out in these verses. It is the perfecting or preparing of the saints for mutual edification in obedience to the law of Christ, which I have called "the ministry." We will examine the nature of this lay "ministry" in the next section of this study.

Perfecting the Saints

The Greek word translated "perfecting" or "preparation" is *katartismon*, which has less the meaning of "completing" or "perfecting" the saints than of "equipping them for a particular purpose" (Thielman, 2010, p. 279). The noun is rare, appearing only here in the New Testament and seldom outside of medical texts prior to the first century. In medicine, this word was used to indicate that one had set a joint or put a broken bone back into place (Wood, 1987, p. 58). It also appears in nonliterary texts from roughly the time of Ephesians, where it refers to outfitting a guest room with furniture, the "equipment" that goes along with a couple of beds. Thielman (2010, p. 279) maintains that Paul had this meaning in mind. Similarly, O'Brien (1999, p. 268) insists that the notion of equipping, in the sense of making someone adequate or sufficient for something, best suits the context.

In the New Testament this word, in its verb form, is used to describe the activity of the sons of Zebedee, who were preparing their fishing nets when Jesus called them to follow him (Mt. 4:21; Mk. 1:19).[13] The use of this term to describe the two brothers "mending their nets" and "putting them to rights" (Amplified Bible) mirrors the notion that pastors (and the others mentioned by

13 We find the verb form of this word in the New Testament to speak of the "restoration" of someone who is caught in a sin (Gal. 6:1; 2 Cor. 3:11). It can also refer to the realization of a project (1 Cor. 1:10; 1 Th. 3:10) or training in character (Lk. 6:40; Heb. 3:21; 1 Pet. 5:10).

Paul) serve primarily to make ordinary Christ-followers adequate for their task of mutual edification.

All the people Paul mentions, in their special functions, have only one reason for being: equipping the saints, or the ordinary Christ-followers, and thus enabling them to serve their risen Lord by building each other up in their obedience to Christ's revised *Shema*. In other words, "The ministry of the officials does not find its fulfilment in their own existence but only in the activity of preparing others to minister" (Best, 1998, p. 173). Their job is to see that those to whom the Lord Jesus has given an appropriate measure of grace will do the work of helping each other move steadily away from their former way of life, with its fragmentation and susceptibility to deception (Thielman, 2010, p. 284; Lincoln, 1990, p. 258), and toward a union with Christ in all its fullness (Thielman, 2010, p. 280).

Building up the Body of the Christ

What the apostles, prophets, evangelists, and pastor-teachers do for others, and also what the saints themselves do through the exercise of their Spirit-given grace, is for the building up of the body of Christ.[14] According to Old Testament prophetic literature, the restoration of Israel after the judgment of the exile is promised in terms of *Yahweh* building a people for himself (Jer. 24:6; 31:4; 33:7). In Matthew 16:18, Jesus expresses the same idea, claiming that he is the one who builds or establishes the renewed communion of the new people of God: "I will build my *ekklēsia*, and the gates of Hades will not overcome it." Charles Talbert (2007, p. 87) offers some pertinent information about the use of the image of the *sōma* (body) in Mediterranean antiquity: "At times *sōma* (body) referred to the *polis* (= *ekklēsia*) or the state. ... This was because the state, composed of many parts, is like the human body. ... So the state could be said to be the body of the emperor, who is the state's head."

Paul has already affirmed in this letter that the resurrected and reigning Christ is "head over everything for the *ekklēsia*, which is his *sōma* (body)" (Eph. 1:22–23), emphasizing the particular relationship his followers have with

---

14 Throughout Paul's letters, body terminology and its constituent parts refer to the mutual relations and obligations of the members of the Christ-followerships (Rom. 12:4–5; 1 Cor. 12:12–27). Peter O'Brien (1999, p. 142) maintains that "the idea of the body of Christ can partly be explained in terms of the Old Testament concept of corporate personality where the movement between the one and the many can be expressed by the one term and yet have overtones of solidarity. For Paul, Christ as the last Adam and second man is representative of the new humanity (Rom. 5:12–21; 1 Cor. 15:22, 45–49), so that one is either 'in Adam' or 'in Christ.'" Jipp (2015, pp. 182–183) links this participation in Adam and his primal kingship to humanity's Adamic, embodied existence which has become morally incapacitated. Jipp (2015, p. 186) rightly insists that it was precisely through his bodily flesh that the incarnate eternal Son identified with enslaved humanity and presented himself as "a sin offering" (as I have explained in chapter 9 above).

him (O'Brien, 1999, p. 145). Annemarie Mayer (2002, pp. 147, 149) argues that all the references, taken in context, point to an understanding of the *sōma* of Christ in Ephesians as referring to a corporate entity, the people who belong to their ruler. Dunn (1992) summarizes the use of the *ekklēsia* as the *sōma* of Christ in Ephesians to setting forth Paul's understanding of the communion of Christ-followers as an equivalent to the state, a counterculture over against the state.

This Pauline use of *sōma* to describe the saints assembled in the network of Ephesian Christ-followerships deserves further attention. He writes, for instance, that those who have graciously been saved by the Creator through *pistis* (2:1–9) are nothing less than a new creation in the Christ (2:10; a thought he will come back to in 4:24). Paul maintains that regardless of our background in Adam, in the body of "his flesh" the messianic second Adam has "created for himself one new man" (2:11–16). Jipp (2015, pp. 276-277) demonstrates that there is a close relationship between the Pauline notions of "head" and "body" and participation in the reign of either the "first Adam" or that of the "last Adam."

The contrast that begins in Eph. 2:11–13 continues as Paul employs citizenship and household images to describe the members of the *ekklēsia* (2:19-22). Whatever the rules may have been that once determined their participation as "fellow members of a socio-political unit—'fellow citizens'" (Louw & Nida, 1989, § 11.72), they now belong as fellow members of God's household. This terminology in the Pauline corpus sheds light on the relations those who adhere to the Christ should have with each other (1 Tim. 3:15; 2 Tim. 2:20, 21).

The Temple Where the Father Dwells

In Ephesians 2:20, the apostle's imagery changes once again. The Christ-followers are not only intimate members of the Father's household; they also have a privileged position in his construction of a "household" or "temple" where he dwells.[15] I will not inquire further here into Paul's use of the language of building on a foundation and of a temple indwelt by the Spirit (which also appears in 1 Corinthians 3:9–17). Nor will I enter into the debate surrounding the identity and foundational role of the apostles (see O'Brien, 1999, pp. 196–197) or the prophets (O'Brien, 1999, pp. 197–198). The most important facet here is that Jesus of Nazareth, the Christ, is preeminently highlighted. He is the vital cornerstone. All is built on and supported by the Christ, and the shape of

---

15 Card (1976, pp. 60–61) rightly notes the play on the word "house" (*oikos*) in 2 Samuel 7:5–11 to denote both a building and a dynasty. Talbert (2007, p. 85) explains that in the dominant perspective of the early Christ-followers, the believers constitute the eschatological temple and the hoped-for remnant community that were widely expected by Jews of their day.

the continuing building is determined by the Lord Jesus, the rabbi from Nazareth. In him we are becoming a "holy temple" (2:21).

In Ephesians 3:11–13, Paul refers to the "mysterious" plan of the Creator for creation that he was called to make known. This mystery is the main focus of the letter. In 1:9–10, he refers to the mystery of God's will to unite all things through Christ; in 3:5–6, the mystery is revealed to apostles and prophets that Jew and Gentile are to be united in one *sōma*; in 3:3, this mystery is revealed to Paul; in 3:4, it is the mystery of Christ; in 3:9, it is a mystery hidden for ages; in 6:19, it is the mystery of the gospel ("the gospel mystery"). There are four elements here: (1) God's will, (2) hidden for ages, (3) revealed to someone now, and (4) associated with Christ and the gospel (Talbert, 2007, p. 98). In 3:10, Paul tells the Christ-followers of Ephesus why he is working on behalf of this mystery, concealed through the ages but now revealed: in order that through the *ekklēsia* the manifold wisdom of the Creator will be made known to the rulers and authorities in the heavenly spheres. This divine purpose—the restoration of the cosmos—now made known to the unruly powers is an eternal purpose, which he accomplished by means of the Christ, Jesus our Lord (*en tō Christō*), through whom we continually have boldness and access with confidence (cf. Heb. 4:16; 10:19) thanks to his faithfulness.

Paul's desire for the members of the Christ-followerships of Ephesus, expressed in the short prayer that follows (3:14–21), is that the Spirit's presence in their inner self would stimulate a desire that Christ may dwell in their hearts, to the point of filling them with the fullness of God. It is as though on an experiential level Paul recognizes the synergistic action of the Father, the eternal Son incarnate, and the Spirit in the realization of the Creator's project. As we saw in chapter 13, Christ-followers do not experience Christ except as Spirit and do not experience the Spirit except as Christ. The same phenomenon seems to be found in Eph. 3:14–19 (Lincoln, 1990, p. 206).

This rapid overview summarizes the logic of the Apostle in Ephesians 1–3, the first main section of this letter. Chapters 4–6 consist of four large units of thought: 4:1–16; 4:17–5:21; 5:22–6:9; and 6:10–20. We have already dealt with 4:7–16 and the place of communion leaders (apostles, prophets, evangelists, pastor-teachers) in the Christ-followership. We saw that the saints need guidance, visual models (like Paul, who refers to himself in this way in 1 Corinthians 11:1), and "outfitting" that will make them adequate or sufficient to help each other grow in "putting off" their old ways of relating, and in "putting on the new self." Growth continues until all attain unto (*eis*) the unity of the faith (cf. 4:5) and of the knowledge of the Son of God (cf. 3:18–19), unto (*eis*) a mature person, unto (*eis*) a measure of the stature of the fullness of the Christ (4:13). The thrice-repeated preposition *eis* indicates that the three phases are parallel to one another. They are three dimensions of one goal, which encompasses both believing in the Christ and enacting allegiance to him as their one Lord in their relationships (cf. 4:5). In Ephesians, the pattern is distinctive. The goal is that both as corporate bodies (the *ekklēsiae*) and as members (*hagiōn* or saints) of those groups, they would grow into the likeness of their ideal king.[16] The Ephesian Christ-followers would have understood that they are called to grow to reflect the character, words, and actions of their head, the Christ (4:15).

Church Growth

This type of "church growth" is focused on the inner growth of the *ekklēsia* rather than on its mission to the world (Lincoln, 1990, p. 268). This is seemingly in contrast to Acts 1:8, where the gift of the Spirit is often understood as intended to empower the missional activity of church planting. However, in Acts 1:8, the mission is specifically described as witnessing to the Christ. Unfortunately, a person *can* establish a new (local and indigenous) Christian church (with a separate life of its own) *without* intentionally focusing everything on growth in the likeness of the Lord Jesus, the Christ (discipleship). But it is also true that one *cannot* get together with someone to focus their attention and energies on "putting off" the old man and "putting on" the image of the Lord Jesus *without* being the *ekklēsia* (Matt. 18:15–20). The Christ is the measure by which spiritual growth is measured, and growth in likeness to the Lord Jesus is the measure of the *ekklēsia*. The church is the by-product of discipleship to the Christ, not the other way around.

Learning to Put on the Lord Jesus Together

Together, the "ministers" (v. 11) and the saints (v. 12) serve the goal of learning a new lifestyle from and with each other. In fact, their new relationship with each other in Christ places them in the ideal situation in which to learn to live according to Christ's pattern. When they are truly being the *ekklēsia* together, they *practise* putting away falsehood (4:25); *learn* not to sin when they get angry (4:26); *rehearse* being honest and hard-working (4:27–28); *exercise* not using unwholesome language (4:29); *rid* themselves of bitterness and rage and anger and shouting and slander (4:31); *model* being

---

16 In this regard, Charles Talbert (2007, pp. 115–116) writes, "Ancient Mediterranean auditors would have heard this statement against the backdrop of discussions about ideal kings. Plato believed that government was ideal when the state was ruled by a king who lived his life in accordance with the law of nature and was able to legislate out of his person (*Pol.* 33a). Aristotle counseled Alexander the Great to lead a virtuous life because 'the greatest pare of humankind regulate their conduct either by law or by your life and principle' (*Rhet. Alex.* 1420b). Hence the ideal ruler embodied a superior form of law. The highest law was that of the king's character. ... Musonius Rufus shows the ancient tradition continued into the Common Era when he says, 'it is of the greatest importance for the good king to be faultless and perfect in word and action, if ... he is to ... [effect] good government and harmony, suppressing lawlessness and dissension'" (*That Kings Also Should Study Philosophy* 8).

kind and compassionate to others (4:32); and *train* in forgiving (4:32). This is what it means to "learn Christ" (4:20–21).

In this sense, we can say that the saints are called to accompany, stimulate, encourage, teach, discipline, and be models for each other, exhibiting embodied allegiance (*pistis*) to the Lord Jesus, the king. The reason why leaders of the *ekklēsiae* (assemblies) exist is that the *hagiōn* (saints) have been set apart to help each other to "watch carefully" how they "are walking, so that they are *not* as unwise but *wise*" (cf. 5:15). This the Apostle equates with being "filled with the Spirit," which results in three things. First, people speak to one another with psalms and hymns and spiritual songs, singing and making music in their hearts to the Lord Jesus (5:19). Second, it issues in giving thanks always for all things in the name of the Lord Jesus to God the Father (5:20). Third, being filled with the Spirit also leads to willing subjection to one another in reverence for the Christ (5:21).

Hence, contrary to those who, like Michael Horton (2011, p. 526), claim that "Christ reigns secretly and invisibly over all empires and nations for the ultimate purpose of building his church," I maintain that the Christ reigns over his *ekklēsia* for the ultimate purpose of fashioning the *hagiōn* so that his own likeness becomes increasingly visible.

Questions to Think About

1. I argue in this chapter that Christology must determine ecclesiology and not the reverse—that the church's work should be guided by its vocation, not its institutional character. What does your local congregation or your denomination do to ensure that this principle is fulfilled? Or conversely, do you see ways in which your church or denomination is held back from fulfilling its calling by institutional features that need to be reconsidered?
2. How could a proper reading of the New Testament epistles counter the common "Holy Man Myth" that sees the pastor as the person responsible for enabling a local church to thrive (a) spiritually, (b) numerically, and (c) financially?
3. This chapter presents two possible interpretations of Ephesians 4:11–12. Which one do you believe represents Paul's intended meaning, and what are the implications of this passage for overcoming the clergy-laity distinction that remains common in modern Christianity?
4. As I explain in the last section of this chapter, Ephesians 4–5 presents a great number of things that the members of the *ekklēsia* should be doing together. Which ones would you say your church is good or not so good at doing? How could you contribute to improvement where the church's performance is weak?

15. A Gospel-Driven Theology of Mission

In chapter 3, we looked at the authoritative words the resurrected Jesus of Nazareth spoke to his first followers shortly before his ascension and enthronement at the right hand of the Father: "Go and make disciples of all nations (*ethnē*)" (Mt. 28:19). Surprisingly, the Apostle Paul never explicitly told his fellow Christ-followers in his extant letters that they should go outside their assembly to evangelize others or make disciples. He did, however, urge others to follow his example (1 Cor. 4:16; 11:1; Phil. 3:17), and he modeled both components of the missionary task (i.e., evangelism and discipling).

For instance, Paul speaks of "imploring others on Christ's behalf" to be reconciled to the Creator, explaining that God was in the process of "reconciling the world to himself in Christ" (2 Cor. 5:18–21). He sets this reconciling action of God in the context of the new creation, the vanguard of a new world (foreseen by the prophet Isaiah; see 65:17; 66:22) that was inaugurated by the resurrection of Jesus of Nazareth (2 Cor. 4:6) as its first fruits (1 Cor. 15:20, 23). Those who hope to share Jesus' resurrection fully (2 Cor. 4:14; 5:1–4) have a present foretaste in the Spirit (2 Cor. 4:10–11; 5:5). In this new creation, our harmonious relationship with the Creator and the glory of humanity as creatures made in God's image—blessings that were partly lost in Adam (cf. Rom. 5:12–21; 1 Cor 11:7)—are being restored in the Lord Jesus, the Christ (cf. 2 Cor. 3:18; 4:4; 1 Cor. 15:49; Rom. 8:29). This new creation comes from the triune God and is the result of a reconciliation effected by the *pistis* of Jesus of Nazareth in his unwavering allegiance through death (2 Cor. 5:14–15; Rom. 5:10), and we actualize it when we embrace the apostolic gospel in *pistis* (1 Cor. 15:1–2).

Although Paul writes in 2 Cor. 5:19 that the Creator in principle reconciled the world to himself in Christ (who died for all, 5:14–15; cf. Ps. 32:2 as quoted in Rom. 4:8), the world has not yet become completely a new creation (5:17). Therefore, Paul refers to himself as willing to surrender his cultural and religious "rights" for the sake of others (1 Cor. 9:1–18; 2 Cor. 4:5). When he was with the Jews, he practised Jewish customs and the Torah to win the Jews. But when he was with the Gentiles, Paul was willing to compromise some of his Jewishness for the opportunity to "gain" many (1 Cor. 9:19–23). Such flexibility could obviously be criticized as hypocrisy or at least inconsistency. Although he saw himself as technically "free" from the constraints of the Law of Moses (1 Cor. 9:1, 19), he willfully made himself a slave (*doulos*) to everyone (1 Cor. 9:19). Paul was flexible among both Jews and Gentiles (1 Cor. 9:20), reducing things that might cause offence (1 Cor. 10:32) so as to win both groups for the Christ. Thomas Schreiner (2001, p. 62) appropriately points out that when Paul writes of "winning" (*kerdaninō*) or "saving" (*sōzō*) people in 1 Corinthians 9:22, this cannot be speaking of an initial conversion, since the "weak" being won in the text are people who have already exercised *pistis* toward the Lord Jesus, the Christ. "Salvation" here has to do with persevering in *pistis* until the end.

How do we explain Paul's abandonment of his former devotion to the ancestral traditions and his inconstant practice of his religious heritage?[1] Paul says that he did all this "for the sake of the gospel" (1 Cor. 9:23). Gordon Fee (1987, p. 415) appropriately remarks that "his [Paul's] renunciation of his 'rights' … is attributable to his singular passion for the gospel. Everything is done so as not to hinder the gospel." Paul said that this communication of the Good News was not something he chose to do (1 Cor. 9:17), but something he was convinced he *must* do. He was obligated to "*gospel*" (1 Cor. 9:16, Greek *euangelizōmai*, see chapter 10) the Good News of the Lord Jesus because of the divine design for his life (Fee, 1987, p. 419).

But Paul was not only passionate about reaching out to others with the Good News of the Christ. Paul also modelled the practice of accompanying others in obedience to the Lord Jesus. Although he never used the word "disciple" (Greek *mathētēs*) to speak of this process, he did use the verb *manthanō* (which is the verbal form of *mathētēs*) 15 times.[2] This verb signifies "to learn, to be instructed" (within both formal contexts and informal relationships) through experience and often carries the additional idea of reflection (Louw & Nida, 1989, p. 327). Although Paul did not call the people he accompanied

---

1 In his letter to the Christ-followers in Galatia, Paul says that before he placed his *pistis* in the Christ he was "formerly in Judaism" (Gal. 1:13). The word formerly (*pote*) surely implies that he is no longer part of Judaism. Don Garlington (2007, p. 42) informs us that the name "Judaism" was used in conscious reaction to "Hellenism" in Paul's day. James Dunn (1992, p. 28) says, "Characteristic of early Judaism was the sense of Israel's distinctiveness and privilege as the people chosen by God and marked out from the other nations by this covenant relation and by the Torah practice of those loyal to this covenant (and thus to God)." Over time, particularly in view of the Syrian and Roman conquests of Palestine, "'Judaism' became synonymous with 'zeal for the law' and an implacable nationalism that was prepared to deal harshly with even an apparent usurpation of power over the law and the temple. For this reason, Paul's subsequent struggle against circumcision and the law was not least a 'betrayal of Judaism' in the eyes of his Jewish opponents because of its 'ethnic political consequences'" (Hengel, 2003, pp. 307–308).

2 Rom. 16:17; 1 Cor. 4:9; 14:31; Gal. 3:2; Eph. 4:20; Phil. 4:9, 11; Col. 1:7; 1 Tim. 2:11; 5:4, 13; 2 Tim. 3:7, 14; Tit. 3:4.

"disciples," he considered the process of guiding their development to be disciple making (Wilkins, 1988, p. 160).

In fact, Paul's instruction to his followers flows through each chapter of the epistle to the Philippians: "I thank God every time I remember you ... because of your partnership in the gospel ... And this is my prayer: that your love may abound ... so that you may be able to discern what is best and may be pure and blameless until the day of Christ, filled with the fruit of righteousness ... to the glory and praise of God. ... Whatever happens, conduct yourselves in a manner worthy of the gospel of Christ. Then, ... I will know that you stand firm in one spirit, contending as one man for the faith of the gospel ... Do everything without complaining or arguing, so that you may become ... children of God without fault in a crooked and depraved generation, in which you shine like stars in the universe. ... But whatever was to my profit I now consider loss for the sake of Christ ... I press on toward the goal ... I press on to take hold of that for which Christ Jesus took hold of me. ... All of us who are mature should take such a view of things ... Join with others in following my example. ... Whatever you have learned or received or heard from me, or seen in me—put it into practice" (Phil. 1:3–11, 27–30; 2:14–16; 3:7–21; 4:9). Paul deliberately called laymen and laywomen to imitate his example in living out the gospel.

But when the faithful lay believers of his day looked at Paul's life, what did they see? Did they observe only how he preached to crowds or the miracles that God did through him? Or did they watch him witness to the centrality of the Lord Jesus of Nazareth day after day as he plied his trade? Undoubtedly, they did both. I can hardly imagine the Apostle who constantly sought opportunities to lead others to believe in and live out faithfully allegiance to the Jesus of Nazareth, the eternal Son incarnate, not sharing his own faith as he made tents. Acts 18 seems to justify this conviction. There we read that Paul found Aquila with his wife Priscilla, and because he was a tentmaker as they were, he stayed and worked with them (verse 3). Luke describes Aquila as a Jew who had been chased out of Rome by Claudius, the Roman Emperor. The book of Acts uses the title "Jew" to designate Jews who did not believe in Jesus as the Messiah. Apparently, Paul led Aquila and Priscilla to persevere and grow in their *pistis* in and toward the Lord Jesus as they laboured side by side in their workshop.

In Acts 19, we find other fascinating details about the Apostle's practice. Luke informs us that Paul "had discussions daily in the lecture hall of Tyrannus," and that this went on for two years (Ac. 19:9). A bit further on, he explains how the sick brought "handkerchiefs and aprons" that had been touched by the apostle and they were healed (19:12). This is the only place where Acts mentions this kind of practice. But what were those "handkerchiefs and aprons"? The Greek word *soudarion* means a facecloth used for wiping perspiration, and *simikinthion* means a workman's apron. Luke is telling his readers that Paul's sweat-cloths and work-aprons used in his trade of tent-making and leather working were taken out to the sick and those afflicted by demons, and through their application cures occurred. It seems that Paul was using the hall between the hours of 11:00 a.m. and 4:00 p.m.—the time of the usual midday rest and after Tyrannus had dismissed his students and Paul had completed his morning's work. The text indicates that he went to the hall in his work clothes, taught for a while, and then returned to his work. According to Acts 20:31, Paul encouraged the Ephesian elders by claiming that he "had not ceased day and night" to warn each of them with tears. Quite evidently, this incessant activity by the Apostle included the hours when he was busy making tents. Apparently other Christ-followers even came to his workplace to meet with him and learn from him.

This total modeling of a way of life is attested by the way Paul describes his relationship to Timothy in 1 Corinthians 4:17: "I am sending you Timothy, my son whom I love, who is faithful (*pistōn*, from *pistis*) in/to the Lord [Jesus]. He will remind you of my way of life in Christ Jesus, which agrees with what I teach everywhere in every *ekklēsia*." The relationship between Paul's Christ-centred way of life and his Christ-centred teaching (cf. Rom. 4:21; Col. 1:28; 2:7), along with his transmission of both to Timothy, is clear.

The notion of transmission is also evident in Paul's exhortation to Timothy to entrust to faithful and reliable men the things he had heard the Apostle say in the presence of many witnesses. Paul says that those men should also be "qualified to teach others as well" (2 Tim. 2:2). Most commentators do not believe that this verse envisions a line of apostolic succession (Twomey, 2009, p. 130). Davies (1996, p. 68) maintains, on the contrary, that this is an appeal to put "the teaching into practice" in a visible way. Rather than emphasizing the need to transmit orthodoxy or apostolic doctrine (important as these might be); Paul is instructing Timothy to pass on *orthopraxy* or a correct way of living (which I call discipleship or conformity to Jesus of Nazareth, the Christ). Just as Paul passed on his Christ-centred way of life and his Christ-molded teaching to Timothy, Timothy was to entrust (the verb form of the noun "deposit" in 2 Tim. 1:14; cf. 1 Tim. 6:20) that deposit to others who would reliably repeat the process (cf. 1 Tim. 1:12).

After exhorting Timothy to pass on to others what he had received, Paul uses three analogies (military, athletics, farming) to urge Timothy to be wholeheartedly devoted to this ministry (2 Tim. 2:4–5). And just as Paul had urged each of the Ephesian Christ-followers to do their part according to the grace they had received (Eph. 4:7), he exhorts Timothy to "be strong in the grace that is in Christ Jesus" (2 Tim. 2:1). This is not just grace that Timothy received as the means of his salvation, but also the grace by which he, like all Christ-followers, is enabled to grow with others in Christ-likeness (cf. 2 Tim. 1:9; Rom. 5:2). Just in case Timothy might miss the point, Paul adds that "the Lord Jesus will give you insight into all this" (2 Tim. 4:7).

In short, everything in this understanding of our mission is "gospel-driven." For instance, Paul places the specific imperatives of his missions appeal within the context of the gospel when he writes: "Don't be ashamed to testify about our Lord Jesus" (2 Tim. 1:8). His exhortation to Timothy to "Take your share of suffering like a good soldier of Christ Jesus" (2:3) is also grounded in this gospel orientation, as is his injunction to "Keep what you heard from me as the pattern of sound teaching, with faith and love in Christ Jesus" (1:13). And just as he had done with Timothy, Paul instructs him to "Entrust those things to those who are reliable or trustworthy people" (2 Tim. 2:2). All this while he keeps in mind "Jesus Christ, raised from the dead, descended from David." This, he states, "is my gospel, for which I am suffering" (2:8). The mission, as Paul describes it, is all about the Lord Jesus of Nazareth, the Christ, with Paul as his secondary agent and ambassador. As a way of wrapping up his gospel-driven understanding of our mission, Paul cites a trustworthy (*pistōs*) saying:[3] "Take your share of suffering for the Lord Jesus" (2:3). He further reminds Timothy, to keep in mind his risen Lord "because if we have died with him, we shall also live with him," and so on (2:11–13).

I will organize the rest of this final study around three key elements involved in a gospel-driven theology of mission. First, I will show why mission guided by a gospel-driven theology of discipleship spontaneously spawns "church planting." Second, I will argue that it also promotes respectful relationships with other believers with whom we may have doctrinal disagreements and fosters unity in the Christ. Finally, I will argue that a gospel-driven theology of discipleship naturally promotes intentional efforts to cross ethnic, religious, cultural, and linguistic barriers for the sake of the Christ.

A Gospel–Driven Theology of Discipleship and Church Planting

It is widely recognized that the Apostle Paul was first and foremost a missionary. Not only was he specifically commissioned as the Apostle to the Gentiles, but he had a great passion to establish or plant churches in virgin Gentile territory, or areas where the Good News of Jesus of Nazareth, the Christ had not previously been proclaimed. If by this we mean that Paul intentionally drew people into relationships in which they could learn from and challenge each other, modeling to each other what new life under the reign of the resurrected Lord Jesus looks like, then the understanding reflects the gospel. If on the other hand, we view Paul's concern for "planting" (1 Cor. 3:6–9; 9:7, 10, 11), laying foundations (Rom 15:20; 1 Cor. 3:10), or giving birth (1 Cor. 4:15; Phm. 10) as more focused on creating a network of churches, this would project on him a theology which developed later, under the influence of Christendom with its established institutions.

The New Testament writers, including Paul, believed that adherence to the Christ involves the obedience of *pistis* (Rom. 1:1–5; 16:25–27), and that a lifestyle "worthy of Christ" (Phil. 1:27–30) happens only when his followers

---

3 The formula "faithful or trustworthy saying" recurs three more times in Paul's correspondence with Timothy (1 Tim. 1:15; 3:1; 4:10, see also Titus 3:18).

continuously learn with and from each other how to "take off the former way of life" (Eph. 4:22; 1 Pet. 2:1)[4] and "put on the new self" (Eph. 4:24; Rom. 6:4). This passion to see Christ formed in his followers motivated Paul's mission. His mission and his letters to the first clusters of Christ-followers were not about establishing the church *per se*. Rather, his concern was to see those who had placed their confidence in the Lord Jesus learn how to live under Christ's reign and persevere in their allegiance to him in each new situation. When this takes place, *ekklēsia* happens. The goal is the dynamic of life transformation in conformity to the Lord Jesus of Nazareth (Von Speyr, 1993, p. 82).

This intentional joining with others for mutual accompaniment in learning how to live as disciples of the Lord Jesus (cf. Mt. 18:20) was labelled the *ekklēsia* by the time Pliny (23/24–79 CE) came into contact with Christ-followers. About this term, Robert Louis Wilken (2003, p. 33) states that "in common usage in Greek and Latin *ekklēsia* referred to the political assembly of the people of a city." The politico-religious nature of *ekklēsia* helps us understand Jesus' authoritative response to Peter, who had just confessed him as the Christ (*ho Christos*) (Mt. 16:16): "I will build my *ekklēsia*" (Mt. 16:18). Jesus was saying that he, not Peter, would build the community around himself, as its members enacted *pistis* in him.[5] Jesus further stated that the understanding of his identity as co-regent of the true kingdom had been revealed to Peter by the Father (Mt. 16:17). Because of this divine revelation, Peter, in this passage, is portrayed as the guarantor of the correct understanding of Jesus' identity (Overman, 1990, p. 138).

Intentional discipleship to the Lord Jesus was the goal long before the word *ekklēsia* was used for gatherings of the disciples. Their coming together reflected Jesus of Nazareth's surprising affirmation in Matthew 18:20: "Where two or three come together in my name, there am I with them." Coming together in the name of someone, like Jesus of Nazareth was, in the ancient Mediterranean world, a way for the group to identify themselves, as well as to identify the one around whom they gathered. The followers of the Christ were thereby confessing their readiness to be known by reference to this Lord Jesus. James Dunn (1996, p. 240) points out that this was no light matter: "'The

---

4 Ephesians 4:22-24 expresses the thought that the followers of Jesus in Ephesus have "learned Christ" (v. 20)—a phrase not found elsewhere in the Greek Bible without any obvious pre-biblical Greek documentary source. Grenz (2001, p. 259) surmises from this observation that this is in contrast to the Jewish emphasis on learning Torah, and that instead they were "taught in him" (v. 21). He writes: "by means of an explicit reference to "Jesus" (v. 21), the writer points out that this instruction centred on the historical Jesus, who is the risen Christ" (2001, p. 259).
5 Michael Wilkins (1988, p. 195) observes that Matthew points to Peter as a model for all disciples to follow: "Peter, as the representative disciple who gives the first personal declaration of the Messiah's identity, is the one in the book of Acts who opens the door of the kingdom to all peoples. Through his authoritative preaching and presence, the kingdom was opened to Jews (Ac. 2), Samaritans (Ac. 8), and Gentiles (Ac. 10)."

name' was one of the chief ways in the ancient world by which a person could be known, by which her or his character could be disclosed." The words of Matthew 18:20 follow Jesus' teaching about sin, conflicts, and the need to hold one another accountable for actions with humility and repentance. We can therefore understand that Jesus was going far beyond giving the simple promise that he would be present when people gathered in a faith community. Rather, he was speaking specifically of his presence in the midst of two or three persons who have come together for mutual accompaniment in learning how to live as his disciples—that is, as the *ekklēsia*.

From Ekklēsia *to "Church"*

During the first years of Paul's ministry, the clusters of Christ-followers whom he accompanied acted with the conviction that every disciple of Jesus refines his or her daily lifestyle in interaction with others as an expression of his or her *pistis* (Neill, 1990, p. 22). Paul's approach produced a network of small clusters of Christ-focused disciples that were immediately autonomous and reproducing. This is one factor that explains the tremendous advance of the gospel during those early years.[6]

Initially, the *ekklēsia* was an illegal movement,[7] more or less clandestine, whose members had the threat of the sword hanging over their heads. The faithful (*pistōs*) in this movement were recruited from among the lower middle class: artisans and workers, liberated slaves, and the large class of domestic and "industrial" servants. The spreading of the network of Christ-focused clusters was the result of the changed lives and resulting allegiance to the Lord Jesus displayed by thousands of anonymous believers, who spontaneously began to win others to the Christ in their random trips and haphazard meetings.[8] This growth through relational and informal networks, which I have labelled an "*ekklēsia*-movement" (Bjork, 2015, pp. 174–186), was largely the product of

---

6 Anglican evangelist David Watson (1978, p. 121) has underscored the fact that "During the first two centuries, the church met in small groups in the homes of its members ... Those two centuries witnessed the greatest advance that the church has ever experienced. The absence of church buildings was not an obstacle to the rapid expansion of the church, it seems rather to have had a positive effect."

7 I define a movement as a diffuse, heterogenous, and polycephalic group united by a common purpose, vision, or ideal.

8 Robert Tuttle (2006, p. 100) offers the following example, among many, of the amazing spread of this movement: "The church—named Church of the East—that would eventually identify with the Nestorian cause was founded by Assyrian Christians in Persia in 45 CE. By the time of the Jerusalem Council the Church of the East had 100,000 converts in all twelve provinces of Persia. Two of the twelve Apostles—Judas son of James and Simon the Zealot—are said to have begun the work around 35 CE. In the face of relentless hostility—especially among the Zoroastrian priests—these Assyrians began a ministry that will probably outlive them forever. They preached, they organized, they suffered, but mostly, they were martyred."

its illegal status. The Roman government, which sought to control the inhabitants of the Empire, felt threatened by this movement.[9]

But in the fourth century, the situation was reversed. The emperor Constantine, in the Edict of Milan of 313 CE, granted Christianity an official character, and the movement that had known itself by the name *ekklēsia* was transformed. It is commonly held that Constantine's conversion marks the beginning of "Christendom," in the sense of the identification of the *ekklēsia* with the whole of organized society (Dawson, 1965, pp. 49–50; Southern, 1970, p. 16). Thus, gathering with a few others in apprenticeship to the Lord Jesus of Nazareth, or being the *ekklēsia*, meant something different for the first generations of Christ-followers in the Roman Empire than it did after the Christian faith was institutionalized by Charlemagne.

Quickly a permanent ecclesiastical organization came into being, mirroring that of the state. At the Council of Nicea, in 325 CE, foundational principles were laid for the hierarchy. After that, subsequent councils worked to make things function smoothly in the church; old procedures were confirmed, and rules were adopted to respond to immediate needs. Like today's clergy, that of the fourth century was clearly distinguished from the faithful and constituted a distinct social category.

The institutional *ekklēsia* was a great success—numerically. But its growing identification with all of contemporary society meant that overall, one could affiliate with Christianity without necessarily being committed to lifestyle conformity to the Lord Jesus. With the Edict of Thessalonica, issued in 380 CE by the emperor Theodosius, every citizen of the Empire was to abandon the ancient gods and embrace Christianity or else risk experiencing the wrath of the Roman state. This threat provoked a massive entry of "converts" into the *ekklēsia* (the formerly clandestine movement) that further contributed to its mutation into an institution. The "committed soul" was being replaced by, in the words of Péguy, "the accustomed soul" (quoted by Rakotoarison, 2014). "Going to church," lamented John Chrysostom, "is often a question of habit. … It used to be that houses were churches, now it is the churches that appear to be no more than ordinary houses!" (quoted by Pargoire, 1900, p. 156).

---

9 As an example, around the year 110, to formulate the opposition between the kingdom of God and the Roman Empire, the author of the Letter to Diogenes used the following expression: "Christians … live in their own countries as though they were passing through. They play their full role as citizens, but labour under all the disabilities of aliens. Any country can be their homeland, but for them their homeland, wherever it may be, is a foreign country" (Spiritual Theology Department of the Pontifical University of the Holy Cross, 2021). Origen (*Contre Celsus* III.29-30) explained that the Church of Jesus Christ had one *politeia*, or conception of citizenship, which was different than that of those who worshipped demons. And he argued that although the Christians were foreigners and from humble origins, they were much wiser than the pagans. He concluded by affirming that because of their moral conduct, even the least perfect among their leaders were superior to the existing civil authorities.

The Constantinian alliance of *ekklēsia* and state in Christendom would remain a defining feature of European history from the fourth to the eighteenth century, or from Constantine to Voltaire.[4] Commenting on this fact, Southern (1970, p. 18) writes:

> In an extensive sense the medieval church was a state. It had all the apparatus of the state: laws and law courts, taxes and tax-collectors, a great administrative machine, power of life and death over the citizens of Christendom and their enemies within and without.

Not only did the *ekklēsia* wield state-like powers within Christendom, but it also constituted a compulsory society:

> From a social point of view a contractual relationship was established between the infant and the church from which there was no receding. For the vast majority of members of the church baptism was as involuntary as birth, and it carried with it obligations as binding and permanent as birth into a modern state, with the further provision that the obligations attached to baptism could in no circumstances be renounced. (Southern, 1970, p. 18)

Southern's analysis would lead us to question the extent to which individuals were learning from each other how to enact voluntary allegiance to Christ under Christendom.[10] Certainly some did. However, pagan beliefs and allegiances also persisted beneath the cultural surface of Christendom. A suitable image of the situation is that of two streams flowing simultaneously, one on the surface, in plain sight (Christianity), and the other subterranean, hidden from immediate view (paganism). Thus, within the scope of

---

10 Prior to Christendom there was the firm conviction among the followers of the Jesus of Nazareth that he was the *imago dei* into which Adam was created. Irenaeus expressed the thinking of the primitive Jesus followers:
And then, again, this Word was manifested when the Word of God was made man, assimilating himself to man, and man to Himself, so that by means of his resemblance to the Son, man might become precious to the Father. For in times long past, it was *said* that man was created after the image of God, but it was nor [actually) *shown'*, for the Word was as yet invisible, after whose image man was created. Wherefore also he did easily lose the similitude. When, however, the Word of God became flesh, He confirmed both these: for He both showed forth the image truly, since He became himself what was His image; and He re-established the similitude after a sure manner, by assimilating man to the invisible Father through means of the visible Word. (*Against Heresies* 5.16.2, in *The Ante-Nicene Fathers,* 1:544.)
Drawing also from the teaching of Irenaeus's contemporary, Clement of Alexandria, Grenz (2001, p. 147) correctly writes, "God created Adam with a future goal in view—namely, that he develop into the fullness of the divine image and likeness, which is the Son." There was, however, an important shift away from the centrality of Christ as the divine image that has characterized the second-century fathers, such as Irenaeus, with the inauguration of Christendom (Grenz, 2001, p. 158).

Christendom, while many individuals maintained their pagan allegiances and worldview, the now-institutionalized *ekklēsia* which furnished Western societies at the surface level with their spiritual values, their moral standards, and their conception of their place in the universe:

> The church was much more than the source of coercive power. It was not just a government, however grandiose its operations. It was the whole of human society subject to the will of God. It was the ark of salvation in a sea of destruction. It was membership in the church that gave men a thoroughly intelligible purpose and place in God's universe. So the church was not only a state, it was the state; it was not only a society, it was the society—the human *societas perfecta*. Not only all political activity, but all learning and thought were functions of the church. Besides taking over the political order of the Roman Empire, the church appropriated the science of Greece and the literature of Rome, and it turned them into instruments of human well-being in this world. To all this it added the gift of salvation—the final and exclusive possession of its members. And so in all its fullness it was the society of rational and redeemed mankind. (Southern, 1970, p. 22)

Within the context of Christendom, to be Christian was to share a common tradition, customs, festivals and sacrifices. This understanding was associated with a territorial Christianity and a perception of human society under which it was assumed that a single people must have a single set of customs. The received traditions had little to do with faith and everything to do with identity as a people.

Christendom and Mission Theology

Thus, although Western civilization in Europe and America is the direct successor and heir of Christendom, we would be naive to believe that the inhabitants of these lands have embraced the person and precepts of Jesus of Nazareth and pledged their allegiance to him.[11] As the missiologist and

---

11 What exactly do missiologists mean when they say that a people group or country is "unchurched"? Does not this term inherently assume that those it describes would become committed Christ-followers if they would take advantage of the presence of the church? As far as Western Europe is concerned, some scholars question the legitimacy of this assumption, because they recognize that a non-Christian Europe has always existed within the confines of historic Christendom (Luneau & Ladrière, 1989; Wessels, 1994). These scholars question whether large numbers of Europeans ever shifted their allegiance from their pagan roots when introduced to Christianity:
The Church ... showed no disposition to trample on the paganism which it had supplanted. In many households the men remained pagan when their women-folk accepted the new faith; this continued as late as the time of Jerome, for some of his most notable disciples had pagan husbands. (Elliott-Binns, 1957, p. 399)

historian of Christian mission Wilbert Shenk (1994, p. 9) has affirmed, a study of literature, history, theology, and sociology reveals that the leitmotif running through the modern period is the bankruptcy of Christendom as an expression of Christian reality. This view is shared by a former missionary to China who commented on the negative effect of this spiritual and moral bankruptcy on emerging nations that are seeing their own cultures being gradually transformed into Western culture. Comparing the spiritual condition of these peoples and that of countries once dominated by Christendom, he wrote:

> The churches in the homelands of those early European missionaries are now sick and in their dotage. When Christians from the "younger" churches visit their "mother" churches, they are frequently shocked and puzzled. They often ask, "Why are we, the offspring of eighteenth- and nineteenth-century European mission, now so strong and growing while European Christianity is weak, uncertain, and confused? Does a European fate await us if the main cause of European church frailty is the erosive effect of certain elements in Westernization?" (Beeby, 1994, p. 7)

An examination of the situation in Italy, Spain, and France after the collapse of the Roman Empire in the West reveals the persistent paganism that continued through the ages, both outside and within the Church:

The old idolatry died slowly in the country areas of Italy. When Benedict came to Monte Cassino in 529 he found the peasants worshipping at a shrine of Apollo. The Lombards of the sixth century, although outwardly Christian, worshipped sacred trees and images of snakes. Pagan cults flourished in Sicily well into the seventh century. The Arianism of the Ostrogoths and Lombards in the Peninsula did not disappear until late in the seventh century.

Spiritual conditions in Spain were very similar to those in Italy. Paganism and Arianism (in the case of the Visigoths) plagued Iberic Christianity as well as did the religious superficiality prevalent everywhere. Spain, apparently, never had had a solid evangelical basis for Christianity; rather she had had only the form of Christianity and a resultant worldliness that was destructive of spiritual effectiveness. ... The Christianity that soon was to face the onslaught of Islam was one of superstition, magic, and tradition; and although a part of the social fabric of the nation, it was devoid of spiritual power.... The same was largely true of Gaul (France) in the early medieval centuries. (Edman, 1949, pp. 177–178)

Furthermore, European observers note that non-Christian Europe has continued to exist, uninterrupted, up to the present despite the presence of the church. One example of this phenomenon is the contemporary "New Right," formed by Alain de Benoist, which radically rejects the entire Christian tradition and calls for "a return to the 'authentic' pre-Christian roots of the West" (Luneau & Ladrière, 1989, p. 40). The permanence of this pagan tradition was firmly emphasized in de Benoist's famous book *Comment peut-on être païen?* (On Being a Pagan). William Edgar (1983, p. 308), Professor in Christian Apologetics at the Free Faculty of Reformed Theology, Aix-en-Provence, France, summarized de Benoist's position: "Paganism has never been far away from us, both in history and in the sub-conscious mind, as well as in ritual, in literature, and so forth."

Why, you might ask, is all this important? It is important because much of our understanding of our mission has been highly impacted by this historic shift. A gospel-driven understanding of mission affirms that the true *ekklēsia* is marked by Christ-centred allegiance and the pursuit of concrete lifestyle alteration, with the accompaniment of at least one other person in growing conformity to Jesus. However, Christendom contends that wherever there is a "legitimate" form of the *ekklēsia* (seen in a more institutional sense), lifestyles are being altered to resemble the Christ.[12] Everyone agrees that transformation of all areas of a person's human existence cannot be restricted to his or her initial decision to confess the Lord Jesus (Rom. 10:9–10). My argument is that the Western church has failed by descending into institutionalism and defining Christian obedience largely in terms of passive worship attendance and perhaps outward morality rather than bold lifestyle conformity and witness. In 2 Peter 3:18 (cf. 1:3–11), which exhorts its readers in this sense, it is remarkable to note how this process is linked to the glory of Jesus the Christ. Peter, the Jew, who would have learned by heart the solemn words of Isaiah 42:8—"I am *Yahweh*; that is my name! I will not yield my glory to another"—attributes glory to Jesus of Nazareth, the one whom he had accompanied on the dusty paths of Palestine. This is a powerful confession of his supremacy as the risen Christ now reigning with the Father (Blum, 1981, p. 289).

A Gospel-Driven Theology of Discipleship
and Mutually Affirming Interaction

From the perspective of a gospel-driven theology, the new life in the perfect God-man, the second Adam, constitutes a restoration of the first creation along with a reestablishment of humanity. Our new life in Jesus of Nazareth, the Christ, implies that we do not live under his reign as separate individuals but grow together in his image as we help each other to fully develop. This renewal of the Creator God's original intent is being fulfilled from start to finish focusing on the eternal Son incarnate in Jesus of Nazareth. A gospel-driven theology of discipleship reflects this diversity and builds on this paradigm of one living and true God in three persons, acting in a fundamental and absolute unity (as described by the Greek word *perichoresis*).[13]

---

12 This observation holds whether one is formed by either the Catholic or episcopal model, the presbyterian or Reformed model, or the congregationalist model. It also influences our various approaches to church offices and our understanding of the proper roles of the individual and the community.

13 The term *Paraklētos* as a designation of the person of the Spirit occurs only in John's gospel (14:16, 26; 15:26; 16:7). When theologians speak of the relationships that exist among the members of the Trinity, they sometimes use the word *perichoresis*. The most basic meaning of this word is "a complete mutual interpenetration of two substances that preserves the identity and properties of each intact" (Harrison, 1991, p. 54). This is

The Missional Basis of Trinitarian Reflection

A friend of mine likes to say, "God had only one Son, and he was a missionary." These words reflect the fact that only in the context of God's missionary activity of renewing or restoring his creation can the believing community be led into the mystery of his tri-personhood. The Father sends the eternal Son; the incarnate Son after his death and resurrection breathes the Spirit upon his disciples (Jn. 20:21) and says to them, "As the Father has sent me, I am sending you." The divine project revealed in the Scriptures begins with the heavenly conceived and initiated mission of the eternal Son of God, and it ends with our being sent, empowered by the Spirit of Jesus, to the ends of the earth.

Missionary thinkers have often reflected on the implications of the outward manifestations of the divine persons of the Trinity. Often, we have looked at the Father as the one who sends both the Son and the Spirit. We have examined the Son who was sent, and we have reflected on the ramifications of his sending of his first followers. We have also examined the close link between Jesus of Nazareth and the work of the Spirit. Here I will approach the missional connotations of the Trinity from a different perspective. Instead of looking at the distinctions between the persons of the Godhead, I will consider what lessons we can learn from their interrelatedness. I believe a gospel-driven theology of discipleship can be enhanced if we examine the way in which the three-person Creator God has manifested his oneness.

The doctrine of the Trinity was developed for the precise purpose of explaining to non-believers the interrelatedness of the eternal Son incarnate and the Father. Hence, not only is the tri-personhood of God inextricably linked to his own missional activity, but history demonstrates that it has been best understood and communicated in the context of the missionary endeavours of God's people. In his little book *Trinitarian Faith and Today's Mission*, Lesslie

---

a fascinating concept. It contains the image of intimacy and of pure reciprocity which does not result in confusion or loss of identity. Quoting Petavius, Pohle (1950, p. 283) writes:

Perichoresis in the Godhead originates in the unity of the Divine essence, and it consists in this, that one Person cannot be divided or separated from another, but they mutually exist in one another without confusion and without detriment to the distinction between them.

Butin (1994, p. 161) uses *perichoresis* to understand the unity of the three persons that focuses on their mutual indwelling or existence, their intimate interrelationship, and their constantly interacting cooperation. Hill (1982, p. 272) stresses that the Greek Fathers made much of *perichoresis* (literally, "dancing around") to suggest that the unity found in the Godhead is "a joyous sharing of divine life." He writes, "Liberty is a property of the divine nature but it is exercised only by the persons, who within the Trinity interrelate one to another in the pure creativity of uncreated freedom and love." *Perichoresis* stresses a oneness produced as each member of the Trinity is defined based upon his dynamic relationship with the other two (LaCugna, 1991, p. 270).

Newbigin (1964) explains that when the faithful enacted allegiance (*pistis*) to the Lord Jesus, the Christ, in their daily lifestyle in the pagan world, they very quickly found themselves compelled to articulate a fully Trinitarian doctrine of the God whom they confessed:

> It is indeed a significant fact that the great doctrinal struggles about the nature of the Trinity, especially about the mutual relations of the Son and the Father, developed right in the midst of the struggle between the Church and the pagan world. ... The vehemence of the doctrinal struggles which centred on the formulation of the Trinitarian doctrine, and especially on the question of the relation of the Son to the Father, is evidence of the centrality of this issue for the whole Christian witness to the pagan world of that time. (1964, p. 32)

Newbigin expounds on his point by contrasting this phenomenon with what took place under the influence of Christendom. He contends that when the missional activity of the faithful subsided under the institutionalized *ekklēsia*, the doctrine of the Trinity did not occupy a comparable place in the thought of Christians to what it had previously.

Beyond the missionary activity of the triune God, and beyond the Trinitarian reflection that took place when the followers of Jesus attempted to explain his relationship to the Father within a pagan context, there is another reason why the gospel-driven missionary enterprise provides the basis for trinitarian reflection. We find that rationale in the prayer of Jesus recorded in the seventeenth chapter of John's gospel:

> My prayer is not for them [those whom you gave me out of the world] alone. I pray also for those who will believe in me through their message, that all of them may be one, Father, just as you are in me and I am in you. May they also be in us so that the world may believe that you have sent me. (John 17:20–21)

In this prayer, Jesus establishes his oneness with the Father as a pattern for his followers in the context of his mission in the world.

Is this call for us to "be one" possible today? Is the unity for which Jesus prayed only wishful thinking? If it is true that in the Christ the old divisions of race, gender, and even religion have been abolished (Rom. 10:12; 1 Cor. 7:19; Gal. 3:28; Col. 3:11), and if there is "one body and one Spirit ... one Lord, one faith, one baptism; one God and Father of all, who is over all and through all and in all" (Eph. 4:4–6), then how can we make our unity visible?[14]

---

14 Contrary to our actual practice, as Donald Bloesch (1983, pp. 64–65) has pointed out, one of our fundamental beliefs as evangelical Christians is that we must work to promote the unity for which Jesus prayed in John 17:

Christian disunity is a contradiction of Christ's prayer that his people be one (John 17:20–23). It also conflicts with Paul's declarations that there is only "one body and one Spirit ... one Lord, one faith, one baptism" (Eph. 4:4, 5). Disunity on theological and

A Gospel-Driven Perichoretic Theology of Mission

Despite our affirmation of the oneness and catholicity of the *ekklēsia*, we are unsure of the nature of the unity we should seek with the faithful believers (*pistōn*) of other Christian denominations.[15] A gospel-driven theology of discipleship, grounded in the relationship between the persons of the Trinity (as described by the word *perichoresis*), can guide us as we seek to overcome some the glaring reality of Christian disunity. In what follows, I argue that a gospel–driven theology of discipleship informed by the *perichoresis* forces us to learn new ways of learning from and with all Christ-followers not just as a kind of side activity, but as an imperative for all his disciples. It compels us to work synergistically with disciples of the Christ who hold different doctrines, traditions, methods, goals, and orientations from our own by intentionally coming alongside them for the explicit task of stimulating faith, enabling response, and empowering witness.

In the face of ever-increasing diversity within global Christianity, a gospel-driven theology of discipleship holds that it is appropriate for Christ followers to act "paracletically" by coming alongside the followers of Jesus from different ecclesial traditions for a period of time, whether brief or extended, in partnership with the Spirit, so as to enter into the fullness and depth of our common missionary mandate. This approach involves at least three key dimensions: (1) a gospel-driven, "paracletic" model of mission is *particular*, taking seriously the story that is being written in the lives of other followers of Christ; (2) it is *participative*, or a ministry of involving oneself in what the triune God is already doing in the lives of other followers of Christ; and (3) it is *purposive*, with a trajectory, aim, target, and goal.

---

even sociological grounds betrays an appalling ignorance of the nature of the church. Indeed, the classical marks of the church of Jesus Christ are oneness, holiness, apostolicity and catholicity. The last term denotes universal outreach and continuity with the tradition of the whole church ... In my view, there will never be real evangelical unity, let alone Christian unity, until there is an awakening to the oneness and catholicity of the church.

15 Evangelicals were also encouraged to work together with other Christians by the Lausanne Congress on World Evangelization, which met in Lausanne, Switzerland in July 1974 (Stott, 1975; Lausanne Committee for World Evangelism, 1989, paragraph 7). That call for co-operation and involvement with other kinds of Christians was repeated in the Thailand Statement (Lausanne Movement,1980), one of the last paragraphs of which reads, "We joyfully affirm the unity of the Body of Christ and acknowledge that we are bound together with one another and with all true believers. ... We must nevertheless strive for a visible expression of our oneness." The Manila Manifesto of 1989 recognized that co-operation is possible between Evangelicals and other kinds of Christians without full doctrinal agreement or compromise: "We recognize that there are many churches which are not part of the Evangelical movement. ... All Evangelicals are aware that serious theological differences between us remain. ... Where appropriate, and so long as biblical truth is not compromised, cooperation may be possible" (Lausanne Committee for World Evangelization, 1989, paragraph 17).

A Gospel–Driven, Paracletic Model of Mission Is Particular

When Jesus of Nazareth trained his first disciples, he did not crush their personalities or force them to act according to his example. Instead, he positioned himself as their servant and as the slave of all (Mk. 10:45). In like manner, when the Spirit teaches us (Jn. 14:26; 15:13), brings things to our mind, and helps us to understand them, he does so in a way that does not violate the particularities of our personhood. He does not impose himself on us in an approach that eradicates the story of our existence. Instead, he comes alongside us in a manner that emboldens us to look deeply into the events of our lives, much as Jesus of Nazareth did with Peter (cf. Mk. 8:31–33). The Spirit does not overlook or ignore the sinful twists and turns of our being. But even as he leads us into all truth (Jn. 16:13), he does so as a comforter, helper, and counsellor who enables us to face our shortcomings with respect and critical honesty.

Our Lord Jesus of Nazareth demonstrated the conviction that his Father would "give" him all those whom the Father had already prepared for his coming (cf. Jn. 6:37, 39; 17:2, 6, 9, 24). In the same way, a gospel-driven, "paracletic" model of mission builds on the conviction that our Lord Jesus' activity precedes us through his Spirit. Christ-followers operating out of this missional paradigm learn a story is also being written in the lives of Christ-followers who are members of other faith traditions. They pay close attention to that story and recognize there the already-present action of their Lord Jesus, the Christ. They do not attempt to invent or rewrite that story. Rather, they understand that one aspect of their role as followers of Jesus of Nazareth, the Christ, is to assist these other believers to grow in their conformity to him. In fact, the success or effectiveness of such a relationship may be related to the ability to move beneath the most immediate, visible Christian rituals and creeds—to "read between the lines," as it were—so as to discover lessons relevant to all the followers of Jesus who participate together.

A Gospel-Driven, Paracletic Model of Mission Is Participative

The Creator's restorative mission is totally participative, in that it is the mission of the Father and the Spirit in the Son that includes the *ekklēsia* (adapted from Moltmann, 1977, p. 64). Similarly, when Christ-followers act "paracletically", they ask questions like these: What is our Lord Jesus up to in this situation? Where is his hand at work in the people whom he has led me to accompany at this time? What role would he have me play, as a welcomed guest, in their adventure of *pistis*?

Acting "paracletically" neither denies nor belittles the importance of the various Christian traditions (Congar, 1963). It does not involve rejecting the constraints of tradition and community. Nor does it mean that the disciple of the Christ becomes "one of them." However, involving oneself "paracletically" does entail drawing close enough to the *pistōn* of the other Christian tradition that a safe place for mutual discovery, learning, and growth is created. It means operating out of the conviction that each of our Christian traditions contributes a witness to the Christ that corrects, expands, and challenges all other forms of witness to him in the worldwide *ekklēsia*. And it entails continually embracing the unsettling discovery that faithfulness to the Lord Jesus (*pistis*) can, in cultures and traditions unlike our own, look quite different from the patterns we have evolved and become accustomed to (Guder, 2000, p. 90). It also implies confronting the realities, limitations, and ambiguities of our traditions and allowing the Spirit to teach us how to better enact *pistis* to the Lord Jesus. It may include assertive and forceful intervention in the life of that local *ekklēsia*, but always with attention to the movement and personality of the Spirit of Christ and what he is already doing there.

This interrelationship among groups of believers deals not only with the past, but also with the unfolding narrative of the life of the other Christ-followership being experienced. None of our spiritual stories are static. As we come alongside other Christ-followers to learn to better enact *pistis* to the Lord Jesus the Christ together, empowered by the Spirit, we discover over time the fullness and depth of our common calling and missionary mandate. As we make that discovery, we encounter the Lord Jesus, the Christ, in ways that broaden and deepen our understanding of the gospel and the story of our own experience. Rather than relating to other Christian traditions out of a hermeneutic of suspicion, a gospel-driven, "paracletic" model of mission creates a place where we can listen to the triune God, to the Scriptures, and to our shared and particular stories in a manner that opens new spaces of meaning and action.

A Gospel-Driven, Paracletic Model of Mission Is Purposive

Throughout these pages, I have insisted that Jesus of Nazareth has called us to one task. In Matthew 4:19, he says to Peter and his brother Andrew: "Follow me, and I will make you fishers of men." Like them, we are called to follow the rabbi from Nazareth, the Christ, and accompany others as they learn to live under his reign. This is what the risen Lord Jesus has defined as our purpose— *to make disciples who can make disciples.* Walter Henrichsen (1974, p. 5) puts it like this: "Make disciples is the mandate of the Master. We may ignore it, but we cannot evade it."

A gospel-driven, "paracletic" model of mission recognizes that a person can be a disciple of Jesus of Nazareth and an Evangelical Protestant, or a Pentecostal, or a Roman Catholic, or a Presbyterian, or a Lutheran, etc. Discipleship is not a question of ecclesiastical affiliation. Belonging to a specific Christian tradition does not automatically make a person a disciple of Jesus, the Christ. Neither does it exclude a person from growth in *pistis* to him!

The purpose of mission is not the expansion of the Christian tradition with which a person is associated. The various Christian traditions offer precious resources that can encourage, sustain, and deepen *pistis* to the Lord Jesus. However, our mission consists in promoting Jesus of Nazareth, the Christ, and not our faith tradition. The Lord Jesus of Nazareth, the eternal Son incarnate, is the Good News. He is the gospel, the heart of the Christian message and experience.

A Gospel-Driven Theology of Discipleship and Contextualization

A gospel-driven theology of discipleship refuses to ignore the dynamics of culture. The eternal Son became flesh in a specific time–space setting. As we saw in chapter 5, this event had cultural implications. For the eternal Son, the incarnation meant not only a new expression of his divine nature; it meant a human, *Jewish* expression of his nature. It meant not only a new expression of his life and a new way of relating to others, but a Jewish way of expressing his life and relating to others, within a Jewish culture and Jewish customs. It also meant subordination in a Jewish family setting. The Apostle Paul sums it up succinctly: "For I tell you that Christ has become a servant of the Jews on behalf of God's truth" (Rom. 15:8). He who is the prototype of humanity, the one in whom and for whom all has been created, became a "servant" (*diakonos*) of the Jews!

The Incarnation of the Eternal Son

The examples of our Lord Jesus and (as discussed at the beginning of this chapter) of Paul show us that with respect to culture, the messenger must change before the hearer of the message can. A gospel-driven theology of discipleship, based on the incarnation of the God-man, recognizes that witness to the Christ should not establish unnecessary barriers derived from our own cultural background. This point is clearly demonstrated in John 4:9, 27, where we learn that the disciples were shocked to discover Jesus bridging the cultural gap between himself and the Samaritans. The disciples were unwilling to relate to the hated Samaritans, enemies of the pure Jews, who held wrong doctrines and polluted their race with Gentile blood. All the disciples could see that day was the hardness of the Samaritans and their distance from the truth. In stark contrast, Jesus of Nazareth essentially declared, "The Samaritans are a ripe harvest field" (see Jn. 4:35). The problem was not the Samaritans, but the hearts of Jesus' followers.

Had the Lord Jesus shared the opinions of his disciples, he would not have entered into a relationship with any Samaritans. Pride in his own nation, ethnicity, culture, status, gender, and religion would have kept the rabbi of Nazareth aloof and distant from them.

When the Samaritan woman inquired as to where one should worship, Jesus of Nazareth raised the concept of worship above specific forms and places. He stated that the time was coming when the true worshipers would worship neither on the mountain of Samaria nor in Jerusalem, but that the important thing was to worship the Father in spirit and in truth (Jn. 4:22–23). Jesus of Nazareth presented himself to the Samaritans as the Messiah and Saviour, but significantly he left the question of the physical form of worship undefined. John says that the Samaritan response to Jesus was enthusiastic and open, so much so that they "urged Jesus to stay with them" (Jn. 4:40). Would the woman's testimony have had the same favorable reception if her message had been, "He told me everything I ever did, *and he commands us to worship God as the Jews of Jerusalem do*"? Would the townspeople have been able to place their *pistis* in the Lord Jesus, or would their own religious, cultural, and ethnic prejudices have kept them from discovering that "this man is the Saviour of the world" (Jn. 4:42)?

The Missionary Example of Paul

Paul's gospel-driven theology of discipleship led him to follow his Lord in the same way. He wrote, "From now on we regard no one from a worldly point of view" because of the resurrected one whose self-sacrificial love teaches us to no longer live for ourselves (cf. 2 Cor. 5:14–16). Because Paul intentionally taught and modelled a gospel-driven theology of discipleship that focuses on life in the new creation under the reign of the God-man, the Jesus movement was carried by ordinary laypeople beyond the initial boundaries of ethnicity, language, culture, and religion. Stephen Neill points out that the spread of the early *ekklēsia* happened as lay people empowered by the Spirit began living out their renewed humanity in submission to the Lord Jesus. Underscoring the fact that the entire body of believers (*pistōn*) was active in this process, Neill (1990, p. 22) adds:

> Where there were Christians, there would be a living, burning faith, and before long an expanding Christian community. In later times great Churches were much set on claiming apostolic origin—to have an apostle as founder was a recognized certificate of respectability. But in fact few, if any, of the great Churches were really founded by apostles. Nothing is more notable than the anonymity of these early missionaries.

Robert Tuttle (2006, p. 122) observes along this line that the message of Christ had a greater impact on non-believers when it came from poor and simple folk rather than from people of power or prestige. He adds:

> In the midst of persecution, Christianity was predominantly a lay movement. Until the end of the empire-wide persecutions, ministry was—for the most part—lay led and rural. Not that there were no great urban bishops and priests; there

were, and they died under the sword—in droves. It's just that for the first 150 years of Christendom every Christian was a priest. Then for the next 150 years, most lay Christians continued to take the Great Commission as a personal mandate to spread the word. (p. 132)

In his study of the propagation of the gospel by the primitive *ekklēsia*, Michael Green highlights the amazing diversity of the people who participated in that work. The spreading of the gospel was not reserved for the most zealous or for the religious professionals. On the contrary, it was the prerogative and the responsibility of each member of the community. "The ordinary church member saw it as his responsibility: Christianity was supremely a lay movement, spread by informal missionaries" (Green, 2001, p. 332).

The problem with movements is that sooner or later, they quit moving (Neill, 1990, p. 440). Eventually, over time, inertia imposes itself. This is particularly true of attempts to establish and maintain a movement of intentional discipleship to the Christ today. But intentional discipleship can be recovered if we purposefully and resolutely embrace the Christ-centred, gospel-driven theology that sustained the initial generations of Christ-followers.

The Task Before Us

The restoration of a gospel-driven theology of discipleship will not be easy. To some degree, we are all products of our own culture, Christian tradition, and hermeneutical choices. Our contexts influence the kinds of things we allow ourselves to see and emphasize. We all only "know in part" (1 Cor. 13:12), and we often feel uncomfortable with alternative understandings and other perspectives. However uncomfortable we might be with a gospel-driven theology of discipleship, it is I believe, the most appropriate foundation for missions. It draws on the humanity of the eternal Son incarnate, Jesus of Nazareth the second Adam, the *imago hominis*. It focuses on the apostolic proclamation of his faithful obedience (enacted *pistis*) to his Father all the way to his death on the cross. It highlights how he undid what Adam had done, thereby initiating the restorative project of the triune Creator as the Father raised him from the dead and set him at his right hand. It maintains that we are restored as humans to our place of glory as we enter into his *pistis* by our Spirit-enabled *pistis* toward him. And it stresses that the purpose of Christ-followerships (*ekklēsia*) is to practise together how to live under the law of self-giving service to others as subjects of our self-giving Lord Jesus, the Christ. All these themes are in the Bible, but they are often not connected together in this way in our thinking. When they are connected properly, our efforts to foster intentional discipleship to the Lord Jesus, the Christ will flourish in ways that are both biblically faithful and meaningful to others.

Conclusion

As we conclude, let me remind you of the foundations of a gospel-driven theology of discipleship. The witness of the Scriptures features the eternal Son, incarnate in the man from Nazareth, and emphasizes his perfect obedience to the Father. Philippians 2:6-11 highlights Jesus' willingness to submit where Adam had failed, even in his humiliation on the cross, resulting in his exaltation and enthronement as Lord. The centrality of Jesus of Nazareth in the Creator's redemptive plan comes through in both, for in his self-giving he manifested the love of the godhead for people of all cultures, though in Adam they have followed their own schemes and fallen short of his intent. When the Father accepted the Spirit-enabled, obedient life of the Son incarnate and sat him at his right hand he made him the mediator of a new covenant. Those who place their confidence in him, receive his Spirit by whose enablement they are empowered to a substantial degree to "put on" a life that reflects their Lord, the Christ. Hence, the incarnation of the eternal Son in the rabbi from Nazareth, the death, resurrection and enthronement of that God-man, inaugurated a new era in which the promise to bless all peoples, made so long ago to Abraham, is becoming a reality.

This, the apostolic witness testifies, is the gospel. The gospel is the message that in the Lord Jesus of Nazareth, the man designated by the Father to reign with him over his kingdom, the triune Creator's promise to bless all peoples has now been fulfilled. This not only highlights the incarnate Son on the cross, with its degradation and suffering, but also puts him in the limelight as the model of Spirit empowered living today. This is true because Jesus of Nazareth is not only the visible expression of the invisible God, he is also the perfect example of human whole-hearted love of the Creator and love for our neighbour.

Learning to re-pattern our lives to resemble Jesus of Nazareth is what a gospel-driven theology of discipleship is all about. Because the Lord Jesus, the Christ, sends us to accompany men and women of all peoples in discipleship to himself, I have not presumed to know the forms that process will take in your setting. You will need to work that out yourself. However, although love of God and neighbor will express itself differently in each human culture, to be true to the gospel it will always be discipleship to the Lord Jesus, where his lordship is being worked out in every aspect of our individual and communal living. The Apostle Paul wrote to the Christ-followers in Corinth that he did not want to tell them exactly how to put their allegiance to the Lord Jesus into practice, but to work together with them so that they would "stand firm" in their *pistis* (2 Cor. 1:24).

A gospel-driven theology that undergirds discipleship to the Lord Jesus incessantly directs us to obedient service to our one Lord, Jesus Christ, through whom all things came into being and through whom we live (1 Cor. 8:6).

Questions to Think About

1. I argue in this chapter that Paul's ministry, his theology, and his daily life, were centred on the Lord Jesus of Nazareth, and that this is what he modeled to those around him. Why is it important for our spiritual lives to keep in mind this example?
2. How could a proper reading of 2 Timothy 2:2 in the context of its surrounding verses counter the common equation of Christian discipleship with spiritual disciplines or methods of follow-up after a personal conversion experience?
3. I propose that a fundamental shift happened in how being a follower of Jesus of Nazareth was understood and lived in the 4th century CE. Do you agree? If so, what might the implications be for Christian theology and missions?
4. This chapter presents three possible elements involved in a gospel-driven theology of mission. Which ones would you say your church is good or not so good at doing? How could you contribute to improvement where the church's performance is weak?
5. As I explain in the last paragraph of this chapter, our contexts influence the kinds of things we allow ourselves to see and emphasize. What are some of the elements of the gospel-driven theology of discipleship you would say your church or denomination is good or not so good at seeing and emphasizing? How could you contribute to improvement in this area?

Bibliography

Akala, A. (2019). Sonship, Sending, and Subordination in the Gospel of John. In M. F. Bird & S. Harrower (Eds.), *Trinity Without Hierarchy: Reclaiming Nicene Orthodoxy in Evangelical Theology* (pp. 23–37). Grand Rapids, MI: Kregel Academic.

Althaus, P. (1966). *The Theology of Martin Luther.* Philadelphia, PA: Fortress Press.

Anderson, C. (2020). DMMs—More than a Fad or Amazing Strategy. *Mission Frontiers*, January, 23–25.

Anderson, P. N. (1999). The Having-Sent-Me Father: Aspects of Agency, Encounter, and Irony in the Johannine Father–Son Relationship. In A. Reinhartz (Ed.), *God the Father in the Gospel of John* (pp. 33–57). Atlanta, GA: Society of Biblical Literature.

Atwood, C. D. (2004). *Community of the Cross.* University Park, PA: Pennsylvania State University Press.

Aulén, G. (1969). *Christus Victor: An Historical Study of the Three Main Types of the Idea of Atonement.* New York, NY: Macmillan.

Baggott, B. (2012). Le Baptême à Quel Nom ? Au Nom du Père, du Fils et du Saint-Esprit, ou au Nom de Jésus Seul ? [Baptism in Which Name? In the Name of the Father, of the Son, and of the Holy Spirit, or Only in the Name of Jesus?] *Chemin de Vérité, 7* (3), https://chemindeverite.com/archives/486

Baillie, D. M. (1990 [1948]). *God Was In Christ.* New York, NY: Charles Scribner's Sons.

Balmer, R. (1999). *Blessed Assurance: A History of Evangelicalism In America.* Boston, MA: Beacon Press.

Barclay, J. (2015). *Paul and the Gift.* Grand Rapids, MI: Eerdmans.

Barrett, C. K. (1968). *Commentary on the First Epistle to the Corinthians.* New York, NY: HNTC.

Barrett, C. K. (1991). *A Commentary on the Epistle to the Romans* (2nd ed). Black's New Testament Commentaries. London: Black.

Barth, K. (2010). *Church Dogmatics* 2nd (second) Edition. Peabody, MA: Hendrickson Publishers.

Barth, M. & Blanke, H. (1994). *Colossians: A New Translation with Introduction and Commentary.* AB 34B (A. B. Beck, Trans.) New York, NY: Doubleday.

Bates, M. W. (2017). *Salvation by Allegiance Alone: Rethinking Faith, Works, and the Gospel of Jesus the King.* Grand Rapids, MI: Baker Academic.

Bates, M. W. (2019). *Gospel Allegiance: What Faith in Jesus Misses for Salvation in Christ.* Grand Rapids, MI: Brazos.

Bauckham, R. J. (1998). The Worship of Jesus in Philippians 2:9–11. In R. P. Martin & B. J. Dodd (Eds.), *Where Christology Began* (pp. 128–139). Atlanta, GA: Westminster John Knox Press.

Bauer, W., Gingrich, F. W., Arndt, W. F., Danker, F. W. (Eds). (1969). *A Greek-English Lexicon of the New Testament and Other Early Christian Literature.* Chicago, IL: University of Chicago Press.

Beale, G. K. (2011). *A New Testament Biblical Theology: The Unfolding of the Old Testament in the New.* Grand Rapids, MI: Baker.

Beasley-Murray, G. R. (1962). *Baptism in the New Testament.* Carlisle: Paternoster.

Beasley-Murray, G. R. (1986). *Jesus and the Kingdom of God.* Grand Rapids, MI: Eerdmans.

Bebbington, D. (1992 [1989]). *Evangelicals in Modern Britain: A History from the 1730s to the 1980s.* Grand Rapids, MI: Baker.

Beckwith, R. T. (1988), Saint. In S. B. Ferguson, D. F. Wright, & J. I. Packer (Eds.), *New Dictionary of Theology* (pp. 609–610). Downers Grove, IL: InterVarsity Press.

Beeby, D. H. (1994). A White Man's Burden. *International Bulletin of Missionary Research, 18* (1), 6–8.

Bennema, C. (2002). *The Power of Saving Wisdom: An Investigation of Spirit and Wisdom in Relation to the Soteriology of the Fourth Gospel.* Tubingen: Druck Partner Rubelmann.

Best, E. (1998). *Ephesians.* International Critical Commentary. Edinburgh: T. & T. Clark.

Bird, M. F. (2009). *Colossians and Philemon: A New Covenant Commentary.* Cambridge: Lutterworth Press.

Bird, M. F. (2013). *Evangelical Theology: A Biblical and Systematic Introduction.* Grand Rapids, MI: Zondervan.

Bird, M. J. (2019). Theologians of a Lesser Son. In M. F. Bird & S. Harrower (Eds.), *Trinity Without Hierarchy: Reclaiming Nicene Orthodoxy in Evangelical Theology* (pp. 9–12). Grand Rapids, MI: Kregel Academic.

Bivin, D. (2005). *New Light on the Difficult Words of Jesus.* Holland, MI: En–Gedi Resource Center.

Bjork, D. E. (1997). *Unfamiliar Paths: The Challenge of Recognizing the Work of Christ in Strange Clothing.* Pasadena, CA: William Carey Library.

Bjork, D. E. (2015). *Every Believer a Disciple.* Carlisle: Langham Global Library.

Black, M. (1981 [1973]). *Romans.* New Century Bible Commentary. Grand Rapids, MI: Eerdmans.

Blizzard, R., & Bivin, D. (2013). *Study Shows Jesus as Rabbi.* Bible Scholars, http://www.biblescholars.org/2013/05/study-shows-jesus-as-rabbi.html

Bloesch, D. G. (1983). *The Future of Evangelical Christianity: A Call for Unity amid Diversity.* Garden City, NY: Doubleday.

Blum, E. A. (1981). 2 Peter. In F. E. Gaebelein (Ed.), *The Expositor's Bible Commentary* (pp. 255–289). Grand Rapids, MI: Zondervan.

Boersma, H. (2011). *Heavenly Participation: The Weaving of a Sacramental Tapestry.* Grand Rapids, MI: Eerdmans.

Boersma, H. (2016). *Sacramental Preaching: Sermons on the Hidden Presence of Christ.* Grand Rapids, MI: Eerdmans.

Boettner, L. (1943). *The Person of Christ.* Eugene, OR: Wipf and Stock.

Bonhoeffer, D. (1979 [1937]). *The Cost of Discipleship* (R. H. Fuller, Trans.). New York, NY: Macmillan.

Borgen, P. (2014). *The Gospel of John: More Light From Philo, Paul and Archaeology.* Supplements to Novum Testamentum (Vol. 154). Leiden: Brill.

Bosch, D. (1995 [1970]). *Transforming Mission.* Maryknoll, NY: Orbis Books.

Bowman, R. M., & Komoszewski, J. E. (2007). *Putting Jesus in His Place: The Case for the Deity of Christ.* Grand Rapids, MI: Kregel Publications.

Boyarin, D. (2012). *The Jewish Gospels: The Story of the Jewish Christ*. New York, NY: New Press.

Bratcher, R. G., & Nida, E. A. (1982). *A Translator's Handbook on Paul's Letter to the Ephesians*. London: United Bible Societies.

Bridge, D. & Phypers, D. (2008 [1977]). *The Water That Divides: The Baptism Debate*. Fearn, Ross-shire: Christian Focus.

Bright, J. (1957). *The Kingdom of God: The Biblical Concept and Its Meaning for the Church*. Nashville, TN: Abingdon.

Brown, R. E. (1965). Does the New Testament Call Jesus God? *Theological Studies, 26*(4), 545–573.

Brown, R. E. (1966). *The Gospel According to John* (Vol. 2). New York, NY: Doubleday.

Brown, R. E. (1997). *An Introduction to the New Testament*. New Haven, CT: Yale University Press.

Bruce, A. B. (1955). *The Humiliation of Christ*. Grand Rapids, MI: Eerdmans.

Bruce, F. F. (1984). *The Epistles to the Colossians, to Philemon, and to the Ephesians*. Grand Rapids, MI: Eerdmans.

Bruce, F. F., & Martin, W. J. (2018). *The Deity of Christ: Was Jesus a Fraud or Was He God?* Nashville, TN: Kingsley Books.

Bruner, F. D. (1990). *Matthew, a Commentary* (Vol. 2). Dallas, TX: Word.

Brunner, E. (1939). *Man in Revolt: A Christian Anthropology* (O. Wyon, Trans.). London: Lutterworth.

Brunner, E. (1953). *The Christian Doctrine of Creation and Redemption* (O. Wyon, Trans.). Philadelphia, PA.: Westminster.

Brunner, E. (1955). *The Christian Doctrine of God: Volume 1: Dogmatics*. Cambridge: Lutterworth Press.

Bullinger, E. W. (1995). *Figures of Speech Used in the Bible*. Grand Rapids, MI: Baker.

Burkett, D. (2004). *The Son of Man Debate*. London: Cambridge University Press.

Butin, P. W. (1994). *Revelation, Redemption and Response*. New York, NY: Oxford University Press.

Butner, D. G. (2018). *The Son Who Learned Obedience: A Theological Case Against the Eternal Submission of the Son*. Eugene, OR: Pickwick Publications.

Byrne, B. 2007 [1996]). *Romans*. Sacra Pagina (Series 6). Collegeville, MN: Liturgical Press.

Calvin, J. (1979). *Commentaries on the Epistles of Paul the Apostle to the Philippians, Colossians, and Thessalonians* (J. Pringle, Trans.). Grand Rapids, MI: Eerdmans.

Calvin, J. (1998). *1, 2 Timothy and Titus*. Wheaton, IL: Crossway Books.

Campbell, D. A. (2005). *The Quest for Paul's Gospel: A Suggested Strategy*. London: T. & T. Clark International.

Campbell, T. A. (2009). *The Gospel in Christian Traditions*. Oxford: Oxford University Press.

Card, G. B. (1976). *Paul's Letters from Prison: Ephesians, Philippians, Colossians, Philemon, in the Revised Standard Version*. Oxford: Oxford University Press.

Carson, D. A. (1984). Reflections on Contextualization: A Critical Appraisal of Daniel von Allmen's "Birth of Theology." *East Africa Journal of Evangelical Theology, 3*(1), 52–53.

Carson, D. A. (1991). *The Gospel According to John*. Grand Rapids, MI: Eerdmans.

Carson, D. A. (2010). What is the Gospel ?—Revisited. In C. S. Storms & J. Taylor (Eds.), *For the Fame of God's Name: Essays in Honor of John Piper* (pp. 147–170). Wheaton, IL: Crossway.

Carson, D. A. & Keller, T. J. (Eds). (2012) *The Gospel as Center: Renewing Our Faith and Reforming Our Ministry Practices.* Wheaton, IL: Crossway.

Carter, M. (2001). *Matthew and Empire: Initial Explorations.* Harrisburg, PA: Trinity Press International.

Carter, M. (2005). Matthaean Christology in Roman Imperial Key: Matthew 1:1. In J. Riches & D. C. Sim (Eds.), *The Gospel of Matthew in its Roman Imperial Context* (pp. 143–165). New York, NY: T. & T. Clark.

Carter, W. (2006). *The Roman Empire and the New Testament: An Essential Guide.* Nashville, TN: Abingdon Press.

Casey, M. (2009). *The Solution to the Son of Man Problem.* New York, NY: T. & T. Clark International.

Chandler, D. J. (Ed) (2016). *The Holy Spirit and Christian Formation: Multidisciplinary Perspectives.* Cham: Palgrave Macmillan.

Chandler, M. & Wilson, J. C. (2012). *The Explicit Gospel.* Wheaton, IL: Crossway.

Christoph, M. (2015). *Christian Theology and Its Institutions in the Early Roman Empire: Prolegomena to a History of Early Christian Theology* (W. Coppins, Trans.). Waco, TX: Baylor University Press.

Clarke, H. W. (2003). *The Gospel of Matthew and Its Readers: A Historical Introduction to the First Gospel.* Bloomington, IN: Indiana University Press.

Clowney, E. P. (2003). *Preaching Christ in All of Scripture.* Wheaton, IL: Crossway.

Collins, R. F. (2013). *Second Corinthians.* Paideia Commentaries on the New Testament. Grand Rapids, MI: Baker Academic.

Congar, Y. (1963). *La Tradition et les Traditions: Essai Théologique* [The Tradition and the Traditions: A Theological Essay]. Paris: Fayard.

Congar, Y. (1969). *The Meaning of Tradition.* San Francisco, CA: Ignatius Press.

Cranfield, C. E. B. (1975, 1979). *The Epistle to the Romans.* 2 vols. Edinburgh: Clark.

Crisp, O. (2009). *God Incarnate: Explorations in Christology.* New York, NY: T. & T. Clark.

Culver, R. (2005). *Systematic Theology: Biblical and Historical.* Fearn, Ross–Shire: Mentor.

Cunningham, D. (1998). *These Three Are One: The Practice of Trinitarian Theology.* Oxford: Blackwell.

Danby, H. (Trans.) (1980 [1933]). *The Mishnah: Translated from the Hebrew with Introduction and Brief Explanatory Notes.* Oxford: Oxford University Press.

Danker, F. W. & Bauer, W. (Eds.). (1969). *A Greek-English Lexicon of the New Testament and Other Early Christian Literature.* Chicago, IL: University of Chicago Press.

Davies, G. N. (2015). *Faith and Obedience in Romans: A Study in Romans 1-4.* London: Bloomsbury Academic.

Davies, M. (1996). *The Pastoral Epistles.* Sheffield: Sheffield Academic.

Dawe, D. G. (1963). *The Form of a Servant: A Historical Analysis of the Kenotic Motif.* Philadelphia, PA: Westminster.

Dawson, C. (1965 [1960]). *The Historic Reality of Christian Culture.* New York, NY: Harper.

De Lacey, D. R. (1982). "One Lord" in Pauline Christology. In H. H. Rowdon (Ed.), *Christ the Lord* (pp. 191–203). Leicester: Inter-Varsity Press.

Delbridge, A., & Bernard, J. R. L. (Eds.) (1994). *The Compact Macquarie Dictionary.* Macquarie, NSW: Macquarie Library.

Demarest, B. (1997). *The Cross and Salvation.* Wheaton, IL: Crossway.

Demaris, R. E. (1994). *The Colossian Controversy: Wisdom in Dispute at Colossae.* Sheffield: JSOT.

Dennay, J. (2010). *The Christian Doctrine of Reconciliation.* Piscataway, NJ: Gorgias.

Dickson, J. (2010). *The Best Kept Secret of Christian Mission: Promoting the Gospel with More than Our Lips.* Grand Rapids, MI: Zondervan.

Dodd, B. (1995). Romans 1:17: A Cruxinterpretum for the *Pistis Christou* Debate? *Journal of Biblical Literature, 114,* 470–473.

Dodd, C. H. (1932). *The Epistle of Paul to the Romans.* London: Hodder & Stoughton.

Dodd, C. H. (1964). *The Apostolic Preaching and Its Developments.* New York, NY: Harper & Row.

Dollar, C. (2006). *Not Guilty: Accept God's Gift of Acceptance and Freedom.* New York, NY: Faith Words.

Dubis, M. (2010). *1 Peter, A Handbook on the Greek Text.* Waco, TX: Baylor University Press.

Dunn, J. D. (1962). The Holy Spirit. In J. D. Douglas (Ed.), *The New Bible Dictionary* (pp. 1136–1141). Downers Grove, IL: Inter-Varsity Press.

Dunn, J. D. (1988). *Romans 1–8.* Word Biblical Commentary 31A. Dallas, TX: Word Books.

Dunn, J. D. (1992). *The Partings of the Ways: Between Christianity and Judaism and Their Significance for the Character of Christianity.* Harrisburg, PA: Trinity Press International.

Dunn, J. D. (1996). *The Epistles to the Colossians and to Philemon: A Commentary on the Greek Text.* Grand Rapids, MI: Eerdmans.

Dunn, J. D. (1997a). Once More, *Pistis Christou.* In E. Johnson & D. Hay (Eds.), *Pauline Theology IV: Looking Back, Pressing On* (pp. 61–81). Atlanta, GA: Scholars Press.

Dunn, J. D. (1997b [1975]). *Jesus and the Spirit: A Study of the Religious and Charismatic Experience of Jesus and the First Christians as Reflected in the New Testament.* Grand Rapids, MI: Eerdmans.

Dunn, J. D. (1998). *The Theology of Paul the Apostle.* Edinburgh: T. & T. Clark.

Earley, D. & Dempsey, R. (2013). *Disciple Making Is ....: How to Live the Great Commission with Passion and Confidence.* Nashville, TN: B. & H. Publishing Group.

Edgar, W. (1983). New Right—Old Paganism: Anatomy of a French Movement. *Nederlands Theologisch Tijdschrift, 37,* 304–313.

Edman, V. R. (1949). *The Light in Dark Ages.* Wheaton, IL: Van Kampen Press.

Elliott, N. (2000). Paul and the Politics of Empire. In R. Horsley (Ed.), *Paul and Politics: Ekklesia, Israel, Imperium, Interpretation* (pp. 17–39). Harrisburg, PA: Trinity Press International.

Ellingworth, P. (1993). *The Epistle to the Hebrews: A Commentary on the Greek Text.* New International Greek Text Commentary. Grand Rapids, MI: Eerdmans.

Elliott–Binns, L. E. (2019). *The Beginnings of Western Christendom.* Greenwich, CT: Seabury.

Emerton, J. A. (1958). The Origin of the Son of Man Imagery, *Journal of Theological Studies, 9,* 231–232.

Erickson, M. J. (1991). *The Word Became Flesh.* Grand Rapids, MI: Baker.

Erickson, M. J. (1995 [1983]). *Christian Theology.* Grand Rapids, MI: Baker.

Evans, C. A. & Brackney, W. H. (Eds.). (2007). *From Biblical Criticism to Biblical Faith.* Macon, GA: Mercer University Press.

Faust, J. (2020). Discipleship, https://www.beliefnet.com

Fee, G. D. (1987). *The First Epistle to the Corinthians.* Grand Rapids, MI: Eerdmans.

Fee, G. D. (1944). *God's Empowering Presence: The Holy Spirit in the Letters of Paul.* Peabody, MA: Hendrickson.

Fiorenza, F. S., & Galvin, J. P. (1991). *Systematic Theology: Roman Catholic Perspectives* (Vol. 1). Minneapolis, MN: Fortress Press.

Fitzmyer, J. A. (1983). *The Gospel According to Luke*. New York, NY: Doubleday & Co.

Fitzmyer, J. A. (2008). *First Corinthians: A New Translation with Introduction and Commentary*. New Haven, NY: Yale University Press.

Frame, J. M. (1987). *The Doctrine of the Knowledge of God*. Phillipsburg, NJ: Presbyterian and Reformed Publishing.

France, R. T. (2007). *The Gospel of Matthew*. Grand Rapids, MI: Eerdmans.

Frankovic, J. (1994). Is the Sage Worth His Salt? *Jerusalem Perspective, 45*, 12–13.

Fruchtenbaum, A. G. (2005). *The Messianic Jewish Epistles: Hebrews, James, First Peter, Second Peter, Jude*. San Antonio, TX: Ariel Ministries.

Fudge, E. (1973). *Our Man in Heaven: An Exposition of the Epistle to the Hebrews*. Athens, AL: C. E. I. Publishing.

Gallaty, B. (2015). *Rediscovering Discipleship: Making Jesus' Final Words our First Work*. Grand Rapids, MI: Zondervan.

Garlington, D. (2007). *An Exposition of Galatians, Third Edition: A Reading from the New Perspective*. Eugene, OR: Wipf and Stock.

Gentry, P. J. & Wellum, S. J. (2012). *Kingdom through Covenant: A Biblical-Theological Understanding of the Covenants*. Wheaton, IL: Crossway.

Georgi, D. (1997) God Turned Upside Down. In R. Horsley (Ed.), *Paul and Empire Religion* (pp. 148–157). Harrisburg, PA: Trinity Press.

Gerlach, L. P. & Hine, V. H. (1970). *People, Power, Change: Movements of Social Transformation*. Indianapolis, IN: Bobbs-Merrill.

Gilbert, G. (2010). *What is the Gospel?* Wheaton, IL: Crossway.

Giles, K. (2006). *Jesus and the Father: Modern Evangelicals Reinvent the Doctrine of the Trinity*. Grand Rapids, MI: Zondervan.

Giles, K. (2012). The Trinity without Tiers. In D. W. Jowers & H. W. House (Eds.), *The New Evangelical Subordinationism? Perspectives on the Equality of God the Father and God the Son* (pp. 262–287). Eugene, OR: Pickwick Publishers.

Gillespie, B. (1991). *The Dynamics of Religious Conversion: Identity and Transformation*. Birmingham, AL: Religious Education Press.

Gilliland, D. S. (1983). *Pauline Theology and Mission Practice*. Lagos: Tryfam Printers.

Ginzberg, L. (2021). *The Legends of the Jews— Volume 2: From Joseph to the Exodus* (J. M. Rodwell, Trans.) Original Sources, http://www.originalsources.com/Document.aspx?DocID=8JVRAVUWX4DS9GD

Glancy, J. A. (2006 [2002]). *Slavery in Early Christianity*. Minneapolis, MN: Fortress Press.

Goldsworthy, G. (2000). *Preaching the Whole Bible as Christian Scripture*. Grand Rapids, MI: Eerdmans.

Goldsworthy, G. (2006). *Gospel-Centered Hermeneutics: Foundations and Principles of Evangelical Biblical Interpretation*. Downers Grove, IL: IVP Academic.

Goldsworthy, G. (2012). *Christ-Centered Biblical Theology: Hermeneutical Foundations and Principles*. Downers Grove, IL: IVP Academic.

Gombis, T. G. (2010). *The Drama of Ephesians: Participating in the Triumph of God*. Downers Grove, IL: IVP Academic.

Gonzalez, J. L. (1970). *A History of Christian Thought, vol. I, From the Beginnings to the Council of Chalcedon*. Nashville, TN: Abingdon Press.

Goranson Jacob, H. (2018). *Conformed to the Image of His Son: Reconsidering Paul's Theology of Glory in Romans*. Downers Grove, IL: InterVarsity Press.

Gordon, T. D. (1994). Equipping Ministry in Ephesians 4. *JETS, 37*, 69–78.

Gorman, M. J. (2001). *Cruciformity: Paul's Narrative Spirituality of the Cross.* Grand Rapids, MI: Eerdmans.

Gorman, M. J. (2004). *The Apostle of the Crucified Lord: A Theological Introduction to Paul and His Letters.* Grand Rapids, MI: Eerdmans.

Gorman, M. J. (2009). *Inhabiting the Cruciform God: Kenosis, Justification and Theosis in Paul's Narrative Soteriology.* Grand Rapids, MI: Eerdmans.

Gorman, M. J. (2015). *Becoming the Gospel: Paul, Participation, and Mission.* Grand Rapids, MI: Eerdmans.

Green, M. (2001). *Evangelism in the Early Church.* Eugene, OR: Wipf and Stock.

Grenz, S. J. (2000). *Renewing the Center: Evangelical Theology in a Post-Theological Era.* Grand Rapids, MI: Baker.

Grenz, S. J. (2001). *The Social God and the Relational Self: A trinitarian Theology of the* Imago Dei. Louisville, KY: Westminster John Knox.

Grudem, W. (1994). *Systematic Theology: An Introduction to Biblical Doctrine.* Grand Rapids, MI: Zondervan.

Grudem, W. (2016). Doctrinal Deviations in Evangelical-Feminist arguments about the Trinity. In B.A. Ware & J. Starke (Eds.), *One God in Three Persons: Unity of Essence, Distinction of Persons, Implications for Life* (pp. 17–46).

Guder, D. L. (2000). *The Continuing Conversion of the Church.* Grand Rapids, MI: Eerdmans.

Gundry, R. H. (1994). *A Survey of the New Testament* (3rd ed). Grand Rapids, MI: Zondervan.

Gunton, C. E. (2003). *Father, Son and Holy Spirit: Essays Toward a Fully Trinitarian Theology.* New York, NY: Continuum.

Gupta, N. K. (2013). *Colossians.* Macon, GA: Smyth & Helwys.

Gupta, N. K. (2020). *Paul and the Language of Faith.* Grand Rapids, MI: Eerdmans.

Gurbikian, G. (2011). *The Deity of Jesus Christ in the Old & New Testaments.* Maitland, FL: Xulon Press.

Hagner, D. A. (1991). Paul's Christology and Jewish Monotheism. In M. Shuster & R. Muller (Eds.), *Perspectives on Christology* (pp. 28–29). Grand Rapids, MI: Zondervan.

Hamann, H. P. (1988). The Translation of Ephesians 4:12—A Necessary Revision. *Concordia Journal* (14): 42–49.

Hamilton, N. Q. (1957). *The Holy Spirit and Eschatology in Paul, Scottish Journal of Theology, Occasional Papers No. 6.* Edinburgh: Oliver & Boyd.

Harris, M. J. (1999). *Slave of Christ: A New Testament Metaphor for Total Devotion to Christ.* Downers Grove, IL: InterVarsity Press.

Harris, M. J. (2008). *Jesus as God: The New Testament Use of* Theos *in Reference to Jesus.* Eugene, OR: Wipf & Stock.

Harrison, V. (1991). Perichoresis in the Greek Fathers. *St. Vladimir's Theological Quarterly, 35*(1): 53–65.

Hart, H. (1972). *Will All the King's Men.* Toronto, CA: Wedge Publishing Foundation.

Hartman, L. (1997). *'Into the Name of the Lord Jesus': Baptism in the Early Church.* Edinburgh: T&T Clark.

Hauerwas, S. (2016). *Discipleship as a Craft, Church as a Disciplined Community.* Discipleship as a Craft, https://jochenteuffel.files.wordpress.com/2016/01/hauerwas-discipleship-as-a-craft-cc.pdf

Hay, D. (1989). *Pistis* as "Ground for Faith" in Hellenized Judaism and Paul. *Journal of Biblical Literature, 108*(27): 461–476.

Hays, R. (1997). *Pistis* and Pauline Christology: What is at Stake? In E. Johnson & D.
   Hay (Eds.), *Pauline Theology IV: Looking Back, Pressing On* (pp. 35–60). Atlanta,
   GA: Scholars Press.
Hays, R. (2002). *The Faith of Jesus Christ: The Narrative Substructure of Galatians
   3:1–4:11* (2nd ed.). Grand Rapids, MI: Eerdmans.
Heil, J. P. (2007). *Ephesians: Empowerment to Walk in Love for the Unity of All in
   Christ.* Leiden: Brill.
Heil, J. P. (2010). *Colossians: Encouragement to Walk in All Wisdom as Holy Ones in
   Christ.* Atlanta, GA: Society of Biblical Literature.
Hengel, M. (2003 [1974]). *Judaism and Hellenism: Studies in their Encounter in
   Palestine during the Early Hellenistic Period*, Vol. 1 (J. Bowden, Trans.). Eugene,
   OR: Wipf and Stock.
Henrichse, W. A. & Garrison, W. N. (1983). *Layman, Look Up: God Has a Place for
   You.* Grand Rapids, MI: Zondervan.
Henrichsen, W. (1974). *Disciples are Made-Not-Born.* Wheaton, IL: Victor Books.
Hertig, P. (2001, July). The Great Commission Revisited: The Rule of God's Reign in
   Disciple Making. *Missiology: An International Review, 29*, 343–354.
Hiebert, D. E. (1978). Titus. In F. Gaebelein (Ed.), *The Expositors Bible Commentary*
   (Vol. 11, pp. 419–450). Grand Rapids, MI: Zondervan.
Higgins, A. J. B. (1980). *The Son of Man in the Teaching of Jesus.* London: Cambridge
   University Press.
Hill, M. (1968). *Entering the Kingdom: A Fresh Look at Conversion.* Bromley:
   Christian Research Library.
Hill, W. J. (1982). *The Three–Personed God: The Trinity as a Mystery of Salvation.*
   Washington, DC: Catholic University of America Press.
Hirsch, A. (2006). *The Forgotten Ways: Reactivating the Missional Church.* Grand
   Rapids, MI: Brazos.
Hirsch, A. (2011). *Fast Forward to Mission: Frameworks for a Life of Impact.* Grand
   Rapids, MI: Baker Books.
Hirsch, A., & Catchum, T. (2012). *The Permanent Revolution.* San Francisco, CA:
   Jossey-Bass.
Hochner, H. W. (2002). *Ephesians: An Exegetical Commentary.* Grand Rapids, MI:
   Baker Academic.
Hodge, C. (1952). *Systematic Theology.* Grand Rapids, MI: Eerdmans.
Hodge, C. (1995). *Epistle to the Romans.* Albany, OR: Sage Software.
Hodgson, R. (1987). The Kingdom of God in the School of St. John. In W. Willis (Ed.),
   The Kingdom of God in 20th Century Interpretations (pp. 163-174). Peabody, MA:
   Hendrickson.
Hooker, M. (1989). *Pistis Christou*: Faith in Christ or the Faith of Christ: A New
   Testament Analysis. *New Testament Studies 35*(3): 321–42.
Hoover, R. (1971). The Harpagmos Enigma: A Philological Solution. *Harvard
   Theological Review 64*: 95–119.
Hordern, W. (1969). *Speaking of God: The Nature and Purpose of Theological
   Language.* New York, NY: Macmillan.
Horrell, D. (1997). Whose Faith(fulness) is it in 1 Peter 1:5? *Journal of Theological
   Studies 48*(1): 110–115, https://doi.org/10.1093/jts/48.1.110
Horton, M. (2011). *The Christian Faith: A Systematic Theology for Pilgrims on the
   Way.* Grand Rapids, MI: Zondervan.
Horsley, R. A. (2003). *Jesus and Empire: The Kingdom of God and the New World
   Disorder.* Minneapolis, MN: Fortress Press.

Horsley, R. A. ed. (1997). *Paul and Empire: Religion and Power in Roman Imperial Society.* Harrisburg, PA: Trinity Press International.

Horsley, R. A. ed. (2004). *Paul and the Roman Imperial Order.* Harrisburg, PA: Trinity Press International.

Horsley, R. A. & Hanson, J. S. (1985). *Bandits, Prophets, and Messiahs: Popular Movements in the time of Jesus.* Minneapolis, PA: Winston Press.

Houghton, M. J. (1996). A Reexamination of 1 Corinthians 13:8–13. *Bibliotheca Sacra, 153,* 344–356.

Hughes, K. (2006). *2 Corinthians.* Wheaton, IL: Crossway Books.

Hull, B. (2016). *Conversion and Discipleship: You Can't Have One Without the Other.* Grand Rapids, MI: Zondervan.

Hultgren, A. (1980). The *Pistis Christou* Formulation in Paul. *Novum Testamentum 22,* 248–263.

Hunt, T. W. & King, C. V. (1998 [1994]). *The Mind of Christ.* Nashville, TN: LifeWay Press.

Hunter, T., & Wellum, S. (2018). *Christ From Beginning to End: How the Full Story of Scripture Reveals the Full Glory of Christ.* Grand Rapids, MI: Zondervan.

Hurtado, L. (1992). Christ. In J. Green, S. McKnight, & I. H. Marshall (Eds.), *Dictionary of Jesus and the Gospels* (pp. 106–117). Downers Grove, IL: InterVarsity Press.

Hurtado, L. (2003). *Lord Jesus Christ: Devotion to Jesus in Earliest Christianity.* Grand Rapids, MI: Eerdmans.

Hurtado, L. (2005). *How on Earth Did Jesus Become a God? Historical Questions about Earliest Devotion to Jesus.* Grand Rapids, MI: Eerdmans.

Hurtado, L. (2015). *One God.* London: T. & T. Clark.

Instone-Brewer, D. (2002). *Divorce and Remarriage in the Bible: The Social and Literary Context.* Grand Rapids, MI: Eerdmans.

Instone-Brewer, D. (2004). *Traditions of the Rabbis from the Era of the New Testament.* Grand Rapids, MI: Wm. B. Eerdmans.

Jamieson, R., Fausset A. R., & Brown, D. (2019). 1 Timothy 3 :16, *Jamieson–Fausset-Brown Bible Commentary,* https://biblehub.com/commentaries/jfb/2_timothy/3.htm

Jenkins, P. (2010). *Jesus Wars: How Four Patriarchs, Three Queens, and Two Emperors Decided What Christians Would Believe for the Next 1,500 Years.* San Francisco, CA: Harper One.

Jenson, R. W. (1997). *Systematic Theology*, Vol. 1. New York, NY: Oxford University Press.

Jeon, J. K. (2017). *Biblical Theology: Covenants and the Kingdom of God in Redemptive History.* Eugene, OR: Wipf and Stock.

Jewett, R. & Kotansky, R. D. (2007). *Romans: Hermeneia-A Critical and Historical Commentary on the Bible.* Minneapolis, MN: Fortress Press.

Jipp, J. W. (2015). *Christ is King: Paul's Royal Ideology.* Minneapolis, MN: Fortress Press.

Johnson, L. T. (1982). Romans 3:21–6 and the faith of Jesus. *Catholic Biblical Quarterly 44*(1), 77–90, https://www.jstor.org/stable/i40149935

Johnson, L. T. (2006). *Hebrews: A Commentary.* New Testament Library. Louisville, KY: Westminster John Knox.

Johnson, L. T. (2013). Life-giving Spirit: The Ontological Implications of Resurrection in 1 Corinthians. *Contested Issues in Christians Origins and the New Testament.* Leiden: Brill.

Johnson, M. P. (2013). *One with Christ: An Evangelical Theology of Salvation.* Wheaton, IL: Crossway.

Johnston, E. A. (2016). *Intra–Trinitarian Subordination: Reflections on the Ontological Relationship of the Father, Son, and Holy Spirit* [Unpublished manuscript]. Columbia Evangelical Seminary, https://academia.edu/26871543/Intra_Trinitarian_Subordination

Johnston, R. K. (1979). *Evangelicals at an Impasse: Biblical Authority in Practice.* Atlanta, GA: John Knox.

Jowers, D. W. (2012). The Inconceivability of Subordination within a Simple God. In D. W. Jowers & H. W. House (Eds.), *The New Evangelical Subordinationism? Perspectives on the Equality of God the Father and God the Son* (pp. 375–410). Eugene, OR: Pickwick Publications.

Kaiser, W. C. (1998). *The Christian and the Old Testament.* Pasadena, CA: William Carey Library.

Kaiser, W. C., & Silva, M. (2007 [1994]). *Introduction to Biblical Hermeneutics.* Grand Rapids, MI: Baker.

Käsemann, E. (1994). *Commentary on Romans.* Grand Rapids, MI: Eerdmans.

Kasulis, T. (1992). Philosophy as Metapraxis. In F. Reynolds & D. Tracy (Eds.), *Discourse and Practice* (pp. 169–195). Albany, NY: SUNY Press.

Kasulis, T. (1993). The Body—Japanese Style. In T. P. Kasulis, R. T. Ames, & W. Dissanayake (Eds.), *Self as Body in Asian Theory and Practice* (pp. 299–320). Albany, NY: SUNY Press.

Kasulis, T. (2004). *Shinto: The Way Home.* Honolulu, HI: University of Hawai'i Press.

Keener, C. (2003). *The Gospel of John: A Commentary* (Vol. 1). Grand Rapids, MI: Baker Academic.

Keener, C. (2005). *1–2 Corinthians.* Cambridge: Cambridge University Press.

Keener, C. (2009). *Romans.* Cambridge: Lutterworth Press.

Kennison, Q. P. (2010). Shepherd or One of the Sheep: Revisiting the Biblical Metaphor of the Pastorate. *Journal of Religious Leadership, 9*(1): 59–91.

Kim, S. (1983). *The "Son of Man" as the Son of God.* Tübingen: J. C. B. Mohr.

Kim, S. (2008). *Christ and Caesar: The Gospel and the Roman Empire in the Writings of Paul and Luke.* Grand Rapids, MI: Eerdmans.

Kinneavy, J. (1987). *Greek Rhetorical Origins of Christian Faith: An Inquiry.* New York, NY: Oxford University Press.

Kirk, J. R. D. (2008). *Unlocking Romans: Resurrection and the Justification of God.* Grand Rapids, MI: Eerdmans.

Kitchen, M. (1994). *Ephesians.* London: Routledge.

Kline, M. (1999). *Images of the Spirit.* Eugene, OR: Wipf and Stock.

Kline, M. (2006). *Kingdom Prologue: Genesis Foundations for a Covenantal Worldview.* Eugene, OR: Wipf and Stock.

Kolatch, A. (1990). *Le Livre du Juif Pourquoi?* [Why the Book of the Jew?] (A. Kokos, Trans.). Paris: Editions MJR.

König, A. (1988). *The Eclipse of Christ in Eschatology.* Grand Rapids, MI: Eerdmans.

Köstenberger, A. J. (1998). *The Missions of Jesus and the Disciples According to the Fourth Gospel: With Implications for the Fourth Gospel's Purpose and the Mission of the Contemporary Church.* Grand Rapids, MI: Eerdmans.

Kraemer, H. (2005 [1958]). *A Theology of the Laity.* Vancouver, CA: Regent College Publishing.

Kuen, A. (1998). *Qui Sont les Evangéliques?* [Who Are the Evangelicals?] Saint-Légier: Éditions Emmaüs.

Kupp, D. (1996). *Matthew's Emmanuel: Divine Presence and God's People in the First Gospel.* Cambridge: Cambridge University Press.

LaCugna, C. M. (1991). *God for Us: The Trinity and Christian Life.* San Francisco, CA: Harper.

Ladd, G. E. (1993). *A Theology of the New Testament.* Cambridge: Cambridge University Press.

Ladd, G. E. (2000 [1959]). *The Gospel of the Kingdom: Scriptural Studies in the Kingdom of God.* Grand Rapids, MI: Eerdmans.

Lane, W. (1991). *Hebrews 1–8.* Word Bible Commentary 47B. Dallas, TX: Word Books.

Larkin, W. J. (2009). *Ephesians: A Handbook on the Greek Text.* Waco, TX: Baylor University Press.

Lausanne Committee for World Evangelization. (1989). *Manila Manifesto an Elaboration of the Lausanne Covenant.* Lausanne: Lausanne Committee for World Evangelization.

Lausanne Movement. (1980). *The Thailand Statement: Consultation on World Evangelization Pattaya, Thailand* (June 16-27, 1980). Lausanne Movement, https://lausanne.org/content/statement/thailand-statement

Lenoir, F. (2008). *Petit Traité d'Histoire des Religions* [A Short History of Religions]. Paris: Plon.

Lewis, J. P. (1980). Qahal. In H. R. L. Archer, & B. K. Waltke (Eds.), *Theological Dictionary of the Old Testament* (Vol. 2, p. 790). Chicago, IL: Moody.

Lincoln, A. T. (1990). *Ephesians.* Word Biblical Commentary 42. Dallas, TX: Word.

Lindars, B. (2010 [1986]). *Behind the Fourth Gospel.* Eugene, OR: Wipf and Stock.

Livius. (2020 [2007]). *Augustus, Res Gestae.* https://www.livius.org/sources/content/augustus-res-gestae/

Lohse, E. (1971). *Colossians and Philemon* (W. R. Poehlmann & R. J. Karris, Trans.). Philadelphia, PA: Fortress Press.

Longenecker, B. (1993). ΠΙΣΤΙΣ in Romans 3.25: Neglected Evidence for the 'Faithfulness of Christ'? *New Testament Studies, 39*(3), 478-480. https://doi:10.1017/S0028688500011334.

Longenecker, B. (1996). Defining the Faithful Character of the Covenant Community: Galatians 2.15–21 and Beyond: A Response to Jan Lambrecht. In J. Dunn (Ed.), *Paul and the Mosaic Law* (pp. 75–98). Tübingen: Mohr Siebeck.

Longenecker, R. N. (1970). *The Christology of Early Jewish Christianity.* Naperville, IL: Alec R. Allenson Inc.

Louth, A. (2003 [1983]). *Discerning the Mystery: An Essay on the Nature of Theology.* Oxford: Clarendon Press.

Louw, J. P., & Nida, E. A. (1989 [1988]). *Greek-English Lexicon of the New Testament Based on Semantic Domains*, 2 vols. New York, NY: United Bible Societies.

Luneau, R., & Ladrière, P. (1989). *Le Rêve de Compostelle* [The Dream of Compostelle]. Paris: Centurion.

MacDonald, M. Y. (2000). *Colossians and Ephesians.* Sacra Pagina 17. Collegeville, MN: Liturgical Press.

Marshall, H. (1966). The Synoptic Son of Man Sayings in Recent Discussions. *New Testament Studies, 12*, 350–351.

Marshall, H. (1978). *The Epistles of John. New International Commentary*. Grand Rapids, MI: Eerdmans.

Marshall, H. (2004). *New Testament Theology: Many Witnesses, One Gospel.* Nottingham: Apollos.

Martin, R. P. (1967). *Carmen Cristi: Philippians 11:5–11 in Recent Interpretation in the Setting of Early Christian Worship.* Cambridge: Cambridge University Press.

Martyn, J. (1997). *Theological Issues in the Letters of Paul.* Edinburgh: T. & T. Clark.

Matlock, R. B. (2000). Detheologizing the *ΠΙΣΤΣ ΧΡΙΣΤΟΥ* Debate: Cautionary Remarks From a Lexical Semantic Perspective. *Novum Testamentum, 1,* 1–23. Leiden: Brill.

Matlock, R. B. (2002). "Even the Demons Believe": Paul and πίστις Χριστου. *The Catholic Biblical Quarterly, 64*(2), 300-318, http://www.jstor.org/stable/43727394

Mayer, A. C. (2002). *Sprache der Einheit im Epheserbrief und in der Ökumene* [Language of Unity in Ephesians and Ecumenism]. Wissenschaftliche Untersuchungen zum Neuen Testament 2/150. Tübingen: Mohr Siebeck.

Mbende, J. Y. N. (2015). Healing as an Approach for Discipleship in the Bible: A Missiological Perspective. *Journal of Adventist Mission Studies, 11*(1), 61–66.

McCall, T. (2010). *Which Trinity? Whose Monotheism? Philosophical and Systematic theologians on the Metaphysics of Trinitarian Theology.* Grand Rapids, MI: Eerdmans.

McCormic, A. E. (2016). *Nicene Trinitarian Theology: Refuting the Eternal Subordination of the Son and the Spirit.* Redding, CA: A. W. Tozer Seminary.

McGrath, A. (2001). *Christian Theology: An Introduction.* Oxford: Blackwell.

McKnight, S. (2005). *Jesus and His Death: Historiography, the Historical Jesus, and Atonement Theory.* Waco, TX: Baylor University Press.

McKnight, S. (2009 [2004]). *The Jesus Creed.* Brewster, MA: Paraclete Press.

McKnight, S. (2016 [2011]). *The King Jesus Gospel: The Original Good News Revisited.* Grand Rapids, MI: Zondervan.

Meyer, H. (1832). Commentary on Matthew 18:1. *Heinrich Meyer's Critical and Exegetical Commentary on the New Testament,* http://www.studylight.org/commentaries/hmc/view.cgi?bk=39&ch=18

Milne, B. (1993). *The Message of John.* Downers Grove, IL: Inter-Varsity Press.

Minor, M. (2009). *2 Corinthians.* Smyth & Helwys Bible Commentaries. Macon, GA: Smyth & Helwys.

Mlakuzhyil, G. (1987). *The Christocentric Literary Structure of the Fourth Gospel.* Analecta Biblica 117. Pontifical Bible Institute, 264–267, https://biblico.it/series.html

Moffitt, D. M. (2011). *Atonement and the Logic of Resurrection in the Epistle to the Hebrews.* Supplements to Novum Testamentum (Vol. 141). Leiden: Brill.

Moltmann, J. (1977). *The Church in the Power of the Spirit: A Contribution to Messianic Ecclesiology.* London: SCM Press.

Moltmann, J. (1989). *The Way of Jesus Christ: Christology in Messianic Dimensions* (M. Kohl, Trans.). London: SCM Press.

Moo, D. J. (1996). *The Epistle to the Romans.* New International Commentary on the New Testament. Grand Rapids, MI: Eerdmans.

Moo, D. J. (2008). *The Letters to the Colossians and to Philemon.* Grand Rapids, MI: Eerdmans.

Moore, R. (2004). *The Kingdom of Christ: The New Evangelical Perspective.* Wheaton, IL: Crossway.

Morgan, T. (2017 [2015]). *Roman Empire and Christian Faith:* Pistis *and* Fides *in the Early Roman Empire and Early Churches.* Oxford: Oxford Scholarship Online.

Morris, L. L. (1989). *Jesus Is the Christ: Studies in the Theology of John.* Grand Rapids, MI: Eerdmans.

Morris, L. L. (1990 [1986]). *New Testament Theology.* Grand Rapids, MI: Zondervan.

Morris, L. L. (1994). *Expository Reflections on the Letter to the Ephesians.* Grand Rapids, MI: Baker.

Moule, C. F. D. (1957). *The Epistles of Paul the Apostle to the Colossians and to Philemon.* Cambridge: Cambridge University Press.

Moule, C. F. D. (1962). *The Birth of the New Testament.* London: Black.

Moule, C. F. D. (1991 [1957]). *The Epistles of Paul the Apostle to the Colossians and to Philemon.* New York, NY: Cambridge University Press.

Mounce, W. D. (1993). *The Analytical Lexicon to the Greek New Testament.* Grand Rapids, MI: Zondervan.

Mouw, R. J. (2000). *The Smell of Sawdust: What Evangelicals Can Learn From Their Fundamentalist Heritage.* Grand Rapids, MI: Zondervan.

Muddiman, J. (2001). *The Epistle to the Ephesians.* Black's New Testament Commentary. Peabody, MA: Hendrickson.

Muller, R. (1985). *Dictionary of Latin and Greek Theological Terms: Drawn Principally from Protestant Scholastic Theology.* Grand Rapids, MI: Baker.

Murray, A. (1908). *The Full Blessing of Pentecost: The One Thing Needful* (J. P. Lilley, Trans). London: James Nisbet.

Murray, D. P. (2013). *Jesus on Every Page: 10 Simple Ways to Seek and Find Christ in the Old Testament.* Nashville, TN: Thomas Nelson.

Murray, J. (1978 [1955]). *Redemption Accomplished and Applied.* Grand Rapids, MI: Eerdmans.

Neill, S. (1990). *A History of Christian Missions.* New York, NY: Penguin Books.

Newbigin, L. (1964). *Trinitarian Faith and Today's Mission.* Richmond, VA: John Knox.

Newman, C. C. (1992). *Paul's Glory-Christology: Tradition and Rhetoric,* Supplements to Novum Testamentum 69. Leiden: Brill.

Niebuhr, H. R. & Williams, D. D. (Eds.) (1983). *The Ministry in Historical Perspectives.* San Francisco, CA: Harper & Row.

Nixon, R. E. (1994). Glory. In J. D. Douglas (Ed.), *New Bible Dictionary* (pp. 423–424). Downers Grove, IL: InterVarsity Press.

O'Brien, P. (1982). *Colossians, Philemon.* Waco, TX: Word.

O'Brien, P. (1999). *The Letter to the Ephesians.* The Pillar New Testament Commentary. Grand Rapids, MI: Eerdmans.

O'Collins, G. (2008). *Jesus: A Portrait.* London: Darton, Longman and Todd.

O'Day, G. R. & Hylen, S. E. (2006). *John.* Louisville, KY: Westminster John Knox Press.

Ogden, G. (2010 [2003]). *Unfinished Business: Returning the Ministry to the People of God.* Grand Rapids, MI: Zondervan. ePub Edition March.

Osborne, L. (2008). *Sticky Church.* Grand Rapids, MI: Zondervan.

Ouaknin, J. (2002). *L'âme Immortelle. Précis des Lois et Coutumes du Deuil dans le Judaïsme* [The Immortal Soul: An Explanation of the Jewish Customs of Mourning]. Paris: Editions Bibliophane-Daniel Radford.

Overman, J. A. (1990). *Matthew's Gospel and Formative Judaism: The Social World of the Matthean Community.* Minneapolis, MN: Fortress Press.

Owen, J. (1968). *The Works of John Owen.* 16 vols. Edinburgh: Banner of Truth Trust.

Packer, J. I. (1988). God. In S. Ferguson & J. I. Packer (Eds.), *The New Dictionary of Theology* (pp. 274–277). Downers Grove, IL: InterVarsity Press.

Packer, J. I. (1994). Conversion. In J. D. Douglas, F. F. Bruce, & J. I. Packer (Eds.), *New Bible Dictionary* (pp. 228–229). Downers Grove, IL: InterVarsity Press.

Pannenberg, W. (1970). *What Is Man? Contemporary Anthropology in Theological Perspective.* Philadelphia, PA: Fortress Press.

Pargoire, J. (1900). *Les Homélies de Saint Jean Chrysostome en Juillet 399* [The Sermons of Saint John Chrysostome in July 399]. *Echos d'Orient 3*(3), 151–162.

Paul, I. (2019). The Trinitarian Dynamic in the Book of Revelation. In M. F. Bird & S. Harrower (Eds.), *Trinity Without Hierarchy: Reclaiming Nicene Orthodoxy in Evangelical Theology* (pp. 85–107). Grand Rapids, MI: Kregel Academic.

Peeler, A. B. (2014). *You Are My Son: The Family of God in the Epistle to the Hebrews.* London: Bloomsbury.

Pelikan, J., & Lehmann, H. T. (Eds.). (1972). *Commentary on Romans*, Luther's Works. Philadelphia, PA: Fortress Press.

Pieterse, G. J. P. (2016, February). *The Word of Faith Movement: Towards a Constructive Engagement.* Thesis, South African Theological Seminary.

Pinnock, C. H. (1996). *Flame of Love: A Theology of the Holy Spirit.* Downers Grove, IL: InterVarsity Press.

Piper, J. (2011). *God is the Gospel: Meditations on God's Love as the Gift of Himself.* Reprint, Wheaton, IL: Crossway.

Poliakov, L. (1976). *Le Racisme* [Racism]. Paris: Seghers.

Pohle, J. (1950). *The Divine Trinity.* St. Louis, MO: B. Herder.

Poole, M. (1985). *Commentary on the Whole Bible* (Vol. 3). Peabody, MA: Hendrickson.

Porter, S. E. (2011). Paul Confronts Caesar with the Good News. In S. Porter & C. L. Westfall (Eds.), *Empire in the New Testament* (pp. 164–197). Eugene, OR: Wipf and Stock.

Porter, S. E., & Cross, A. R. (1999). *Baptism, the New Testament and the Church: Historical and Contemporary Studies.* Sheffield: Sheffield Academic Press.

Przybylski, B. (1980). *Righteousness in Matthew and his World of Thought.* Cambridge: Cambridge University Press.

Rakotoarison, S. (2014). Charles Péguy, la Rigueur Intellectuelle et l'audace dans l'Action [Charles Péguy, Intellectual Rigor and Audacity in Action], http://mobile.agoravox.fr/culture-loisirs/culture/article/charles-peguy-la-rigueur-155470

Rambo, L. (1993). *Understanding Religious Conversion.* New Haven, CT: Yale University Press.

Rasmussen, C. G. (1989). *NIV Atlas of the Bible.* Grand Rapids, MI: Zondervan.

Richard, L. J. (1982). *A Kenotic Christology in the Humanity of Jesus the Christ, the Compassion of Our God.* Washington, DC: University Press of America.

Richards, W. L. (1968). *2 Corinthians: God's Way Is the Best Way.* Nampa, ID: Pacific Press.

Richardson, N. (1995). *Paul's Language about God.* Sheffield: Sheffield Academic.

Richey, L. B. (2007). *Roman Imperial Ideology and the Gospel of John.* Washington, DC: Catholic Biblical Association of America.

Ridderbos, H. (1978). *The Coming of the Kingdom* (H. St. Catharines, Trans.). Jongste, CA: Paideia Press.

Robertson, N. W. (1910). Commentary on Matthew 18:1. *The Expositor's Greek Testament*, http://www.studylight.org/commentaries/egt/view.cgi?bk=39&ch=18

Rosner, B. S. (2000). Biblical Theology. In B. Rosner, T. D. Alexander, G. Goldsworthy, J. Laansma, & D. A. Carson (Eds.), *New Dictionary of Biblical Theology* (p. 10). Downers Grove, IL: InterVarsity Press,

Rubenstein, J. L. (2007). Social and Institutional Settings in Rabbinic Literature. In C. E. Fonrobert & M. S. Jaffee (Eds.), *The Cambridge Companion to the Talmud and Rabbinic Literature* (pp. 58–74). Cambridge: Cambridge University Press.

Rubenstein, R. E. (2013). *When Jesus Became God: The Epic Fight over Christ's Divinity in the Last Days of Rome.* New York, NY: Mariner Books.

Russ, E. (2010). *Discipleship Defined.* Xulon Press, http://xulonpress.com

Ryrie, C. (1986). *Basic Theology.* Wheaton, IL: Victor.

Ryrie, C. (1997). *The Holy Spirit.* Chicago, IL: Moody.

Safrai, S. & Stern, M. (Eds.) (1976). *The Jewish People in the First Century.* Amsterdam: Van Gorcum.

Sanders, E. P. (1990). *Jewish Law from Jesus to the Mishnah: Five Studies.* London: SCM Press.

Sanders, F. (2010). *The Deep Things of God: How the Trinity Changes Everything.* Wheaton, IL: Crossway Books.

Schaberg, J. (1982). *The Father, the Son, and the Holy Spirit: The Triadic Phrase in Matthew 28:19b.* Chico, CA: Scholars.

Schreiner, T. R. (1998). *Romans.* Grand Rapids, MI: Baker Academic.

Schreiner, T. R. (2001). *Paul: Apostle of God's Glory in Christ.* Downers Grove, IL: InterVarsity Press.

Schreiner, T. R. (2013). *The King in His Beauty: A Biblical Theology of the Old and New Testaments.* Grand Rapids, MI: Baker Academic.

Schneider, J. (1976). God. In C. Brown (Ed.), *The New International Dictionary of New Testament Theology* (pp. 66–82). Grand Rapids, MI: Zondervan.

Schwetze, A. W. (1998). *I Timothy, 2 Timothy and Titus.* St. Louis, MO: Concordia.

Scott, J. M. (1992). *Adoption as Sons of God: An Exegetical Investigation into the Background of Huiothesia in the Pauline Corpus.* Tübingen: J. C. B. Mohr.

Seckler, M. & Berchtold, C. (1988). Foi [Faith]. In P. Eicher (Ed.), *Dictionnaire de Théologie* [The Dictionary of Theology] (pp. 261–270). Paris: Les Éditions du Cerf.

Shelly, M. (2017). The Ever–Broadening Role of the Pastor: Over the Centuries, Shepherding a Flock has Gotten a Bit More Complicated, http://www.christianitytoday.com/pastors/2016/may-web-exclusives/ever-broadening-role-of-pastor-.html

Shenk, W. R. (1994). Encounters with "Culture" Christianity. *International Bulletin of Missionary Research, 8*(1), 8–13.

Shkul, M. (2009). *Reading Ephesians: Exploring Social Entrepreneurship in the Text.* New York, NY: T. & T. Clark International.

Simpson, E. K. & Bruce, F. F. (1957). *The Epistles of Paul to the Ephesians and to the Colossians.* Grand Rapids, MI: Eerdmans.

Slick, M. (2015). What Is the Biblical View of Discipleship? https://carm.org/what-is-the-biblical-view-of-discipleship

Smith, E. (2017). Right–Side–Up–Down. *Outreach Magazine* (May/June), 81–87.

Sommer, J. (2016). *Trinitarian Roles Are Necessarily Restricted to the Economic Trinity: A Biblical-Theological Response to Eternal-Relational Authority-Submission* [unpublished manuscript]. Academia.edu, https//:academia.edu/32722840/TRINITARIAN_ROLES_ARE_NECESSARILY_R ESTRICTED_TO_THE_ECONOMIC_TRINITY

Southern, R. W. (1970). *Western Society and the Church in the Middle Ages.* Grand Rapids, MI: Eerdmans.

Spangler, A., & Tverberg, L. (2018 [2009]). *Sitting at the Feet of Rabbi Jesus.* Grand Rapids, MI: Zondervan.

Spiritual Theology Department of the Pontifical University of the Holy Cross. (2021, April). *The Christians in the World.* From a letter to Diognetus: The Christians in the world, https://www.vatican.va/spirit/documents/spirit_20010522_diogneto_en.html

Stackhouse, J. G. (2000). Evangelical Theology Should Be Evangelical. In J. G. Stackhouse (Ed), *Evangelical Futures: A Conversation on Theological Method* (pp. 39–60). Grand Rapids, MI: Baker.

Stamm, C. (1983). *The Pastoral Epistles of Paul the Apostle.* Germantown, WI: Berean Bible Society.

Stamm, C. (1988). *Commentary on the First Epistle of Paul to the Corinthians.* Chicago, IL: Berean Literature Foundation.

Stamm, C. (1992). *Commentary on the Second Epistle of Paul to the Corinthians.* Chicago, IL: Berean Literature Foundation.

Stauffer, E. (1977). Christology. In G. Kittel & G. Friedrich (Eds.), *The Theological Dictionary of the New Testament* (Vol. 3). Grand Rapids, MI: Eerdmans.

Stedman, R. C. (1995 [1972]). *Body Life: The Book That Inspired a Return to the Church's Real Meaning and Mission.* Grand Rapids, MI: Discovery House Publishers.

Stott, J. R. W. (1975). *The Lausanne Covenant: An Exposition and Commentary.* Minneapolis, MN: World Wide Publications.

Stott, J. (1986). *Pour une foi Equilibrée* [For a Balanced Faith]. Cergy-Pontoise: Sator.

Stovell, B. (2012). *Mapping Metaphorical Discourse in the Fourth Gospel: John's Eternal King.* Leiden: Brill.

Stowers, S. (1989). ἐκ πίστεως and διὰ τῆς πίστεως in Romans 3:30. *Journal of Biblical Literature, 108*(4), 665-674. doi:10.2307/3267186

Strong, J. (2009 [1890]). *Strong's Concordance.* Peabody, MA: Hendrickson.

Stubbs, D. (2008). The Shape of Soteriology and the *Pistis Christou* debate. *Scottish Journal of Theology, 61*, 137–157.

Talbert, C. (2007). *Ephesians and Colossians.* Grand Rapids, MI: Baker Academic.

Tanner, K. (2010). *Christ the Key.* Cambridge: Cambridge University Press.

Taylor, D. (1999). Conversion: Inward, Outward and Awkward. In C. Lamb & D. Bryant (Eds.), *Religious Conversion: Contemporary Practices and Controversies* (pp. 35–50). New York, NY: Cassell.

Taylor, J. (2004). From Faith to Faith: Romans 1.17 in the Light of Greek Idiom. *New Testament Studies, 50*, 337–348.

Temple, W. (1961). *Readings in John's Gospel.* New York, NY: Macmillan.

Tenney, M. C. (1981). The Gospel of John. In F. Gaebelein (Ed.), *The Expositor's Bible Commentary* (Vol. 9, pp. 3–206). Grand Rapids, MI: Zondervan.

Thayer, J. H. (1996). *Greek-English Lexicon of the New Testament.* Peabody, MA: Hendrickson.

Thielman, F. (2010). *Ephesians.* Grand Rapids, MI: Baker Academic.

Thiselton, A. (1992). *New Horizons in Hermeneutics.* Grand Rapids, MI: Zondervan.

Thiselton, A. (2000). *The First Epistle to the Corinthians,* New International Greek Text Commentary. Grand Rapids, MI: Eerdmans.

Thompson, J. L. (2007). *Reading the Bible with the Dead: What You Can Learn from the History of Exegesis That You Can't Learn from Exegesis Alone.* Grand Rapids, MI: Eerdmans.

Thrall, M. E. (1994). *Introduction and Commentary on II Corinthians I–VII.* Vol. 1 of *The Second Epistle to the Corinthians: A Critical and Exegetical Commentary.* International Critical Commentary. Edinburgh: T. & T. Clark.

Tödt, H. E. (1965). *The Son of Man in the Synoptic Tradition.* London: SCM Press.

Tozer, A. W. (1961). *The Knowledge of the Holy.* New York, NY: Harper Collins.

Tomson, P. J. (2008). Transformations of Post–70 Judaism: Scholarly Reconstructions and Their Implications for Our Perception of Matthew, Didache, and James. In H. Van de Sandt & J. K. Zangenberg (Eds.), *Matthew, James, and Didache: Three Related Documents in their Jewish and Christian Settings* (pp. 91–122). Atlanta, GA: Society of Biblical Literature.

Torrance, T. F. (1996). *The Christian Doctrine of God: One Being Three Persons.* Edinburgh: T. & T. Clark.

Treat, J. R. (2014). *The Crucified King: Atonement and Kingdom in Biblical and Systematic Theology.* Grand Rapids, MI: Zondervan.

Trueblood, E. (1952). *Your Other Vocation.* New York, NY: Harper & Brothers.

Trueblood, E. (1967). *The Incendiary Fellowship.* New York, NY: Harper & Brothers.

Tuttle, R. G., Jr. (2006). *The Story of Evangelism: A History of the Witness to the Gospel.* Nashville, TN: Abingdon Press.

Tverberg, L. (2012a). *Walking in the Dust of Rabbi Jesus.* Grand Rapids, MI: Zondervan.

Tverberg, L. (2012b). Covered in the Dust of Your Rabbi: An Urban Legend? https://ourrabbijesus.com/covered-in-the-dust-of-your-rabbi-an-urban-legend/

Twomey, J. (2009). *The Pastoral Epistles Through the Centuries.* Malden, MA: Wiley-Blackwell.

Van der Kooi, C. & van den Brink, G. (2017). *Christian Dogmatics: An Introduction.* Grand Rapids, MI: Eerdmans.

Vellanickal, M. (1973). Evangelization in the Johannine Writings. In L. Legrand, J. Pathrapankal & M. Cellanickal (Eds.), *Good News and Witness* (pp. 121–168). Bangalore: Theological Publications in India.

Vermes, G. (1993). *The Religion of Jesus the Jew.* Minneapolis, MN: Fortress.

Volpe, M. A. (2013). *Rethinking Christian Identity: Doctrine and Discipleship.* Chichester, West Sussex: Wiley–Blackwell.

Voltaire (1843). Apostles. *A Philosophical Dictionary from the French of M. de Voltaire.* Vol. 1. London: W. Dugdale.

Von Rad, G. (1962). *Old Testament Theology. Volume 1. The Theology of Israel's Historical Traditions.* New York, NY: Harper and Row.

Von Speyr, A. (1993). *The Letter to the Colossians* (M. J. Miller, Trans.). San Francisco, CA: Ignatius Press.

Wallis, I. (1995). *The Faith of Jesus Christ in Early Christian Traditions.* New York, NY: Cambridge University Press.

Walvoord, J. F. (2011 [1953]). *Every Prophecy of the Bible: Clear Explanations for Uncertain Times.* Colorado Springs, CO: David C. Cook.

Wanamaker, C. A. (1987). Philippians 2:6–11: Son of God or Adamic Christology? *New Testament Studies, 33,* 179–193.

Ward, R. A. (1974). *Commentary on 1 & 2 Timothy and Titus.* Waco, TX: Word Books.

Watson, D. (1978). *I Believe in the Church.* Grand Rapids, MI: Eerdmans.

Wax, T. (2011). *Counterfeit Gospels: Rediscovering the Good News in a World of False Hope.* Chicago, IL: Moody.

Webster, J. (2007). Jesus Christ. In T. Larsen & D. Treier (Eds.), *The Cambridge Companion to Evangelical Theology* (p. 60). Cambridge: Cambridge University Press.

Weiss, J. (1985 [1971]). *Jesus' Proclamation of the Kingdom of God* (R. Hiers & D. L. Holland, Trans.). Chico, CA: Scholars Press.

Weiss, J. (2010 [1911]). *Christ: The Beginnings of Dogma.* London: Kessinger.

Wenham, D. (1995). *Paul: Follower of Jesus or Founder of Christianity?* Grand Rapids, MI: Eerdmans.

Wessels, A. (1994). *Europe: Was It Ever Really Christian?* London: SCM Press.

Westcott, B. F. (1998). *St. Paul's Epistle to the Ephesians.* Eugene, OR: Wipf and Stock.

Wilken, R. L. (2003 [1984]). *The Christians as the Romans saw Them* (2nd ed.). New Haven, CT: Yale University Press.

Wilkins, M. (1988). *The Concept of Disciple in Matthew's Gospel as Reflected in the Use of the Term "Mathetes."* Leiden: Brill.
Wilkins, M. (1992a). *Following the Master.* Grand Rapids, MI: Zondervan.
Wilkins, M. (1992b). Discipleship. In J. B. Green, S. McKnight, & I. H. Marshall (Eds.), *Dictionary of Jesus and the Gospels* (pp. 176–189). Downers Grove, IL: InterVarsity Press.
Willaime, J.-P. (2000). Le Développement du Protestantisme Evangélique et des Campagnes d'Evangélisation [The Development of Evangelical Protestantism and of Evangelism Campaigns]. In J. M. Mayer (Ed.), *Histoire du Christianisme* (pp. 293–297). Paris: Desclée.
Willard, D. (1998). *The Divine Conspiracy: Rediscovering Our Hidden Life in God.* San Francisco, CA: HarperCollins.
Willard, D. (2010). Discipleship. In G. McDermott (Ed.), *Oxford Handbook of Evangelical Theology* (p. 236). Oxford: Oxford University Press.
Williams, S. (1980). "The 'Righteousness of God' in Romans." *Journal of Biblical Literature, 99*, 241–90.
Williams, S. (1987). Again *Pistis Christou. Catholic Biblical Quarterly, 49*, 431–447.
Wilson, W. (1987). *New Wilson's Old Testament Word Studies.* Grand Rapids, MI: Kregel.
Witherington, B., III. (2005). *The Problem with Evangelical Theology: Testing the Exegetical Foundations of Calvinism, Dispensationalism, and Wesleyanism.* Waco, TX: Baylor University Press.
Witherington, B., III., & Hyatt, D. (2004). *Paul's Letter to the Romans: A Socio-Rhetorical Commentary.* Grand Rapids, MI: Eerdmans.
Wittman, T. R. (2019). *Dominion naturale et oeconomicum*: Authority and the Trinity. In M. F. Bird & S. Harrower (Eds.), *Trinity Without Hierarchy: Reclaiming Nicene Orthodoxy in Evangelical Theology* (pp. 141–164). Grand Rapids, MI: Kregel Academic.
Wood, A. S. (1978). *Ephesians: The Expositor's Bible Commentary* (Vol. 11). Grand Rapids, MI: Zondervan.
Wright, N. T. (1986). *The Epistles of Paul to the Colossians and to Philemon: An Introduction and Commentary.* Downers Grove, IL: InterVarsity Press.
Wright, N. T. (1992). *The New Testament and the People of God.* Minneapolis, MN: Fortress Press.
Wright, N. T. (1993). *The Climax of the Covenant: Christ and the Law in Pauline Theology.* Minneapolis, MN: Fortress Press.
Wright, N. T. (1996a). *Jesus and the Justification of God.* London: SPCK.
Wright, N. T. (1996b). *Jesus and the Victory of God: Christian Origins and the Question of God* (Vol. 2). Minneapolis, MN: Fortress Press.
Wright, N. T. (2000). Paul's Gospel and Caesar's Empire. In R. Horsley (Ed.), *Paul and Politics: Ekklesia, Israel, Imperium, Interpretation* (pp. 160–183). Harrisburg, PA: Trinity Press International.
Wright, N. T. (2004). *Romans, Part 1: Chapters 1–8.* Vol. 1 of *Paul for Everyone.* London: SPCK.
Wright, N. T. (2006). *Simply Christian: Why Christianity Makes Sense.* New York, NY: HarperCollins.
Wright, N. T. (2011). *Simply Jesus: A New Vision of Who He Was, What He Did, and Why He Matters.* New York, NY: HarperCollins.
Wright, N. T. (2012). *How God Became King.* New York, NY: HarperOne.
Wright, N. T. (2015). *The Paul Debate: Critical Questions for Understanding the Apostle.* Waco, TX: Baylor University Press.

Wright, T. (1996). *Jesus and the Victory of God.* New York, NY: SPCK.

Wuest, K. S. (1953). *Ephesians and Colossians in the Greek New Testament.* Grand Rapids, MI: Eerdmans.

Wu, J. (2015). *One Gospel for all Nations: A Practical Approach to Biblical Contextualization.* Pasadena, CA: William Carey Library.

Yarbrough, R. W. (1996). In W. A. Elwell (Ed.), *Evangelical Dictionary of Biblical Theology* (Baker Reference Library). Grand Rapids, MI: Baker Biblical Theology.

Young, B. (1995). *Jesus the Jewish Theologian.* Peabody, MA: Hendrickson.

Young, B. (1998). *The Parables: Jewish Tradition and Christian Interpretation.* Peabody, MA: Hendrickson.

Ziesler, J. (1989). *Paul's Letter to the Romans.* New Testament Commentaries. Valley Forge, PA: Trinity Press International.

Zerbe, G. (2013). Discipleship as Citizenship. *Canadian Mennonite, 17*(24), 4–8.

Appendix
Working Definitions of Theology and Discipleship

What we know today as Christian theology began with "the overwhelming personality of a Jew, the revelation of the Jewish God in a person who awakened faith and created community among non-Jews as well" (Christoph, 2015, p. 5). Among the first witnesses to the resurrection, this faith was neither known in fixed formulas nor systematized, though it was already being reflected on. However, according to Christoph, in "an astonishingly short time theologies emerged" (p. 5). From the earliest Christian theologies, certain theological *topoi* became accepted as orthodoxy at an early stage, whereas others were excluded as "heresies" from the second century onward. At the end of this development, from the fourth century on, stands the "dogmatization" of certain *theologoumena* in the empire-wide councils of late antiquity.[1]

The classic definition of theology is "faith seeking understanding" (*fides quaerens intellectum*). That definition comes from Augustine (354–430 CE) for whom it meant "I believe, therefore I understand." In other words, he saw theology as rational discussion respecting the deity which can be seen in Chapter 1, Book 8 of *The City of God*.

Anselm of Canterbury (1033–1109 CE) viewed theology as the effort of one who has faith to understand the one in whom he or she believes.

Theology has long been considered the "science of divine things." This understanding is the foundation for the definition offered by *The Compact Macquarie Dictionary*: "The science which treats God, his attributes, and his relations to the universe; the science or study of divine things or religious truth" (Delbridge & Bernard, 1994, p. 1045). For Charles Hodge (1952), an orthodox Calvinist theologian who influenced the fundamentalist and neo-Evangelical traditions, theology is the science of the facts of divine revelation concerning the nature of God and our relationship with him as his sinful creatures, the subject of his redemption (p. 21). Charles Ryrie (1986) said that theology is "thinking about God and expressing those thoughts in some way" (p. 9). According to the Baptist theologian Robert Culver (2005), "Christian

---

1 Prior to the fourth century we have no clear examples of the term *theologian* among followers of Christ (Christoph, 2015, p. 13).

Theology is study or organized treatment of the topic, God, from the standpoint of Christianity" (p. 2). The Anglican theologian Alister McGrath (2001) also identified theology with the "God whom Christians worship and adore" (p. 137).

These definitions are generally correct. However, they do not reflect theology as it is defined by the gospel. Instead, they are rooted in the reigning philosophical framework of the fourth century and the medieval realisms of both Plato and Aristotle (Bird, 2013, pp. 33–40). As a result, they mistakenly begin with the attempt to establish the existence of a God who is then to be scientifically studied. Instead, I maintain that as Christ-followers, our entry into theology should begin by specifically reflecting upon or speaking of the God who is revealed in the person of Jesus of Nazareth, and the fruit of that activity. This seems to be the conviction of two contemporary Dutch theologians, Cornelius van der Kooi and Gijsbert van den Brink (2017), who argue that our theology as Christians understands itself as "having been evoked by this shocking experience that God as he really is has made himself visible in Jesus" (p. 148). In other words, our theology must be "gospel-driven" from start to finish. This is in fact what being "evangelical" is all about. As Stanley Grenz (2000, p. 337) writes:

> To be "evangelical" means to be centred on the gospel. Consequently, evangelicals are gospel people. They are a people committed to hearing, living out, and sharing the Good News of God's saving action in Jesus Christ and the divine gift of the Holy Spirit, a saving action that brings forgiveness, transforms life, and creates a new community. As a gospel people, evangelicals continually set forth the truth that the centre of the church is the gospel and that the church, therefore, must be gospel centred.

Bird sums this up succinctly: "Theology has its agenda and energy derived from the Good News of Jesus Christ. It is, dare I say, the beauty of the gospel that matures our theological reflection on who God is toward us in Jesus-Christ" (2013, p. 41). Bird quotes John Webster (2007) to substantiate his claim:

> The best evangelical work emerges from the delight in the Christian gospel, for the gospel announces a reality which is in itself luminous, persuasive, and infinitely satisfying. That reality is Jesus Christ as he gives himself to be an object for creaturely knowledge, love, and praise. To think evangelically about this one is to think in his presence, under the instruction of his Word and Spirit, and in the fellowship of the saints. And it is to do so with cheerful confidence that his own witness to himself is unimaginably more potent than any theological attempts to run to his defense. (Bird, 2013, p. 60)

Robert Jenson (1997, p. 5) underscores the role of theology in the communication of the good news of Jesus Christ. He maintains that theological reflection is necessary and that we are not called to simply repeat the message that we have received. Rather, theology allows the contextualization of revelation, making it pertinent. Even though the truths of the gospel are timeless, its content must be communicated in a specific language and thought forms that are understandable and significant in a culture, and at a precise moment in time. For this reason, Jenson (1997, p. 5) defines theology as reflection that permits the verbal articulation of the gospel either toward humanity in the form of a message, or toward God in the form of praise and worship.

Toward a Working Definition of Discipleship

Like "theology," the word "discipleship" is also used in various ways. For some, such as Gordon Zerbe (2013) and Medi Volpe (2013), it is simply a different label for Christian identity. For Zerbe (2013, p. 8), it indicates a new identity that cuts across all other citizenship identities in sometimes complementary, and in others conflicting ways. Volpe (2013, p. 225) maintains that discipleship is the practice of Christian identity that stresses our constant need of formation and reflection on participating in the faith. Matt Slick (2015) claims that discipleship is a mandatory requirement for being a Christian.

The word "discipleship" is commonly used in a general way to mean learning to live as God wants us to live and by the wisdom of his Word. A quick internet search reveals that for many, discipleship consists of modeling and teaching to other Christians the precepts of the Bible—mainly prayer, doctrine, Christian living, and worship. Eric Russ (2010) links discipleship to spiritual formation, seeing it as growth from spiritual infancy to spiritual maturity. The progressive nature of discipleship as advancing in "spiritual maturity" or "righteous living" (denoted by the term "sanctification" in systematic theology) is emphasized in some definitions. In an article entitled "A Biblical Basis for Discipleship," for instance, James Faust states that discipleship "includes many things. It is chastity. It is tithing. It is family home evening. It is keeping all the commandments. It is forsaking anything that is not good for us" (Beliefnet, 2020).

I find these proposed definitions too vague to be useful. I prefer understandings that specifically link discipleship to the person of Jesus of Nazareth, the Christ. The definition offered decades ago by Dietrich Bonhoeffer (1979, p. 63) comes to mind: "Discipleship means adherence to Christ, and, because Christ is the object of that adherence, it must take the form of discipleship." The Cameroonian Jacques Yves Nganing Mbende (2015, p. 63) is even more precise: "It is a matter of renunciation of oneself; it is about setting aside one's own aims, goals, ambitions, and desires in life. It involves sacrifice for the sake of the Lord Jesus Christ."

Since evangelical theology delights in the good news of who God is toward us in Jesus Christ, then discipleship must be specifically linked to Jesus. I find scriptural basis for this claim in 2 Corinthians 4:4, where the Apostle Paul writes that the god of this age has blinded the intelligence of unbelievers so that they cannot see the light of the gospel of the glory of Christ, who is the image of God. Paul goes on, in verse 6, to reinforce this idea that the glory of Jesus of Nazareth, the Christ, is the heart of the gospel: "For God, who said, 'Let light shine out of darkness,' made his light shine in our hearts to give us the light of the knowledge of the glory of God in the face of Christ."[2] Moreover, according to Romans 14:7–9, the goal of the death and resurrection of Jesus of Nazareth is precisely that he should be recognized as the exalted Lord. According to Romans 8:34, Paul can see, in the Exalted One who sits at the right hand of the Father, the goal of the total event of salvation (Schweitzer & Peacock, 1955, p. 93).

For this reason, I propose an understanding of "discipleship" as ordering one's life, personal story, symbols, worship, preaching, finances, relationships, ambitions, and hopes around the most important confession of faith: that Jesus of Nazareth is Lord (Bird, 2013, p. 455).

Doing theology is intimately related to this process. Theology is not primarily a question of words; it deals with reality. And the most solid of all realities is encountering God in the person of Jesus of Nazareth, the Christ (Louth, 2003, p. 89). Evangelical theology has the task of thinking about and rethinking, in a sustained, regular, and deep way, the person and teaching of Jesus of Nazareth, the Christ. He is the one in whom all the fullness of God was pleased to dwell (cf. Col. 1:15–19; Jn. 14:10). I am convinced that such theological reflection leads to discipleship. This is also the opinion of the well-known theologian Stanley Hauerwas (2016), who maintains that theology fulfils its role correctly only when it initiates us into the life of Jesus the Christ, and thereby into discipleship.

The Transformation of Theology

Unfortunately, theology today, even evangelical theology, does not automatically lead to the centring of life in Jesus of Nazareth, the Christ. Even if Evangelicals hold to the importance of the cross, for centuries ecclesiastical and missional practice has often accentuated other things than centring one's life in Jesus. This is also true of our theological disciplines. One can be an evangelical who does theology without doing it in a distinctly evangelical way. One can even be an evangelical theologian and develop theology that is not shaped by the gospel. This in fact is often the case in evangelical seminaries!

Sometimes this problem occurs because we have inadvertently allowed our practice to determine our theology. This problem has been labelled "metapraxis" by Thomas Kasulis (1992, 1993, 2004). Kasulis defines

---

2 Paul similarly affirms in 2 Thessalonians 2:14 that God has called us through the gospel to share in "the glory of our Lord Jesus Christ."

metapraxis as the explanation or defense of religious practices by theological or philosophical arguments. He maintains that a constant challenge for any religious tradition is to integrate its convictions concerning reality (metaphysics) and the beliefs of its followers concerning their religious practices (metapraxis).

To clearly illustrate what Kasulis and Geertz are speaking of, let us consider a concrete situation. In Europe in the nineteenth century, some referred to the curse of Ham to justify the enslavement of black Africans on the grounds that they were descendants of Ham. Georg Horn, History Professor at the University of Leyden, seems to have been the first scholar, in 1666, to propose a classification of the races according to the model of the descendants of Noah in Genesis (Poliakov, 1976, p. 57). In 1677, Jean Louis Hannemann, drawing from a commentary on Genesis 9, argued that the Ethiopians had become both black and enslaved because of the curse of Ham. In this way, in the context of a very literal interpretation of the Bible dating back to the Protestant Reformation, slavery was justified among some groups of Christians in the West.

Our interpretations of the Scriptures often function to justify our emphasis on converting "souls" and church planting. I am not opposed to these practices *per se*, though I am convinced that they are insufficient to enable discipleship. Overemphasizing them as if they constitute the goal of missions even stifles proper discipleship to Jesus of Nazareth. We erode discipleship not by frontal assault but by placing the emphasis elsewhere. This leads to inadequate emphasis on whole-life obedience to the Lord Jesus.

Perhaps our real problem is hermeneutical. Robert Johnston (1979, pp. vii–viii) points to our often contradictory interpretations of Scripture as a sign that although Evangelicals proudly hold to the "sola Scriptura" battle cry associated with the Protestant Reformation, we do not agree with each other on how it is to be understood. And these differences of interpretation are, as John Stott (1986, p. 7) affirms the most important challenge facing Evangelicals. Why is this the case? Because as we will see in the studies in this series, the meanings we attach to the Scriptures are crucial. For this reason, Ben Witherington (2005) argues convincingly that Evangelicals must be willing to ask themselves critically to what extent their current preaching and teaching is actually grounded in God's Word. Witherington adds:

> Hermeneutical principle number one is this: what the text could not have possibly meant to the original inspired biblical author, it cannot possibly mean today. For example, John of Patmos was addressing first-century churches in Asia Minor at the end of the first century AD *in terms they could understand*. I must insist that what it meant then is still what it means today; that is the very nature of treating the Bible's authors with the respect they deserve and letting them have their own say in their own words, rather than trying to put words in their mouths. (2005, p. x; emphasis in original)

In this sense, strange as it sounds, the trouble with our Bible-centred evangelical form of Christianity is that it is not nearly biblical enough (Witherington, 2005, p. xi).

The Theological Method of Recovery

If the evangelical scholars I have just referred to are correct, our most crucial and fundamental problem seems to be that of hermeneutics (how we interpret the Scriptures). We defend the authority of the Scriptures, but we do not sufficiently measure the way in which historical and cultural forces influence our understanding (Johnston, 1979, pp. vii–viii). We must establish some basis for a theology of intentional discipleship to Christ. To do this, we need what could be called a "theology of recovery." I borrow that term from some Reformed theologians who have recently begun listening afresh to their forebears to discern if their own exegesis and theological interpretations are valid, or where they might need readjustment (see for instance Thompson, 2007).

To illustrate what I am talking about, I use one of the greatest artistic restoration projects in history—the restoration of Michelangelo's masterpiece in the Sistine Chapel in Rome—took 13 years to complete. Before the project began, art experts and religious and political leaders all agreed that the refurbishment was necessary to save the work and restore the brilliance it once had. But some opposed the project. Some critics feared that it would damage or distort Michelangelo's original work. Even after the restoration was completed and the results were revealed, the outcome was criticized. Some claimed that the dull, darkened colours before the restoration represented the artist's intent or that the brilliant colours that had been revealed once again were not the colours of Michelangelo.

I see many parallels between this artistic restoration project, along with the resistance it provoked, and what I am attempting to do here. I think that our understanding of discipleship and our ecclesial practice need a kind of cleaning up, yet any attempt to alter these things provokes fierce opposition. That opposition can also reside within us, in our own thinking. Someone has said that our ignorance does not keep us from moving forward as much as what we think we know. We are convinced that we have solid biblical reasons for "doing church" as we do, and for making it the centre. We find it difficult to admit that our practices might be based on preconceived notions that we refuse to examine critically. It will take patience, perseverance, and lots of grace to scrape away the layers of understanding that we have learned from previous readings of the Scriptures, from theological training that was not firmly grounded in the gospel, and from our evangelistic heritage and practices. However, without this process, all our efforts to foster intentional apprenticeship to Christ will produce only short-lived fruit.

Subject Index

Author Index

Scripture Index

2.5	222	1.18	182, 192, 195
2.5-11	179	1.19	113
2.6	50, 68	1.20	44, 114, 117, 157
2.6-7	45, 67, 68	1.20-22	43
2.6-8	113, 177, 222	1.21-22	194
2.6-11	53, 188, 259	1.21-23	185
2.7	90, 103, 104	1.23	170, 231
2.8	44, 193	1.25	231
2.9	82, 97, 106, 139	1.27	11, 83, 185, 204, 207
2.9-11	37, 130, 182	1.28	11, 187, 201
2.11	41	1.28-29	186
2.14-16	241	1.29	201
3.6	176	2.2	185
3.7-8	193	2.2-3	216
3.7-10	11, 90	2.3	50, 51, 185, 189
3.7-21	241	2.5	170
3.8	50	2.6	185, 204
3.8-9	187	2.7	170, 185
3.8-11	172	2.8	185
3.9	193	2.9	50, 97, 113, 193
3.10	50, 77, 105, 113, 193, 195	2.10	192, 193
3.10-11	104	2.12	162, 170, 187, 193
3.12-14	193	2.14	44
3.17	213, 239	2.15	191
3.18	44	2.16	185
3.20	125, 179	2.18	185
3.21	130, 195, 196	2.20	162
4.9	240, 241	3.1	35, 162, 185, 190, 204
4.11	240	3.1-4.6	185-6
4.12-13	140	3.2	117
		3.3	212
Colossians		3.4	117
1.2	193, 225	3.5	162, 206
1.3	98	3.6	212
1.4	170, 184	3.8	212
1.5	184	3.8-9	206
1.5-8	185	3.9	190
1.7	54, 184, 231, 240	3.10	190
1.9-13	219	3.11	252
1.12-14	157	3.12	206
1.13	38, 39, 125, 139, 140, 184, 206, 213	3.14	212
1.13-14	113, 130, 184, 192, 200	3.16	212, 215
1.14	117	3.17	41, 70, 98, 113, 144, 212
1.15	48, 97, 113, 189, 191, 192, 195	3.18	212
1.15-16	216	3.24	47, 140
1.15-17	33	4.3	187
1.15-20	11, 113, 157, 185, 188	4.3-4	187
1.16	117, 191	4.7	54
1.16-17	53	4.12	54
1.17	192		